Robin Odell was born in Hampshire in 1935. After training as a laboratory technician and developing an interest in forensic science, he turned to crime writing as a pastime. His first book, *Jack the Ripper in Fact & Fiction*, published in 1965, is still regarded as an important contribution to the subject. In a writing career spanning over forty years, he has written or co-written eighteen books in the fields of true crime, forensic investigations and criminal history. He won an Edgar Award from the Mystery Writers of America in 1980 for *The Murderers' Who's Who* and again in 2007 for *Ripperology*. He also lectures extensively to clubs and societies on crime cases.

Also available

The Mammoth Book of
Bizarre Crimes

Robin Odell

RUNNING PRESS
PHILADELPHIA · LONDON

Constable & Robinson Ltd
3 The Lanchesters
162 Fulham Palace Road
London W6 9ER
www.constablerobinson.com

First published in the UK by Robinson,
an imprint of Constable & Robinson, 2010

A copy of the British Library Cataloguing in Publication
Data is available from the British Library

UK ISBN 978-1-84529-781-7

1 3 5 7 9 10 8 6 4 2

First published in the United States in 2010 by Running Press Book Publishers

9   8   7   6   5   4   3
Digit on the right indicates the number of this printing

US Library of Congress number: 2009929933
US ISBN 978-0-7624-3844-0

Running Press Book Publishers
2300 Chestnut Street
Philadelphia, PA 19103-4371

Visit us on the web!
www.runningpress.com

Printed and bound in the EU

In Memory of
Wilf Gregg

Contents

Acknowledgments

There have been many pathfinders on the trail of bizarre murders. Detectives, lawyers, judges, pathologists, coroners, forensic scientists and criminologists have published accounts of the murders they have encountered in the course of their professional careers. Their books offer a feast for researchers, historians and crime writers.

Then there are the crime reporters, journalists and true crime writers themselves, who collect, interpret, analyse and expand on particular murders for the benefit of a wider audience. Playwrights, film script writers and dramatists add their contribution to the murder mix, exposing social issues and using drama to probe for explanations.

I pay tribute to this college of crime cognoscenti in the exercise of their knowledge, descriptive skills and analytical acumen. The literature of true crime is vast, well-documented and supplemented by the internet. The writers are too numerous to acknowledge individually, beyond a select bibliography, but I would like to salute them collectively.

I would like to express personal thanks to Pete Duncan and Duncan Proudfoot of Constable & Robinson for welcoming me to the inner circle of Mammoth authors. A big thank you goes to Annie Hepburn who processed all the words and provided encouragement and helpful comment.

And finally, my thanks to Non Davies for her loving support throughout.

Introduction

Setting the Crime Scene

"Tis strange – but true; for truth is always strange; stranger than fiction."

Lord Byron

This book of bizarre murders was conceived in the gentle ambience of a garden party. The late Wilf Gregg, a chronicler of the criminous, held an annual lunch at his Middlesex home attended by friends, fellow crime writers and criminologists of every denomination.

One of the benefits of Wilf's hospitality was to browse in his extensive library of books on true crime and his meticulously archived collection of press cuttings. While idly turning the pages of books and leafing through press reports of murder cases, we commented not only on the sheer variety of murders but on the esoteric nature of the events described. Exclamations such as unbelievable, weird and bizarre came readily to mind.

It might be thought that murder presented as fictional entertainment on cinema and television screens is frequently implausible. Yet in its bizarre, extraordinary and frequently farcical consequences it is invariably bettered by the real thing – truth really is stranger than fiction. This is often borne out in real life. It certainly applies to the realm of murder where it is underwritten by the circumstances and exotic details of many crimes. The reported details of murders featuring in the news media frequently fall into that category where the conclusion is, "You couldn't make it up!" Why not, we thought, compile a collection of true murder stories distinguished by their stranger-than-fiction content?

A cursory glance at a few randomly selected newspaper headlines illustrates the point. A German man weighing 127 kg (280 lb) squashed his wife to death following a domestic dispute. In China, a woman was reported to have killed her lover by kissing him while releasing a capsule containing rat poison which she held in her mouth. And, in Britain, a promiscuous married woman disposed of her unwanted husband by spiking his steak and kidney pie with toxic garden chemicals. The victim ill-advisedly kept a supply of paraquat in the garden shed and his wife saw her opportunity (*see* Chapter 13).

Apart from the variety of methods, what many of these murders have in common is that they were committed in a domestic setting and were conceived as a way of solving personal problems. These incidents also underline one of the important common denominators of murder which is that murderer and victim, more frequently than not, are known to each other.

Murder seems to attract weird behaviour beyond the basic elements of one person killing another. Tremayne Durham, for instance, a murder suspect in custody in the USA, became fed up with the monotonous institutional food he was served in prison and arranged a plea-bargain whereby he would admit guilt in return for a chicken dinner. The internet has inspired a boom in the sale of prison memorabilia manufactured by prison inmates serving life sentences for murder. Self-portraits of serial killers are popular and form part of a new merchandising sector which has been called psychopathic handicrafts.

Murder is rooted in the ordinary and, sometimes, extraordinary, activities of human beings hence they encompass the full scope and depth of human diversity. For example, the motive that drove a grandfather to sacrifice his ten-year-old granddaughter in India in 2009 was to ensure a good harvest. While every excess of which the human mind is capable has probably been catalogued in one form or another, a killing such as this seems to belong to a primitive era.

The acid test of murder is intention and what the law calls *mens rea* or guilty mind. Guilty intention is described as malice aforethought and it is this which distinguishes it from manslaughter. The classic definition of murder based on malice aforethought goes back to English Common Law and takes account of the age and mental status of the offender. This was set out by Lord Chief Justice Edward Coke (1552–1634) when he referred to "a man of sound memory and at the age of discretion". In practical terms, this meant an individual who was not insane and aged at least ten years.

While intention is all-important and constitutes the essence of what murder is, there are other factors that give structure to the act of killing. These broadly come together as modus operandi and may be defined as motive, method and opportunity. No matter how bizarre the circumstances of a particular murder, it will be given substance by the perpetrator's attention to these three principles. They are the factors that energize and give form to the intention to kill.

Other behavioural patterns emerge periodically and these are reflected in official figures and studies of homicide. Analysis of homicide statistics over a ten-year period in New York City has shown that while murder rates in general have declined there are peaks during the summer months, July to September. This is a time when people socialize more frequently and when drinking and drug-taking become more prevalent. Emotional temperatures tend to rise, creating an environment in which violence lurks in the shadows. When murder erupts, it is in a familiar context involving husbands, wives and lovers.

The weapon of choice in these scenarios is the handgun. Fears about possible curbs on the purchase of firearms in the USA in 2009 led to a boost in weapon sales. The arguments about gun control were emphasized by a spate of shootings in several states, including the killing of Dr George Tiller, a late-term abortion doctor gunned down in the lobby of the Lutheran church in Wichita, Kansas where he worshipped.

Homicide figures in the UK for 2007/8 showed a decline in the annual murder rate for England and Wales. Patterns indicated that female murder victims were most likely to be killed by someone known to them. One reason given for the decline in homicide was more effective emergency medical treatment of knife and gunshot wounds. Injuries which would have resulted in murder were not fatal and thus the crime reduced to attempted murder.

In common with all human activities, murder has evolved over time, absorbing and reflecting changes in social conditions with greater awareness and self-knowledge on the part of individuals. Yet underlying this sophistication lie dark forces that come to the surface when triggered by elemental drives such as self-preservation, ambition, power, aggression and domination.

The collision of basic instincts and moral values has been explored by some of the great novelists such as Emile Zola and Fyodor Dostoevsky. In *La Bête Humaine* Zola gives a portrait of a personality tormented by the struggle between his social nature, or better self, and a desire to test his powers to the absolute limit. It is not the intention of this book to dwell on the psychology of murder. This has been admirably achieved by others and, in particular, by Colin Wilson in his book, *Order of Assassins*. We are concerned here, though, with what happens when the threshold of intention, of malice aforethought, is crossed and actions lurch into the unpredictable realm of the extraordinary and idiosyncratic.

Premeditation should, theoretically at least, afford the best possibility for committing the perfect murder. This seems logical compared with crimes of passion which, by their nature, pay scant regard to either caution or discretion. They just happen.

Most murders are committed by people who in the ordinary course of events would be regarded as normal and rational. They are the sort of people who would be expected to make some sort of risk assessment before investing their money or committing themselves to a new business venture; the sort of people who, having formed the intention to extinguish the life of another human being, might formulate some kind of murder management plan after taking into consideration factors such as method and opportunity, assessing risk factors and allowing for contingencies. *But how often do they?*

There are exceptions, such as the teenage daughter of a millionaire businessman who compiled what amounted to a murder blueprint. Her intention was to enrich herself by killing a wealthy elderly person. She committed a detailed action plan to paper, together with a list of equipment needed for the task. Her mistake was to leave the blueprint where it could be found and provide incriminating evidence against her (*see* Chapter 13).

The murderer's chief aim is to fulfil the intention while minimizing the chances of being caught – the essence of perfect murder. Yet, at the very moment when planning is called for, calm detachment quickly turns into unforeseen turmoil. Rationality gives way to the beast within and events take an uncharted and erratic course. The release of elemental forces precipitates unthinking responses to the trauma of death, once the murderer's intention is made real. Confronted with his victim's corpse, possibly bloodied by violence, the first decision is whether to stay or flee. Already, the forensic trail has been started and every subsequent action is likely to leave a footfall, fingerprint or fibre behind. After all, it is the detectives' mantra that every murderer makes mistakes.

There are at least two groups of people who should, theoretically at least, be competent at carrying out the intention to kill: first, those who choose not to bloody their hands and can afford to pay someone else to do their dirty work for them, which puts distance between themselves and their victim. Such plans often come unstuck, however, because the hit man lacks guilty intention and falls down on attention to detail but the converse of this is politically motivated assassination where resources and professionalism come together with lethal efficiency (*see* Chapter 9).

The second group that might be expected to have a head start over everyone else consists of members of the medical and nursing professions, who have the knowledge, skills and agents at their disposal. In practice, though, they frequently turn out to be bunglers when it comes to murder and their professional acumen deserts them when they most need it. An example is the Austrian doctor who successfully murdered his mistress but kept her head as a sort of trophy in a jar of preserving fluid (*see* Chapter 3).

Accounts are given here of nearly three hundred murder cases. For convenience, they are grouped under chapter headings such as, *Parts and Parcels, Justice Delayed* and *Motive, Method and Opportunity,* which are broadly descriptive. The classification is fairly loose as many of the murders would fit into several categories.

Thomas de Quincey wrote an essay, published in 1827, entitled, *On Murder Considered as a Fine Art.* He talked about a Society of Connoisseurs of Murder who he thought might be called "murder fanciers". They would meet from time to time to discuss the latest crimes and offer a critique of them in a similar way to making an appraisal of a work of art.

Perhaps the murderer's canvas is his crime scene on which he leaves his bloody brush strokes, either by design or by default? The Dali Murders (*see* Chapter 7) are possibly the best example of death imitating art. Thomas Griffiths Wainewright was an artist who turned to murder and Walter Sickert painted murder victims, although none were claimed by him, unless the accusation that he was Jack the Ripper is ever substantiated.

But the demise of Isidor Fink in a locked room in New York City probably best qualifies as murder considered as a fine art. The fatal shooting of the thirty-three-year-old laundryman has defied resolution for eighty years. In every sense, it is the perfect murder (*see* Chapter 14).

While we might share the fascination of De Quincey's connoisseurs of murder, we might also be mindful that every murder claims a victim. Murder is undeniably part of the human condition with its roots in the primitive recesses of the brain where moral restraints are overridden by the dark forces of malice. To read about murder is to open a door into the territory occupied by those who transgress the boundaries observed by civilized society. We may be shocked, entertained or informed by what we read, while knowing that in murder cases the unbelievable is all too often true.

In 2009, Vincent Bugliosi, the US attorney who led the prosecution in the Manson murder trial in the late 1960s, was reported as saying that the killings were the most bizarre murders in the history of American crime. He commented that, "If they had been written as fiction no one would have read it. It would have seemed too far out." And, as Thomas de Quincey reminded his readers, using a question framed by Lactanius, the Roman poet; "What is so dreadful; what so dismal and revolting, as the murder of a human creature?"

Robin Odell

CHAPTER 1

The Dog and the Parrot

Animals frequently play a part in the chronicles of crime. Their role has usually been in a supporting capacity and only occasionally as killers. London newspapers in 1876 reported a "Murderous Attack by a Gorilla" armed with a cut-throat razor in France. The Victorians were fascinated by images of young maidens being attacked by snakes, cats and sea monsters.

The savage natural instincts of animals have sometimes been harnessed by murderers for their capacity to destroy evidence of a crime. Thus in 1937 did Joe Ball, proprietor of The Sociable Inn in Elmendorf, Texas, dispose of his victims by feeding them to crocodiles and, in 1960, the Hosein brothers, in all likelihood, fed the remains of their murder victim to the pigs at Rooks Farm.

Only rarely are the lethal attributes of animals used as a murder weapon. Robert James thought he had found a novel way of disposing of his wife by setting rattlesnakes on to her. They failed to kill her quickly enough, though, so he resorted to drowning to make sure.

Whether kept as domestic pets or farm animals, dogs are often encountered by unwanted visitors and are only too willing to attack intruders or alert their owners. Sir Arthur Conan Doyle referred to "The curious incident of the dog in the night time", when a dog did not bark because it recognized the intruder intent on stealing a racehorse. The dog kept by the landlady of the Cross Keys Inn in London's Chelsea area clearly knew the individual who robbed and killed its mistress in 1920. The dog did not bark but the killer gave himself away by other means.

Possibly the most unusual intervention by an animal was that of a green parrot which witnessed the killing of its owner in a New

*York bar in 1942. Gifted with the power of calling out the names of
people it knew, the parrot acted as a police informer by identifying
the murderer.*

Listen To The Parrot

The Green Parrot Restaurant in Harlem, New York City, was
a popular watering hole and the bar was presided over by the
owner's parrot. The bird had a useful vocabulary and knew
many customers by their first name. Max Geller, the owner,
refused all offers to sell his parrot, one of whose tricks was to
insult the patrons.

On the evening of 12 July 1942, there was a shooting at
the Green Parrot Restaurant. A man came into the bar and
demanded a drink, a request that was refused by Max Geller
because the man was already drunk. The angry customer
pulled a gun, shot Geller and disappeared into the busy street.

Max Geller died three weeks later. The gunshot wound
he sustained in the throat had damaged his vocal cords and
he was unable to speak. When the police arrived at the bar,
they questioned people who had been present but with little
positive result. Pedestrians talked of seeing a man fleeing from
the bar with a gun in his hand. The most vocal witness was
the Green Parrot. The bird was agitated and kept shouting,
"Robber! Robber!" The police captain summed up progress
with the words "we have a dying victim who can't talk, twenty
witnesses who won't and a squawking parrot we can't shut
up!"

The usual suspects were questioned but to no avail and the
investigation into the murder was beginning to founder when
someone suggested that the parrot, known for addressing
patrons by their first name, might not be saying, "Robber!
Robber!" but "Robert, Robert". With this new line of enquiry,
detectives began checking on the late Max Geller's customers
who were called Robert. By a process of elimination, they
arrived at the name of Robert Butler.

Butler was a cab-driver who frequented the Green Parrot
but had disappeared since the shooting. His friends had no

knowledge of his whereabouts and a year went by with no progress in the efforts to locate him. But determined detective work eventually traced Butler to the Bethlehem Steel plant at Baltimore.

Officers were waiting for him when he came off the late night shift. Butler said he had left New York after a quarrel with his wife but agreed to accompany detectives back to Harlem. Asked if he knew anything about the shooting of Max Geller he responded with a question of his own; "What makes you think I did it?" One of the officers enquired, "What do you think of Geller's parrot?" "Smart bird", came the reply. When told that the parrot had named him, Butler said, "I never did like that bird".

Charged with murder, Butler said that he had got into trouble over gambling and armed himself for protection. He had a few drinks because he was scared and was angry when Geller refused to serve him. In his fury, he drew his gun and shot the restaurant owner. Tried for murder in February 1944, Butler was convicted and sentenced to up to fifteen years in Sing Sing. History does not relate what happened to the parrot.

Silent Pooch

The dog that did not bark in the night added a strange dimension to an unsolved murder in the UK's capital in 1920.

Fifty-three-year-old Frances Buxton was the licensee of the Cross Keys Inn in Chelsea. She was regarded as rather eccentric, living alone at the pub since her estrangement from her husband and having as her sole companion a pet Pomeranian dog. She was thought to be secretive and a bit of a hoarder.

On the night of 18 January 1920, a policeman patrolling in Lawrence Street noticed smoke coming from the Cross Keys Inn. He promptly called the fire brigade and the blaze was put out. A search of the premises revealed Frances Buxton's body in the cellar. She was dead from head wounds inflicted with an axe or knife. The body had been covered with sawdust and sacking which had been set on fire.

Examination of the body showed the full extent of the battering she had received; her features were practically unrecognizable. It also appeared as if an attempt had been made to strangle her. The dead woman's pet dog was found in the room behind the bar, unharmed and apparently unalarmed. Curiously, the dog had not reacted to the disturbance by barking. Neighbours found this odd as the animal had a shrill bark with which it greeted strangers.

The motive for the murder seemed to be robbery. Frances Buxton was in the habit of keeping her bar takings in a basket beside her bed. She also had a collection of valuable jewellery including diamond brooches, gold rings and bracelets, which had disappeared, presumably stolen by her attacker.

Her ex-husband was interviewed by detectives and was cleared of suspicion. There was, though, talk of a tall stranger who had visited the Cross Keys Inn and taken a fancy to the lady behind the bar in her sparkling jewellery. In the manner of the day, bar staff thought he was their employer's fancy man. This individual was never traced and neither was the stolen jewellery.

The murder investigation was losing impetus when a witness at a magistrates' hearing four years later into an assault case announced that one of his relatives had information about the Chelsea murder. Like other possible leads, this came to nothing. There was a similar negative outcome to an alleged confession made by a man being held in a French prison. This turned out to be a hoax. Another suggestion regarding a motive other than robbery for killing Frances Buxton, a lady with a string of lovers, was that she had infected one of them with venereal disease and he took his revenge.

If the dead woman's pet dog was performing to type by not barking, it seems likely that the intruder on the winter's night was not a stranger.

Inside Job

In the early hours of 1 August 1980 an intruder gained entry to the house of the Marques de Urquizo in the Somosauguas district of Madrid in Spain. The family dog did not react and the security system was disarmed. The quiet assassin shot the fifty-seven-year-old Marques with one bullet through the brain while he was sleeping and then shot the Marquesa with two bullets through the throat. The live-in maid registered no disturbance, possibly because she was drugged.

The Urquizo family were wealthy members of the Spanish establishment. The Marques was head of one of the country's most important commercial banks. The house contained a priceless art collection but nothing was stolen by the deadly intruder. The circumstances of the killings suggested someone with inside knowledge.

Suspicion fell on the dead couple's son-in-law, Rafael Escobedo. In 1978, Escobedo, the son of a lawyer, married the Urquizos' only daughter Miriam de la Sierra against the wishes of her family. The marriage proved to be unhappy with heated disagreements and came to a head when the Marques cut off his daughter's finances with a divorce pending.

Escobedo was interviewed by the police in April 1981 during which he allegedly made a confession that he subsequently retracted. More importantly, detectives found a cache of .22 calibre ammunition at the home of his parents where he had set up a firing range. Ballistics tests allegedly matched some of these rounds to the bullets fired at the crime scene.

In June 1983, Escobedo appeared on trial at Madrid's Palace of Justice charged with murdering his wife's parents. His estranged wife attended court supported by an American friend. The prosecution argued that the bullets found at Escobedo's home matched those used in the fatal shooting. The problem was that this vital firearms evidence had disappeared since it was taken into safe-keeping by the police.

Another plank in the prosecution case was the handwritten confession that was said to have been made by Escobedo. He retracted this, saying he had only written it to save his family from harassment. In a further embarrassment for the police, this document had also disappeared.

Newspaper coverage of what was billed as "The Trial of the Century" emphasized the social standing of the participants, with Escobedo being described as a playboy. Due to police ineptitude, the evidence against the defendant was mainly circumstantial. The dog that did not bark in the night suggested an inside job and disagreements with the family over his marriage provided Escobedo with a possible motive. There were also strong suggestions that he had not acted alone.

"The Trial of the Century" concluded on 7 July 1983 with a conviction for murder. Escobedo was sentenced to a jail term of fifty-three years.

Snakes Alive!

Robert James was a Californian barber who earned the nickname "Rattlesnake" on account of his novel method of murder. On 5 August 1935, James called the police to his home in La Canada telling them that he had found his wife dead in the garden pond.

Detectives found twenty-five-year-old Mary James, who was pregnant, lying face down in six inches of water in the lily pond. Doctors established that one of her legs was badly swollen, possibly from an insect bite. It was thought that she might have become dizzy as a result of the bite and fallen into the pond.

Accidental death was recorded and, several weeks later, the grieving husband collected a modest insurance payout. There matters might have rested if James had not drawn attention to himself. He ran a barber's shop in Los Angeles and apparently made an offensive suggestion to a woman passing by in the street. She reported the incident to the police, which prompted the authorities to take a closer look at James' background.

They uncovered an extraordinary trail of failed marriages and questionable deaths. It seemed that James had been unlucky in his choice of partners. His first wife divorced him claiming that he had tortured her; the second marriage also ended in divorce and his third wife drowned in the bathtub. In each case, James had collected the insurance. His fourth wife was more astute. She refused to be insured, saying that strange things happened to people with life insurance.

In the course of their now intensified enquiries, detectives came across a character called Charles Hope who had helped James in his barber shop. He had an interesting story to tell after investigators discovered that he obtained snakes on behalf of Robert James. Receipts were found for two rattlesnakes bought from a dealer in Long Beach known as "Snake Joe" at the going-rate of 75 cents per pound.

Hope said that James had asked him to buy the snakes and he duly turned up at La Canada with two reptiles called "Lethal" and "Lightnin". He was then drawn into James' scheme to kill his wife by posing as a doctor. He told Mary that she did not look well and thought that having the baby would endanger her life. There and then, she agreed to have an abortion.

"Dr" Hope prescribed whisky as an anaesthetic and once the "patient" was inebriated, James produced a box containing the two rattlesnakes and placed Mary's foot inside. The two men then went into the garage for a smoke and to await developments. Checks were made and although Mary's leg was badly bitten, she was still alive. "The damned snakes didn't work," exclaimed James, adding, "I'm going to drown her." The semi-conscious woman was put in the bathtub and then transferred to the garden pond where she finally expired.

Armed with Hope's confession, police went in search of James who they found engaging in a spot of sado-masochism with one of his consorts. In due course, Charles Hope was sentenced to life imprisonment for his part in the murder. Robert James was given the death sentence and spent four years on Death Row in San Quentin where, unsurprisingly, he was known as "Rattlesnake". He was hanged on 1 May 1942, and was the last man in California to be so executed. After this, death sentences were carried out in the gas chamber.

A Dog That Barked

The violent death of a wealthy widow, signalled by the barking of her dog, was judged on first appearances to be a mysterious murder in a locked room. The eventual explanation proved to be more commonplace.

In the summer of 1969, tragedy struck a residential suburb of Salisbury, Rhodesia, with the death of fifty-eight-year-old Mrs Whitworth. A widow, she lived alone, except for her dog, and led an active life looking after her garden and engaging in sporting pursuits.

Neighbours were disturbed by the constant barking of Mrs Whitworth's dog throughout the night. The following morning, a near neighbour telephoned to ask if everything was OK. There was no reply, so he walked over to the bungalow and knocked on the door. Again, no reply. When he looked through the bedroom window, he could see a pair of feet on the floor close to the bed. Fearing there had been an accident, he called the police.

Officers entered the bungalow through an unsecured side door but when they reached the bedroom found it locked. They burst the door open and as they did so, heard the key drop to the floor inside. Mrs Whitworth lay on the floor, dead from injuries to the head. She had marks on her face and had bitten her tongue, resulting in a great loss of blood, which had choked her.

When it was discovered that she was epileptic, investigators believed she might have locked herself in her room if she felt unwell and was then overcome by a fit, which proved fatal. A search of the bungalow threw doubt on this explanation. Mrs Whitworth was known to be a meticulously tidy person, yet there was an empty beer bottle in the fireplace and a corned beef tin that had been crudely opened with a penknife. Thoughts began to gather about a possible intruder.

Fingerprints in the bungalow were matched to a man called Mpani who was a temporary gardener. He was known to the police on account of convictions for assault. He admitted having asked Mrs Whitworth to lend him money or at least to give him an advance on his pay. Then he claimed that an accomplice had assaulted his employer while he simply ran away. The accomplice was tracked down and proved to have an unshakeable alibi. Mpani now admitted that he had killed Mrs Whitworth.

His story was that she had refused to lend him money and threatened him with a poker to which he responded by attacking and strangling her. When she fell, she hit her head which accounted for the injuries to her face. The mystery of the locked room was resolved by a simple explanation. What officers believed was the key falling inside the bedroom when they broke down the door was actually the latch-plate, which had broken on impact.

Mpani explained that he dragged his victim's body into the bedroom and placed it on the floor. When he left the room, he locked the door from the outside and, using a piece of newspaper, slid the key under the door and into the room. Pathologists established that Mrs Whitworth had been strangled which resulted in her badly bitten tongue.

Mpani was brought to trial for murder and found guilty. He told the court, "I did not mean to kill her but a devil got into me".

CHAPTER 2

Parts and Parcels

One of the first challenges facing a murderer is what to do about the victim's body. The first instinct is probably to escape from the scene of the crime and abandon the body to forensic scrutiny by investigators. This is a risky strategy, however, especially if there has been contact between victim and perpetrator, as this usually yields important investigative evidence. Strangling, stabbing and bludgeoning offer ample opportunity for the transfer of contact traces such as blood, hair and fibres. Shooting, on the other hand, puts distance between victim and killer, but firearms evidence has powerfully incriminating qualities. While it may involve close contact, poisoning is subtle and gives scope to ingenuity on the part of the clever operator, with many ways to disguise his true purpose and simulate natural causes.

Disposal of a body requires both method and resourcefulness. The chief purpose is concealment or, at least, to delay discovery of the crime with the idea that no body equals no crime, which, as many murderers have discovered, is not necessarily the case.

Burial may seem an obvious choice but the perpetrator immediately encounters the first challenge. Moving the body of an adult, when it is literally a dead weight, is not an easy task for one person without assistance. A burial also requires a degree of secrecy and is usually carried out during the hours of darkness. Then there is the inconvenient product of burial which is the soil excavated from the grave. Disturbed soil is a dead giveaway for search parties.

To overcome the difficulties of moving and transporting a corpse, murderers readily incline towards dismemberment. Reducing the body to small components allows parts to be parcelled up for easier disposal – at least, that is the theory. In practice, there is the revelation that the process is, to a very high degree, messy. For a start, the average human body contains at least six and a half litres of blood. Once this major body fluid is released, it gets everywhere – it drips, splashes, stains and leaves trails.

For this problem, and where dismemberment is part of a pre-conceived plan, the murderer may have noted the availability of a bath in which to place the body or have had the foresight to acquire some plastic sheeting. Choice of tools for dismemberment may involve visits to hardware stores to buy knives, saws, axes and other implements of the slicing and dicing trade. Some operators, such as Simone Weber in 1985, have recourse to an electric saw, which provides speedy lopping of the limbs but tends to increase the mess factor. For the medical practitioner turned murderer, there is the option of risking identification by demonstrating skill at disarticulation. In 1928 Dr Frank Westlake's dismemberment of his victim betrayed his medical background.

The object of dismemberment is to render the victim's body to manageable proportions. Using her particular technique, Mme Weber, filled seventeen plastic bags with human remains. The astute murderer will target his victim's head for severance and separate disposal, hence the high proportion of headless torsos that turn up lacking the most obvious means of identification.

Once the body has been reduced to a number of basic components, the resultant parts may be individually wrapped for disposal. Unless carefully thought out in advance, this usually means the murderer grabs whatever clothing, bedsheets, blankets or sacks that may be at hand to make a bundle or parcel. Newspaper has proved to be a popular material for this purpose, even though this may well offer clues as to the place and date of the crime. Dr Ruxton wrapped parts of one of his victims in a special edition of a Sunday newspaper, which conveniently provided investigators with vital co-ordinates of his crimes.

Having rendered the victim's remains into a number of conveniently-sized bundles or parcels, the murderer still faces the problem of disposal. The chronicles of crime amply demonstrate the extraordinary lengths to which murderers are prepared to go to accomplish this task. In 1851 William Sheward dumped parcels of body parts in and around the city of Norwich and James Greenacre made several trips on foot and by omnibus with a similar mission in London in 1836.

Transportation by car and casual disposal in a stream close to the roadside was the method favoured by Dr Ruxton in 1935. While Donald Hume, a decade later, took to the skies in a light aircraft to drop his airmail parcels over the Essex mudflats. Others have used car transport and rail services to deliver unwanted body parts to distant places using suitcases and trunks.

Trunk murderers occupy a special place in the pantheon of odious criminals. Prominent among this band of luggage specialists was Winnie Ruth Judd, who in 1931, accompanied the dismembered remains of her two victims packed in trunks on a train journey from Phoenix to Los Angeles. Trunk murderers, and those who delay too long in deciding on their disposal option, face the inevitable consequences of decomposition and its accompanying stench.

A popular disposal method is to dump parcels of remains in water. This offers the temporary satisfaction of putting grisly remains out of sight and out of mind, but water has the uncanny knack of delivering up the dead, as Donald Hume discovered. In 1927 James McKay dumped his murdered mother's body parts in the River Clyde but they came back to haunt him.

Even destruction by fire or acid is not foolproof and, as many killers have discovered, the human frame is remarkably resilient. Teeth, in particular, possess amazing powers of indestructibility. John Perry in 1990 went to great lengths to destroy his wife's remains, including her skull, but there were enough teeth left to provide identification.

What to do with the head of the victim is a problem that has taxed the ingenuity of many murderers. Fred Thorn went to the trouble of encasing his victim's head in plaster of Paris while Dr Herman Schmitz kept his trophy in a jar of preservative.

Heads and skulls have exerted a special fascination for murderers when dealing with their victims and also for the enforcers of law and order when dealing with murderers. Ned Kelly's skull became the object of controversy when it was stolen in 1990. The Australian authorities were so concerned about the possible desecration of the body after Thomas Griffin was executed in 1868, that his head was removed before burial. The ploy did not succeed and the head ended up as a trophy.

The tragic fate of Fanny Adams in 1867 and the two fingers shown to the authorities in Vienna in 1926 by Dr Herman Schmitz are among the infamous references to body parts.

Sweet Fanny Adams

"Sweet Fanny Adams" was the name given by British sailors in the Royal Navy to canned meat that formed part of their rations. This was a coarse reference to a young girl who had been murdered in a field in Hampshire on a warm summer's day in 1867.

Eight-year-old Fanny Adams, together with her sister and a friend, left their homes in Alton to play in the nearby fields. Their favourite spot was Flood Meadow, which bordered the River Wey and was shallow enough for paddling.

At about 5.00 p.m. on 24 August, Fanny's two companions returned to their homes without her. They explained that they had seen William Baker who worked as clerk to a local solicitor and he spoke to them. He offered Fanny a halfpenny to go with him and he had given money to the other girls who, left to their own devices, continued playing by the river until it was time to go home.

Fanny's mother and a neighbour immediately set out to look for the eight-year-old. Early in their search, they encountered William Baker. They asked him about Fanny and, while he admitted giving money to her friends, said he knew nothing about her. Reassured by their conversation, Mrs Adams returned home, assuming her daughter had gone off to play on her own and would soon return.

When Fanny had not returned home by 7.00 p.m. a proper search was organized and her body was soon discovered in a hop field. The child had been brutally attacked and mutilated. Her head was severed from the body, the eyes and one ear were missing and the abdomen disembowelled. The remains were strewn about on the ground.

As the last person known to have seen the dead girl, William Baker immediately came under suspicion. The twenty-nine-year-old clerk was only saved from a violent end at the hands of Fanny's father by the intervention of the police. Baker was arrested and two small knives, one of which was bloodstained, were found in his possession. There were also traces of blood on his clothes.

A search of Baker's desk at the office where he worked produced the most incriminating evidence. His diary entry for the day of the murder read, "Killed a young girl – it was fine and hot."

Baker, the subject of great public hostility, was tried for murder at Winchester. He was an articulate man and tried to talk his way to innocence by saying the knives found on him were too small for mutilation and that the children had lied about him. In his defence, it was stated that a failed love affair had left him depressed and suicidal and he was stressed by overwork. None of this impressed the jury who found him guilty and were not inclined to mercy. William Baker was executed before a crowd of five thousand at Winchester on Christmas Eve 1867. Poor Fanny's memorial lay in the sailors' reference to the contents of their canned food.

Pre-Nuptials

Briton James Greenacre had contracted several profitable marriages and was planning his fourth wedding, to Hannah Brown, on Christmas Day 1836. On Christmas Eve, they met at his house in Camberwell, London, to discuss their plans. His tactic was to call off the wedding because he believed Hannah had been using his name to obtain credit while, contrary to his expectations, she had no money of her own. Hannah was not seen alive again, although parts of her began appearing in different places.

On 28 December, a package was found on the Edgware Road lying in a pool of frozen blood. When the sacking was pulled open, a female trunk emerged with the arms intact but legs and head missing. Just over a week later a head was retrieved from the Regent's Canal at Stepney. This second find matched the torso found earlier. Two months later, a large bundle was found in a ditch at Camberwell. This contained the legs belonging to the other body parts already recovered.

It would be another three weeks before the dismembered body, now re-assembled, would be identified. A man whose sister had been missing for three months identified the remains as Hannah Brown. It was known that she had last been seen in the company of James Greenacre, the man she intended to marry.

Greenacre was preparing for flight with a female companion, Sarah Gale, heading for America. Some of their trunks were already on board their passenger ship. These were taken for examination and the contents included cloth identical to the wrapping used on some of the body parts. Greenacre was arrested along with his lady friend, whom he attempted to absolve from any involvement in the crime.

His explanation was that Hannah had tipped up her chair and fallen badly, damaging her head. He later changed his story, saying that he was so incensed by Hannah's false statements regarding her property that he hit her with a wooden roller and killed her. Following his confession, he gave a detailed account of how he disposed of her dismembered corpse. He thought to disarm any suspicion by dumping his parcels in broad daylight, believing this would appear less furtive than operating at night.

Having been tried and convicted of murder, Greenacre spent his time leading up to execution writing an autobiography. He portrayed himself as an industrious and respectable individual who had been elected to the office of overseer of his parish. His calculation was made evident when he attempted to engineer another marriage after murdering Hannah by advertising for a partner with money. Greenacre ended his life on the scaffold and the woman he planned to take with him to America was sentenced to transportation.

Trophy Cabinet

An Irish immigrant to Australia became Chief Constable at Brisbane and was drawn into crime by the lure of gold. After his execution for murder, the authorities went to great lengths to prevent his head being taken as a trophy. That they failed said a great deal about the lawlessness of the 1860s.

Thomas Griffin took advantage of a free passage offered to former soldiers to start a new life in Australia in 1856. With his new wife he set up a boarding house in Melbourne but, wanting some more excitement in his life, he joined the police and rapidly rose through the ranks.

By 1867, at the height of the gold rush, he was Gold Commissioner at Rockhampton. His job was to buy the precious metal from the miners. On 27 October, he set out with an armed escort to carry notes and coins worth £4,000 across the Mackenzie River to Claremont. Troopers John Power and Patrick Cahill guarded the ten canvas bags containing the money.

When they reached the river crossing on their 200-mile journey, Griffin decided to return to Rockhampton, leaving the two troopers to continue without him. Soon after he arrived back at Rockhampton he called at the police office asking if it was true that the gold escort had been killed. Indeed, the dramatic news had just been received that Power and Cahill had been found dead in the bush and the money gone.

Griffin was very forthright in his theories about what had happened. In response to reports that the troopers had been poisoned, he said it was a false report, ". . . they are shot, you'll see if they aren't." A small group of men, including a doctor, decided to visit the scene. Griffin volunteered to drive the trap but handled it so dangerously that the doctor asked him to step down before they were all killed.

Once they reached the scene of the crime, it became clear that the troopers had been shot, bearing out Griffin's prophecy. The suspicion that had settled on him intensified as a result of a round of drinks he had bought at a tavern in Rockhampton, paid for with a one pound note. The note was part of the consignment that had been stolen and, unbeknown to Griffin, its number recorded.

Griffin was arrested on suspicion of murder and, despite the circumstantial nature of the evidence, was found guilty at his trial in Rockhampton. While in the condemned cell he tried to persuade his jailors to help him escape and made references to the whereabouts of the stolen money. No deals were done and he faced the hangman with the words, "Go on. I am ready."

In an extraordinary sequel to Griffin's career, first as law enforcer and then as law breaker, there were fears that an attempt would be made to remove his head from his corpse. To prevent this, the authorities arranged that another body would be buried on top of his in the same grave. Despite this precaution, his head was removed and the skull displayed as a grisly trophy in the surgery of the doctor who had complained about his driving.

Par Avion

A farm labourer hunting wild fowl in the Essex mud flats in the UK on 21 October 1949 discovered a headless torso in the water. The grisly remains were clad in a silk shirt and underpants wrapped up in a parcel with grey felt and rope. There was evidence of stab wounds in the chest and the lower limbs appeared to have been severed using a sharp knife and saw.

The remains were identified by fingerprints held on file at Scotland Yard. The dead man was Stanley Setty, a car dealer and black marketeer who had a conviction for fraud. He was last seen on 4 October – a day when he had made several car deals for cash. One of Setty's associates was Donald Hume, a former serviceman in the Royal Air Force, who held a civilian pilot's licence.

The police checked up on Hume's movements and learned that he had hired a light aircraft from the United Services Flying Club at Elstree on 5 October. He had taken off from the airfield carrying two parcels as freight. Hume was located on 26 October and questioned about the purpose of his flight.

His explanation was that he had agreed for a payment of £50 to ditch at sea two parcels containing parts of a printing press used to produce counterfeit petrol coupons. On his return, the man with whom he had been dealing offered him a further £100 to dump another parcel. Hume described the parcel as bulky and there was a gurgling noise when he moved it which made him think it might be a body.

Nothing Hume had said could be corroborated and he was arrested and charged with murdering Stanley Setty. At his Old Bailey trial in January 1950, the prosecution set out a scenario whereby Hume killed Setty in the living room of his flat and then had the carpet cleaned and wiped the place clean of fingerprints. The jury were unable to agree a verdict and were discharged. A new jury was sworn in and as the prosecution declined to offer any evidence against him, the judge directed that they should return a verdict of not guilty. He was, though, found guilty of being an accessory to murder and was sentenced to twelve years' imprisonment.

Hume was released from Dartmoor Prison in February 1958 and in May, he travelled to Switzerland. In June, his confession to murder appeared in a Sunday newspaper, with the headline, '*I killed Setty . . . And Got Away With Murder*'. He was safe in the knowledge that he could not be charged again with the same offence.

He was involved in bank robberies in the London area in 1958 before returning to Switzerland. On 30 January 1959, in the aftermath of robbing the Gewerbe Bank of Zurich, he shot and killed a taxi-driver. As he fled from the scene, he was pursued by members of the public who held him captive until the police arrived.

Hume was tried for murder in a Zurich court in September when he pleaded guilty. The jury found him guilty of murder, attempted murder, robbery and other offences. He was sentenced to life imprisonment with hard labour. In August 1976, having served seventeen years, Hume was returned to Britain. Following psychiatric examination, he was admitted to Broadmoor where he died, aged sixty-seven, in 1988.

If The Shoe Fits . . .

A rail track inspector working on the line between Aberdeen and Edinburgh in Scotland on 24 March 1969 found a parcel. On inspection it was found to contain the severed leg of a human female, the limb still clad in a nylon stocking. On the same day, another parcel was found about four miles away; it contained the other leg.

Pathological examination determined that the remains were those of a female in the age range of thirty to forty. The police checked all the missing persons lists for the United Kingdom and used the broad description of the dismembered woman in a process of elimination. The police made an appeal on press and television for anyone with information about a missing neighbour or acquaintance to come forward.

On 26 March, a thirty-five-year-old man, James Keenan, reported that his wife, Elizabeth, was missing from their home in Lanark. She had been gone about six days following a domestic argument, leaving their baby to be looked after by her mother. The report had the sound of a fairly commonplace domestic upset and no immediate action was proposed.

As part of the ongoing process of eliminating women from the missing persons register, detectives asked Keenan if he would give them a pair of his wife's shoes. When the shoes were tried on the amputated limbs, they were found to fit perfectly. At the end of April, in a copse about a mile from the Keenan's home, a headless torso wrapped in a blanket was discovered by passers-by. A check on fingerprints and an abdominal scar proved that these were the remains of Elizabeth Keenan.

Keenan's house was searched and investigations found evidence in the bathroom of an intensive clean up. Traces of blood were found in the bath waste outlet. Keenan, nicknamed "Tarzan" by his workmates on account of his bodybuilding, was arrested and charged with murder.

Keenan admitted killing his wife with an axe following a quarrel and described how he cut up her body with a hacksaw and wrapped it in pieces of blanket. He put the parcelled-up segments of the body in the boot of his car and drove his child to his mother-in-law's house for her to look after, then drove around distributing his parcels. He led police to a wooded area near Carnwath where he had left the head of his murdered wife.

James Keenan was tried at the High Court in Edinburgh on 3 June 1969 where he pleaded guilty to murder. He said that after he killed his wife he drank a bottle of whisky and the next thing he remembered was seeing her cut up in the bath. He was sentenced to life imprisonment.

Kelly's Head

The notorious Australian bushranger Ned Kelly became a cult figure after his execution in 1880. Unlike many criminals of this era, he had not been transported to Australia from England, although his father had. Kelly senior was transported to the penal settlement at Van Diemen's Land (modern Tasmania) in 1842. He worked on convict gangs for seven years before being released. His years of servitude brought a hatred of law and order which was inherited by his son, Ned.

The Kelly gang were notorious for their exploits, roaming at will and using their knowledge to hide when trouble loomed and to protect their friends. They had virtual free reign because the police were spread so thinly; in the northeast of New South Wales, an area of over 10,000 square miles, there were fifty officers.

It was in this sprawling territory, known as Kelly country, that Ned Kelly shot and killed Constable Thomas Lonigan. This was the crime committed at Stringybank Creek in October 1878 for which Kelly would eventually have to answer. During the next two years there was a spate of bank robberies and other escapades. But, on 27 June 1880, Kelly and three of his gang were located at Glenrowan. The police called for back-up and the rebels were surrounded by fifty armed officers. Wearing improvised armour consisting of pieces of scrap iron and cooking pots, Kelly tried to shoot his way to freedom.

In the fire-fight that followed, all of Kelly's followers were killed and he was taken prisoner. In due course, Ned Kelly was tried at Melbourne for the murder of PC Lonigan. He was convicted of the crime and sentenced to death. The judge, in passing sentence, used the customary words, "And may the Lord have mercy on your soul" to which Ned Kelly reputedly replied, "Yes, I will see you there." Kelly was hanged on 1 November 1880 and Mr Justice Barry died two weeks later.

Kelly became a figure of legend and folklore, featuring in films and books. After he was executed, his head was removed from his corpse and his skull was subsequently displayed in an anatomical museum before ending up in the prison museum at Melbourne. There the gruesome relic remained until 1978 when it was stolen. In 1999, a man living in Western Australia admitted stealing the skull from the museum. He said that as "an angry young man" he could not understand how someone's skull could end up in public custody. He reportedly believes that Ned Kelly's home at Beveridge in Victoria should be restored. He refused to say where the missing skull was but said he wanted it to be buried near Kelly's home.

A Lot Of Work!

In July 1927 in the US, parcels wrapped in brown paper began appearing in the Brooklyn area of New York. The first was spotted by a policeman patrolling in Battery Park, a second was found in a churchyard and a third near a theatre. The contents of the parcels included dismembered portions of a human body.

Several more parcels were discovered in various parts of the city and the combined parts constituted two female bodies, minus their heads. The only available clue was the brown wrapping paper which originated from the Brooklyn branch of Atlantic and Pacific grocery stores.

The police checked missing persons registers and began to focus on the disappearance of a Mrs Bennett who had last been seen entering a boarding house in Prospect Place, Brooklyn. Officers called and asked to speak to Sarah Brownell who ran the establishment. They were admitted to the house by one of the tenants, thirty-eight-year-old Ludwig Lee, a Norwegian who described himself as an odd-job man.

Questioned about Miss Brownell's whereabouts, Lee said, after some hesitation, that she had gone to stay with relatives. During this interview, one of the detectives with a keen nose, picked up the unmistakably cloying smell of decomposition which seemed to pervade the air around Lee. A search of the basement revealed various human body parts and the head of Mrs Bennett. Leaning against the furnace was a large axe which had evidently been cleaned recently.

When other boarders at Prospect Park were interviewed, detectives became acquainted with Christian Jensen who worked as a clerk at Atlantic and Pacific grocery stores. He told them that he had given a quantity of wrapping paper to Lee who wanted it to wrap up gifts to be sent to Norway. Jensen identified his handwriting which appeared on one of the body part parcels.

Doctors pieced together the remains of Mrs Bennett and Miss Brownell on the table in the kitchen of the boarding house. Confronted with their macabre reconstruction, Lee vigorously denied killing the women. The discovery in his room of Sarah Brownwell's savings book showing deposits of $4,000 told a different story. In a final piece of theatre, the police brought Lee and Jensen together. The store clerk confirmed that he had provided Lee with wrapping paper. At this point, Lee broke down and confessed to murdering the two women.

He said Mrs Bennett had come down to the basement looking for Miss Brownell and caught him in the process of disposing of her body. He killed Mrs Bennett to conceal the first murder. "There was nothing to do but chop them into little pieces . . ." he said, adding with reference to his parcel deliveries, "it was a lot of work – doing all that running around." New York's self-confessed parcel murderer was convicted in 1928 and went to his death in the electric chair.

The Sausage Maker

Adolf Luetgert emigrated to the US from Germany and set up a business in Chicago. He brought with him the skills he had learned in making sausages and his products were sought after. He was a man of considerable size, weighing around 109 kg (240 lb). The forty-nine-year-old also had a big sexual appetite, keeping several mistresses and installing a bed at his factory just in case the opportunity for coupling should arise.

Not surprisingly Luetgert's wife, Louisa, became fed up with his ill-disguised antics; she was also worried by the declining state of their business. For his part, Luetgert was tired of his wife and wanted her out of the way so that he would be free to entertain his lovers.

Louisa disappeared on 1 May 1897 and, when her absence was noted, Luetgert told friends that he would hire private detectives to find her. Eventually, Louisa's family reported her as a missing person and the police started to take an interest.

Several searches were made of Luetgert's sausage-making factory and investigators began to take a close look at some of the equipment, including the numerous steam vats. The vats were systematically drained and in one of them police found pieces of bone, some teeth and two gold rings, one of which was engraved with the initials L.L.

Confronted with these discoveries, Luetgert tried to explain away the bone fragments as being of animal origin. He found it difficult to account for his wife's wedding ring, however, particularly as it was known that because her finger joints were swollen she was unable to remove her rings.

Luetgert was charged with murder and sent for trial. One of his employees testified that he had bought a large quantity of potash and given instructions that it was to be crushed and put in one of the steam vats. Luetgert was seen late one evening tending the vat and next morning his workers cleaned up a sticky sludge that had run out on to the floor.

While all this was circumstantial evidence, the sausage-maker's mistresses used his trial to take their revenge. One of these ladies said he told her he hated his wife and "could take her and crush her". Another of his mistresses told the court that he had given her a bloodstained knife for safe-keeping after Louisa disappeared.

Luetgert consistently maintained his innocence but the jury at his trial in 1898 found him guilty and he was sentenced to life imprisonment. He died at Joliet State Penitentiary in 1911. Chicago's appetite for sausages declined after Luetgert's trial but it was by no means certain that Louisa became sausage meat. Her sad fate was to be boiled into sludge.

Bunker Mentality

Men towing a barge on the River Clyde in Scotland on 15 October 1927 spotted an odd-looking bundle on the bank. They retrieved it and on unwrapping it their curiosity was rewarded by the discovery of a collection of human remains. There was a head, two legs sawn off below the knee, an upper leg and an arm. The grisly remnants also included bits of clothing and a newspaper dated 9 October 1926.

The body was quickly identified as Agnes Arbuckle whose home was in Main Street, Glasgow. The police lost no time in making a house call where they found the dead woman's son, James M'Kay, sitting by the fire eating a meal. In answer to questions, he said, "She is dead – she died about ten days ago. I put part of her in the Clyde and the rest is in the bunker."

The bunker, which was in the main room of the house, contained coal, underneath which was buried the rest of Mrs Arbuckle's dismembered remains. In the style of popular reporting, the discovery was referred to as "The Body in the Bunker".

Local enquiries elicited the information that M'Kay had sought help from a friend to move a large, heavy trunk from Mrs Arbuckle's house to his lodgings. This occurred on 12 October and, the following day, M'Kay was observed returning to Main Street with the trunk. A neighbour gave a graphic description of his dishevelled appearance, dirty clothes and shoes and with his hair standing on end above his wild, staring eyes.

A few months before she died, M'Kay had insured his mother's life and when arrested he had writing materials on the kitchen table where he was attempting to forge a will and other documents. Mrs Arbuckle had been a thrifty person and had a nest egg in the bank amounting to eighty-three pounds, which she had not touched for fourteen years.

M'Kay was tried for murder at Glasgow in December 1⁣ An insanity defence was put forward on his behalf but the jury found him guilty as charged and he was sentenced to death. So desperate was he to profit from his mother's death that he removed her dentures and attempted to sell them. After he was sentenced to death for murdering her, he called out to his wife, "Cheer up!"

The case made Scottish legal history by being referred to the High Court of Judiciary at Edinburgh. It was the first appeal of its kind under newly enacted legislation. The Court was asked to accept that while M'Kay had dismembered his mother's body, it was not proved that he had murdered her. It was argued that he might have come home and found her already dead and, believing that he would be held responsible, decided to conceal the body.

This was not an argument that carried much conviction and the prosecutor asked the court to consider the kind of man who would kill and dismember his own mother and then remove the dentures from her mouth and try to sell them. The Court dismissed the appeal and James M'Kay was hanged at Duke Street Prison, Glasgow on 24 January 1928.

Body In The Boot

Twenty-year-old Stephanie Skidmore lived in West Auckland, New Zealand, in a part of the city devoted to the sex trade. She lived with her boyfriend, Jason Menzies, and twenty-month-old baby. She was last seen alive on 12 May 1996 when she left home after a disagreement.

Concerned about the loss of contact, Stephanie's mother, who lived in the USA, made several repeated telephone calls to Auckland. She spoke to Menzies who explained that Stephanie had left him. He disagreed that he should report her disappearance to the authorities. The couple had frequent arguments and Stephanie had apparently gone off before.

After further phone calls, Menzies agreed to report her as a missing person which he did on 11 June, nearly a month after she was last seen. The police concentrated their enquiries in the red light district where Stephanie had involvement with prostitution and nightclubs. They pieced together a picture of an erratic young woman with a history of running away from home. She had met Jason Menzies in 1993 and, from all accounts, the couple had a troubled relationship.

Police enquiries established that money had been withdrawn from Stephanie's bank account six days after she went missing. Only she could have done this unless someone else had access to her PIN number. Her friends were convinced that it was unlikely she would have abandoned her baby.

On 27 June, Menzies appeared on nationwide television seeking information from the public in the search for Stephanie. By this time, police were beginning to take a keen interest in Menzies who had made a number of decisions about income support and other matters which suggested he did not expect Stephanie to return.

Officers visited Menzies' home. It seemed he liked cars and there were six vehicles parked at the rear of his flat. These were searched and in the boot of one of them was a bundle wrapped in an assortment of plastic sheeting and bedclothes tied up with cord. Once unravelled, the bundle was found to contain the decomposing body of Stephanie.

Menzies was arrested and charged with murder. He was tried at the High Court in May 1997. The prosecution case was that he had strangled Stephanie in their flat. He claimed her death was an accident arising over an argument about who should make scrambled eggs. He said she was high on drugs and out of control. She attacked him with a knife and in the struggle that followed he throttled her.

Once she was dead, he wrapped the body up and kept it in the flat for several days while he went about his normal affairs, including looking after the baby. He elicited the help of friends to move the body into the boot of the car where it was eventually found by the police.

The prosecutor dismissed Menzies's claims that he had acted in self-defence, saying that he lied to save his skin. The jury found him guilty of murder and he was sentenced to life imprisonment. His failure to dispose of the body had inevitably led to his certain downfall.

The Sunday Roast

Forty-seven-year-old John Perry, a factory worker from Wales in the UK, met his future wife on a holiday in the Philippines in June 1984. Arminda was half his age and had a young daughter. They joined Perry in Wales and Arminda, who changed her name to Annabelle, became his wife.

Their marriage soon got into difficulty due chiefly to Annabelle's promiscuous ways. She made herself available to other men, which infuriated Perry and arguments ensued. One of the problems was that he worked a nightshift, which enabled the marital bed to be used by Annabelle to entertain her men friends.

In 1990, Annabelle asked for a divorce to which Perry responded by unsuccessfully trying to have her deported. A settlement was agreed whereby Perry would pay her a lump sum and regular maintenance for her daughter. Payment was due in February 1991 and it was then that neighbours noticed Annabelle's absence. Perry explained that she had gone to London to work as a prostitute.

On 28 February, police called at Perry's home to enquire about his missing wife. To the question, "What happened to your wife?", he replied, "I've killed her." This startling response was delivered against a background of activity in the kitchen which seemed to involve a great deal of roasted meat.

Examination of the kitchen, apart from the smell, revealed a coating of grease on every surface, an oven coated with fat and piles of cooked flesh cut into small pieces. In the garage were plastic containers filled with portions of cooked flesh and other body parts. Little remained that could be identified and Perry explained that he had destroyed his wife's skull. He had not entirely defeated the skills of forensic science, though, for enough remained of the jaws to confirm by dental identification that the remains were those of Mrs Perry.

John Perry was tried for murder at Mold Crown Court in November 1998. When he gave evidence he related how his world collapsed when he realized his wife was having an affair. He described an argument when she threatened to cut her wrist with a kitchen knife. He struggled with her to gain possession of the knife – then everything went blank. He tried to revive her without success and then decided to dispose of her body. At first he thought of burial but he wanted to make sure her remains would never be found so he opted for dismemberment and rendered the remains. Asked why he cooked the body parts, he said he remembered from his school days that a human body was composed of seven-tenths water. He believed that by cooking the body he would reduce it to a condition that would make its disposal easier. He used a popular family medical guide containing diagrams of human anatomy to dismember her body. When questioned, he admitted cooking the remains and feeding some to the cat.

The jury returned a majority verdict of guilty. The judge spoke about Perry's chilling and ruthless efficiency and the fact that he had not shown the slightest remorse at what he had done. The self-taught anatomist was sentenced to life imprisonment.

Secret Burial

While working as an airline official at Manchester airport in the UK in 1959, Peter Reyn-Bardt met thirty-two-year-old Malika Maria de Fernandez and within three days they had married. Their wedding photograph showed a happy, smiling couple, but for Reyn-Bardt, it was a marriage of convenience. He was a homosexual and he believed that being married would give him credibility with his employer.

Friction soon intruded on the marital scene and the couple decided to lead separate lives. Reyn-Bardt moved to a cottage near Wilmslow, Cheshire, where he lived with his homosexual partner. In the space of nine months he and Malika married, argued and split-up.

In October 1960, Malika turned up at the cottage demanding money. In his statements to the police, Reyn-Bardt claimed that she came at him, clawing at his face, after he refused her demands. He remembered grabbing her around the neck and shaking her. Then she was lying dead at his feet. He said the attack was not premeditated. "Something just boiled over inside me," he said. He could not remember how he killed her.

Faced with the dead body of his wife, Reyn-Bardt decided on dismemberment. He used an axe to sever the head and limbs and attempted to burn them in his garden. When this failed, he buried the remains.

Then, twenty-two years later, came the discovery of a human skull in the peat bog close to Reyn-Bardt's cottage. An excavator driver digging out peat for a commercial contractor unearthed the skull about 300 yards from the property. The fact that the skull was that of a female aged around thirty fitted Malika. Questioned by the police in June 1983, Reyn-Bardt admitted killing her.

He was sent for trial at Chester Crown Court in December 1983. Reyn-Bardt pleaded not guilty to the charge of murder. His defence was that he had struggled with his wife after she attacked him but he could not recall what happened afterwards. The supreme irony of the case was provided by testimony from a professor at Oxford University's department of archaeology. He said that the age of the human skull had been carbon dated to around the year 410 AD.

The jury brought in a majority verdict of guilty and Reyn-Bardt was sentenced to life imprisonment. Among the mysteries concerning Malika was that her remains have not been found and her origins were not clear either. On her marriage certificate she was described as a portrait painter and her father's name was recorded as Benjamin Mendoza de Fernandez. Attempts to locate him proved fruitless.

"Piggy Palace"

The Downtown-Eastside district of Vancouver in Canada was a rundown area and home to drug addicts, pimps and prostitutes. A third of the population of the area fell into one or other of these categories, and the rate of HIV infection was the highest in North America. Initially, when young women began disappearing without trace in Vancouver in 1983, the police were reluctant to accept that a serial killer was at large. They believed they were dealing with a transient population and when one of their number suggested that the statistical concentration of missing people indicated something more sinister, he was not taken seriously. But, eventually, after a period of twenty years, when more than sixty women had gone missing and bowing to pressure from missing women's families and the media, an investigation team was assembled.

The investigative trail led to a farm at Port Coquitlam, twenty miles east of the city, run by the Pickton brothers, and to the stabbing of a prostitute. Robert Pickton was charged with this offence but the case was dropped.

Slowly, a pattern emerged at what life down on the farm was like. Pickton ran a late night drinking den in a barn, which he called Piggy Palace. Female drug addicts and prostitutes were among the clientele. A notice on the farm gate warned off intruders – "This property protected by a pit bull with AIDS".

Police began to receive calls from the public about activities at the farm and in 2002 Robert Pickton was arrested in connection with an enquiry about weapons. A search of the premises turned up some interesting artefacts in the freezer: two human heads and assorted severed hands and feet. This discovery led to a two-year investigation by forensic teams who searched through 370,000 cubic metres of mud and farm waste looking for human remains. They also took over 200,000 DNA samples. Traces of thirty women were found on the seven-hectare farm.

As news of the grim discoveries reached the press, fears were expressed locally that human remains might have found their way into food products via Pickton's pig feed. It later transpired that he put body parts through a wood chipper.

Robert Pickton, who liked to be called Willy, was a regular user of prostitutes, many of whom had a $500-a-day drug habit. He associated with Hell's Angels and was thought by many to be weird. Apart from his parties at Piggy Palace, he kept a low profile. He was charged with the murders of twenty-seven women and sent for trial on six counts based on the identification of human remains found at his barn.

Initially, he pleaded not guilty but then claimed he had killed forty-nine women. He allegedly told a fellow remand prisoner, "I was going to do one more and make it an even fifty." The evidence against him was unchallengeable but the jury at British Colombia's Supreme Court took ten days to reach their verdict in December 2007. They found fifty-eight-year-old Pickton guilty of six murders and he received an automatic life sentence. He still faces charges over twenty other deaths and police investigations into forty other missing women continue.

Two Fingers!

In Austria, Vienna's Police Commissioner Weitzel was startled to find he had been sent the well-manicured, surgically removed digit from a woman's right hand. This surprise package, received on April Fools' Day in 1926, was followed some days later by another finger, complete with a gold ring.

Inspection of the surface of the ring indicated it had been etched with what investigators believed might have been the type of acid used to remove tattoos. Microscopic examination of the finger confirmed this theory with the discovery of faint tattoo marks in the form of a snake.

While detectives visited tattoo parlours in the city to find a source for the snake design, enquiries took an unexpected turn when the headless body of a woman, minus two fingers from the right hand, was found in swampy ground. A footprint left in soft soil near the body suggested the involvement of a heavily built man and the surgical skill evident in the removal of the fingers led detectives to think their quarry was a surgeon.

By a process of elimination, they came up with the name of Dr Herman Schmitz. He fitted the weight criteria and his medical background was highly relevant. The doctor had suffered a decline in his practice following charges of malpractice. Despite being exonerated of any wrongdoing, the stigma remained.

Enquiries revealed that Dr Schmitz was married with two

children and that he also had a mistress, all of whom were fit and well. Further scrutiny of his background showed that his mistress frequented a particular dress shop where her purchases were charged to the doctor's account. Significantly, his previous mistress, Anna Stein, had enjoyed the same privilege and she was now missing.

Attention immediately switched to the woman's body, minus its head and two fingers, which lay in the mortuary. Next came a search of Dr Schmitz's consulting rooms where officers found the head of Anna Stein immersed in preservative. The outcome of tests on the body was that she had been poisoned with cyanide.

It was presumed that the doctor had killed her to make way for his new lover. He then hit on the idea of literally giving two fingers to the police to taunt them and perhaps to get his own back for what he saw as the injustice of being prosecuted for malpractice. Unfortunately for him, his taunt came at a price because he had failed to remove all traces of the identifying tattoo.

While in custody, Dr Schmitz made a bid for freedom and, in the course of his escape, fell from the top of a building. He made a dying confession of murder and Vienna's police museum acquired a new exhibit in the form of two fingers.

A Secret No More

A man out walking his dog in Norwich in the UK on a summers' day in 1851 was surprised when the animal rooted out a piece of flesh which turned out to be a human hand. The discovery was reported to the police and there was great public curiosity at the prospect of finding more human remains.

Search parties aided by dogs scoured the countryside and in the days following the initial discovery, a foot, pelvis, several vertebrae and sundry gobbets of flesh were retrieved. Doctors examining the remains believed they were of a woman aged between sixteen and twenty-six.

Posters were printed seeking information, especially about any missing women. Meanwhile searches continued in a radius of two to three miles from the centre of Norwich and further discoveries were made. Another foot and hand turned up, together with some intestines and pieces of flesh, all in different locations.

Curiously, there was no coroner's inquest and interest waned as other events captured the public imagination. The unidentified remains were preserved in spirit and after several months, were emptied into a hole dug in the basement of Norwich Guildhall and covered with lime.

Time went by and the remains of the woman lay out of sight and out of mind. Then, eighteen years later, out of the blue, came a confession to murder. On 1 January 1869, a man appeared at Walworth Police Station in London and declared, "I have a charge to make against myself." Asked to explain himself, he said that he had murdered his first wife at Norwich, adding, "I have kept the secret for years and can keep it no longer." He identified himself as William Sheward.

Sheward was put in a cell overnight and questioned the following morning. He stated that he cut his wife's throat with a razor on 15 June 1851 and then cut up the body. He was charged with murder and remanded pending enquiries in Norwich. Many of those involved in the original investigation had since died. Relatives of Martha Sheward provided a description of her, with particular reference to her golden hair. The man who had found a piece of skin back in 1851 remarked on the golden colour of the hair attached to it. Direct comparison with the remains mouldering in the earth under the Guildhall proved impossible; all that was left were a few bones.

Sheward was sent for trial at Norfolk Assizes where he appeared in March 1869. After hearing the evidence the judge advised the jury that they needed to answer three questions: was Martha Sheward dead? was she murdered? were the remains hers? All the answers appeared to have been affirmative when the jury returned its guilty verdict. The judge pronounced sentence of death and Sheward was taken to the City Gaol.

While awaiting execution, he made a confession. He said he and Martha had "a slight altercation" over money. "Then I ran the razor into her throat." He continued by giving a detailed account of which body parts he disposed of on which days. He had put his wife's head in a saucepan and boiled it before breaking it up for disposal.

Execution was set for 20 April when fifty-seven-year-old Sheward, badly crippled with rheumatism, shuffled to the gallows. The hangman did his work while 2,000 people waited outside the prison gates. His confession was published and *The Times* described it as a "shocking and disgusting narrative ...".

Out Of The Deep

Visitors to the Coogee Beach aquarium in Australia admired a tiger shark and its graceful movement in the water when the creature experienced what might be described as a stomach upset. Out of the shark's mouth came a human arm which, on closer inspection, was seen to bear a tattoo of a pair of boxers squaring up to each other. This exotic discovery in April 1935 sparked off one of Australia's most enduring murder mysteries.

With the evidence of the tattoo and by taking fingerprints from the severed arm, investigators were able to identify its owner as James Smith, a forty-year-old ex-boxer. Smith was employed at the Sydney boatbuilding yard operated by Reg Holmes and had been missing for two weeks.

Smith had spent a holiday in a rented cottage at Cronulla with Patrick Brady who was known to the police as a forger. The police had stumbled on an intricate web of underworld dealings. Brady was questioned and denied killing Smith but implicated Reg Holmes in criminal activities.

While Brady was in custody, there was an incident in Sydney harbour involving Holmes. His speedboat was stopped after a chase and when police boarded it they found Holmes lying injured with a bullet wound to the head that turned out to be superficial. He claimed that he had been trying to get away from a gunman who was attempting to kill him. Holmes admitted knowing Brady and accused him of killing Smith and disposing of his body.

Brady was charged with Smith's murder and while he was in custody, Reg Holmes was shot dead in his car. Telling his wife he was meeting a friend, Holmes left his home on the evening of 11 June saying he would be home before 9.30 p.m. A witness living at Miller's Point saw a man leaning into Holmes' car and then heard three shots. The man walked away and was never identified.

The fatal shooting of Reg Holmes occurred on the eve of the Coroner's inquest into the Shark Arm affair at which he was due to appear as a witness. Medical evidence featured prominently at the inquest and doctors stated that the arm had been severed with a sharp knife, although not as part of any surgical operation. Another expert was confident that the arm had been removed from a dead body by the shark. Brady's lawyer argued that an arm did not by itself constitute a body and contended that there was no conclusive proof that Smith was in fact dead.

The inquest proved to be a stormy affair with first the widow of James Smith giving testimony and then the statement previously given to the police by Reg Holmes. The question hanging in the air was how much of a body was legally required for it to be accepted as a body within the meaning of the Coroner's Act? The outcome was that, at a special hearing, Mr Justice Halse Rogers decided that an identified part of a body and evidence that it came from a dead body were insufficient for a Coroner's jurisdiction.

Patrick Brady was committed for trial but, on the basis of the circumstantial evidence put to the court, the judge acquitted him. Brady, who had protested his innocence throughout the Shark Arm saga died in hospital on 11 August 1965. It was believed that both Holmes and Brady had been involved in murky underworld activities. Had he lived, Holmes would have been a star trial witness. Two men charged with his murder were subsequently acquitted.

An international forensic expert who examined the Shark Arm believed that Smith's body had been dismembered and put into a trunk for disposal at sea. The arm would not fit inside the trunk so it was roped to the outside, worked loose in the sea and was swallowed by a shark. The police believed that the elimination of Reg Holmes dispelled any hopes of solving the mystery.

The Handless Corpse

Amateur scuba divers in the UK discovered a naked man's body in a quarry on 14 October 1979. The hands had been cut off at the wrists and the face mutilated to obscure the identity of the dead man. Initial thinking was that he had been executed in some kind of gangland killing or was possibly an IRA victim.

Then, out of the blue, two women appeared at Leyland police station to tell an amazing story about a drugs syndicate operating in several countries and turning over millions of pounds. Julie Hue had been in Spain with a friend, Barbara Pilkington, when she was told that the syndicate had killed her boyfriend. Fearing for her own life, she returned to the UK.

The handless corpse was the boyfriend, twenty-seven-year-old New Zealander Martin Johnstone, a member of the drug syndicate. Sometimes known as "Mr Asia", Johnstone ran the syndicate's operations in south-east Asia. Hue and Pilkington were afraid of Andrew Maker, who had worked with Johnstone.

Maker had sidetracked Johnstone to work on a fictitious deal in Scotland and it was Maker who shot his business associate and mutilated his body before dumping it in the flooded quarry. Others were involved in supplying weights to make sure the body sank in the water and providing the murder weapon.

As the investigation spread its net, the path led to Alexander Sinclair, known as "Mr Big", a New Zealander with a criminal record. He and his associates criss-crossed the globe moving drugs and money about and keeping a tight rein on their operatives. Johnstone had, apparently, stepped over a few boundaries and Sinclair gave instructions that he was to be eliminated.

In July 1981, the plotters were put on trial at Lancaster Castle. Eight men and one woman appeared in court in proceedings that lasted 121 days. Alexander Sinclair, who was believed to have made £25 million from drug-dealing denied murder. Andrew Maker pleaded guilty to murder and conspiracy. James Smith who helped dispose of the body, denied murder. Keith Kirby denied murder; Frederick Russell, who supplied the weapon, pleaded guilty; Leila Barclay, the syndicate's banker, pleaded guilty to drug conspiracy charges; Errol Hincksman, Christopher Blackman and Sylvester Pidgeon denied drug conspiracy charges.

The jury listened to detailed allegations of an international drug operation that ended in the sordid execution of one of the main players. After deliberating for thirty-eight hours, they found Sinclair, Maker, Smith and Kirby guilty of murder; Russell had already pleaded guilty. Three others were convicted on drug conspiracy charges.

Sentenced to life imprisonment and wanted in Australia in connection with five murders, Sinclair was confined in Parkhurst Prison. His death in prison was reported in 1983. He was thirty-nine years old and most of his drug-dealing fortune remained intact.

I.D. On A Plate

Daryl Suckling was a caretaker at Wyrama Station, a remote community in New South Wales, Australia. In March 1988, he and his supposed niece were invited to dinner by neighbours. During the evening, Sophie Carnie, detached herself from Suckling and privately told her host that she was being held captive by him against her wishes. The dinner host discreetly informed the police and a bizarre story began to unravel.

Under questioning, twenty-six-year-old Sophie related how she had befriended Suckling, a man twice her age, who had served time in Pentridge Prison. She felt sorry for him because he seemed friendless when he was released. She invited him to live with her and her husband in Melbourne. Events took a turn for the worse when Suckling teamed up with her husband to carry out burglaries. Both men ended up with prison sentences.

On his release in 1987, Suckling sought to re-establish his relationship with Sophie but she made it clear that she did not want to know. In March 1988, Suckling kidnapped Sophie, held her captive at his home and repeatedly raped her. He threatened to kill her saying that he had "a body buried down the wood already".

Sophie's strategy was to comply with her captor's wishes to the point where he allowed her limited freedom. This culminated in the dinner with neighbours and her opportunity to escape from his clutches. When police searched Suckling's home, they found chains, handcuffs and drugs which amply supported Sophie's story. They also found articles of female clothing, not belonging to Sophie, and, significantly, discovered a denture discarded in a waste disposal sack.

Further searches turned up photographs of naked women and one in particular who appeared to be distressed and drugged. She was identified as Jodie Marie Larcombe, a twenty-one-year-old Melbourne prostitute, missing since December 1987. Confirmation of her identity came from the discovery of her dental plate found at Suckling's home.

Suckling was charged with Larcombe's murder, although there was no body. Intensive searches using police divers and aerial surveys failed to recover the missing woman. The only evidence against Suckling was circumstantial. In the meantime, he was charged with the abduction and rape of Sophie Carnie but the young woman died of a drug overdose before the trial.

In August 1989, Suckling was committed for trial for the murder of Jodie Larcombe but proceedings were dropped due to lack of evidence. The case remained open and police achieved a breakthrough in 1994 when a man who met Suckling in prison revealed the admissions his fellow inmate had divulged. Suckling told him that he had abducted and murdered a woman several years previously. The informer co-operated with investigators and in bugged conversations Suckling boasted about getting away with murder and described some of his acts of mutilation in horrific detail.

Suckling finally stood trial for the murder of Jodie Larcombe in September 1996. New evidence was put forward, including a statement from a relative who said Suckling had volunteered the information that he had cut the girl's body into pieces and buried them. Together with admissions he had made while in prison, there was, finally, sufficient evidence to convict him of murder. He was found guilty and sentenced to life imprisonment. Jodie Larcombe's body has not been found.

"Jigsaw Murder"

The first piece of New York's "Jigsaw Murder" turned up in the form of part of a man's upper body found by two boys swimming in the harbour on a summer's day in 1897. During the following few days, further pieces of a dismembered corpse were retrieved, sufficient to piece together a complete body with the exception of the head.

Two teenagers cooling off in the murky waters of a disused dock had discovered a parcel wrapped in distinctive red oilcloth. Excited by their mysterious find, they removed the wrapping and, to their horror, revealed part of a man's torso. The next day, two different boys, picking wild fruit along the banks of the Harlem River came across another parcel similarly wrapped in red oilcloth. Later in the same week sailors at Brooklyn Navy Yard found a pair of human legs.

Investigators put the pieces of the human jigsaw together and they fitted to complete a human corpse save the head. Significantly, a piece of skin had been cut away from the chest, suggesting that a distinctive mark, possibly an identifying tattoo, had been removed. Another feature of the torso was that it was well developed and the hands were smooth and well cared for.

While the police scratched their heads about the possible occupation and identity of the "Jigsaw Murder" victim, a young medical student came up with a possible answer. He thought the physical characteristics of the corpse indicated that in life the man might have been a masseur.

There were numerous Turkish bath establishments in New York City and enquiries revealed that a masseur at one of the baths, a man called Willie Guldensuppe, had not reported for work for a few days. A description of the missing masseur matched the human remains in the post-mortem room and it was confirmed that Willie had a tattoo on his chest.

It appeared that Willie lived with a lady called Augusta Nack who was separated from her husband and had acquired a number of lovers. With the masseur now missing, Augusta had a new man in her life, one Fred Thorn. It appeared that he had been on the scene before but had been frightened off by Willie.

Fred Thorn and Augusta Nack were arrested on suspicion of murder and clinching evidence of violence was provided by bloodstained water which had drained into the street from the soakaway of Augusta's house. Faced with this discovery, Augusta told police that she had lured Willie to her house where Fred Thorn lay in wait. Thorn shot the masseur and put the body in the bath where it was dismembered.

Augusta had bought a supply of red oilcloth for the purpose of parcelling up the remains. She and Thorn embedded the head in Plaster of Paris, which, unlike the oilcloth bundles, sank when jettisoned in the harbour. At their trial for murder, Augusta turned States Evidence and pleaded guilty to manslaughter. For her part in the killing of Willie Guldensuppe, she was sentenced to fifteen years imprisonment, while Fred Thorn went to the electric chair at Sing Sing in August 1898.

Power Assisted

Simone Weber, who restored vintage cars in her spare time, was widowed in 1980 when the elderly man she had married three weeks earlier died suddenly. When Marcel Fixart, a retired gendarme, left the world unexpectedly, she inherited his house and assets. Her neighbours in Nancy in eastern France gave full reign to gossip and rumour. This increased in December 1983 when she met forty-eight-year-old Bernard Hettier, the foreman at a local factory with a reputation as a ladies man.

The sixty-year-old and her toy-boy became lovers, but she proved to be too obsessive and Hettier tried to break off their relationship. In June 1985, he disappeared along with his Renault car and personal documents. The tongues wagged and Weber was questioned by the police about her paramour's disappearance. While there was suspicion, there was no evidence.

The police decided to consult Examining Magistrate, Gilbert Thiel, a man with a determined streak in his personality. As a result of this consultation, police tapped Weber's telephone. She made calls to her sister in Cannes and there were references to "Bernardette". This turned out to be a nickname for Bernard Hettier's car.

Investigators discovered that an elderly couple living on the ground floor of the building in Avenue de Strasbourg, where Weber had an apartment, had observed some strange goings on. In June 1985 they had seen her with a man who appeared to be drunk. On the evening of 22 June they heard a noise that sounded like a vacuum cleaner or an electric motor of some kind. The next day they were surprised to see Weber carry down seventeen plastic refuse bags which she took away in her car.

It was known that Weber had hired an electric saw but failed to return it, saying it had been stolen. Sensing a breakthrough in their enquiries, police recollected that in September 1985 a fisherman had reeled in a suitcase from the River Marne. The suitcase belonged to Bernard Hettier and contained a torso, minus head and limbs. Pathologists believed the dismemberment had been effected with an electric saw.

It took Examining Magistrate Thiel four years to accumulate enough evidence to put Weber on trial for murder. Incredibly there were no traces of blood or tissue in Weber's apartment although she had acquired guns, dynamite and a collection of official rubber stamps. Bernard Hettier's car was found in a rented garage in Cannes. Weber had left a trail of deception including false documents, forged prescriptions and false names.

Tried for the murders of Hettier and Fixart in March 1991, La Sorcière, as she had been dubbed by the press, was found guilty of killing Hettier and sentenced to twenty years imprisonment. She was cleared of murdering Fixart due to lack of evidence.

Fancy Knifework

A father and son out scavenging along the banks of the river near Lynwood, California, in the US in April 1928, found the torso of a young woman floating in the water. This was the start of what became known as the "Lynwood Torso Mystery".

A post-mortem carried out on the torso determined that the limbs and head of the corpse had been detached by someone with dissection skills using surgical instruments. The immediate problem facing investigators was to identify the body. They began by checking reports on missing persons but, six weeks after the grim discovery of the torso, there was still no identification.

The big question was, where was the missing head? This was dramatically resolved on 18 May when some boys were seen fooling around with a head on a pole. Horrified residents of Lynwood at first thought the head was some kind of mask but then came the grim reality that it was a human skull.

Pathologists matched the head to the torso and were able to assess the age of the corpse as around forty to fifty years. Investigators continued to check out missing persons reports and sought help from the public to help identify the woman.

The breakthrough came when a man reported that his former wife, Laura Bell Sutton, had been absent from her Los Angeles home since 17 May. Another man, describing himself as a friend, also came forward saying Laura Bell had been distressed by the recent death of her mother and might have left for that reason. The informant was Frank Westlake, a recently widowed businessman.

Laura Bell was a forty-five-year-old divorcee who lived alone but was known to have an active social life and several men friends. Frank Westlake was one of these. Investigators talked to Laura's family and friends and established that she was last seen alive on 29 March when she paid a visit to her attorney. When it was discovered that fresh flowers had been put on her mother's grave, it led to speculation that Laura was still alive.

The missing woman's dentist was consulted and he was able to confirm that, without doubt, the remains retrieved from the river at Lynwood were those of Laura Bell. Investigators turned their attention to the dead woman's male companions and, in particular, Frank Westlake.

It seemed that while he may have been Laura's lover, he was also her business manager. They shared a joint bank account and he was the beneficiary of her life assurance. When it turned out that Westlake had worked as a surgeon in Illinois, the police began to take a closer interest in him. They were mindful about the skill shown in dismembering the body.

Westlake told investigators that he and Laura planned to marry and said he had forsaken his medical career to come and live in California. With their suspicions growing, detectives followed Westlake on a trip he made to visit his son in Pasadena. In the garage roof of his son's house, officers retrieved a set of surgical instruments wrapped in a newspaper dated 24 March.

Further enquiries about the doctor's background established that at least five people close to him had died suddenly, leaving their properties and financial assets to him. There were also rumours that he had been involved in carrying out illegal abortions.

A coroner determined that Laura Bell had died of a blunt trauma to the head and traces of blood found in Westlake's bathroom led to his arrest for murder. The evidence against him was circumstantial and he maintained that Laura was still alive.

Dr Westlake was sent for trial in August 1929 when Laura Bell's mortal remains were exhibited in full view of the court. The prosecution case was that he had killed the woman, cut up her body in the bath and disposed of it in the river. The doctor continued to state his belief that she was still alive and protested his innocence.

After many hours deliberation, the jury brought in a guilty verdict but declined to recommend the death penalty. On 8 September, Dr Westlake was sentenced to life imprisonment in San Quentin. He was released on parole after serving fourteen years and he died in January 1950 at the age of eighty.

CHAPTER 3

Playing God

Sir Arthur Conan Doyle trained as a doctor and practised medicine for eight years before starting his illustrious career as a writer. With this experience and his characteristic insight, he had Sherlock Holmes comment that when a doctor goes wrong he is the "first of criminals" because he has both nerve and knowledge.

As a profession, doctors command all the skills and means to execute murder to perfection if that is where their mind takes them. By their very nature little is known of such crimes because subtlety and secrecy direct their commission. Yet doctors form an unusually large category in the annals of murder with the names of many well-known and infamous practitioners such as Crippen, Palmer, Pritchard, Ruxton, Webster, Petiot, Bougrat and others.

It is to be assumed that when doctors fall prey to the human frailties that inspire criminal activity, they do so for the same motives that drive others; gain, lust, elimination and jealousy. Once they have crossed the Hippocratic threshold of not preserving life but of extinguishing it, they have a number of attributes in their favour.

They are trusted and respected members of the community who enjoy access to people's homes and private lives in the performance of their duties. Drs John Bodkin Adams and Harold Shipman were examples of medical men who exploited privileged knowledge of their patients' lives for gain. Doctors, dentists and nurses have legitimate and regular access to drugs and possess the knowledge to guide their choice of unusual lethal agents that are difficult to detect. Dr Paul Vickers used a rare drug to poison his wife and Dr Carlo Nigrisoli employed curare with the same intention. Operating on a different principle, the expectation of disguising murder as fatal illness, Dr Warren Waite and Dr John Hill plied their victims with lethal concoctions of death-dealing bacteria.

Given the attractive subtleties of poisoning or administering a lethal overdose of a prescription drug, it is surprising that doctors even think of using violent means. Yet Dr Geza de Kaplany opted for the use of acid, ostensibly only to disfigure his wife but, nevertheless, condemning her to a horrific death. Dr Yves Evenou's choice of a weapon to murder his wife was a knife, although he directed someone else to use it.

While doctors may sometimes by accused of playing god, it is a role better suited to the destructive impulses of nurses and carers who are entrusted with administering treatment to patients usually in hospital or nursing homes. The problems of dealing with sick, elderly and, sometimes fractious, patients can overwhelm the ethics of caring to the point where they opt for elimination. One such carer, Colin Norris, grew to despise those he was supposed to care for while Waltraud Wagner disposed of patients who were a nuisance. Access to hypodermic syringes, intravenous drips and prescribed drugs provided ample means.

Apart from the elimination of troublesome patients on hospital wards and in nursing homes, another motive is that of satisfying a craving for self-importance. Genene Jones thrived on emergencies in the wards where she cared for babies as did Beverly Allitt and, between them, they were responsible for at least five infant deaths. Jane Toppan was a nurse who enjoyed the power she had over patients because they trusted her. Robert Diaz had visions of grandeur and asked to be called "doctor" while Robert Harvey maintained the pretence that he was carrying out mercy killing. Between them this deadly trio accounted for the deaths of over eighty patients and possibly more.

With the notable exception of Harold Shipman who murdered 215 of his patients, doctors tend to limit themselves to one or two victims. Dr Michael Swango however, is an exception in every sense. Known to his colleagues at medical school as Double-O-Swango (licensed to kill), Swango left a trail of death behind him wherever he practised, accounting for thirty-five murders using lethal injections. He was obsessed with poisons and addicted to playing God.

Licensed To Kill

In 1984, Ohio State University Hospital in the US dispensed with Dr Michael Swango's services following the mysterious deaths of several patients. The following year, while working as a paramedic at Quincy's Blessing Hospital in Illinois, he poisoned five colleagues with arsenic but with no fatalities. He was tried for these offences but the evidence was regarded as inconclusive. The judge determined that Swango did not intend to kill his poison victims but only wanted to study their reactions. He was given the minimum sentence of five years' imprisonment.

Hospital colleagues recalled that Swango kept files of newspaper cuttings dealing with cases of poisoning, including the umbrella murder of Georgi Markov in London in 1978 using ricin. In conversation, he gave his view that poisoning was a good way to kill people. He went a step further while watching a television programme about serial killer Henry Lee Lucas when he suggested it would be a treat "to travel around the country killing people".

On release from prison, Swango easily secured a post as a physician at the Veteran Affairs Medical Center in Iowa by the simple device of concealing his criminal record. When his past caught up with him, the hospital authorities dismissed him. Yet, once again, he quickly found new employment, this time at the Veterans Affairs Medical Center in Northport, New York state. He worked at Northport for four months in 1993. During that time four patients in his care died. Again, the authorities dismissed him when they learned of his record. But the damage had already been done by the doctor's toxic injections. Perhaps feeling the heat, he absconded to foreign parts.

For eight months in 1994/95, he worked as a physician at Mnene Mission Hospital in Zimbabwe. His presence was marked by the death of patients and a warrant was issued for his arrest in connection with five fatal poisonings. Dr Swango left Zimbabwe in 1997 en route to a new medical post in Saudi Arabia but encountered difficulties over his visa. This meant taking a flight to a destination in the USA, which would issue the necessary document. On arrival in Chicago, he was arrested for a minor offence.

In due course, Swango was charged with three counts of murder related to the deaths at Northport, New York State. He was suspected of killing as many as thirty-two other patients. At his trial in New York, he admitted to killing a sixty-year-old man. "I did this," he said, "by administering a toxic substance which I knew was likely to cause death. I knew it was wrong."

Swango's favourite film was *Silence of the Lambs* and he was also apparently influenced by a number of books about murder. He made notes on one of them in which he recorded of the central character that, "He could look himself in the mirror and tell himself that he was one of the most powerful and dangerous men in the world. He could feel that he was a god in disguise."

Prosecutors described Swango as a person who killed for thrills; "He used his skills to search for victims and take their lives." During his professional career as a doctor, sixty of his patients died. He was obsessed with poison and detectives searching his apartment found a virtual laboratory stocked with poisonous compounds.

Dr Swango was found guilty of murder and given three life sentences to run consecutively. His philosophy was perhaps summed-up by one of the quotations found in his notebook which read. "I love it. Sweet, husky, close smell of an indoor homicide." A press headline accurately captured the nature of the man with the title, "Doctor Death".

Sister Knows Best

"You're looking terrible, let me give you a tonic ... Sister knows best." These were some of the last words heard by many of Nurse Toppan's patients.

Jane Toppan was a child adopted by a family in Lowell, Massachusetts, in the US, whom she impressed with her religious and scholarly diligence. After being jilted and surviving a suicide attempt, she took up nursing. In 1882 she enrolled for training and again impressed her tutors with her eagerness to learn. It was noted, though, that she had a particular fascination with post-mortem work.

Her early promise remained unfulfilled when she was dismissed from one of her early jobs following the unexpected deaths of two patients. After she was turned down for a position at a hospital because she was unqualified, she decided to pursue a different path by providing nursing care to people in their own homes.

At the age of twenty-six, Toppan had established a reputation among many New England families as a dedicated, caring nurse. She lost patients in the course of her work but, as she moved from job to job, no one was keeping count. In 1901 she arrived at the Davis home in Cataumet and four members of the family died from strange illnesses.

When the husband of one of the family members returned home after a long sea trip to an empty house, he demanded an explanation and wanted his wife's body exhumed. The result was that she had died of morphine poisoning. This perplexed the family doctor because when he examined the woman there was no pin-pointing of the pupils of the eyes which is indicative of morphine poisoning.

Suspicion began to grow around "Nurse" Toppan with first a trickle and then a flood of allegations about her activities. Throughout Massachusetts graves were opened up of persons who had perished while she was caring for them. "I wouldn't kill a chicken" was her response to suggestions that she had murdered many of her patients.

Enquiries eventually led detectives to a pharmacist who had regularly supplied Toppan with morphine on doctors' prescriptions. It was shown that the signatures on the forms were forged. Taken in to custody, Toppan made a confession naming thirty-one of her victims. "Oh, I killed so many of them," she said. Her cunning method was to counteract the telltale pin-pointing of the pupils caused by morphine by adding atropine which had the opposite effect. By this means she was able to kill using morphine without being detected and doctors had no difficulty issuing death certificates.

With the angel of the sick room at their bedside, her patients absorbed ever-increasing doses of her deadly mixture. They suffered painful breathing and convulsions and died, while "Nurse" Toppan moved on to her next assignment.

"Everybody trusted me," she said, "It was so easy. I felt strange when I watched them die . . . it was the only pleasure I had . . . I had to do it." She was tried for murder in June 1902 and a plea of not guilty by reason of insanity was entered on her behalf. She reacted strongly to this, declaring in court. "I understand right from wrong! That proves I am sane."

Jane Toppan was sent to Taunton State Asylum for the Criminally Insane where she died, aged eighty-four, in 1938.

Love Pills

In April 1955 police investigations of a murder in Minneapolis in the US led them to the office of Dr Arnold Axilrod. Twenty-one-year-old Mary Moonen had been strangled and her body left lying by the roadside in a fashionable part of the city. Post-mortem examination revealed that she had recently had sexual intercourse and was three months pregnant.

When enquiries showed that the dead woman had visited Dr Axilrod on the day before her death, detectives decided to question the dentist. They discovered that he was in the habit of administering a pill to his female patients, which in some cases, incapacitated them for several hours. One patient said that she had taken a pill and alleged that the dentist had made suggestive comments to her.

Further evidence of the dentist's practice came from Mary Moonen's doctor who said that she had told him that Axilrod had assaulted her in his surgery and that he was the father of her child. As the investigation progressed, several women came forward relating how they had been given pills by the dentist and been knocked out for as much as five or six hours.

Axilrod was arrested and questioned about Mary Moonen. He flatly denied that he had sexually assaulted her while she was under the influence of drugs administered by him. He could not recall what happened on the night of the murder because he had experienced a black-out. He admitted, though, that she had discussed her pregnant condition with him and they had argued.

Dr Axilrod was put on trial for murder in September 1955. The case of the dentist and his "love pills" made popular reading in the newspapers. The prosecution case was that he took advantage of his female patients by first drugging and then sexually molesting them. When he was arrested and questioned about Mary Moonen, it was alleged that he confessed saying, "I guess I did it, no one else was there." This was later denied.

Axilrod maintained that he had never had sexual relations with Mary Moonen and that he had not murdered her. He was convicted of manslaughter and sentenced to five to twenty years' imprisonment.

Acid Doctor

Thirty-six-year-old Dr Geza de Kaplany was a Hungarian who had emigrated to the USA and worked as an anaesthetist at a hospital in San José, California. In July 1962 he married a fellow Hungarian immigrant, twenty-five-year-old Hajna Piller, a former model, and they moved into a new apartment.

Loud music coming from the de Kaplany apartment disturbed the neighbours on the morning of 28 August. Partly concealed by the music were eerie wailing noises. The police were called because of the disturbance and their knock on the door was answered by Dr Kaplany in his underclothes. A search of the apartment revealed the source of the distressed sounds, which the loud music was intended to disguise.

The bedroom was virtually a torture chamber. The naked body of Hajna corroded with acid burns lay on the bed. She was rushed to hospital suffering third-degree burns from which she died just over a month later. The bedclothes had been reduced to rags and there was a large hole in the mattress where the acid had burned through. There was a case containing bottles of hydrochloric, sulphuric and nitric acid and rubber gloves. A chilling message written on a prescription form was an instruction to Hajna not to shout out if she wanted to live.

Dr de Kaplany was arrested and charged with murder. It appeared that he had tortured his wife for about an hour before being interrupted. He had made small incisions all over her body and then poured acid into them.

At his trial for murder in January 1963 he made a joint plea of "not guilty" and "not guilty by reason of insanity". He was calm at first saying that he never intended to kill his wife, he only wanted to disfigure her so that she would not be attractive to other men. When the prosecution showed photographs of the acid-wrecked body of Hajna, his composure broke and he became hysterical shouting, "I am a doctor. I loved her. If I did this – and I must have done this – then I'm guilty."

The defence argued that de Kaplany suffered from multiple personality syndrome, moving between caring and cruel modes of behaviour depending on external stimuli. The idea was that when he heard rumours of his wife's possible infidelity, he flipped and reacted in a cruel and irrational way.

The jury returned a guilty verdict on 1 March 1963 and "The Acid Doctor", as he had become known, was sentenced to life imprisonment. He served thirteen years of his sentence and was granted parole in 1976. In a curious footnote to the case of Dr Kaplany, it seems that he was released early to enable him work as a doctor in a Taiwan hospital. Later reports noted that he had settled in Germany.

Personal Magnetism

Dr Etienne Deschamps was a French-born dentist who established a practice in the US in the 1880s. Not only did he pull teeth but he also practised magnetic physiology, which often involved administering small doses of chloroform.

Deschamps had fought in the Crimean War and been wounded. He developed a liking for politics but gave that up for dentistry and discovered the wonders of magnetic physiology. He began to explore the occult and convinced himself that magnetism had great curative properties. He decided to exploit his skills in the New World and rented rooms in New Orleans.

Although the doctor built up a successful practice, based as much on his magnetic consultancy as his dentistry, he had many patients though few friends. But in 1888 he made the acquaintance of Jules Deitsch, a fellow Frenchman, who first consulted him as a patient and then became an ardent disciple of all things magnetic.

Deitsch, a widower, had two daughters, one of whom was twelve-year-old Juliette. She was just the medium Deschamps was looking for to aid him with his magnetic and hypnotic powers. He had already confided in Deitsch that he had a scheme based on his treatments which would make him rich and which he was prepared to share.

Deitsch was impressed by his friend's intellect and generosity and readily fell in with his plans. These included the assistance of young Juliette. She and her younger sister became regular visitors to the doctor's rooms and little by little he groomed Juliette for the role he had in mind.

On 30 January 1889, Deitsch's youngest daughter appeared to be distressed when she came home. Asked where her sister was, she told her father that Juliette was asleep in the doctor's house. Deitsch immediately went to Deschamps's rooms but could not get a response. In a state of some concern, he fetched the police who entered the room. Lying naked on the bed was Juliette next to the doctor, also unclothed.

Juliette it appeared was not asleep but dead and the doctor had several wounds in his chest, which were self-inflicted. Enquiries established that Deschamps had used chloroform to render Juliette unconscious but had overdone the dosage. The dead girl's sister said that she had often seen Juliette and the doctor lying naked together. A post-mortem examination revealed that Juliette had been sexually assaulted over a long period.

Deschamps recovered from his injuries and made several statements. He claimed that Juliette's death was an accident that had occurred when he was hypnotizing her. He stated that the use of chloroform to assist the process was an accepted practice and that he was simply a scientist.

He attempted to hang himself in his custody cell but was saved by prison guards. A trial date was set for 29 April and the doctor again tried to circumvent justice with an attempt on his own life but was unsuccessful.

The dead girl's sister gave evidence at his trial and described some of the doctor's practices. Deschamps did not testify and was found guilty of murder. He appealed against the verdict and won a second trial, which began in March 1890.

Deschamps had mustered a more effective defence for the second trial and claimed there was no premeditation involved in Juliette's death. As before, the dead girl's sister gave evidence and reiterated that she had seen Juliette and the doctor naked together in bed many times. She had sworn not to tell her father. The jury verdict, again, was guilty as charged.

Questions were now raised about Deschamps' sanity. Certainly his behaviour as a prisoner was eccentric, if not mad. Nevertheless, he was sentenced to death, his execution being set for 18 January 1891. But a commission of doctors obtained a stay of execution on the grounds that he was insane. Application was made for a reduction in his sentence which, in due course, was rejected.

Meanwhile, Deschamps acted up in his prison cell by talking to the moon. Following further procedural delays, a new date was set for execution. This too was overtaken by events with yet another reprieve. Rumours began to gain currency about sinister forces at work to save the mad doctor. Finally, on 12 May 1892, loudly proclaiming his innocence, Dr Deschamps was hanged, three years after Juliette's untimely end.

Playing Doctor

When twelve patients died in Californian hospitals in the US in the space of several weeks, suspicions were aroused.

Between 29 March and 25 April 1981, the small, thirty-six bed community hospital at Perris near Riverside experienced the deaths of eleven patients, male and female, aged between fifty-two and ninety-five. The cause of death appeared to be a mystery and it was some time before the unusually high number of possible suspicious deaths was reported.

A curious feature of the deaths was that they tended to occur at the same times of day in the critical care unit – at 1.00 a.m., 4.00 a.m. and 7.00 a.m. Autopsies revealed the presence in some patients of large amounts of lidocaine, a powerful medication used to stabilize the heart rhythm. One similar death was also reported at a nearby hospital in Banning. An initial theory was that the supplies of the drug kept in the hospital had become contaminated, but enquiries showed this was unlikely.

At this point, investigators began to examine the roles played by hospital staff and their attention fell on a forty-two-year-old male nurse, Robert Diaz. He worked on the critical care unit and was on duty at the times when fatalities occurred. He was questioned and his home in Apple Valley was searched. Supplies of lidocaine and a syringe were found there. Diaz said he had been concerned about the high death rate and had questioned whether the supplies of lidocaine were contaminated.

Diaz was arrested on 23 November 1981 after an investigation that had taken over six months, and charged with twelve counts of murder. He responded by filing a lawsuit against his employers for violation of his civil rights.

He was sent for trial in November 1983 before Judge John J. Barnard sitting without a jury. Colleagues testified that Diaz liked "playing doctor" during medical emergencies. Nurses said he had been seen going from room to room in the hospital "like a butterfly" giving injections that were not authorized. Diaz denied this, saying he only administered injections to save life and then strictly within hospital protocols.

Diaz came from a large family and was brought up in Gary, Indiana. He joined the US Marines when he was aged eighteen but deserted and subsequently enrolled for nursing studies. Fellow students commented that he liked to be introduced as "Doctor Diaz". Nursing colleagues recalled that he sometimes predicted the time when an apparently stable patient would die and was often proved right.

He spent six days on the witness stand giving his account, strongly denying the allegations made against him. He said that if on occasions he appeared to act like a doctor, it was because physicians on duty failed their patients. On 30 March 1984, Judge Barnard delivered a guilty verdict on all twelve murder charges. "Special circumstances" applied to the verdict, which meant, under Californian law, multiple pre-meditated murder, and carried the possibility of a death penalty.

Two weeks after the verdict was announced Diaz was sentenced to death in the gas chamber at San Quentin Prison. He was allowed to give an interview on local radio when he condemned the hospital in which he had worked and said there was a cover-up of patient death rates. He described the place as "a slaughterhouse".

Commenting on Diaz's character, a psychologist who spoke to him was of the opinion that he was unable to accept authority or responsibility. As to his motive, the prosecution's stated view was that he killed for "amusement and entertainment".

Brink Of Death

Over a nine-week period around Christmas 2003, in the Accident and Emergency department at Horton Hospital in Banbury, Oxfordshire in the UK, eighteen patients suffered a respiratory collapse, two of whom died.

Hospital doctors were alarmed at the crises affecting patients not admitted with life-threatening conditions. Investigations showed that a common factor in all these cases was that they had been dealt with by Benjamin Geen. Police were called in and suspicions voiced. Geen was arrested when he arrived for duty and was found to be carrying a syringe in his pocket. Analysis of residues in the syringe showed the presence of two drugs used in operating theatres: vecuronium, a muscle relaxant, and midazolam, a sedative.

Records showed that sixty-two-year-old Anthony Bateman, believed to be suffering with cancer, was admitted in December 2003. A saline drip was set up by Geen. The patient declined rapidly and his breathing failed. Efforts to resuscitate him were hampered by his generally poor health and he died. Over the next few weeks, there were numerous crises in A&E involving the resuscitation of patients with respiratory collapses. David Onley, aged seventy-five, had health problems and died following breathing difficulties on 21 January 2004.

Enquiries concluded that some of these patients had received muscle relaxants not prescribed by doctors and probably administered via saline drips. Geen was charged with murder and committed for trial at Oxford Crown Court in April 2006. The prosecution described the evidence against him as overwhelming, although circumstantial. The hypodermic syringe found on him when he was arrested was referred to as a "smoking gun". Traces of unprescribed drugs were found in the urine of a patient who survived; the same drugs that Geen had in the syringe.

The police called Geen a self-centred narcissist who abused his position of trust. Hospital staff regarded him warily as he did not always follow instructions. He appeared elated when an emergency situation arose and remarked to a colleague, "There is always a resuscitation when I'm on duty."

The suggestion was that Geen secretly administered drugs that had the effect of bringing patients to the brink of death. Then he would gain satisfaction from observing the emergency efforts needed to save them. The run of emergencies at Horton Hospital was a rare sequence of events and the common denominator was that Benjamin Geen was on duty at the time. He claimed to be innocent.

The jury found him guilty of two murders and of inflicting grievous bodily harm on fifteen others. On 10 May 2006 Mr Justine Crane passed down seventeen life sentences and told Geen he would spend at least thirty years in prison.

A Friend In The Woods

Josephine Burnaby lived in Providence, Rhode Island, in the US. She was the estranged wife of a wealthy clothing store owner. Her doctor, Thomas Thatcher Graves, treated her for minor ailments and when Mr Burnaby died, the doctor persuaded his widow to give him power of attorney.

The late Mr Burnaby had left his wife a small annuity, which Graves thought was somewhat miserly. He advised Mrs Burnaby to contest the will and, after due process, the will was reversed. This gave Dr Graves access to a considerable sum of money and he proceeded to milk the widow's account.

He also wanted Mrs Burnaby out of the way so, in his capacity as her doctor, he advised her to go on long visits to California for health reasons. On returning from one of these trips at the end of 1892, Mrs Burnaby decided to break the journey by staying with a friend in Denver, Colorado.

When she arrived, her friend told her there was a parcel waiting for her which had been sent through the postal service. Opening the package, Mrs Burnaby found a bottle of whisky with a note attached. The handwritten note bore the message, "Wish you a Happy New Year. Please accept this fine old whisky from your friend in the woods."

The two women decided to drink some of the whisky which they described as "vile stuff". Within a few days, both were dead. Mrs Burnaby's daughter arranged for a private autopsy to be carried out and poisoning was confirmed as the cause of death. The contents of the whisky bottle were believed to have disguised the poison.

Mrs Burnaby had voiced concerns about the way Dr Graves was managing her affairs and suspicions began to form about his true intentions. Certainly, he had attempted to profit from her wealth. The newspapers began to hint at the doctor's involvement, although he strongly denied the allegations. In any case, there was no evidence to link him with sending the bottle of whisky. Meanwhile, his patients rallied round in support.

Despite the lack of firm evidence of guilt, Dr Graves was charged with murder and put on trial. The prosecution case was faltering until a surprise witness appeared. Joseph M. Breslyn testified that he had been approached by Dr Graves in November 1890 at Boston Railway Station who asked him a favour. Explaining that he was unable to write a note to accompany a gift, he asked the young man to write a message at his dictation. Thus was the provenance of the note sent to Mrs Burnaby established and the identity of the sender revealed.

Dr Graves was convicted of murder and sentenced to death. He appealed and was granted a retrial but in April 1893 he committed suicide in his prison cell using poison that he had smuggled in.

Murder By Omission

In the US, Joan Robinson was the adopted daughter of a Texas oil tycoon and made a name for herself as a horsewoman. She married Dr John Hill, a rising star in the field of plastic surgery, and the couple lived in style at River Oaks, Houston.

By the late 1960s, the marriage began to break up and, in March 1969, Joan Hill became sick and was taken to hospital by her husband after he had treated her at home for four days. She died on 19 March and following a hurried post-mortem, the body was prepared for burial before cause of death had been properly established. The contention at the time was that she had died of a liver infection.

Joan Hill's father, Ash Robinson, refused to accept the account given of his daughter's death and began openly to accuse Dr Hill of allowing her to die. These allegations triggered a lawsuit for slander and when Hill remarried three months later, speculation was renewed.

In November, Joan Hill's body was exhumed and a second post-mortem was carried out. Doctors examining the brain, preserved from the first autopsy, concluded that meningitis was a factor to be taken into account. It was pointed out, though, that there was no such indication in the brain stem, giving rise to the suggestion that the brain was not that of Mrs Hill.

Three grand juries considered the case before an indictment was brought against Dr Hill. The decision was based on a provision in Texas law whereby a case could be brought under the heading of murder by omission.

Dr Hill was tried for murder in 1971 when his second wife, whom he had divorced, gave evidence against him. She alleged that he had tried to kill her by deliberately crashing their car in which she was a passenger, against the side of a concrete bridge. The car was extensively damaged but Hill's wife, though shocked, was uninjured. In a sensational development she said that he tried to inject her with procaine hydrochloride while she sat in the wrecked car. She fended him off but, had he succeeded, she might well have died with every appearance of being fatally traumatized by shock.

A mistrial resulted, but further accusations continued to be revealed in the press. Dr Hill was alleged to have kept bacterial culture dishes in the bathroom and to have injected his first wife with a concoction made from "every form of human excretion", including pus taken from a boil.

Before a second trial could be held, Hill was overtaken by a dramatic turn of events when he was shot dead by a hired gunman who, in his turn, was killed by a police officer. There were suspicions that Joan Hill's father had paid for a hired killer to eliminate his son-in-law. Allegations of various kinds continued to rumble around like distant thunder, including a suggestion that Dr Hill was alive and well, living in Mexico.

Mercy Killer

In the US, thirty-five-year-old Donald Harvey's killing spree ended in 1987 when an alert doctor at Drake Memorial Hospital in Cincinnati, Ohio, smelled arsenic in the room where a patient had died and suspected Harvey of foul play. He was arrested in April and admitted killing twenty-five patients to "put them out of their misery".

Harvey grew up in rural Kentucky where he dropped out of school. While his teachers remembered him as a pleasant, outgoing youth, psychiatrists who examined him recorded that he had been abused as a child. In an interview, Harvey denied he had killed out of pleasure or, as had been suggested, due to repressed homosexuality. Armed with notes to aid his memory, he recounted the time, place and method of many of the deaths for which he was responsible. He used cyanide and arsenic and introduced air into intravenous tubes. In two cases he used a petroleum-based cleaning product as a poison. He said that although many believed in mercy killing, few had the nerve to carry it out. He was not concerned about being discovered.

Harvey's lawyer negotiated a plea bargain whereby he would escape the death penalty if he made a full confession of his murderous activities. A grand jury spent six weeks considering the evidence against him. This included a three-month investigation into deaths at Drake Memorial Hospital carried out by a local television station which first drew attention to the especially high number of deaths on the ward where Harvey worked.

The County Prosecutor described Harvey as a pathological killer who had ". . . a compulsion to kill like some of us have . . . a compulsion for cold beer". A chart displayed in the court room listed the names of Harvey's victims and detailed the manner of their deaths. This death list showed that his modus operandi ranged from poisoning with arsenic put in pies and puddings to asphyxiation using plastic bags and wet towels.

Evidence that he had attempted to kill others who were not hospital patients supported the idea that he was a compulsive murderer. Some of his colleagues said he was not trusted by them and there was evidence that he was fascinated by Satanism. Family members of some of his victims were not impressed by Harvey's demeanour in court, especially when he appeared to be joking with his advisers.

The "Angel of Death" who had plea-bargained his way out of a death sentence was given four life sentences for murdering twenty-five people. Harvey will be eligible for parole when he is ninety-five years old. His admission that he had killed fifty people would make him one of America's most prolific serial killers, overtaking the infamous Ted Bundy and John Wayne Gacy.

By Lethal Injection

In Germany, Stephan Letter, a twenty-seven-year-old hospital worker, was dubbed "The Nurse of Death" by the German press.

Letter's activities came to light after staff at the hospital where he worked in Sonthofen, Bavaria, noticed that drugs had been going missing. He had started work in the internal diseases ward in 2003 and during a period of a year and a half there had been several deaths of elderly patients. It was noticed that many of the deaths of patients who were not seriously ill coincided with times when Letter was on ward duty. When he was questioned, he admitted killing the patients. A search of his apartment turned up a supply of drugs sufficient to kill several people.

This prompted an intense investigation with concerns over the deaths of seventy patients. Forty-two bodies were exhumed for post-mortem examination. Among them were six women aged between seventy and eighty-nine and four men aged between sixty and sixty-eight. They had died from lethal injections administered by Letter because he claimed he could not stand by and see them in pain.

He was tried for murder in November 2006. Letter repeated that he had killed them out of compassion but admitted he did not know how many. The prosecution said, "He killed as if it were an assembly line." He had known some of his victims only a few hours before snuffing their lives out. His activities went unnoticed for so long because deaths among a population of elderly patients were not unexpected. His defence lawyer suggested that he had been given too much responsibility at too young an age. The judge said Letter was of above-average intelligence. He showed no emotion as he was convicted of killing twenty-eight patients with lethal injections and entered the records as Germany's worst serial killer. The "Nurse of Death" was sentenced to life imprisonment with a ruling that he would have to serve at least fifteen years. In an ironic rider, the court ruled that he would never be allowed to work again as a nurse.

"Dr" Death

The German Odd Fellows' Home in the Bronx, New York, provided care for up to eighty elderly people. Over a period of four months, between August 1914 and January 1915, seventeen residents died. The authorities expressed concern but no action was taken. The attrition rate might have continued but for an extraordinary confession.

Frederick Mors, an Austrian from the Tyrol, clad in lederhosen and sporting an Alpine hat complete with feather, presented himself at the Criminal Courts building in New York and asked to speak to an attorney. With the aid of a German interpreter, Mors announced that he was responsible for eight of the deaths at the old people's home. He explained that he worked there as a nursing assistant.

Mors had arrived in the USA from Liverpool on the *Aquitania* on 26 June 1914. He originated from Vienna where he had worked as a forester. Once in New York he began looking for work and found a job as a porter at the German Odd Fellows' Home. Having advanced to nursing orderly, he came under the influence of the Home's superintendent who enlisted Mors' help in disposing of troublesome patients.

Mors enjoyed his work but became concerned that poisoning with opium, morphine and arsenic left traces in the body. In consequence, he perfected a technique of administering death with chloroform. First he anaesthetized his victim using drops of chloroform on a pad clamped over the nose. Then he poured chloroform into the mouth producing fatal poisoning which could not be detected. When an undertaker observed burn marks around the mouth of one of the victims, he made up some plausible explanation and realized he needed to refine his method. He did this by greasing his victim's faces with Vaseline to prevent burns.

Mors had free rein at the Odd Fellows' Home with access to drugs and no supervision of his activities. Enquiries about his background in Vienna elicited the information that he was so fascinated by death that he had changed his name to Mors, a corruption of the Latin word for death. Following his interrogation by police, Mors was sent for psychiatric examination.

To the suggestion that he was imbalanced, if not insane, he told detectives where to find his supply of chloroform which he kept hidden. Asked why he killed the people he was supposed to be caring for, he said he brought death to them to relieve their suffering. In April 1915, Mors was declared insane by a lunacy commission and sent to Matteawan State Prison for the Criminally Insane.

Mad or not, Frederick Mors, a man obsessed with death, contrived to escape from prison in the 1920s. He was clever enough to avoid recapture and was never heard of again.

Strychnos Toxifera

Dr Carlo Nigrisoli came from a family of distinguished medical men. He lived in Bologna, Italy, with his wife Ombretta and three children where he had a successful practice. When he met Iris Azzali, he fell for her charms and began to lead a double life. His lover became pregnant and he arranged an abortion for her. But at this point, Mrs Nigrisoli realized that her husband's attention was increasingly being diverted. She suspected another woman had entered the picture and was understandably distraught.

Family friends became aware of Ombretta Nigrisoli's concerns and one of them, a physician, discussed the lady's nervous condition with Nigrisoli. They agreed she should receive treatment in the form of injections given by the doctor friend. Then, for convenience, and knowing nothing about Nigrisoli's dalliance with Iris, the doctor friend agreed that Carlo should administer the treatment to his wife.

With Nigrisoli spending more time away from home, Ombretta's worries increased to the point where she became a burden. On 14 March 1963, late at night, Nigrisoli summoned help saying that his wife had suffered a heart attack. Ombretta died without regaining consciousness. Her husband said that he had given her a stimulant by injection but she had failed to respond. He then pressed his fellow doctors to register Ombretta's death as caused by coronary thrombosis.

They declined to meet his wishes explaining that they were insufficiently aware of the facts leading up to his wife's death. At this point, Nigrisoli produced a pistol, declaring that unless his wishes were met, he would kill himself.

The attending physicians calmed him down and he ended up being questioned by the police. When officers discovered that Nigrisoli had been giving his wife injections, their suspicions were immediately aroused. A post-mortem was carried out on Ombretta and the results showed that she had died from the administration of curare.

Curare, the legendary and notorious poison used by South American Indians for hunting and vanquishing their enemies is extracted from tree bark. When it enters the blood stream it causes paralysis of the motor and respiratory muscle. It has a use in modern surgical practice as a relaxant prior to surgery.

Nigrisoli was charged with murder. His trial began on 1 October 1964, although he did not appear in person. He gave his testimony from his cell that was relayed to the court room. He proclaimed his innocence. The prosecution said he had given his wife a fatal dose of curare and callously waited for it to take effect. Evidence was given describing how Ombretta had found a bottle of curare in the bathroom and feared it might be intended for her. A friend advised her to go to the police. The next day she was dead.

Dr Nigrisoli, Italy's first convicted curare poisoner, was found guilty and sentenced to life imprisonment.

Forecasting Death

Colin Norris was a staff nurse at Leeds General Infirmary in the UK who had the knack of forecasting when a patient would die. When Ethel Hall, an eighty-six-year-old patient recovering from a hip operation went into a coma at 5.10 a.m. on 20 November 2002 and died shortly afterwards, Norris' uncanny accuracy over the old lady's demise alerted a doctor who took a blood sample. It was found that Ethel Hall had abnormally high levels of insulin in her body.

Following this incident, other deaths of elderly patients were investigated. It was discovered that Doris Ludlam, Bridget Bourke and Irene Crooker had all died within a six-month period in similar circumstances. All three were recovering from hip operations and were not terminally ill. They went into a coma and expired. The common feature was that they died when Colin Norris was on duty.

During his nursing training Norris had expressed the opinion that he did not like the idea of looking after geriatrics. Once he started work as a nurse he made clear his dislike of changing the soiled bed linen of elderly patients and other duties, which he found menial and distasteful. He was also arrogant and disrespectful.

Norris was tried for murder at Newcastle Crown Court in February 2008. He was charged with killing three patients at Leeds General Infirmary and one at St James' Hospital. There was an additional charge of attempted murder. The deaths occurred between June and December 2002.

In the course of an investigation that lasted three years, West Yorkshire police considered seventy deaths that had occurred at Leeds General Hospital. They eventually narrowed down their list of suspicious deaths to eighteen. Some of the bodies had been cremated, thereby ruling out further consideration.

During their enquiries, detectives learned a great deal about Nurse Norris and his attitude to patients under his care. A view was expressed that had he not been found out, many patients' lives would have been at risk. Comparisons with British mass-murderer Dr Harold Shipman (*see pages 44, 45*) were inevitable. Some of the most damning character assessments voiced at the trial came from hospital patients. One recalled, "he was very nasty – he didn't like us old women." Colleagues also testified to Norris' attitude when on duty. On one occasion he remarked that whenever he was on night duty someone died and it was his luck to have to do all the paperwork.

Norris had shown no remorse and simply denied the charges. Much of the evidence against him was circumstantial and the judge, Mr Justice Griffith Williams, expressed his puzzlement over the motive for the murders. The jury found Norris guilty of committing four murders and one attempted murder. Sentencing him to life imprisonment, the judge said it was clear that he regarded geriatric nursing as a waste of time and, ". . . only you know why that dislike was so much that you decided to kill."

Student Of Surgery

A woman's body was washed up at Godinot Bay in Trinidad in April 1954. She was white, blonde and aged between twenty-five and thirty-five. The body had been wrapped in a sack that also contained a medallion and a charm bracelet. The post-mortem examination confirmed death by strangulation and it was evident that the jugular vein had been opened to drain off the blood and that the internal organs had been removed.

While the pathologist was conducting his post-mortem, another doctor turned up asking to borrow some medical books. He took a keen interest in what was going on and behaved suspiciously. The police decided to question him. He was Dr Dalip Singh, a medical practitioner in Port of Spain who was married to a lady of German origin, Inge, a professional optician with a successful practice.

Dr Singh told detectives that he last saw Inge on 6 April when she walked out on him. He said that she was subject to depression and had done this before. He heard that a body had been washed up on the coast and decided to take a look, hence his appearance at the post-mortem. The identity of the corpse was confirmed and the medallion and bracelet belonged to Inge.

Singh had drawn suspicion to himself by his actions but the evidence against him was circumstantial. At about this time, the police received an anonymous communication stating, "I sorry for Dr Singh he is not guilty." The message was written on notepaper of a type used by the doctor.

When detectives interviewed Dr Singh's houseboy he threw some interesting light on the doctor's behaviour. Singh met Inge at the airport on 6 April and they returned home together. During the evening, there was a heated argument and the doctor went out in his car, returning alone in the small hours. Inge did not turn up for breakfast.

Dr Singh was tried for murdering his wife and evidence was put forward depicting him as an intensely jealous personality. He believed Inge was having an affair and had tried to hire a private detective three weeks before she went missing, with a view to tracking her movements. It also came out in court that at the beginning of April, he had borrowed a book on surgery. The inference was that he swotted up on the procedures involved in eviscerating a body with the intention that it would not float when put into the sea.

Unfortunately for Dr Singh, on this occasion, despite his best efforts the sea gave up its dead. He was found guilty and sentenced to death. His execution took place on 28 June 1955.

Prescription For Murder

Paul and Margaret Vickers had been married seventeen years. Forty-seven-year-old Dr Vickers was an orthopaedic consultant at Gateshead Hospital on Tyneside in the UK. He was successful professionally and had aspirations to enter the political world. His wife was a shy person, prey to illness, and was being treated for schizophrenia.

Vickers had a succession of lovers and, in March 1976, he met Pamela Collison who worked as a researcher in London at the House of Commons. They were deeply attracted to each other and wanted to share their lives. Margaret, frequently sick, stayed at home in Gosforth, but her health gradually declined to the point where in February 1979, she was admitted to hospital.

Doctors were vexed by the cause of her illness and her condition continued to deteriorate. On 13 June, she had a major heart attack and died the following day, just short of her seventeenth wedding anniversary. Cause of death was attributed to aplastic anaemia, a disease which destroys the bone marrow. Margaret Vickers was buried in an unmarked grave.

Dr Vickers was now free to make plans to marry Pamela Collison and the couple set a date for their wedding. Then, within a few short months, their relationship cooled off and the wedding plans were cancelled. On 1 May 1980, Collison made some startling revelations to detectives at Barnet police station in north London.

She told them of her suspicions that Dr Vickers had killed his wife. She explained how he had used her to pick up prescriptions from a pharmacy in London on a regular basis prior to his wife's death. Detectives headed north to interview Vickers who readily admitted giving the anti-cancer drug, CCNU, to his late wife to treat a brain tumour. He also admitted his affair with Pamela Collison.

CCNU was a product of pharmaceutical research in the USA used as an effective treatment for some cancers. It was not generally available in the UK except through a pharmacy in London. Dr Vickers wrote regular prescriptions for the drug to treat his wife and asked Pamela Collison to pick up the capsules. In order to minimise the appearance of overdosing his patient, he wrote out prescriptions for non-existent patients.

Vickers and Collison were arrested on 8 October 1980 and charged with murder. They were tried at Teesside Crown Court a year later. Both denied committing murder and the court proceedings provided a colourful public spectacle. The newspaper headlines told the story; "Surgeon committed professional suicide"; "Vickers renewed liaison a day after wife buried"; "This relentless, blackmailing Boadicea"; and "The surgeon who killed wife for ambition's sake".

The trial judge, Mr Justice Boreham, reminded the jury that "The charge is murder, not adultery. This is a court of law, not morals." On 20 November 1981, the jury cleared Pamela Collison of the charges and found Dr Vickers guilty of murder. He was sentenced to life imprisonment. An appeal was turned down in 1983 and his case came to the Court of Appeal again in 1994 on the basis of new medical evidence purporting to show that Margaret Vickers did not die from the administration of drugs but from mental illness. The appeal was turned down and the original conviction upheld.

A Bad Man From Egypt

Dentist Dr Warren Waite worked for a company in South Africa before returning to the US in 1914. The following year, he married the daughter of John E. Peck who had made his money in the timber business. Peck funded a fashionable Manhattan apartment for the couple and also made them a monthly allowance. It seemed that Dr Waite grew less interested in his profession and chose to spend his time socializing. One of the doctor's sidelines was research on germ culture.

In January 1916 he invited his mother-in-law to come and stay with them in New York. While there, she contracted a sudden illness and died. The Peck family was shocked and recalled how kind and considerate Waite had been to his mother-in-law. After his wife was cremated, grieving John Peck went to New York to spend some time with his daughter and son-in-law. Within a few weeks he too was dead, apparently of kidney disease.

The family declined Waite's insistence on cremation and took Mr Peck's body back to Grand Rapids for burial. Following an autopsy and the discovery of arsenic in the dead man, suspicion was aroused and all eyes focussed on Dr Waite who was now a potential beneficiary of the Pecks' fortune.

During their searches, police found an atomizer that Waite had used to treat Mr and Mrs Peck; it was laden with anthrax and typhoid germs. At first, Waite tried to laugh off this discovery but when suspicion mounted, he attempted to commit suicide by taking sleeping pills. His next ploy was to feign insanity with garbled accounts of being possessed. By way of explanation, he said, "A bad man from Egypt dwells in my body. He makes me do bad things. He struggles for possession of my soul."

In due course, he confessed to a string of fraudulent claims about his professional qualifications and, worse, to his designs on Peck's fortune. He admitted doctoring Mrs Peck's food with germs and spraying her throat with bacteria, commenting that it took just ten days to take effect. He adopted the same procedure with his father-in-law but the old man proved fairly resilient so he had to consider other means. When arsenic failed, he suffocated his victim. Asked why he wanted to kill his in-laws, he replied quite simply, "It was for the money."

Waite was put on trial in May 1916 and pleaded not guilty. He played to the gallery with his smiling, matter-of-fact delivery of the facts about his bacteriological assault on Mr and Mrs Peck. If the members of the jury were amused they did not show it and took twenty minutes to find him guilty. He greeted the verdict with a sigh and the comment, "What a relief." He was sentenced to death and sent to Sing Sing pending appeal.

The Court of Appeal confirmed his sentence in April 1917 and on 1 May he was strapped into the electric chair. Looking around at the apparatus that would end his time on earth, he was reported to have said, "Is this all there is to it?"

Just For Fun

Killing to ease the stress of a bad day was part of the strategy adopted by care assistants Catherine Wood and Gwendoline Graham at the Alpine Manor Nursing Home in Walter, Michigan in the US. To make their game more fun, they selected their elderly victims in a sequence whereby the first letter of their names spelled out the word, M.U.R.D.E.R.

The plan had to be abandoned when some of the designated victims put up too great a struggle and disrupted the sequence. But Wood and Graham carried on killing anyway, "just for fun", as Graham put it later.

Wood and Graham were lesbian lovers and while they both received satisfactory job reviews, their nursing home colleagues had suspicions about their behaviour. For one thing, the pair liked to boast about the callous way they treated some of the patients suffering from Alzheimer's disease in their care, which included taking souvenirs such as trinkets and ornaments. Colleagues were not sure how seriously to take things they were told.

After a series of eight deaths at the nursing home, some of these boasts landed on fertile ground. Wood's ex-husband heard stories about patients being suffocated and, after months of indecision, eventually went to the police. The two women were arrested in December 1988 and charged with murder.

It seemed that Wood and Graham had made a lovers' pact that they would be bound together for eternity, bonded by their knowledge of the secret killings. But Wood, who was led by Graham's strong personality, turned against her partner and offered to testify in court.

Wood told her ex-husband in August 1987 that she and Graham had killed six patients chosen for their frailty. "You wouldn't believe the things we've done," she told him. Their strategy in the nursing home was for Graham to suffocate the victim with their bedclothes while Wood kept a lookout.

The bodies of two of the patients who had died, one of them aged ninety-eight, were exhumed and subjected to postmortem examination. The original cause of death from natural causes was changed to asphyxia by suffocation. This was based less on medical evidence than the insistence of the police that the deaths were not natural.

Wood and Graham were put on trial at Grand Rapids in 1989. Some of Graham's friends and former colleagues testified that she had freely discussed the murders she had committed. The general reaction was disbelief or the feeling that the claims were a sick joke. Wood said of her partner, "She was always happy when one of the patients died." Wood also said she feared that if she were not stopped, Graham might turn to killing babies.

Wood was convicted of second-degree murder and sentenced to twenty to forty years imprisonment while Graham, found guilty of six murders, was sentenced to life with no hope of parole.

Oral Hygiene

"Oral hygiene" was the code name for murder used by nursing auxiliaries at an Austrian hospital in the 1980s. The term signified killing by pouring water into the lungs of the victim and blocking the throat with the tongue. Waltraud Wagner was implicated in the deaths of thirty-nine elderly patients using this and other means at the Lainz General Hospital in Vienna.

Wagner was a nursing auxiliary who worked the night shift on wards that housed mostly geriatric patients. Over a seven-year period a hundred patients died in the hospital, many of them at the hands of Wagner and her three cohorts, Irene Leidolf, Stephenie Mayer and Maria Gruber.

Against a background in which patients were frequently argumentative and ungrateful, Wagner was overheard openly discussing with her colleagues methods of disposing of them. "Sending a patient down to the cellar" was code for a death sentence to be meted out and signified that the victim would end up in the mortuary.

This conversation had been noted by a detective who was posing as a patient in one of the hospital wards tended by Wagner where there had been many deaths. With suspicion mounting, a doctor confronted Wagner over an unprescribed dose of insulin given to a woman patient. She denied it, but the doctor's suspicions were confirmed at post-mortem.

Wagner was arrested in April 1989. She broke down under questioning and confessed to killing ten patients. She went on trial in March 1991 in proceedings that aroused huge public interest. There appeared to be no gain to the perpetrators in killing the elderly people apart from being rid of them as inconvenient nuisances. In court, Wagner offered the excuse that she was relieving her patients of pain.

The trial provoked public consternation about the way the sick and elderly were cared for. Recrimination followed about the lack of supervision and procedural failures. Shocked by the turn of events, some had likened the procession of death to the atrocities of Auschwitz. In the media there were lurid stories about witchcraft and sex on hospital wards.

Also brought into the discussion was the status of the nursing auxiliaries who were low-paid and overworked, and faced daily demands from patients who were often fractious and hostile. In some quarters, Wagner and her assistants were regarded as scapegoats for an incompetent system that was attempting to cover up the wider issues.

But for the persistence of a suspicious doctor, the killings might have gone on longer. The four defendants were found guilty: Wagner of fifteen murders, seventeen attempted murders and two instances of causing bodily harm, and she was sentenced to life imprisonment. Her accomplices were found guilty on various counts of murder and attempted murder, and received commensurate sentences.

CHAPTER 4

On Demand and by Request

Willingness to commit the ultimate crime as a test of love and obedience has its roots in control patterns of behaviour. Murder on demand usually involves a dominant male figure directing a woman to kill at his bidding as an act of slavish devotion.

When Jacques Algarron instructed his lover to kill her child as a sacrifice, he did so from a mind-set steeped in Nitzschean philosophy. This involved the subjugation of women, especially if it empowered the man. The elevation of evil to a higher plane of thinking was part of this outlook and strength of will was paramount.

Similar but less well articulated thoughts guided Felix Roques when he demanded that his lover kill her husband as an act of obedience, even to the extent of acknowledging her task in writing. The same principle was shown to operate in the family context when David Brown cajoled his daughter into killing her stepmother with the infamous rejoinder that she would do it if she really loved him.

The peculiar talent of the control freak is the ability to bend others to his will. Thus, when Dr Yves Evenou decided to eliminate his wife, he enlisted a dull-witted woman who became his slave and carried out his murderous bidding. The master thereby exerted his dominance in keeping with Nietzschean concepts of male superiority.

Murder by request, on the other hand, is less about gender domination and more about opportunity. When Marthinus Roussouw admitted killing his employer, it was on the basis that Baron Dieter von Schauroth had requested him to do it. The dead man was a diamond dealer who had taken out heavy life insurance and, allegedly, handed his bodyguard a revolver and money with instructions to kill him. It was possible that von Schauroth, in the realization that his business dealings were under scrutiny, took out life insurance to provide his family with financial security, while he opted for oblivion. Roussouw's obedience to his employer's instructions did not absolve him from responsibility, however, and he was tried, convicted and, eventually, hanged for murder.

Armin Meiwes advertised on the internet for volunteers willing to be killed and eaten. His request found a respondent who was duly consumed in a cannibalistic feast. Despite the willing co-operation of his victim, Meiwes too was convicted of murder. A harsher fate awaited a young Eskimo tribesman called Aligoomiak who answered a request from a relative to eliminate a rival in a tribal love affair. Pursued across thousands of miles of Canada's frozen north, the Eskimo hunter was put to death by the hangman, proving that killing at someone else's request is still murder.

Ritual Murder

A young, unmarried mother, Denise Labbé, aged twenty, had a two-and-half-year-old daughter resulting from a previous affair. She took a job as a secretary at the National Institute of Statistics at Rennes in France and became involved in the social side of student life. In May 1954, she met twenty-four-year-old Jacques Algarron who was an officer cadet at the prestigious Saint-Cyr military school.

They engaged in a one-sided relationship in which Algarron was the master. He was considered a brilliant mathematician but aside from his academic abilities, his mind was occupied by the "Superman" philosophy of Friedrich Nietzsche. He considered women as subject to his will and demonstrated his mastery by directing Denise to sleep with other men so that she could ask for his forgiveness.

This bizarre instruction was simply the prelude to an even more sinister demand. In August 1954, during dinner at a Paris restaurant, he told her that the love she felt for him could only be proved by murdering her baby daughter, Cathy.

Denise was so much under his influence that she had gone along with his previous demands but she initially baulked at the idea of making her daughter a sacrifice. Worn down by the psychological pressure he applied, however, she made two failed attempts to kill Cathy. On the first attempt, she pulled back from dropping the child from a bridge and, on the second, she retrieved her daughter after putting her into a canal. All of this was rejected by Algarron as weakness.

Finally, on 8 November, while staying with her sister at Vendôme, Denise held Cathy's head down in a water-filled basin and drowned her. She said the child died as the result of an accident and to Algarron she wrote: "Catherine deceased. See you soon." He replied, "It is all very disappointing. It means nothing to me now."

Friends became suspicious about the little girl's death and when police questioned her, Denise admitted being responsible saying, "Yes, I killed my daughter but it was a ritual murder." She named Algarron who was promptly arrested.

The couple were tried for murder at Blois in May 1955. Algarron appeared arrogant and cold-hearted and put the blame for what had happened on Denise. She expressed her love for him and sorrow over the loss of her child. Powerful speeches were made by counsel for both parties who simply blamed each other.

The jury took three hours to reach a verdict and found Denise guilty of murder with extenuating circumstances and Algarron guilty of having provoked a crime. She was sentenced to penal servitude for life and Algarron was given twenty years' hard labour.

"You Are To Be Obeyed"

Jeanne Daniloff Weiss married in 1886 when she was eighteen. Soon afterwards, her husband Lieutenant Weiss was posted to a French army unit in Algeria. During the next three years, the couple had two children and appeared to be a contented family.

This aura of domestic bliss was punctured in 1889 when Jeanne met Felix Roques, an engineer working on the Algerian railways. She fell madly in love with him and became his mistress and slave. Alarmed at the turn of events, Lieutenant Weiss took his wife and family on holiday in France in the hope of breaking up the relationship. But, by that time, Jeanne was pregnant with her lover's child.

When they returned to Algeria, Jeanne met Roques to discuss their future plans. They ruled out elopement as an option and settled on a course of action that would enable them to marry, namely the elimination of Lieutenant Weiss. This task was allotted to Jeanne and she was required by Roques to give him a written undertaking that was spelled out in his pocket book; "I swear that I will murder my husband, that I may belong to you alone – Jeanne".

The plan was to be put into effect while Roques was working in Spain on an engineering project. The implications of what she had agreed to now began to dawn on Jeanne and she had second thoughts. She expressed these in a letter to her lover. He was dismissive, telling her to carry out the plan to which she responded by writing, "It is agreed Felix, you are to be obeyed . . ." But still she was wracked by doubts which prompted Roques to tell her, "You promised to obey me. I implore you to obey me."

In October 1890, Lieutenant Weiss became ill as his wife began systematically to poison his food. He was laid low by bouts of vomiting, convulsions and fevers which gave his friends cause for concern, if not suspicion, about Jeanne's part in his deteriorating health. This suspicion was fuelled by the local post-mistress who was in the habit of reading the letters exchanged between Jeanne and Felix Roques.

On 9 October 1889, one of Jeanne's letters was intercepted and the murderous plot began to unravel. She complained to Roques about her husband's vitality and said she was afraid that she did not have enough of "the remedy" left. She asked him to send a further supply by post. This letter was given to one of Weiss' friends who immediately went to the authorities.

Confronted by the evidence of her plan to poison her husband, Jeanne admitted that Roques was her lover. Quantities of an arsenical preparation, prussic acid and corrosive sublimate were found in her house. Roques was arrested in Madrid and the discovery of Jeanne's letters in his apartment provided conclusive proof of the lover's murderous plans.

Roques avoided justice by taking his own life, thereby leaving Jeanne to face the music on her own. Her husband survived the attempts to poison him and she was tried for attempted murder. Weiss gave evidence in court and declared, "I do not and I never will forgive her . . ."

Jeanne Weiss was found guilty and given a sentence of twenty-five years' penal servitude. Spectators at the trial applauded the verdict. When she was returned to her cell on 29 May 1891 at the end of the trial, she took her own life by ingesting strychnine, which she had concealed in her handkerchief.

Out Of Love

A millionaire computer expert David Brown and his wife, Linda, lived in Santa Ana, California in the US. They had a baby daughter, Krystal, and fourteen-year-old Cinnamon, his daughter from a previous marriage. There were tensions in the marriage and Brown was attracted to seventeen-year-old Patti, his wife's sister.

A fatal shooting occurred at the Brown's house on 19 March 1985. Police officers called to the scene found Linda in the bedroom fatally wounded with gunshot wounds to the chest. The baby and Patti were in the house but Cinnamon was absent. When the property was searched, the girl was found in the yard lying in her own vomit in the dog's kennel. She was ill from a drug overdose. She had written a message on a piece of card that read, "Dear God, please forgive me, I didn't mean to do it."

There were rumours of disagreements between Cinnamon and her stepmother as a result of which she was banished to a trailer in the garden. The teenager admitted firing the gun and was tried for murder as a juvenile. She was convicted and sentenced to twenty-seven years' imprisonment. Some of the investigators had uneasy feelings about the outcome and decided to keep David Brown under surveillance. They discovered that, following Linda's death, Patti began wearing her dead sister's clothing and jewellery. In due course, Brown and Patti were married and had a child.

After serving more than three years of her sentence, Cinnamon began to realize the extent to which she had been used. She confided to investigators that her father had feared Linda was planning to kill him and so he'd enlisted the help of Patti and herself to thwart her ambitions. She said that on the evening of 19 March 1985, her father had made her write a suicide note and directed her to swallow some drugs. He then left the house and, programmed and drugged, Cinnamon took the gun she had been given and shot Linda. He had coerced her into killing her stepmother with the encouraging words that she would do it if she really loved him and out of love for her father she was prepared to admit the killing and accept the punishment that followed.

In September 1988, David Brown and his new wife, Patti, were arrested and charged with Linda's murder. The account that Patti gave of events three years earlier confirmed Cinnamon's version. In February 1990, Brown was tried for murder, conspiracy to commit murder and with expectation of financial gain. The evidence against him was deeply incriminating and, despite efforts while he was in custody to persuade a fellow inmate to kill Patti, he was convicted on all charges.

Brown was sentenced to life imprisonment while Cinnamon and Patti remained in prison but with a favourable outlook as far as parole was concerned. Ann Rule's book on the case, published in 1991, captured the essence of the crime in its title, "*If You Really Loved Me*".

Red And Black

Dr Yves Evenou, an obstetrician and former mayor at Choisy-le-Roi, a town to the south of Paris, married Marie-Claire in 1946. They had a daughter and lived in a three-storey house. Marie-Claire was permanently unwell but she was a dutiful wife. What neither she nor her daughter realized was that the doctor was leading a double life in which wine and women featured strongly.

Evenou met Simone Deschamps when she attended his surgery for a routine appointment. What the forty-three-year-old seamstress lacked in beauty, it seemed she made up for with a vigorous sexual appetite. She responded to all the doctor's demands and received insults and humiliation in response.

Despite this treatment, Simone became one of the family, helping with the chores and mending clothes. Evenou installed her in a room on the ground floor so that she was accessible to meet his needs. To all intents and purposes, she was his slave.

These arrangements continued for about five years until Evenou became bored and decided to extend his repertoire of abuse. During drinking sessions, he told Simone that the present situation could not continue. "We can't go on unless she is removed," he declared. The person he was referring to was Marie and his plan was to murder her or, rather, to get Simone to murder her.

Ever willing to follow her master's instructions, Simone agreed and, having been told that stabbing would be the best method, went out to buy a knife. There was no time to be lost. Having made the decision, Evenou wanted the deed done immediately.

One evening in 1955, the pair returned to the house and Evenou consumed the meal his wife had cooked for him while Simone prepared for her part in the action to follow. She had been instructed to strip off her clothes and wear only her red shoes and black gloves. Thus attired, she went upstairs to where Evenou was waiting. He had given Marie a sleeping draught and she lay on the bed with the blankets pulled over her.

Evenou pulled the bedclothes back and indicated that all was ready for Simone to play her part, which she did with deadly effect, stabbing Marie eleven times. Simone washed the blood from her naked body and hid the knife and gloves, while Evenou called the police to tell them that an intruder had entered the house and killed his wife.

Investigators did not believe his story and, in no time, Evenou was putting the blame on Simone. She, in turn, accused him of planning the murder. In their separate ways they both confessed. But Evenou was taken ill and died before he could be brought to trial and Simone was left to answer for their crime.

Her defence was simply that she had been manipulated by Evenou. She recalled their relationship in such graphic detail that the judge felt obliged to clear the court. Simone was found guilty and the fact that she had clearly been under the influence of an evil man established her credentials as a person acting under extenuating circumstances. She thereby escaped the death penalty and was sentenced to life imprisonment.

Volunteer Victim

Armin Meiwes was a German computer technician who came to be called "The Rotenburg Cannibal" after he confessed to killing and eating a man he met via the internet.

Meiwes advertised online for a "young, well-built man who wants to be eaten". He received a reply from a forty-three-year-old computer engineer, Bernd Brandes, who lived in Berlin. They communicated by e-mail and Brandes noted that they were both smokers, adding, ". . . smoked meat lasts longer . . . maybe you can use my skull as an ashtray . . . I don't want anything left from my ex-person." Meiwes replied, "Don't worry, I am just interested in your flesh. I will get rid of the rest."

The cannibal and the masochist agreed to meet and in March 2001, Brandes took a day off work. After deleting files of masochistic material from his computer, he took a train to Rotenburg. There he met Meiwes and the pair went off to the farmhouse where Meiwes lived alone.

That evening, after cutting off Brandes' penis and feeding him sleeping tablets, Meiwes read a novel while his newfound friend lapsed into unconsciousness. Early next morning, he lay Brandes out on the table in his upstairs "slaughter room" and stabbed him to death. Then he hung the corpse on a meat hook and went to bed.

The next day, he cut off pieces of the body and stored them in his freezer. He later told a magazine reporter that he cooked parts of Brandes with olive oil, garlic, peppers and nutmeg and ate them with sprouts and potatoes. This repast was washed down with a bottle of red wine. He claimed he buried Brandes' bones and other parts in the garden while he read the 23rd Psalm. Meiwes made a video of some of his acts, which he then watched from the comfort of his armchair. He subsequently returned to the internet, placing ads for further volunteers for slaughter.

It was his return to the internet that led to his capture when an Austrian man contacted the police about the ads and details of the killing. Officers turned up at the farmhouse in Rotenburg in December 2002. They found that Meiwes had eaten about 20kg (44 lb) of his victim from the freezer.

His two-month-long trial began at Kassel at the end of 2003. Psychologists testified that Meiwes was mentally fit to stand trial. The prosecution made out a case for sexually motivated murder. It appeared that as a child Meiwes had been completely dominated by his mother who supervised his every movement including any sexual inclinations he had as a young man.

Cannibalism was not illegal in Germany and Meiwes' defence was that Brandes had not been murdered because he was a willing participant in his own death. Judge Volker Mütze was inclined to take the same view, stating in his judgment that, "This was the killing of a person without murder. These were two psychologically sick people. The famous lust for murder was not there."

Judge Mütze rejected the prosecution case and Meiwes was found guilty of manslaughter. He was given a sentence of eight and a half years' imprisonment. The verdict and sentence were greeted with shocked amazement by the German public. One newspaper reported that Meiwes had smiled when sentenced as if he had been served a delicious pudding.

Over press photographs of Meiwes sitting smoking in a restaurant with a bottle of wine on the table, came news that he was planning to write a book and was considering film offers. When the cannibal entered prison he became a vegetarian, supported the agenda of the Green Party and helped fellow inmates by writing letters for them.

The prosecution lawyers maintained that Meiwes was guilty of murder and appealed against his sentence. A re-trial was ordered and the cannibal was served his just desserts when a court sitting in Frankfurt in May 2006 found him guilty of murder and sentenced him to life imprisonment.

Eager To Please

A young Eskimo hunter, called Aligoomiak, killed a tribal chief so that his uncle could take possession of the rival's wife. He left a trail of death in his flight from the Mounties before ending up as a victim of "Neck-Tie Bill".

An Eskimo tribe called Cogmollocks lived in the wilds of northern Canada, on Herschel Island inside the Arctic Circle. Their life was hard and conditions tough and unforgiving. They were skilled hunters and had a reputation for violence among themselves in inter-tribal disputes. White traders and missionaries were not welcomed and periodically ended up dead.

In 1922, a Cogmollock chief was killed in a dispute over ownership of a wife. The widow was taken by one of the dead man's rivals, Pugnana, which left another contender dissatisfied. Tatamangama resolved to eliminate the man who had snatched his prize away. He enrolled his eighteen-year-old nephew, Aligoomiak, as the assassin.

During a hunting expedition with fellow tribe members, Aligoomiak bided his time and killed Pugnana with a single shot. The young man's uncle took his dead rival's wife and possessions and moved into his igloo. He rewarded Aligoomiak by giving him a new rifle and the death of Pugnana was reported as an accident.

When news of the death reached the Royal Canadian Mounted Police, an officer was despatched to Hershel Island to investigate. By bribing a few Eskimos to speak out, he established the broad facts of Pugnana's death. As a result he arrested both Aligoomiak and his uncle and set off to take them to the nearest trading post, which was a long and arduous journey through blizzards and involved living off fish and seal meat. However, when they reached their destination Aligoomiak killed the policeman and the trader manning the post.

Several months later the Mounties finally got their man when Aligoomiak, who had vowed to kill any white man who crossed his path, was once again arrested and charged with murder. At the end of 1923, after an epic journey of four thousand miles, a party consisting of a judge and several court officials arrived at Hershel Island from Edmonton. The group also included a hangman, William Brown, better known as "Neck-Tie Bill" whom the judge had brought along in case he was needed.

Aligoomiak put up a strong defence against the charge of killing the policeman who he said planned to eliminate him rather than bringing him to justice. His aim, he claimed, was to incapacitate the officer. Both Aligoomiak and his uncle were found guilty and sentenced to death. They were then handed over to "Neck-Tie Bill" and on 1 February 1924 the two Eskimos were hanged.

Will You Kill Me?

Late on the night of 10 June 1919, Sutton Police Station in the UK, received a call from a local resident reporting that he had found a man near his house who appeared to have been stabbed. On their way to the scene, officers stopped a young man in the street and questioned him. The answers he gave were not convincing and when he offered them money to let him go as he had a train to catch, he was assured of closer attention.

The injured man had sustained several stab wounds but was still alive. He was taken to hospital and the young man was conveyed to the police station. They each had a story to tell. Seventeen-year-old William Adams said he had encountered the man on the Thames Embankment. He was down on his luck and sixty-year-old George Jones offered him food and shelter. Jones told him that he could not afford to pay his income tax and said that life was not worth living. He said to

Adams, "I've done you a good turn. Now you do me one. Will you kill me?"

No doubt surprised by this request to commit murder, Adams answered, "I would if I had the pluck." By arrangement, he subsequently met Jones and they went by tram to Tooting and then walked towards Sutton. Adams had another man with him, called Charlie Smith, a completely mysterious character who, despite the best efforts of the police, was never traced. The trio stopped by a field in Sutton and Jones repeated his earlier request saying, "I want to die. God help me, I want you to kill me." He pressed into Adams' hand a shoe-maker's awl and said, "Stab me," adding, "The best way is in the neck . . ."

Jones had prepared himself for the end by taking off most of his clothes and lying on the ground. Adams stabbed him three times in the neck and again in the stomach. None of the wounds were fatal and Adams tried to drag Jones to a nearby pond, presumably to drown him, but found his victim too heavy. Smith, apparently, was an observer of all this but not an active participant. Eventually, Jones was relieved of what little money he had on him and was abandoned to his fate.

George Jones, who had convictions for burglary and housebreaking, took three days to die in hospital. During that time, he made a dying declaration. He said that he had met Adams but could not understand why he wanted to stab him: "I have done nothing to him," he said. He confirmed the presence of the mysterious Charlie Smith.

William Adams was tried for murder at Guildford Assizes. The jury found him guilty but, possibly believing him to be feeble-minded, added a recommendation to mercy. The sentence of death passed on him was commuted to life imprisonment by the Home Secretary.

CHAPTER 5

Justice Delayed

Several high-profile murder cases have been solved in recent times after having lain dormant for long periods. This has been due to a combination of factors such as the re-examination of crime-scene evidence under cold-case reviews and the benefits of ground-breaking advances in DNA technology.

The murder of elderly Hilda Murrell in 1984 made big headlines but lapsed into an investigation mired in conspiracy theory. The solution which emerged eighteen years later from a cold-case review aided by DNA evidence, proved to be a killing as a result of a bungled burglary.

The death of Rachel Nickell on Wimbledon Common in 1992 also seized the headlines. The investigation into her murder faltered on bungled procedure and was finally resolved in 2008 after a cold-case review, again aided by DNA evidence, pointed the finger of guilt at a man already convicted of rape and murder.

Thirty-two years was the time delay in solving the murder of eleven-year-old Lesley Molseed in 1975. This was another high-profile case which led to a miscarriage of justice when Stefen Kisko was wrongly convicted of murder and served fifteen years imprisonment before his innocence was established. The forensic sample collected at the crime scene, which proved Kisko's innocence, ironically, also led to the identification of Ronald Castree as the real killer after a further fifteen years had lapsed.

The elements of delayed justice in such cases serve many purposes, not least in demonstrating that crimes will be pursued resolutely for the benefit of society. There is also the benefit of closure for the families of victims and satisfaction for those working in the many disciplines charged with implementing investigative procedures.

More important than capturing the guilty perhaps, is freeing the innocent. The processes involved are often very similar. In the case of "The Cardiff Three", new developments in DNA techniques applied to crime-scene evidence collected nine years previously irrevocably confirmed their innocence. This was vindication after they had been released from prison sentences based on unsafe convictions. A bonus for the judicial system was that a re-examination of the original evidence led, via the national DNA database, to identification of the murderer. This process took thirteen years.

While DNA has become an indispensable part of the crime-scene matrix, there are other powerful factors at work that serve the cause of justice. One of these is the nationwide scope of the news media and the part played by public information. Television programmes such as Britain's "Crimewatch" and "America's Most Wanted" stir memories of things seen and heard which can provide vital investigative clues. Eighteen years after he had murdered his family, John List was recognized by a member of the public from a description broadcast on US television. Thus was the murderer of five brought to justice.

Another American fugitive from justice was Ira Einhorn who remained on the run for twenty-five years. He was tracked down in Europe due to the vigilance of the international justice system. He too eventually faced the consequences of his crime. Ronald Jebson was on the run for thirty years before he was brought to book for the "Babes in the Woods" murders. Jebson was a dangerous paedophile with a string of offences but it took investigators three decades to put all the pieces in place and secure a confession.

Sometimes the truth emerges too late to confront the perpetrator. The murder of Rita Sawyer in 1970 was solved twenty-nine years later by a cold-case review of DNA evidence which established the killer's identity. Although investigators had solved the case, they failed to bring the murderer to justice. He defeated them by dying before he could be confronted with his guilt.

Freeing the innocent is not always possible due simply to the passage of time. The young soldier convicted of killing Nellie Trew in 1918 was wrongly judged and, over eighty years later, a fresh analysis of the evidence showed that another man was the likely murderer. While such cases alter nothing, they show that the drive to achieve justice, no matter how long delayed, is an unending and worthwhile quest.

No Conspiracy

The murder of seventy-eight-year-old Hilda Murrell in 1984 raised a storm of controversy alleging involvement of British intelligence services and a cover-up. The reality of the elderly rose-grower's death, when it was revealed eighteen years later, proved to be rather more mundane, although no less tragic.

Hilda Murrell was a spinster who lived on her own near Shrewsbury and was well known for her successful participation in local and national flower shows. The fact that she was an active campaigner in CND (Campaign for Nuclear Disarmament) won her a reputation as being mildly eccentric.

On 21 March 1984, she was abducted from her home and, three days later, her partly-clothed body was found six miles away on Haughmond Hill. She had been repeatedly stabbed and there were semen traces on her body. Police discovered that her telephone had been tampered with and the initial presumption was that she had been killed by a burglar in a crime that had gone tragically wrong. This view was supported by evidence that her house had been systematically searched and there was evidence of a struggle having taken place.

When the dead woman's involvement in anti-nuclear campaigning came to light, conspiracy theories began to emerge. Speculation increased when it was learned that her nephew had served with naval intelligence during the Falklands War. Theorists had a field day with the idea that the elderly lady was killed by agents looking for hidden documents about the sinking of the Argentine battleship, *General Belgrano*.

The inquest into Hilda Murrell's death concluded that the most probable cause was hypothermia. In December 1984, the Coroner returned a verdict of unlawful killing and West Mercia police stuck to their view that she had been the victim of a random burglary.

Speculation about the death of the rose-grower continued over the ensuing years and became something of a cause célèbre. New developments in DNA testing were to be applied to forensic traces collected at the crime scene. Questions were asked in Parliament and the Home Secretary acknowledged that new DNA tests would be carried out.

In April 2002, West Mercia police launched a cold-case review in the hope of clearing up the unresolved matter of Hilda Murrell's death. Apart from the DNA evidence, the police had fingerprints and a footprint that had possibly been left by the killer.

This intensive re-examination of evidence led the police to Andrew George, a thirty-seven-year-old labourer who, at the time of the murder, was sixteen years old. Semen traces at the crime scene matched George's DNA profile. He was arrested in June 2003.

George was tried for murder at Stafford Crown Court in April 2005. He protested his innocence. The prosecution argued that he broke into Hilda Murrell's home and was disturbed when she returned. She was a feisty women, despite her age, and probably grappled with the intruder. After sexually assaulting her and attacking her with a knife, he drove to the spot where her body was dumped. The DNA match proved George's guilt and the jury returned a unanimous guilty verdict. He was distraught and abusive when the verdict was announced. Mr Justice Wakerley sentenced him to life imprisonment.

Pleased at the outcome and vindicated in their original assessment, West Mercia police acknowledged that the case would have been solved more quickly had modern DNA techniques been available at the time. As it was, it was open to the free rein of wild conspiracy theories which consumed acres of newsprint.

Kill, And Kill Again

The murder of Rachel Nickell on Wimbledon Common in the UK in July 1992 was finally solved in 2008 when a serial rapist and murderer confessed to the crime. This followed a controversial police investigation involving a false accusation and bitter recriminations.

Twenty-three-year-old Rachel Nickell was walking with her young son on Wimbledon Common on 15 July 1992 when she was subjected to a frenzied knife attack. Her assailant stabbed her forty-nine times before getting clean away. She was found dead with her two-year-old son clinging to her body.

News of the murder committed in a public park in London that was frequented by many people for recreational purposes caused outrage and demands for action. A massive investigation was mounted and psychological profiling was used as a means of identifying the type of individual likely to carry out such a crime. A number of likely attributes were suggested. These included a fascination for sadistic sex and an urge to seek domination over women. It was thought such a person would be a low social achiever and probably living alone close to the murder location.

A profile based on these considerations was aired by the BBC's "Crimewatch" programme in September 1992 and photofit images of two men seen on Wimbledon Common on the day of the murder were screened. Following the programme, four viewers called the police to say they recognized the man in one of the photofits as Colin Stagg.

Thirty-one-year-old Stagg lived at Roehampton and admitted being on Wimbledon Common with his dog on the day Rachel Nickell was murdered. Many of his personal characteristics seemed to match those of the psychological profile. This influenced the police in setting up an unprecedented undercover operation – a so-called "honey trap". A policewoman befriended Colin Stagg and attempted, unsuccessfully as it turned out, to draw him into making a murder confession.

Despite the failure of this strategy, Stagg was charged with the Wimbledon Common murder in August 1993. His trial at the Old Bailey in the following year collapsed when Mr Justice Ognall ruled that the prosecution evidence was inadmissible. The police were criticized for attempting to manipulate a suspect and trap him into self-incrimination. Colin Stagg was declared innocent and discharged. He was subsequently awarded over £700,000 in damages.

Running parallel with the enquiry into the murder of Rachel Nickell was an investigation into the activities of a serial rapist in southeast London. It would take sixteen years before the two enquiries converged to produce a common suspect.

In May 1992, a few weeks before Nickell was murdered, a young woman out with her child was raped in Eltham. This was one in a series of attacks in which a rapist targeted young women and which culminated in murder in November 1993. Samantha Bisset and her young daughter were killed in their home at Plumstead by an intruder. The four-year-old had been raped and suffocated while her mother was subjected to a frenzied knife attack.

DNA found at the Plumstead murder scene matched forensic traces left by the serial rapist during his earlier attacks. He was identified as Robert Napper, aged forty-two, a man with a history of mental problems. He had also been identified by two members of the public who recognized him from photofit images compiled from victims' descriptions of the rapist.

Napper, it seemed, had led a charmed life. When questioned by the police, his failure to provide a blood sample was not followed up and he was eliminated from enquiries because he did not match the height of the suspect rapist. A search of his bedsit turned up a pistol, ammunition, knives and documents, which suggested a sinister agenda. He was given an eight-week custodial sentence for firearms offences.

Two years later, he was charged with the Bisset murder on the basis of DNA evidence. Even then, with striking similarities between this murder and that of Rachel Nickell, the crimes were still being treated as separate enquiries. In October 1995, Napper admitted the murders of Samantha Bisset and her daughter and, in addition, acknowledged two attempted rapes and one actual rape. He was committed to Broadmoor high-security hospital.

Forty-two-year-old Napper had a history of psychiatric illness from an early age. He committed his first criminal offence in 1986 and, three years later, was diagnosed as a paranoid schizophrenic with a tendency towards delusions.

By the time the police started to connect Napper with the Wimbledon Common murder, he had been in Broadmoor for nine years.

In 2004, as the result of a cold-case review, the police made the connection between Napper and the murder of Rachel Nickell. At his trial in 2008, he pleaded guilty to diminished responsibility manslaughter and he was returned to spend the rest of his days in Broadmoor.

The fall-out from the trial was considerable. The police admitted errors in the handling of evidence, which had left Napper free to continue his violent attacks and, in particular, to commit the murder of Rachel Nickell. A public apology was offered to Colin Stagg, acknowledging that he had been wrongly accused of murder. Rachel Nickell's family also received apologies for failures in police procedure, which had left Napper at liberty to kill again.

Matching DNA

The murderer of a young girl was convicted by DNA evidence thirty-two years after the crime was committed. In the meantime, an innocent man, wrongly imprisoned, spent fifteen years behind bars.

Eleven-year-old Lesley Molseed left her family home in Rochdale, Lancashire, UK on a shopping errand on 5 October 1975. She did not return and her body was found four days later on isolated moorland between Oldham and Halifax. She had been sexually assaulted and stabbed.

An intense police investigation resulted in the arrest of Stefan Kisko on suspicion of murder in December 1975. He was a man of low mental age who worked as a clerk and lived with his mother. During questioning, he confessed to killing the child. Kisko was tried at Leeds Crown Court in July 1976, found guilty of murder and jailed for life.

Kisko's mother mounted a fierce campaign protesting his innocence and his conviction was quashed on appeal in 1992. It was clear that Kisko could not have committed the murder because he was infertile, while forensic traces gathered at the time from the dead child's clothing including semen containing sperm. Stefan Kisko, the victim of a tragic miscarriage of justice, was released from prison after serving fifteen years and he died two years later.

In 2005, fifty-three-year-old Ronald Castree, a local man, who lived in the same area as the Molseed family, came under public scrutiny. He had been convicted of abducting and assaulting a nine-year-old child months after Lesley Molseed's murder. Thirty years after the event, he gave a DNA sample following an alleged sex attack on a woman in Oldham. As a matter of course, this sample was computed with forensic material from other cases. Castree's DNA proved to be an exact match with the semen traces found in 1975.

Castree was arrested and denied killing the girl, claiming that the DNA had been contaminated. Lesley Molseed died in an era before DNA profiling was possible but evidence from the crime scene preserved in a forensic laboratory provided retrospective proof of his guilt.

Tried for murder at Bradford Crown Court in November 2007, Castree heard that the odds against an error in the DNA evidence that linked him to the crime thirty-two years previously were described as a billion to one. He was convicted of a murder for which an innocent man was wrongly imprisoned and for which, no doubt, he believed he had escaped suspicion. Castree was convicted and sentenced to a minimum of thirty years' imprisonment.

The Cardiff Three

In a case that made criminal history, a miscarriage of justice was corrected when Jeffrey Gafoor pleaded guilty to murder. In November 1990, at Swansea Crown Court, three men were convicted of the murder of Lynette White on evidence that was unsafe.

The Cardiff Three were Stephen Miller, Yusef Abdullahi and Anthony Paris. Along with two other men, they were charged with murdering twenty-two-year-old Lynette White, a sex worker who lived at Butedown in Cardiff's docklands. On 14 February 1988, the young woman was found dead in her flat, the place where she took her clients. She had been savagely attacked. Her body bore fifty-seven stab wounds and her throat had been cut.

The trial was the largest in British criminal history at that time. The prosecution agreed that Stephen Miller, the dead woman's boyfriend, owed money to Abdullahi and Paris. They alleged that he needed her earnings to pay off the debt and when she declined to co-operate, they killed her. Lynette White had been a prostitute for three years, living and working in the murky sub-culture of the docklands. The miserable room in which she met her death bore ample evidence of the horrors enacted there. Traces of blood, hair, saliva and semen were collected, together with fingerprints.

Forensic tests on the three defendants all proved negative and each had an alibi. Convictions were secured on Miller's confession, which he later retracted. Witnesses had seen a dark-haired man with blood on his hands near the murder scene. He disappeared and a photofit failed to produce a suspect. The Cardiff Three were convicted of murder and sentenced to life imprisonment.

There was considerable unease about the trial and the lack of convincing evidence. In December 1992, the Court of Appeal quashed the murder convictions in a landmark decision. Lord Taylor, the Lord Chief Justice, accused the police of using oppressive and bullying tactics in their interview with Miller and had taunted him when he repeatedly denied the accusations made against him. There were emotional scenes outside the court when the Cardiff Three, proven innocent, regained their freedom.

The final twist in the story came five years later. A campaigning journalist who had written a book about the case was convinced that a re-examination of the crime scene evidence would bear fruit, especially in light of new developments in DNA testing. Profiling of material collected at the crime scene in 1988 was found to give a partial match with the DNA of a fourteen-year-old boy on the national DNA database. This meant that the murderer was a close relative of the boy.

The new information stimulated fresh police enquiries and led to thirty-eight-year-old Jeffrey Gafoor. He worked in Cardiff as a security guard. He lived in a rented apartment and was described as "a loner and a bit tormented". On 4 July 2003 at Cardiff Crown Court, Gafoor admitted killing Lynette White. He was sentenced to life imprisonment and legal history was made.

Caught On TV

Before disappearing into anonymity for eighteen years, the murderer of five family members in the US left a written confession acknowledging his guilt and apologising for leaving his mother's body in the attic, saying, "she was too heavy to move".

John List was viewed by all who knew him as a mild-mannered man and a regular churchgoer. His career consisted of taking jobs with impressive titles but offering little satisfaction. In 1965 he took a position with the First National Bank of Jersey City on the strength of which he bought an expensive house in Westfield. He had pushed his commitments beyond the limits of his salary and was soon in financial difficulties.

In less than a year he was out of the job but kept the bad news from his wife and family. For six months he kept up the daily pretence of going to the office until he found a new job. Then he told his wife, who was ill with a degenerative brain disease, that he had moved on but kept quiet about the much reduced salary.

In his neighbourhood, List was regarded as a slightly quaint figure. He was a very private person who was never seen without a jacket and tie, whether it was winter or summer. He taught at the local Sunday School and was co-leader of the cub-scouts pack. He was regarded as being too heavy-handed with discipline.

Mired in debt and with obligations that he could not fulfil, List decided to lighten his burden by disposing of his family and starting a new life somewhere else. On 9 November 1971, he shot dead his wife, daughter and two sons and his eighty-four-year-old mother at their home in Westfield and promptly disappeared. The bullet-ridden bodies of his victims were found three weeks later. He had left behind a letter of confession in which he wrote, "I know that what has been done is wrong . . ."

He went west to Denver, Colorado, where he changed his name to Robert Clark and took work as a kitchen night-shift cook. He remarried in 1985 and moved to Brandermill, Virginia, where he found work as an accountant. He told his new wife that her predecessor had died of a brain tumour.

Having enjoyed eighteen years of anonymity and begun a new life, John List probably thought he had put all his troubles behind him. When Fox Television's *America's Most Wanted* programme featured the List killings in New Jersey and described the fugitive, public curiosity was stirred. A viewer called the programme's hotline to report that a man answering List's description was living in Brandermill.

The knock on Robert Clark's door came on 1 June 1989 when the FBI came visiting. Once his fingerprints had been taken, his true identity was undeniable and John List, fugitive from justice, was taken into custody. He was extradited to New Jersey where he stood trial in April 1990.

After listening to the evidence for seven days, the trial jury found John List guilty on five counts of murder in the first degree. There being no death penalty in New Jersey, he was given five consecutive life sentences.

Fugitive From Justice

Ira Einhorn was a notorious fugitive from justice who defied attempts to secure his return to the US to answer a murder charge. He remained on the run for twenty-five years before finally appearing on trial.

Einhorn was a recognized figure in the 1960s counter culture movement in Philadelphia and taught at the University of Pennsylvania. His ideas about saving the planet were widely listened to and he impressed those he met with his encyclopaedic knowledge. He was an imposing figure with a powerful debating style and a high opinion of his own abilities. He styled himself as "The Unicorn".

In 1972, Einhorn met Holly Maddux, a young Texas girl, and began a passionate affair with her. They lived together in his apartment in Philadelphia and, according to those who knew the couple, the relationship was sometimes strained. In 1977 they went to Europe on holiday together but returned separately.

In September 1977, Holly disappeared. Answering her parents' concern, Einhorn said she left the apartment on 11 September to go shopping but did not return. Weeks went by with no news of Holly and she was reported missing.

During their enquiries into Holly's disappearance, investigators learned that Einhorn had a reputation for ill-treating his girlfriends, although no charges were brought. They also discovered that Einhorn had asked two friends to help him move a trunk that he wanted to dump in the Schuylkill River. The task proved impossible because the trunk was too large to fit in the friends' car.

Detectives arrived at Einhorn's apartment on 28 March 1979 armed with a search warrant. In a closet they found a trunk containing the mummified remains of Holly Maddux. Protesting his ignorance regarding the contents of the trunk and claiming that he had been set up by intelligence agents, Einhorn was arrested and charged with murder.

Before he could be committed for trial, "The Unicorn" jumped bail and fled from the US. He was reported to be in Ireland where he was protected by the lack of an extradition treaty. In 1993 a Philadelphia court convicted him of murder in his absence and, by 1997, he had moved to France. In 2001 he lost his appeal against extradition and he was ordered to be returned to the US. Einhorn's reaction to this decision was to attempt suicide and cast blame for his predicament on the French Prime Minister. Despite appeals to the European Court of Human Rights, he was finally sent back to Philadelphia.

He appeared on trial for the murder of Holly Maddux in October 2002. One of the conditions of his extradition from France was that he would not have to face the death penalty. He was scornful of the charge against him and repeated his earlier defence that he had been framed by the CIA because of the knowledge he possessed about their mind control programme. He was disrespectful of the family of Holly Maddux who had won a civil suit preventing him from profiting by publishing accounts of the case. In court, the prosecutor read from one of Einhorn's poems relating how he had choked a lover who has deserted him. "In such violence, there may be freedom," he had written. "The Unicorn", who had avoided justice for so long, was finally found guilty of first-degree murder and sentenced to life imprisonment.

Babes In The Woods

At Easter time 1970, Susan Blatchford, aged eleven, and Garry Hanlon, aged twelve, disappeared after they had been out playing together near their home in Enfield, north London. They promised to be back in an hour for their evening meal. When they had not returned by 8.00 p.m. the alarm was raised.

A full-scale search was mounted for the missing children and days turned into weeks. Epping Forest was the focus for search teams involving 600 police, frogmen, tracker dogs and helicopters. Over 5,000 acres of woodland were searched and 15,000 people were questioned.

Then, on 17 June 1970, a man walking his dog in Epping Forest discovered the missing children. Their bodies were huddled together in dense undergrowth at a spot on the edge of the forest. The hot weather during the summer had speeded-up decomposition, making it impossible to recover any forensic evidence. There was a suggestion that the youngsters had died of exposure. The manner of their discovery prompted the press to call them "The Babes in the Wood".

The coroner recorded an open verdict and there the case rested until the investigation into the children's deaths was re-opened in 1996. Ronald Jebson, a sixty-one-year-old convicted sex offender, currently serving a prison sentence was questioned about events in 1970. He admitted being involved and, in August 1998, made a full confession.

Jebson was an adopted child who grew up to be a loner. He served in the army on two separate occasions, going absent without leave on his second spell in uniform. He became dependent on alcohol and amphetamines and spent much of his life in prison, serving various sentences for sex offences involving children.

In December 1968 Jebson was jailed for two years for an indecent assault on a six-year-old boy. He was released in March 1970 and a month later, Susan Blatchford and Gary Hanlon, went missing. In April of that year, he assaulted a boy and his conviction earned him five years in prison. He was released in August 1973 when he then raped and strangled an eight-year-old girl. That crime placed him in prison for a long sentence.

Jebson was described by the police as a "highly dangerous, fixated and sadistic paedophile". He confided to a prison psychiatrist, "If I get a few drinks and poppers, nothing would stop me."

Tried at the Old Bailey in May 2000, Jebson pleaded guilty to "The Babes in the Wood" murders and was given two life sentences. The judge described him as "a truly wicked and perverted man". Thus, after a delay of thirty years, justice was finally served.

Killer With No Name

Eighteen-year-old Rita Sawyer spent the evening of 4 September 1970 with her boyfriend in Leamington Spa, Warwickshire. When they parted, she met someone else in the town and went missing. Her body was found the next day at Harbury Windmill, a local beauty spot close to her home. The young woman, who was three months pregnant, had been stabbed repeatedly and her body dumped in a hedge.

Witnesses recalled seeing a Ford Zephyr car in the vicinity where she was found. Traces of semen found on the body would ultimately prove the key to the identity of her murderer. In an investigation lasting four months, Warwickshire Police took hundreds of statements and questioned many people but the search for Rita's killer ground to a halt.

Then in 1999, taking advantage of developments in the world of forensic science, and particularly in DNA testing, Warwickshire Police re-opened their investigation. All the original scene of crime evidence had been carefully stored and this was handed to the Forensic Science Service.

Examiners confirmed that there were semen traces on clothing enabling them to search for a DNA match on the national database. A police spokesman was confident that the review of evidence that had provided a DNA profile would enable the killer to be identified.

In August 1999, Warwickshire Police announced that the mystery of Rita Sawyer's death had been solved. A DNA match had been found with a man from Leamington Spa who had been interviewed in 1970 but was not considered a suspect.

The name of the man, who would have been in his twenties at the time of the murder, was not made public. He had died in 1989 and the view was taken that no purpose would be served by publicly identifying him. Warwickshire Police were entirely satisfied that they had got their man twenty-nine years after he committed murder.

The long arm of forensic investigation had proved its worth but the murderer took his knowledge of a secret crime with him to the grave.

". . . A Man Who Sits And Thinks"

The farming community of Fort Fairfield in New England, USA, was shocked by the disappearance of a fourteen-year-old boy on 26 December 1964. Cyrus Everett, a newspaper delivery boy, left home soon after 5.00 p.m. to start his round but did not return. Local searches failed to locate him and he remained on the missing persons register.

Two months later, the community was hit by a second tragedy when a twenty-four-year-old local girl who worked as a waitress was found murdered. When Donna March failed to turn up for work at the Plymouth Hotel on 24 February 1965, her brother went to the apartment into which she had recently moved. He found her lying dead on the sofa with a towel wrapped around her head. She had been beaten with sufficient force to fracture her skull.

On 9 May 1965, three youngsters playing in an area called Chaney's Grove discovered Cyrus Everett's partially decomposed body. In a tragic irony, he was found in the exact location predicted weeks earlier by a medium using extra sensory techniques.

Fort Fairfield was rife with rumours about the two deaths and there was much gossip, some of it malicious, suggesting that a local politician was responsible. There was, though, a curious connection between the two cases. The last house on Cyrus Everett's delivery round belonged to Philip Adams who was well known to the police. It was an apartment in this same house that Donna March had rented a few days before she died, and it was the place where her body was found.

Philip Adams was questioned by detectives but there was no follow-up action. Donna's murder remained unsolved and some local citizens were unhappy at the outcome of investigations into the paperboy's death. Because his body was badly decomposed, examiners decided that a precise cause of death could not be determined. Dissatisfied with this outcome, a prominent citizen in the town hired a private investigator. He arranged for an exhumation and a second post-mortem was carried out. On this occasion, the examiner found a skull fracture which made murder a likely cause of death.

Donna's death was investigated as a murder and it was found that the twice-divorced young woman dated airmen from the nearby Fort Loring Air Base. One of her dates, a Lieutenant, was known to have argued with her about her promiscuity. He had no alibi for the time Donna was killed and was arrested. He appeared on trial for murder but the evidence against him was so weak that an acquittal was the only possible outcome.

And there the twin tragedies of Fort Fairfield rested until 1984 when the editor of the local newspaper was sent a poem in the mail. Written anonymously, the scribe said, ". . . I know a man who sits and thinks, at the happening a score years ago. The clue to which is buried, where only he knows."

The poem was traced to Philip Adams who, at the time was serving a prison sentence at Somers Correctional Institution. He had been convicted of attacking a ten-year-old boy and had other convictions for sex offences. It seems that Adams voluntarily committed himself to a mental institution in February 1965 and was released six days before Donna March was killed.

At the age of forty-two, Adams was sent for trial in January 1985. Evidence given by his brother amounted to a confession. He revealed that on the night of the murder, he had visited Donna with the intention of borrowing money. He found her asleep and, after searching the apartment, killed her, covering her head to hide the wounds he had inflicted.

So, after twenty years, justice was served when Adams was found guilty of murder and sentenced to life imprisonment. There was no mention of Cyrus Everett other than a cryptic line in Adams' poem about "two unsound corpses".

Murder In Paradise

Norfolk Island, situated in the Pacific Ocean 1,000 miles from eastern Australia, is a place with a small population and a long history. It is home to 1,800 residents and its attractive beaches and beautiful scenery attract many tourists.

The calm of this peaceful place was disrupted on 31 March 2002 when a young woman was murdered. Janelle Patton, a twenty-nine-year-old restaurant manager, had gone out walking on Easter Sunday and went missing. Later that day her body was found wrapped up in a sheet of black plastic. She had sustained several stab wounds and lacerations and her skull was fractured. Cuts to her hands were testimony to the vigour with which she had tried to defend herself against a frenzied knife attack.

There had not been a murder on this island paradise for 150 years. A former penal colony, it had been settled in

1856 by descendents of the HMS *Bounty* mutineers. It was a community where people worked together and enjoyed the benefits of nature. Although it was on Australian territory, Norfolk Island had its own immigration control. The passport of every visitor was checked so that the make-up of the population, both resident and visiting, totalling 2,771 people, on the day of the murder was known.

Detectives from Canberra arrived to begin a murder investigation. A mass fingerprinting exercise was undertaken to include everyone between the ages of fifteen and seventy. In a small community, everyone had an opinion and gossip featured prominently. Janelle Patton came from Sydney and had worked on the Island for just over two years. She was regarded by some as a confrontational person who had been involved in rows with some of the locals. Many residents thought they knew who her killer was and names of suspects were given to detectives.

In an enquiry that lasted four years, suspicion settled on a New Zealander, a twenty-eight-year-old chef, Glenn McNeill, who had since returned to his home in Nelson. Following a preliminary hearing in May 2004, McNeill was ordered to stand trial for murder.

He appeared before the Island's Supreme Court in March 2007, the first murder trial there for 150 years. There was some difficulty in finding twelve impartial jurors. Nearly two-thirds of the hundred people on the jury pool were excused. Some either knew the victim or the defendant and others had made up their minds about who was guilty.

The prosecution set out the case that McNeill had accidentally struck Janelle Patton with his car and, in a panic, put her body in the boot. When the injured woman showed signs of recovering, he silenced her with stab wounds inflicted with a fish knife. McNeill made a confession to the police but later retracted it. Key evidence was that McNeill's fingerprints were found on the plastic sheeting used to wrap the victim's body. Other incriminating forensic traces linking him to the killing were found at his flat and in his car. On 9 March 2007, the jury found McNeill guilty of murder and he was sentenced to life imprisonment. On 23 May 2008, he lost his appeal against the sentence.

Too Clever By Half

Fifteen-year-old Vicky Hamilton was reported missing from her home in Bathgate, Edinburgh, on 11 February 1991. Ten days later, her purse was discovered near the city's rail station. The girl's background led the police to believe she was a runaway and there were indications that she thought she was pregnant. Thousands of statements were taken and many hours of fruitless enquiries were recorded, yet Vicky's disappearance remained a mystery.

In November 2006, the enquiry into Vicky's disappearance was re-opened and five months later came the first glimmer of hope in the investigation. Peter Tobin, a sixty-year-old itinerant handyman, was arrested in connection with the murder of a Polish girl in Glasgow, Angelika Kluk, whose body had been found hidden under the floorboards of St Patrick's Church.

Tobin, a man with a long record of sexual offending had, until this point, successfully eluded the police investigation. He was sentenced to life imprisonment for the murder of Angelika Kluk. Tobin's background came under intense scrutiny and it was shown that he had a string of offences going back to 1969 when he had been sentenced to fourteen years' imprisonment for assaulting two teenage girls at his flat in Portsmouth.

Although he had never been considered a suspect in the disappearance of Vicky Hamilton, it was known that he was living in Bathgate at the time. A search was made at his former home and a knife was found hidden in the loft. Tobin had left the Bathgate house in March 1991 and moved to Margate in Kent. It was here in November 2007, in the back garden, that investigators found the remains of Vicky Hamilton. Her dismembered body had been wrapped in plastic sheeting and buried in a two-metre deep hole in the garden filled in with concrete and soil.

Fingerprints found on the plastic sheeting were identified as Tobin's. Further incriminating evidence was to follow. The dead girl's purse, which had been found in Edinburgh all those years before, was tested for DNA. Tests showed that Tobin's young son had chewed on the purse, leaving genetic material that was matched to his father's DNA. Thus, the clue which the murderer had planted in the belief that it would derail any investigation, came back to haunt him.

If further proof were needed it was provided by the knife found in Tobin's Bathgate home which had a sliver of tissue adhering to the blade. This yielded sufficient DNA to prove it had been used on Vicky Hamilton.

Tobin was tried for murder in Dundee in December 2008. He was convicted of abduction, rape and murder. Sentencing him to life imprisonment, the judge, Lord Emslie, referred to the way he had desecrated his victim's body, which he said, "must rank among the most evil and horrific acts".

For over forty years, Tobin had travelled around the country in his role as a handyman preying on women, immobilizing them with sedatives and committing sexual assaults. He used deception and manipulation to avoid capture. The resolution of Vicky Hamilton's disappearance owed much to the tenacity of the Lothian and Borders police. They never gave up and eventually got their man. Because of his record, several police forces suspect that Tobin may have been involved in at least four other cases of missing women.

Beauty In The Bath

Cynthia Bolshaw, an attractive divorcee living in Heswell, Merseyside, was found dead in the bath at her home on her fiftieth birthday. "The Beauty in the Bath", as the press called her, was a lady with many boyfriends as their names in her diary testified.

Cynthia's diaries contained the names of over 200 men, and it was clear that she lived a sexually active life. In their initial enquiries into her death in 1983, detectives interviewed sixty-four men and took more than a thousand statements.

One of those questioned was John Taft who worked for a double-glazing company. Cynthia asked him to call at the house to provide a quotation for work. They became lovers. In the light of subsequent events, Taft was asked if he had met Cynthia Bolshaw. He denied knowing her. Police enquiries were frustrated by persistent hoax telephone calls and the investigation lost its impetus.

The breakthrough came in April 1999, partly due to advances in testing crime scene DNA, but also to new witness information. A fingerprint voluntarily recorded by Taft in 1983 provided a DNA sample which matched semen traces found in Cynthia Bolshaw's bedroom. Coupled with this was a statement from Taft's ex-wife who said that Taft had admitted visiting Cynthia on the day she died.

Taft was arrested and put on trial for murder. The prosecution case was that he had strangled Cynthia and dumped her body face down in the bath. He said he had sex with her but stated she was alive when he left the house. He had asked his wife at the time to lie on his behalf to prevent him being drawn into the murder investigation.

In November 1999, a case that had dragged on for sixteen years was finally concluded when a trial jury, with a majority verdict of ten to two, convicted Taft of murder. He was given a life sentence.

Not Getting Away With It

On 30 October 1975, teenaged Martha Moxley and some friends visited the Skakel home after an evening of pre-Halloween partying. The fifteen-year-old girl left the house to return home but did not make it. Her body was found the next day under trees at her family home. She had been beaten to death with a golf club and stabbed with a piece of wood from the splintered shaft. Michael Skakel, then fifteen years old, and his brother, Thomas, aged seventeen, were suspects. The Skakel boys were from a prominent family in Bell Haven, Connecticut, and had influential connections to the Kennedys; Robert F. Kennedy Jr was his cousin. It was later suggested that they were spirited away from the scene to mislead investigators.

Little progress was made with police enquiries. Meanwhile, Michael Skakel entered a clinic dealing with mental health and alcohol abuse problems. It was later alleged that during one of these sessions he blurted out an admission that he had killed Martha Moxley. His life moved on and in due course he became a skier and settled down to married life in Palm Beach in an exclusive community with his wife, son and father.

In a sensational development in January 2000, police charged Skakel, then aged thirty-nine, with the Moxley murder. He claimed he was not guilty and a legal question arose as to the procedure that would be used to consider the charge. In 1975, he had been dealt with in juvenile court and his lawyers argued that the new charge should be dealt with in the same way. The implication of this was that the juvenile court was presided over by a single judge with no jury present and no evidence heard, whereas the Superior Court carried more severe penalties in the event of a guilty verdict.

In February 2001, it was decided that his case would be heard in State Superior Court for a trial lasting two months. The prosecutor described how Martha Moxley had met her death by being beaten with a golf club so furiously that the club broke apart. The case had finally come to court thanks to the campaigning efforts of the dead girl's mother.

The golf club was traced to the Skakel home but there were no eyewitnesses to the crime and no linking forensic evidence. It was stated that Michael Skakel had confessed to the crime on several occasions. Testimony was given to that effect by some of his contemporaries back in the 1970s at the rehabilitation clinic. Evidence was given that he had said, "I'm going to get away with murder. I'm a Kennedy."

The court's guilty verdict surprised some legal experts because there was no forensic evidence linking Skakel to the crime. Skakel did not give evidence but after his conviction, he broke down and protested his innocence with several references to God. The judge sentenced him to twenty years to life subject to appeals.

". . . Such Wickedness"

A murderous priest defied all attempts to persuade him to confess, even when dramatically confronted in court with his victim's skull. "Now confess your sin," commanded the judge.

Franz Riembauer was a wayward cleric who failed to practise what he preached. He looked after the faithful in his various livings in the Black Forest region of Germany, but also had a secret life filled with his mistresses and offspring.

In 1805 Riembauer was the village priest in Lauterbach where he lodged with a farmer and his family. When the farmer died, the priest continued to live in the farmhouse with his widow and two daughters. In the summer of 1807, he took the eldest daughter, Magdalena, with him to Munich for several months. While there, the young woman gave birth, an event which excited the gossips back home.

A further source of rumour concerned the disappearance of a young woman, Anna Eichstäder who was employed by a neighbouring priest, who visited Riembauer. When she did not return to her village after several days, questions were asked and Riembauer's response was to deny that she had made the visit.

The following year, Riembauer took the living in a neighbouring village, accompanied by the widow and her two daughters who could not bear to be separated from him. Tragedy followed when, in quick succession, both the widow and Magdalena died after brief illnesses, leaving teenaged Katherina as the sole survivor of the farming family. The priest offered her the position of cook but she declined and left to find domestic work in another parish.

While the tongues wagged about the turn of events, no one dreamed of thinking bad thoughts about the priest until Katherina decided to speak up. She first confided in her new parish priest, claiming that she had seen Riembauer kill Anna Eichstäder and, now that her mother and sister were also dead, she was the only person who knew what had happened. The clergyman advised her to keep quiet to avoid scandal.

But Katherina had a story to tell and she related it to another priest. She went further than before, accusing Riembauer of fraud and of poisoning her mother and sister. The cleric wrote to Riembauer in Latin advising him of the accusations in coded language. Finally, in 1813, Katherina took her story to the magistrates who told her that at the age of seventeen, she was too young to give sworn evidence.

A year later, she finally gave a sworn account of what she had witnessed. She claimed that Riembauer admitted killing Anna Eichstäder, mother of his child, because she had demanded money from him. Incredulous magistrates visited the old farmhouse where they discovered Anna's buried remains.

Meanwhile, the wily priest had moved to another village and, when questioned, claimed that Katherina's family had killed Anna and, of the other allegations, he said, "Only a vicious tongue could utter such wickedness." Nevertheless, Riembauer was taken into custody pending further enquiries which revealed a trail of indiscretions, mistresses and illegitimate offspring.

Eight years after Anna Eichstäder met her death, Riembauer answered murder charges at the Superior Court in Munich. When the judge confronted him in court with Anna's skull and demanded that he confess, he replied, "I was compelled to kill her. Therefore I cannot regard my action as a crime. My conscience is clear." He claimed the witnesses were corrupt and he talked about the purity of his soul.

Finally, in 1830, twelve years after he was arrested, Riembauer was found guilty of murder and sentenced to indefinite confinement. Many believed he was fortunate to escape death by hanging.

Disposal Tips Online

In May 2000, twenty-one-year-old Lucie Blackman travelled to Japan and took a job at a bar in the Roppongi district of Tokyo. Two months after her arrival in the country, Lucie disappeared. She told a friend that she was going out on a drive with a male companion.

Largely due to the persistence of the missing girl's family, Japanese police investigators intensified their efforts to find out what had happened to Lucie Blackman. Their enquiries led to Jogi Obara, a forty-seven-year-old property developer. When questioned, he admitted meeting Lucie although he denied any knowledge of her disappearance.

In February 2001, the dismembered body of Lucie Blackman was found buried at a seaside location within yards of Obara's apartment. The body had been cut into eight pieces and the head embedded in a cement block.

Obara came under close scrutiny and it was discovered that he had many secrets. Videos retrieved from his various apartments showed him sexually assaulting women who had been drugged into insensibility. One of these was an Australian woman who had died in Tokyo in 1992.

Investigators found that Obara had embarked on a shopping expedition at the time of Lucie's disappearance, buying supplies of cement and items such as scissors, hammers and a chainsaw. His computer records showed that he had searched the internet for information about the disposal of bodies.

Under questioning, Obara admitted spending the evening with Lucie Blackman before she went missing. He was arrested in April 2001 and charged in connection with her disappearance and death. He protested his innocence and used his inherited wealth to fund a vigorous defence campaign.

In October 2003, he was charged with abduction, rape resulting in death, and disposal of a body. At his trial in April 2007, he was acquitted on the most serious charge linking him to the death of Lucie Blackman on the grounds of insufficient evidence. He was, though, convicted of multiple attacks on other women and manslaughter and given a life sentence. In accordance with Japanese law, some of the surviving victims of his assaults accepted condolence payments from him.

Prosecutors decided to appeal against Obara's acquittal of the charges relating to Lucie Blackman and the case was heard by appeal judges in Tokyo in December 2008. The allegation was made that he had caused her death by drugging her as a prelude to rape. The court took the view that this could not be proved. The judgment was that Obara was guilty of kidnapping, mutilating and abandoning the young woman's body.

Lucie Blackman's parents welcomed the judgment which, though it partly reversed earlier court verdicts, did not alter Obara's situation. He will continue to serve the life sentence imposed on him in 2007.

Truckload Of Bones

A so-called survivalist, Leonard Lake built a system of underground bunkers in the foothills of the Sierra Nevada. A former US marine, Lake had a pathological hatred of women and shared his fantasies with another former marine, Charles Ng, the son of wealthy parents in Hong Kong. Between them, they were suspected of killing twenty-six victims of both sexes, including children.

In 1985 Ng was spotted shoplifting in San Francisco and he made off in a car driven by Lake. The police followed and Lake was arrested. In the confusion, Ng had managed to escape. Shortly after being taken into custody, thirty-nine-year-old Lake took his own life by swallowing cyanide pills.

When police searched Lake's property in California, they found a house of horror which one of the investigators likened to a Nazi death camp. Human remains were found in three mass graves. They contained decomposing remains of two men, the headless body of a woman, a body stuffed into a sleeping bag and what the police described as a "truckload of bones". A shed was used as a torture chamber, equipped with handcuffs, whips and a one-way mirror. Videotapes were found featuring both Lake and Ng humiliating and torturing female victims. Lake was preparing to confront Armageddon by stocking bunkers with food and weapons. He planned to breed a new race from female sex slaves. Ng was last seen boarding a bus heading across the US/Californian border to Toronto. He kept out of the clutches of the police for several months but, in December 1985, he was arrested in Calgary while attempting robbery. He was convicted of armed robbery and given a four-and-a-half-year prison sentence. He spent his time resisting extradition to the US, but was returned to California to face charges of conspiring to kill twelve people, including two children.

The trial in Orange County lasted four months, involved over 100,000 pages of evidence and cost $14 million. Ng employed delaying tactics, endlessly complaining about procedure and hiring and firing lawyers. He attempted to dissociate himself from Lake's fantasies and denied having anything to do with the killings. Some of the videos shot in the bunker told their own story, although he continued to try to talk himself out of involvement. When he went on to the witness stand to defend himself he declared that he too was a victim. He explained that some of the behaviour seen on the videotapes was just bluff.

In February 1999, the trial jury convicted thirty-eight-year-old Ng of eleven murders and in a separate sitting, recommended the death penalty. It had taken fourteen years to bring Ng to justice but he finally ended up on death row. Prosecutors believed he and Lake may have murdered more than twenty people. His lawyers thought he sealed his fate when he decided to take the witness stand.

No Hiding Place

Justice caught up with Brian Field thirty-three years after he had murdered when a combination of chance and advances in DNA technology enabled a link to be established between victim and attacker.

Fourteen-year-old Roy Tuthill, who lived near Dorking in Surrey, in the UK, went missing in April 1968 on his way home from school. He was last seen alive attempting to hitch a lift. Three days later, his body was found in a copse near Chessington. He had been strangled and sexually assaulted. His attacker had folded the boy's clothing and placed it over his body.

The police search for the attacker produced no immediate results. But, in 1972, suspicions began to form around Brian Field, an itinerant farm machine repairer. He was jailed for attacking and indecently assaulting a teenage boy in Scotland.

This flagged up an amber warning for Surrey Police and Field was questioned about Roy Tuthill's death. No action resulted from this interview and Field went on to offend again in 1986 when he attempted to abduct two teenage boys. They escaped and Field was jailed for four years.

The breakthrough in the police investigation came by chance in 1999 when Field was routinely stopped on suspicion of driving under the influence of drink. New powers enabled the police to take a DNA sample from anyone convicted of a crime and check it on the DNA national database. Field's DNA matched that found on Roy Tuthill's clothing over thirty years previously.

Field eventually confessed to the Surrey murder and he was sent for trial at the Old Bailey in November 2001 where he was convicted and sentenced to life imprisonment. Mr Justice Gordon said that, "advances in modern science techniques should stand as a warning that there is no hiding place for sexual and violent criminals".

Killer Abroad

Volker Eckert was a truck driver who travelled the motorways of Europe trawling for women to murder. Over a period of thirty years, he killed at least thirteen times.

He was arrested in Cologne on 17 November 2006, after his truck was found in a car park at a football stadium in northern Spain. When the vehicle was checked out by the local police it was found to contain the body of a young woman. In the driving cab were incriminating photographs and a length of rope.

Eckert's admission that he was responsible for six killings triggered police investigations throughout Europe and revealed a trail of death. It became evident that he had killed his first victim when he was a mere fourteen years of age. It was only when he qualified as a truck driver in 1999 that he perfected his modus operandi, regularly crossing borders, picking up his victims, killing them and dumping their bodies elsewhere.

Eckert had grown up in the town of Plauen, which at the time was in East Germany. As a child he was fascinated by his sister's toys and, particularly, by a doll with long hair. He practised strangling the doll and playing with her hair. This was an experiment which he turned into reality in 1974 when he fantasized over a schoolgirl and strangled her in a crime that remained unsolved for another thirty years.

A search of Eckert's flat following his arrest revealed a collection of photographs depicting some of his murder victims with ropes around their necks. There were also notes describing some of the murders and, under the bed, a life-size rubber doll decorated with hair and trophies taken from his victims.

Apart from serving six years in prison for attempted murder, he joined the estimated thirty serial killers believed to be active throughout Europe. The E45 highway running from Austria south to Italy was a killing ground where over forty women had been murdered. Prostitutes, along with migrant workers, were successfully targeted by Eckert as being lone, vulnerable women with no fixed address and few family or friends to worry about them when they went missing.

For thirty years, Eckert got away with murder. He confessed to six killings, which was raised to thirteen following police investigations, and there are possibly more. While justice finally caught up with him, Eckert avoided a trial appearance by taking his own life. While awaiting trial at Hof, he hanged himself in his prison cell on 1 July 2007, on his forty-eighth birthday.

Procedural Delay

When a British Royal Navy officer was murdered in New Zealand in 1847, a local man was convicted of the crime and sentenced to death. Only a procedural delay saved him from imminent execution and during that time he was shown to be innocent.

Lieutenant Robert Snow, based at North Shore, Auckland, was in charge of the naval magazine and stores depot at Devonport. He lived locally in a traditional Maori dwelling. On 23 October 1847 in the early hours of the morning, a seaman on board HMS *Dido* at anchor in the harbour reported a blaze on the foreshore.

A cutter and crew were despatched to investigate and found Snow's house on fire. Alert crew members noticed Maori canoes leaving the scene. Once the fire had been extinguished, a search of the remains revealed the bodies of Snow and his wife and daughter. They had been killed with knives and axes.

A naval raiding party rounded up a number of Maoris for questioning. The *New Zealander* reported that there was little doubt the murders had been committed by natives. It was noted that Lieutenant Snow had been involved in disagreements with Maoris who he accused of stealing his crops. Relationships between the Maoris and the authorities became strained and there was talk of war.

Further investigation of the murders led to the arrest of Thomas Duder, a signalman at Mount Victoria. He protested his innocence and, on the basis of very little evidence, he was tried and convicted. The sentence was death by hanging and he was held in custody while the necessary authority to carry out the execution was awaited from London.

During this delay the true facts behind the murders were revealed by chance. A couple brawling in the street at Devonport on a Sunday morning attracted the attention of the police. A man known only as Burns had stabbed his female companion, Margaret Reardon, and then attempted to take his own life. Both survived and information began to emerge about Burns, who was an ex-convict from Sydney.

Enquiries showed that he had been employed by a local Maori chief and, together, they hatched a plan to rob Lieutenant Snow of his monthly salary which he received on specified dates from the Auckland Treasury. Burns involved Reardon and the couple went to Snow's house on the pretext of warning him about trouble brewing among the Maoris. They attacked and killed the Snow family and set fire to the house.

When the murderers fell out, Reardon threatened to inform on Burns. A confession followed and they acknowledged carrying out other murders. In the wake of this development,

Thomas Duder was released and Burns and Reardon were sent for trial. Found guilty, Burns was condemned to death while Reardon was sentenced to penal servitude for life.

Burns was taken to the scene of the crime after being publicly paraded in a horse-drawn cart sitting on his own coffin. On 27 June 1848, he was hanged on the same spot that the Snow family met their deaths. Thomas Duder, an innocent man spared by a trick of fate, went on to prosper in Devonport's business life and a street in the town was named after him.

"Accidental" Murder

The conviction of David Greenwood for "The Button and Badge Murder" in 1918 seemed an open-and-shut case, but a recent review of the evidence suggests that he was an innocent victim of the system.

Sixteen-year-old Nellie Trew was reported missing from home by her father on 9 February 1918. The next morning, the girl's body was found close by Eltham Common in south-east London. She had been raped and strangled. Detectives examining the crime scene found a military badge and a button near the body. The badge depicted the tiger motif of the Leicestershire Regiment and the button had a piece of wire attached to it.

Illustrations of the button and badge featured in newspaper reports of the murder. As a result of this publicity, a man who worked at a factory in London's Oxford Street, spoke to a colleague who usually wore such a badge. He observed that David Greenwood was no longer wearing it. Greenwood's explanation to his workmate was that he had sold it, but he took his friend's advice and reported the fact to the police.

Twenty-one-year-old Greenwood lived in Eltham, a short distance from the spot where Nellie Trew had been found dead. When questioned and shown the badge found near the body, he admitted it was his but explained that he had sold it to a man he met on a tram. Police officers noted that the overcoat Greenwood was wearing had no buttons and that it had a tear as if a button had been torn off. When it was established that the wire attached to the crime scene button was the same as that used in the factory where he worked, suspicion against him hardened.

Greenwood had served his country in the First World War trenches and been injured by an exploding shell when he was buried alive. He was invalided out of the army in June 1917, and was subject to fainting fits and with a weak heart. When discharged from hospital, he took a job as a metal worker.

Charged with the rape and murder of Nellie Trew, he was sent for trial at the Old Bailey in April 1918. The evidence against him was circumstantial. He claimed to have spent the evening of 9 February at the YMCA in Woolwich. Much hinged on the condition of the overcoat, which he had acquired as part of his discharge entitlement. It was established that he had been seen wearing the coat fully buttoned up four days after the murder.

In his defence, it was argued that in view of his physical weakness resulting from his war injury, he would not have been capable of overcoming a strong young woman. This view was supported by Sir Bernard Spilsbury who appeared as an expert witness at the trial. Nevertheless, the jury returned a guilty verdict with a recommendation to mercy in view of the ex-soldier's service to his country. Greenwood spoke from the dock, declaring his innocence, before Mr Justice Atkin sentenced him to death.

An appeal against sentence was refused and it was left to the Home Secretary to consider a reprieve. There was considerable public disquiet about the verdict and a reprieve from execution was granted. In return for his life, Greenwood was given a sentence of penal servitude.

A new slant on the case emerged in 2007 in a book about Sir Bernard Spilsbury by Andrew Rose. During his researches, the author discovered that a man who had been committed to a mental institution in April 1918 confessed to having murdered Nellie Trew. At the time, Albert Lytton was an apprentice at Vickers in Erith where he worked the night shift and frequented Woolwich on Saturday nights. He suffered a mental breakdown and because of his violent behaviour spent most of the rest of his life in mental institutions. He admitted going out with Nellie and "accidentally" murdering her. He said he got blood on his trousers and lost one of the buttons. His mother gave his army greatcoat away. These admissions were made three years after the murder.

Following a sustained campaign to have Greenwood released, the former soldier regained his freedom in 1933, after serving fifteen years in prison. It would take another seventy-three years to establish his innocence.

CHAPTER 6

Final Journeys

The final journey made by many condemned murderers is to their place of execution. It may only be a few short steps from the death cell to the scaffold, gas chamber, electric chair or other designated place of judicial extermination. Historically, those who have made such journeys have done so with equanimity, stoicism, terror, defiance and even humour. And while most have been guilty of the crimes for which they paid the ultimate penalty, some were innocent victims of flawed justice or flagrant prejudice.

Whether administered as a deterrent or as retribution, the manner and procedure of executions exhibit some of the most bizarre aspects of society's efforts to deal with those who transgress. The concept of a life for a life has a long and tortuous history, and executions are wrapped in public spectacle, bungled methods and rituals that may seem more reprehensible than the crimes for which they are the punishment.

Methods of execution in the twentieth century had odd national characteristics. The English preferred hanging, the French retained the guillotine, while the Spanish favoured garrotting. In the US, attempts to introduce new technology with the aim of making the process more humane have led to the introduction of the electric chair, the gas chamber and lethal injection, each with its own quirks and failings.

While many countries have rejected capital punishment in favour of long prison sentences, those that have retained it have yet to find a procedure that is both humane and foolproof. Worldwide, there were 2,390 judicial executions in 2008, more than half of which were carried out in China. The United States called a moratorium on the death penalty in 1967 as a response to public concern over the twelve years it took before the death sentence passed on Caryl Chessman was carried out. The Supreme Court lifted the ruling in 1976 and capital punishment was adopted in thirty-six states. In 2007, there were forty-two executions in the US, which is fewer than in previous years. In Europe, most countries have abolished capital punishment, with the possible exception of a penalty for treason at times of war.

In the present century, the debate about procedure continues to be waged in the US. During an execution in Florida in 2006, a fifty-five-year-old Death Row inmate had taken thirty minutes to die, after the administration of the prescribed cocktail of three lethal drugs. Following a challenge as to the constitutional legality of lethal injection, the Supreme Court called a moratorium on this form of execution but decided in 2008 that the method was not a "cruel and unusual punishment".

As in many aspects of crime and punishment, the grim, gruesome and ugly feature side-by-side with practices that reduce proceedings to a farce. Gallows humour is not without foundation as William Shakespeare observed in his line in Twelfth Night *that, "many a good hanging prevents a bad marriage". And a Scottish judge is credited with the remark about a convicted felon that he would be "none the worse for a good hanging".*

The final journey made by Jack Alderman, whose crime was that he murdered his wife, took thirty-three years. That was the length of time spent on Death Row in Georgia, USA, before being executed in 2008. Appeal procedures by condemned murderers often mean extended time spent on Death Row in the hope of gaining a reprieve, while others, once sentenced, simply want to face the end quickly.

Steven Judy was one of those who walked willingly to the electric chair in 1981, refusing all attempts to seek a stay of execution. By contrast, John Spenkelink exploited every legal loophole available to him during the five years he spent on Death Row. He gained three reprieves but eventually died in the chair. He had some bitter things to say about capital punishment, which he believed was meted out disproportionately to people from poor backgrounds.

In some cases, death alone was not deemed sufficient punishment and judgment decreed that executed felons should forfeit their corpses to the surgeons for dissection. This was the ultimate fate of fourteen-year-old John Any Bird Bell in 1831 and, earlier in the same century, the body of Sylvester Colson, a mutineer convicted in Boston, USA, was subjected to galvanic experiments for no apparent good reason apart from dubious scientific curiosity.

William Kemmler was a pioneer of sorts, being the first person to be despatched in the newly invented electric chair in 1890. His death by "manufactured lightning" at Auburn Prison, New York, was one of many bungled executions using electricity. Things had not changed a great deal forty-six years later when Albert Fish, an odious child murderer, was seated in "Old Sparky" at Sing Sing and precipitated a short-circuit in the apparatus.

Stories with a happy ending are rarely the outcome of these final journeys. But John Lee, famous as "The Man They Could Not Hang", survived three attempts to kill him in 1884. Another remarkable survivor was Anne Greene who was hanged at Oxford in 1650 and her body placed in a coffin ready for the undertaker. She startled all present by defying the rope and, apparently, rising from the dead.

The last laugh on the final journey surely belongs to Kenneth Neu who joked his way through his trial for murder in 1935. He kept up his entertaining ways while in the condemned cell and declared that he was as fit as a fiddle and ready to hang.

Gallows humour aside, it seems strange that the human ingenuity which can put a man on the moon and devise an internet cannot produce a humane and reliable method of judicially terminating life. Perhaps the simple solution is the obvious one, to abolish capital punishment worldwide as an out-dated and unworthy practice. The central proposition that killing people is the way to teach them it is wrong to kill seems an untenable paradox.

"I've Lived My Hell"

"For one time in my life I get something I want", was twenty-four-year-old Steven Judy's comment when he faced death in the electric chair. He declined to make any last-minute appeal against execution and resisted attempts by groups opposing the death penalty to halt proceedings.

Judy's short life had been a violent one. At the age of thirteen he raped a woman and attacked her with a knife and axe. He was confined to a mental institution and was classed as a sexual psychopath. After his release, he embarked on a life of crime which, according to his own account, included numerous rapes, armed robbery and burglary.

His criminal career ended in April 1979 after he killed a young mother and her three children. Twenty-three-year-old Terry Lee Chasteen was driving her children to the baby minder in Indianapolis when another driver flagged her down, indicating there was something wrong with her car. She pulled over and the man offered to help her. He pretended the car was not safe to drive and offered to give the family a lift. Driving off the interstate highway, Steven Judy raped and strangled the mother in front of her terrified children who he later drowned in a nearby river.

Judy was quickly caught and put on trial for murder in Indianapolis. Aware of his violent impulses, he told the jury, "You'd better put me to death. Because next time it might be one of you or your daughter." The jury responded by convicting him and he was sentenced to death in the electric chair.

Judy issued many statements from his prison cell, but none of them contained anything approaching remorse. He said, "I'm not sorry for the things I've done because I've lived my life the only way I knew how . . ." One of his lawyers found redeeming features in his personality and described him as likeable and intelligent.

His execution was scheduled for 9 March 1981, and it marked the first time a person had been put to death in Indiana for twenty years. Despite Judy's welcoming words regarding his own demise, numerous groups were fighting hard to gain clemency on his behalf. And a fellow prisoner asked the Supreme Court to halt Judy's execution on the grounds that if it went ahead it would endanger his own appeal.

Protesters outside Indiana State Prison staged a candle-lit vigil on the eve of execution. Some of them carried placards declaring, "Why do we kill people who kill people to show that killing is wrong." None of this had any effect on the man in the death cell. He was reminded that he could still gain a stay of execution if he changed his mind. He told reporters that he was looking forward to the execution to give him release. "I've lived my hell," he said, indicating that death was what he wanted.

His wish was granted when 2,200 volts surged through his body on 9 March 1981 and he became the sixtieth person to die in Indiana's electric chair.

Six Minutes To Die

Having spent five years on Death Row, during which he was granted three reprieves, John Spenkelink became the first man for twelve years to be executed in the USA against his wishes. The execution at Starke Prison, Florida in 1979 proved controversial, requiring three separate charges of 2,000 volts to kill the prisoner who took six minutes to die.

Spenkelink was a drifter who had been in and out of prison most of his life. While on parole in 1973, he encountered a hitch-hiker who, he claimed, forced him into a sexual act at gunpoint. The two men shared a room at the Ponce de Leon hotel in Tallahassee, Florida, and it was here that Spenkelink shot the hitch-hiker in the back of the head.

Following his conviction for murder and sentence of death, Spenkelink exercised every channel of appeal open to him during the time he spent on Death Row. Finally, on 25 May 1979, the Supreme Court authorized his execution to take place.

There were reports that angry inmates at Starke Prison rattled their metal mugs against their cell doors in a noisy protest at what was about to happen. Spenkelink was taken in manacles to the death chamber containing the electric chair. The executioner was apparently a volunteer, drawn from the prison staff.

Fortified with two shots of whisky, the prisoner was strapped into the chair and the switch was pulled. A doctor applied a stethoscope to his chest and determined that a second charge should be delivered. When this failed to make death certain, a third charge was ordered. Official witnesses were treated to the sights, sounds and smell of smoke and burning flesh. One of those present was reported as saying, "It is un-Christian. It is barbaric."

Following the chaotic nature of Spenkelink's last moments, there were rumours that he had fought with prison guards on his way to the death chamber and was already dead or unconscious when he was put in the chair.

After a moratorium of fifteen years, Florida was back in the execution business. Opponents of capital punishment feared an upsurge of judicial killings. Spenkelink's death raised many controversial issues, including the suggestion that convicted persons from underprivileged backgrounds attracted the greater number of death sentences. Spenkelink was often quoted as commenting, "capital punishment means those without capital get the punishment".

Another issue was the conduct of the execution process, which had been particularly gruesome in Spenkelink's case. This led in 1981 to an order to exhume his body in order that an autopsy could be carried out to establish whether he was indeed dead or unconscious at the time he was electrocuted.

"His Eye Did Not Quail"

John Any Bird Bell, aged fourteen, was convicted of murder in 1831 and publicly hanged before a crowd of 10,000 people at Maidstone, Kent in the UK.

On 4 March 1831, thirteen-year-old Richard Taylor was sent on an errand by his father. He had been instructed to collect a parish allowance due to his family. He had done this on numerous occasions and his habit was to safeguard the money by keeping the coins in his left hand on which he pulled a mitten.

When the boy had not returned by nightfall, his father went in search of him but he remained missing for many weeks. Then, on 11 May, a man out walking near Bridge Wood at Stroud, Kent, found his body lying in a ditch. Richard Taylor was dead from a stab wound to the throat. A search in the undergrowth nearby turned up the presumed murder weapon, a horn-handled knife. The mitten had been cut off his hand and the money was missing.

The knife was traced to the Bell family who lived in a poor house close to Bridge Wood. Fourteen-year-old John Any Bird was the owner of the knife. He and his eleven-year-old brother, James, were taken into custody. The coroner's court decided that the dead boy's body, which had been interred almost immediately after discovery, should be exhumed. The purpose was to search the clothing.

The two boys in custody were taken to the graveyard to witness the exhumation so that their reactions could be observed as possible indications of guilt. John Any Bird declined to take part in the macabre incident that followed. But his brother accepted the invitation to climb down into the grave and search the pockets of the corpse. No money was found, confirming that Richard Taylor had been robbed and murdered.

John and James appeared before the magistrates at Rochester when the younger boy made a confession. He said that he kept watch while John ambushed Taylor and robbed and killed him. The eleven-year-old said that they had noticed Taylor's regular errand to collect money for his father and hatched a plan to rob him. For his part in the enterprise, James was rewarded with one shilling and six pence.

John Any Bird Bell was convicted of murder at Maidstone Assizes and, while being transported from the court to the prison, acknowledged his crime. He even pointed out a pond in which he had washed off his victim's blood. The judge who sentenced him to death told him that his body would be given to surgeons at Rochester for dissection.

The Kent and Essex Mercury reported that the execution on 1 August 1831 drew "an immense concourse of people to witness the sad spectacle". Half an hour before the time of the execution, 10,000 people had gathered near the gaol. John Any Bird Bell had made a full confession to his crime on the eve of execution. Accompanied by the chaplain, he walked steadily to the scaffold and it was reported that, ". . . his eye did not quail, nor was his cheek blanched". After the rope was placed around his neck, he exclaimed in a loud voice, "All the people before me take warning by me!"

". . . The Toes Moved Briskly"

When Sylvester Colson enlisted as crew aboard the US schooner *Fairy* at Boston in August 1820, it was for a voyage that turned him into a mutineer and murderer.

The tone of the voyage to Europe was set at the quayside before sailing when the ship's mate, Thomas Paine Jenkins, had an argument with Charles Marchant, who was reluctant to take orders. Having loaded a cargo of timber, the *Fairy* slipped her moorings and headed out to sea under the command of Captain Edward Selfridge.

From the start, Marchant's rebellious nature affected other members of the crew and he found a willing ally in Colson. They proved to be a troublesome pair, arguing with both the mate and the captain. Matters came to a head when Colson was caught asleep on duty. He and fellow crew member, John Hughes, complained that their watches were too long.

On the night of 24 August 1820, Colson and Marchant resorted to murder. When Hughes enquired as to the whereabouts of the mate he was told casually that both the mate and the captain had been killed and thrown overboard. Marchant had blood on his clothes and he and Colson made preparations to scuttle the ship.

On 29 August, once they had sighted the coast of Nova Scotia, the mutineers sank the ship and rowed ashore with Hughes and another seaman called Murray. They related an implausible tale to the captain of a US ship, requesting him to take them on to Halifax. At this point, Murray decided to inform on the mutineers and they were taken into custody by the Canadian police.

Colson and Marchant were returned to Boston where, in November 1826, they were charged with revolt, piracy and murder. They were tried separately and each was found guilty and sentenced to death. Marchant escaped execution by taking his own life while Colson died on the scaffold. The bodies were taken to Harvard Medical School for anatomical examination.

In February 1827, the corpses were handed over to Dr John White Webster, who, in the fullness of time, would stake his own claim to criminal immortality. Webster was engaged in experiments with galvanic apparatus to observe reactions to electrical stimulation on the nerves and muscles. What happened next was reported in excruciating detail in the *Columbian Sentinel* on 3 February 1827.

Colson's body was connected to a powerful galvanic battery by means of wires inserted in his mouth and urethra. The report noted that, ". . . convulsive motions ensued. Applied to the eye, the organ opened and rolled wildly . . .". Also, ". . . the leg was much agitated at every contact . . . and the toes moved briskly". Dr Webster, whose expertise lay in chemistry and mineralogy, declared the experiment "a great success".

Whatever the doctor may have learned it did little to assist his own criminal ambitions when he murdered fellow academic, Dr George Parkman, in 1850. Like Colson, he felt the hangman's noose around his neck.

Manufacturing Lightning

William Kemmler's crime was that he took an axe to Tillie Ziegler, his mistress, and ended her life. He paid for it by forfeiting his own life in the electric chair, the first murderer to be killed by this new method of electrocution. Kemmler told the witnesses gathered to observe the judicial use of electricity that he believed he was "going to a better place". While that thought might have comforted him, the manner of his going was a woeful spectacle.

The details of Kemmler's crime were lost in the blizzard of publicity accompanying his execution. There was a great deal of press speculation about the new method that was supposed to be more humane than hanging. The authorities debated the type of electrical supply that was to be used. Would it be Edison's direct current (DC) or Westinghouse's alternating current (AC)? Meanwhile, carpenters in Auburn Prison's workshop were building the wooden chair in which Kemmler was to spend his last moments on Earth.

The date of execution was fixed for 6 August 1890. The prison warden brought Kemmler into the execution chamber and introduced him to the assembled witnesses. Among them was a group of doctors, sitting around the chair. Kemmler gave a bow and sat down. He made a brief statement: "The newspapers have been saying a lot of things about me which were not so. I wish you all good luck in the world. I believe I am going to a better place."

Prison officials began preparing him by buckling his arms and legs to the chair and placing the electrodes to his back and to his skull. A mask was then placed over his head and the warden said, "Goodbye William". The executioner, waiting behind a screen, was given the signal and he pulled a switch sending 1,000 volts AC through Kemmler's body. The surge of current lasted seventeen seconds.

To the consternation of those present, Kemmler was not dead and his body arched against the restraints that bound him to the chair. Frantic signals were given to the executioner to send another charge through the chair. This lasted for four minutes before officials decided that Kemmler was dead.

The bungled execution using the new method was universally criticized. One US newspaper declared that Kemmler would be the last man executed in such a manner. The New York *Globe* took the view that, "Manufactured lightning to take the place of the hangman's rope for dispatching of condemned murderers cannot be said to be satisfactory."

Implements Of Hell

Albert Fish was a house painter in New York and father of six children who acquired numerous titles as a result of his perverted sexual activities, including "The Moon Maniac", "Inhuman Monster" and "Cannibal".

Fish was brought up in an orphanage where he grew accustomed to the brutal regime of disciplining children with whips and acts of sadism. He became addicted to pain, subjecting himself to flagellation and other sado-masochistic practices. He burned himself and inserted needles into his body. When there was a full moon, he would eat raw meat.

Not surprisingly, his wife left him and he was abandoned to his perverted practices. He assembled a collection of newspaper cuttings relating to cannibalism, including reports about the German mass murderer, Fritz Haarmann, convicted of twenty-seven killings in 1924.

Over a period of twenty years, Fish was believed to have molested hundreds of children. He had a family cottage in Westchester County where he took his own and neighbours' children and encouraged them to abuse him. His life of perversity came to a crisis point in 1928. He befriended the Budd family who lived in Manhattan, New York, and took a particular interest in Grace, their twelve-year-old daughter.

On 3 June 1928, on the pretext of taking the child to a party, he took her instead to his cottage in Westchester. Grace was strangled by Fish and using what he called his "implements of hell", a butcher's knife, saw and cleaver, he dismembered the child's body. Over a period of several days, he sliced pieces of flesh off the corpse and ate them in a stew with vegetables. This act of cannibalism kept him in a state of sexual fervour.

Grace Budd was reported missing by her family and her fate would have remained a mystery but for Fish's action in writing to her family. Six years after Grace disappeared, he wrote a letter in 1934 informing her mother that he had killed her daughter. The police traced his whereabouts through the letter and he was arrested.

Fish made an extraordinary confession, admitting to six murders and a catalogue of other atrocities, the precise details of which he could not recall. The remains of Grace Budd were recovered from a shallow grave at Westchester.

His trial in March 1934 at White Plains, Westchester County, was a battle of the psychiatrists. His defence contended that he was insane, with ample evidence pointing to that conclusion. He was interested in religion and especially what he saw as the need for purging and physical suffering. He said, "I am not insane, . . . I am just queer. I don't understand myself."

After protracted arguments in court, Fish was judged to be sane; he was duly found guilty of murder and sentenced to death. This meant death in the electric chair at Sing Sing Prison. While awaiting his fate on Death Row, he professed to be looking forward to being electrocuted because that was one thrill he had not previously experienced.

On 16 January 1936, the sixty-six-year-old child molester and cannibal readily made his way to the electric chair. The first electrical charge failed, apparently short-circuited by the needles still in his body. A second charge extinguished the life of the oldest man to be electrocuted at Sing Sing.

"Amazing Grace"

The convicted killer of an elderly couple in Smyrna, Delaware, USA, was given the choice of death by hanging or by lethal injection. He chose hanging and became the first person to be executed in the state by that method for fifty years.

Billy Bailey left a work-release centre in Wilmington on 21 May 1979 and held up a liquor store. He then moved on to a farm occupied by Gilbert and Clara Lambertson, intent on stealing their pick-up truck. In the course of his theft, he killed the couple with a shotgun. Asked later why he did it, he said, "I don't really know. I just know that I feel bad about it . . .".

Bailey was convicted of murder and sentenced to death by hanging. During the time he spent on Death Row, the state of Delaware changed its policy on execution and in 1986 adopted the use of lethal injection. After the appeals process had been exhausted, Bailey was scheduled to be executed in January 1996 and because his original sentence had specified death by hanging, he was given the choice of the noose or injection. The gallows built to hang him in 1980 was still in place and Bailey elected to die by the rope.

Forty-nine-year-old Bailey was taken to the gallows erected in the yard of the Delaware Correctional Center shortly before midnight. The traditional hood was placed over his head and he was attended by two hooded prison guards. He was duly hanged in a manner which his lawyer described as "medieval and barbaric" and witnessed by the children of his victims. Supporters of the death penalty had gathered outside the prison protesting that violent crime deserved violent punishment. Opponents of execution sang "Amazing Grace".

Bailey's execution came at a time when violent crime was on the increase in the US and coincided with a debate about the methods used. This was highlighted by Bailey's decision to be hanged rather than die by lethal injection and by what had happened a day earlier in Virginia. A man who had been on Death Row for twenty years was subjected to lethal injection. It took those administering the fatal chemicals twenty minutes to find a vein into which to insert the needle. In light of this bungled method, death by hanging appeared to be a humane option.

Love, Loot, Lust And Loathing

The secret execution of a White South African woman in Botswana in 2001 was unusual and controversial. Mariette Bosch was hanged at 5.30 in the morning at Gaborone prison without the knowledge of her family or lawyers.

Like many South Africans, fearful of the increase in crime in their country in the 1990s, the Bosch family moved to neighbouring Botswana. They established a new life in a suburb of Gaborone where they became friendly with fellow South Africans, the Wolmarans family. Tragedy struck in 1995 when Justin Bosch was killed in a car accident. Being a good friend, Maria Wolmarans immediately came forward to support the grieving widow and her children.

Tragedy struck a second time in 1996 when Maria was found shot dead in her home. The police investigation into the shooting appeared to make little headway. Meanwhile, Mariette and the widower, Tienie Wolmarans, became close and told their children they intended to marry.

Mariette breathed new life into the stalled enquiry into Maria's death when it became known she had borrowed a handgun from a friend during a visit to South Africa, which she later gave to her brother-in-law for safe-keeping. She had also ordered a wedding dress. Mariette was arrested and charged with murder and, while in custody, married Tienie, whose wife she had allegedly killed.

She went on trial in Botswana in 2000. The prosecution claimed that Mariette was intent on marrying Wolmarans who had promised to divorce his wife. When that did not happen quickly enough for Mariette, she took matters into her own hands by acquiring a firearm and killing Maria. The gun retrieved from Mariette's brother-in-law was tested and proved to be the murder weapon. The prosecution described the case as an example of "the four L's of murder – love, loot, lust and loathing". The trial judge described her as a wicked and despicable woman who had tried to shift the blame for the murder on to a third party. She was found guilty and sentenced to death.

In January 2001, Mariette's appeal was heard by judges from four Commonwealth countries sitting in Botswana's appeal court. She was represented by Desmond de Silva QC, a British barrister with an international reputation. His appeal was dismissed and in the words of Justice Isaac Aboagye, the court could not find "one moral extenuating circumstance". The only lifeline left for her was an appeal to the President of Botswana for clemency.

When Tienie Wolmarans arrived at Gaborone prison on 30 March 2001, he was turned away and told to come back on the following Monday. When he did so, it was to learn that Mariette had been executed. She was the first woman to be hanged in Botswana for thirty years. An application for clemency was apparently being prepared and the fact that a mere two months had elapsed between rejection of her appeal and execution was distressful for her lawyers and family.

"Plop, Plop, Fizz, Fizz"

In 1992 the State of California carried out its first execution for over twenty-five years. Events surrounding the death of a double murderer in the gas chamber at San Quentin Prison were described at the time as the nearest thing to a public execution. Forty-eight people witnessed the death of Robert Harris whose sentence was reprieved and restored four times during the last twelve hours of his life.

Harris entered the gas chamber on 21 April 1992 to be released when his third appeal was granted on the grounds that gassing violated his constitutional rights. In less than an hour, the US Supreme Court overruled this local decision and Harris was returned to the gas chamber where, after fourteen years on Death Row, he was finally executed.

Harris's execution inflamed public opinion. While campaigners supporting capital punishment rejoiced in his death with gross displays of hatred, others railed against the barbaric practice of imposing death sentences. At the time, over 2,500 individuals were held on Death Row throughout the US.

The crime for which Harris was punished with death took place in San Diego on 5 July 1978. He decided to rob a bank and equipped himself with guns stolen from a neighbour, which he first tested in practice firings. He talked two teenagers eating hamburgers in their parked car into driving him to a remote hillside location outside of town. There he shot them dead and finished their lunch before setting off again.

Thirty-nine-year-old Harris had suffered a troubled childhood with an alcoholic mother and an abusive father. He left home at the age of fourteen, lapsed into delinquency, attempted to commit suicide and was diagnosed as a schizophrenic. He became a drifter and when he killed the two youths in San Diego he had been out of prison just a few months following a conviction for manslaughter.

In many ways, he became a statistic in a country where 25,000 homicides were committed annually. The public wanted the violence curbed and some saw the restoration of the death sentence in states such as California as the answer. A poll recorded that seventy-five per cent of the population was in favour of imposing death penalties for premeditated murder.

Once on Death Row, Harris' lawyers fought numerous appeals and secured delays in execution. Days before the due date, the California media ran stories about the impending death sentence in lurid detail. Crowds gathered outside San Quentin Prison bearing grotesque slogans about death by gassing; "Plop, plop, fizz, fizz", referred to the method of dropping cyanide capsules into acid in the gas chamber.

Inside the prison, Robert Harris ate a last meal of Kentucky Fried Chicken and pizza washed down with a soft drink. He asked his jailers to give his fellow inmates ice cream as a treat. His troubled life thus came to an end and provided a spectacle for the pros and cons of capital punishment.

". . . Return To Mother Earth"

A man who was supposed to have died in a house fire as part of an elaborate insurance swindle was forced to play a charade whereby he moved from place-to-place and wore disguises to conceal his real identity. Winfield Scott Goss, aged thirty-seven, was an inventor who had rented a cottage near Baltimore, Maryland, in order to carry out secret experiments. On the evening of 2 February 1872, the cottage was destroyed by fire and the body in the ruins was believed to be that of Goss. Among those gathered to watch the blaze was William E. Udderzook, a toolmaker, who said to one of the onlookers, "I think he is still in the house". When asked who he was referring to, he replied, "Mr Goss".

Udderzook was Goss' brother-in-law. His behaviour at the time of the fire was thought to be odd and, equally strange, was the puzzle of why Goss, a fit and active man, had not escaped from the blazing cottage. Suspicion began to grow that the body was not that of Goss, who, it later transpired, had several life and accident insurance policies to his name.

The insurance companies refused to pay out and further examination of the human remains in the burnt out cottage proved by dental evidence that the fire victim was not Goss. Meanwhile, Udderzook had left the neighbourhood and was seen in the company of a man at Jenneville and other locations. When traces of blood were found in a carriage used by Udderzook and he no longer had a travelling companion, suspicion hardened further.

A week later, a farmer noticed buzzards circling a nearby field. He was intrigued by what had attracted the birds and investigated a wooded area where he found a shallow grave containing a man's body. The true fate of Winfield Goss was thus established over a year after he was supposed to have died in the fire. Udderzook was arrested on 25 July 1873 and taken to West Chester prison.

The full extent of Udderzook's scheming emerged after his arrest. Goss had taken out a large life insurance policy with the intention of faking his death so that he could share the proceeds with his brother-in-law. A cadaver was obtained to provide evidence of a life lost in the fire. Unfortunately, the corpse had a rotten set of teeth, whereas Goss had excellent dentition.

The fraudsters embarked on a charade, moving from place to place, while lawyers grappled with the insurance claim. To keep Goss' true identity hidden, Udderzook made him wear various disguises. When Goss rebelled, his brother-in-law killed him in expectation of eventually reaping all the insurance proceeds.

William Udderzook was tried for murder at West Chester in October and condemned to death. Before facing execution, he stated his wish that his body would be put in the same grave as that of Winfield Goss, "that our bodies may return to the mother earth . . .". Udderzook was executed on 12 November 1874.

Blistered Hands

Smutty Nose is one of a small group of islands called The Shoals lying out in the Atlantic about ten miles off the coast of New Hampshire, in the US. On the night of 5 March 1873, twenty-eight-year-old Louis Wagner, a German immigrant who earned a meagre existence as a fisherman, stole a boat in Portsmouth with the intention of rowing to Smutty Nose.

He was bent on robbing a Norwegian family who lived on the island. He knew them well because they had given him shelter when he was down on his luck. He also knew that on this particular night, the three women were alone because their menfolk were away fishing.

Wagner landed on the snow-covered rocks and headed straight for the Hontvets' home. Karen Christenson awoke when she heard a noise and thought her brother-in-law had returned. The intruder felled her with a heavy blow that aroused the other two women. Maren Hontvet grappled with the assailant and shouted to Anethe to fetch help. Paralysed with fear, all she could do was shout "Louis, Louis, Louis" as she immediately recognized the intruder.

Brandishing an axe, Wagner smashed Anethe's skull with several blows and then attacked Karen who was dazed by the initial assault. He struck her again and again breaking the handle of the axe in the process. Realizing there was nothing she could do except save herself, Maren fled from the house and spent the rest of the night sheltering among rocks. Meanwhile, Wagner went through the house searching for money and then calmly sat down in the kitchen to eat a meal with the corpses of the two women he had killed lying around him.

At daybreak, Maren raised the alarm and men arrived from a neighbouring island. She identified the murderous assailant as Louis Wagner and when her husband returned this news was quickly relayed by boat to the mainland. The murderer had returned to lodgings in Portsmouth and then boarded a train to Boston. Following news of his arrest, angry mobs awaited his return to Portsmouth and marines with fixed bayonets were needed to prevent a lynching.

In June 1873, Wagner was tried for murder and Maren Hontvet gave graphic testimony. Four men gave evidence that Wagner had said he needed money so badly he would murder for it. His bloodstained shirt was retrieved and his blistered hands provided ample evidence of his rowing feat.

He was found guilty of murder and sentenced to death but gained a reprieve pending a decision about the fate of another axe murderer, John True Gordon. It was decided that the two murderers would be hanged together on 25 June 1875. But fate intervened when Gordon stabbed himself, causing potentially fatal wounds. The decision was made to go ahead with the double execution and, while Wagner walked to the scaffold, Gordon was dragged semi-conscious to face the hangman. Thus two axe murderers who, between them, had killed five people, were sent to their doom.

Sudden Passion

Miriam and Isaac Angel lived in two rooms in Batty Street, Whitechapel, London. They attracted a certain degree of envy because, while their neighbours lived in only one room, the Angels had two. Miriam was pregnant and, on 28 June 1887, a friend called in to see how she was. Growing concerned when there was no response to her knock, the friend pushed the door open and entered the room.

Miriam Angel lay on the bed with yellow froth exuding from her mouth, which later proved to be nitric acid. The bedclothes were stained with acid and Miriam had a head injury. A doctor was called and could do little more than pronounce her dead. Noting the obvious signs of corrosive poisoning, he started to search the room for a container.

By this time, a crowd of fellow residents had gathered at the door and a police officer arrived at the scene. He joined the doctor in the search for the source of the poison and, in the process, moved the bed. They heard groaning noises at the disturbance and revealed a man lying beneath the bed. They dragged out twenty-two-year-old Israel Lipski who had marks of corrosive poisoning around his mouth.

Lipski was revived and sent to hospital where he made a full recovery. He explained that he lived in the attic in the same house as the Angels. He alleged that two men who also lodged in the house had murdered Miriam Angel and forced him to drink poison. They pushed him under the bed and, as they departed, one said to the other, "Lipski will soon be dead, too".

His story did not hold up, not least because the door of the murder room had been locked from the inside. Although the body had been covered with a blanket, there were suggestions of a sexual assault. It was proved that Lipski had bought nitric acid and an empty acid bottle was found in the room.

Lipski was charged with murder and sent for trial in July 1887 to appear before Mr Justice James Fitzjames Stephen. The judge's summing up was against Lipski. It was suggested that he had been overcome by a surge of "sudden passion" on seeing Miriam Angel lying in bed. To access his room in the attic, Lipski had to ascend a stairway and pass a window that gave a view into the Angels' room. The trial jury took ten minutes to bring in a guilty verdict.

After the verdict, public opinion swung heavily in Lipski's favour and W.T. Stead, editor of the *Pall Mall Gazette*, campaigned on his behalf. A reprieve was demanded and Mr Justice Fitzjames Stephens was said to be concerned about a possible miscarriage of justice. But Lipski made a full confession the day before he was hanged at Newgate Prison. He said that robbery rather than sexual assault was his motive which, perhaps, helped to ease the judge's conscience.

Meadow Massacre

On 11 September 1857, a large force led by John D. Lee, a Bishop of the Mormon Church, attacked a wagon train in Utah killing 120 men and women in America's greatest civil atrocity.

A party of Arkansas farming families, numbering 140, was headed west to California and had reached a place called Mountain Meadow in Utah. At the time, Utah Territory was in conflict with the United States and was being run as the personal fiefdom of Brigham Young and the Mormon Church. The Mormons were stockpiling weapons and disregarding federal laws.

When the wagon train reached Mountain Meadow, about 300 miles from Salt Lake City, it was surrounded by a band of white renegades masquerading as Indians. The pioneers held off their attackers for three days. Then Lee offered a truce, saying that if the pioneers gave up their gold and livestock they would be allowed to continue their journey westwards. Having secured the truce, the renegades systematically slaughtered 120 people, sparing only seventeen children. Corpses were stripped of clothes and jewellery and the attackers disappeared.

The Mormons were suspected of involvement and Brigham Young was thought to be implicated but there was no evidence to support such allegations. In 1858, Young denied any complicity and put the blame on the Indians. A five-year-old boy who survived the massacre was questioned two years after the event and he related how his father had been killed by Indians but when they washed their faces, they were white men.

In 1870, blame was shifted to Bishop John D. Lee who was excommunicated by Brigham Young. There was talk of a church-inspired cover-up and, in 1875, Lee was arrested. It had taken the federal authorities eighteen years to gather sufficient evidence to charge him. He was tried twice and at the second attempt found guilty. Lee was condemned to death and, on 23 March 1877, he was taken to the scene of the massacre at Mountain Meadow and executed by firing squad.

The massacre inspired a number of novelists intrigued by the drama of events steeped in treachery and atrocity. In 2002 the controversy erupted again with fresh accusations blaming Brigham Young. Two books claimed the case against the Mormon leader was undeniable. Arguing that nothing happened in Utah in the 1870s without his knowledge, the thesis is that he gave his authority for the attack on the pioneers and then perpetrated a cover up.

John Lee wrote about the events of 1857 while he was awaiting execution. He blamed the Indians for attacking the pioneers and claimed that the Mormons joined in reluctantly. Later commentators suggested variously that greed lay behind the massacre or that Brigham Young decided to stage a demonstration of his political power. Contemporary Mormon church historians repeat the official line which was that the massacre was a local incident carried out by renegades. Wherever the truth lies, it is certain that John D. Lee paid the ultimate price.

A Great Escape

When working in Oxford in the UK as a servant to a local dignitary, Anne Greene was seduced by her employer's grandson. Four months later, she delivered a dead child. Horror-struck, she hid the body but her attempt at concealment failed. When the dead infant was discovered, Greene was arrested and charged with murder. She was quickly tried, found guilty and sentenced to death by hanging.

On 14 December 1650, she was placed on the scaffold, declaring before the assembled crowd that she was an innocent victim of her employer's lewdness. That said, executioners pushed her off the ladder. She was a heavy woman and dropped to her intended death at the rope's end. She hung in the air while spectators pulled on her legs until she was senseless.

Greene's body was cut down, put into a coffin and delivered to the house of Dr William Petty, an Oxford surgeon, for autopsy. It was the custom for onlookers to attend such proceedings and a crowd watched when the coffin was opened. To the surprise of all present, the occupant "rattled her throat". A bystander, anxious to snuff out any last vestige of life, stamped on her body.

Dr Petty aided by Dr Thomas Willis, who became famous as a pioneering medical man, tried to revive the woman. They pulled her clenched teeth apart and tickled her throat with a feather, whereupon she coughed her way back to life. The doctors bled her and administered potions of ground-up mummies and rhubarb. The next morning, very much alive, she asked for beer and was soon eating chicken.

The justices wanted to hang Anne Greene a second time but the doctors pleaded for her life. They argued that her premature baby had been dead when born, thus absolving her of the charge of murder and that her revival was a sign of divine providence indicating her innocence.

News of Anne Greene's resurrection from the dead spread far and wide. People paid a fee to see her lying in the coffin in the doctor's chambers and, in due course, she went home taking her coffin with her as a symbol of her great escape. Pamphlets were published describing the miracle of her salvation, including poems written by, among others, Christopher Wren, the great architect to be.

". . . Fit As A Fiddle . . ."

Kenneth Neu's burning ambition was to be a nightclub entertainer but he reserved his best performances for the prison authorities.

On 2 September 1933, when walking in the vicinity of Times Square in New York, Kenneth Neu encountered Lawrence Shead, a theatre owner, who offered to help him. It turned out that Shead had his own agenda and having invited Neu back to his hotel room for drinks made sexual advances towards him.

Neu's response was to lash out and, in a violent encounter, he bludgeoned Shead to death. He then calmly took a shower and dressed himself in one of the dead man's suits and travelled to New Orleans. A few days later, short of money, Neu targeted an elderly man he saw in a hotel. The man, Sheffield Clark, took him up to his room where Neu's demand for money met with a blunt refusal. His response was to bludgeon Clark to death, steal his money and drive away in his car.

In an attempt to thwart efforts to trace the stolen car by means of its registration plate, Neu covered it with a rough, hand-made sign declaring that the car was in transit. It was not long before he was stopped and questioned by a police patrol. He failed to convince officers about his ownership of the car and questions turned to the recent murder of a businessman in New York. Neu's response was, ". . . I killed him. This is his suit I'm wearing now." He also readily admitted killing Sheffield Clark.

Neu's confession made his trial somewhat of a formality. The only issue was his sanity and after hearing defence arguments, the court decided he was fit to stand trial. He was duly convicted of murder, whereupon he offered the jury his best wishes and went into a song and dance number with a rendition of "Sweet Rosie O'Grady". Whether or not the jury joined in was not recorded.

While in prison, he apparently spent his time rehearsing song and dance routines, possibly for his last performance on the scaffold. On 1 February 1935, he entertained guards with his own composition of "I'm as fit as a fiddle and ready to hang". He met his end, if not laughing, at least crooning his way to oblivion.

CHAPTER 7

Out of this World

The association of witchcraft and the supernatural with crime has a long history. It is probably rooted in attempts to explain what on the surface appears to be mystifying, weird or bizarre. The concept of procuring a person's death by applying witchcraft goes back many centuries and is found in many cultures. In modern times, black magic practices have been offered as an explanation for violent crimes. A notable example is the murder of Charles Walton in 1945 in an English county renowned for observances of witchcraft.

Satanism has been adopted by many murderers as a conduit for hatred and violence. In the 1960s, Charles Manson showed that his followers, fuelled with drugs and satanic values, could be controlled and directed to kill. Devil worship has been embraced by some murderers as an expression of their rage against society. This seemed to motivate the Brazilian serial killer, Francisco de Brito, who confessed to killing in revenge for the abuse he received as a child. Over a period of fourteen years, over forty boys were killed and emasculated.

The idea of taking a life as a ritual sacrifice also has its roots in satanism. Ricky Kasso, inspired by a visit to Amityville and the house where Ronald De Feo killed his family in 1974, murdered a teenager as a sacrifice to Satan. An aspect of this mindset is the initiation ritual involving a killing to establish an individual's standing among his peers. Such was the motive behind the two murders committed by Lucifer's Outlaws, Michael Bardell and Stephen Parkinson, to impress their fellow Hell's Angels.

Fantasists of different kinds form a substantial group among convicted murderers. These are often individuals consumed with narcissism who can no longer distinguish between reality and fantasy. Their crimes frequently probe the frontiers of forensic psychiatry. One such was Jean-Claud Romand who led two separate lives maintained by lies and secrecy and ended up by killing his family.

Fantasists often work in pairs, like Marco Furlan and Wolfgang Abel, self-appointed angels of death, whose mission was to kill sinners. Or Jamie Petrolini and Richard Elsey who were obsessed with fantasy heroics and trained for pseudo military missions by using murder as an initiation test. A sense of mission also motivated Fred Klenner who equipped himself with enough weapons to start a private war. He was in a constant state of readiness for Armageddon with his family as the ultimate victims.

Those who fake their own deaths in order to cover up for crimes they have committed or to embark on a re-invented life are indulging in a kind of fantasy. Marie Hilley poisoned her husband and successfully feigned her own death to the extent of publishing an obituary. With echoes of a fictional Reggie Perrin, Robert Healey and John Allen staged their own suicides to escape from their crimes and re-establish themselves in another life.

Practitioners of otherworldly arts are often control freaks, like Arthur Covell, a bed-ridden invalid who directed his nephew to murder his mother. He commanded obedience to his will using a combination of astrology and hypnotism. Herman Billik was another self-appointed wizard who used his malign influence to prey on others and usurp their lives and possessions.

There are also well-documented examples of psychic detection and the part played by clairvoyants in solving crimes. Clarence van Buuren's victim was located by a psychic with uncanny accuracy. Equally astounding was the discovery of Ernest Dyer's victim as the result of a dream experienced by the dead man's mother.

When all other explanations fail, we are simply left with the weird, such as the unsolved Dali Murders. The victims were mutilated in ways which parodied the paintings of the female form by the surrealist artist, Salvador Dali.

Sickle And Fork

The gruesome murder of an elderly farm labourer on St Valentine's Day 1945 in Warwickshire in the UK led to stories of witchcraft. Seventy-four-year-old Charles Walton was a reclusive man who preferred wildlife to human beings. He lived at Lower Quinton with his niece and, despite his arthritis, did handy jobs for the local farmers. At around midday on 14 February he was seen trimming hedges. When he did not return home at nightfall, his niece reported him missing.

A search the next morning located Walton's body in a field close to where he had been seen working. His throat had been slashed with a sickle and a hayfork driven through his body with such force that it took two policemen to pull it free. A cross had also been crudely scratched on his chest.

Local police sought assistance from Scotland Yard and the famed detective, Robert Fabian, was assigned to the murder enquiry at Lower Quinton. Robbery, revenge and an argument seemed possible motives. The dead man was regarded as being eccentric and there were suggestions that he had money. Unusually, in that age and that community, Walton had a bank account.

Detectives questioned prisoners of war held at nearby Long Marston but promising enquiries came to nothing. Fabian's guile as a detective won him few friends in Lower Quinton where local residents remained tight-lipped and unhelpful. When he visited the local pub he recalled that, "silence fell like a blow" and that drinkers got up and left.

The detectives discovered that Warwickshire had a rich folklore and many tales of witchcraft. The nature of Walton's death led to much speculation along these lines. Local historians recorded that in 1875, John Haywood had stabbed an eighty-year-old woman declaring that she was a witch. His chosen murder weapon was a hayfork. Put on trial, Haywood explained that when cattle or farm animals died it was the result of the "Evil Eye" attributed to witches.

Fabian was to have his own encounter with these beliefs with the incident of the Black Dog. While out walking, searching the area around Lower Quinton, he saw a black dog. Next on the scene was a boy who ran off terrified when Fabian asked him if he was looking for the dog. Legend had it that seeing the Black Dog presaged a death.

Despite taking 4,000 statements and sending all manner of samples for forensic testing, Fabian and his team did not succeed in tracing Charles Walton's killer. "We had to leave it," wrote Fabian somewhat ruefully in his memoirs.

In 1987, in a book called *Perfect Murder*, Stephen Knight wrote that Fabian did know the identity of the murderer. Walton was killed by farmer Albert Potter who employed him as a casual labourer and from whom he borrowed money. When Walton pressed for repayment he was killed and the manner of his death disguised with occult symbolism.

Uneasy Verdict

When an elderly spinster was found dead at her home in Pluckley, Kent in the UK, in circumstances suggesting an element of ritual, there were faint echoes of a murder committed thirty-five years earlier.

Gwendoline Marshall's body was discovered in the garden shed at her home on 7 October 1980. She had been beaten, tied up and pinned to the ground with a hayfork. The use of this implement drew comparison with the unsolved murder of William Walton at Lower Quinton, Warwickshire, in 1945 (*see* above). Like her, he had been an elderly recluse and had been pinned down with a hayfork.

Miss Marshall lived alone with her dog in the house she owned with its six acres of ground. She rarely ventured out, grew her own fruit and vegetables and painted country scenes and still lifes. One of the few visitors to her home was Peter Luckhurst whom she called "Master Peter" and allowed to shoot rabbits on her land. In return, he chopped wood for her and picked apples.

Peter visited her around midday on 7 October, cycling from his home to pick some apples. He discussed with her the possibility of obtaining a shotgun licence. On the following day at about 3.00 p.m., a family called at the house to pick apples at Miss Marshall's invitation. They knocked on the door but could not raise her, the house was open and the dog was hiding in the garage.

Venturing into the kitchen, the visitors discovered blood on the floor and then the lounge. There was a trail of blood leading upstairs. The police were called and searches made. There was blood everywhere, including each of the bedrooms. When officers reached the garden shed, they found it padlocked. Inside, they found Miss Marshall, hands tied behind her back, brutally beaten and pinned down with a hayfork. The doctor thought she had died within the last few hours.

Detectives made house-to-house enquiries in Pluckley. They spoke to a local youth who suggested they should talk to Peter Luckhurst because he had found the old lady's dog running loose and took it back to the house. Seventeen-year-old "Master Peter" admitted going to the house and immediately confessed to hitting the old lady with a piece of wood. He later wrote out a statement in which he described hitting her, looking for money, tying her up and putting her in the shed before going home on his bike for tea.

Within twenty-four hours of discovering the murder, police had a suspect, concluding, "Peter did it and he did it on his own". Villagers were shocked as much by the murder itself as by their disbelief that Luckhurst was the culprit. A key question was how the youngster could have carried out a bloody murderous act and yet have so little blood on his clothes.

Villagers united behind him and Luckhurst stood trial at Maidstone in June 1981. He retracted his confession saying that he had innocently stumbled on a murder scene. The jury did not believe him and found him guilty. He was sentenced to be detained at Her Majesty's pleasure. No fingerprints were found at the crime scene and many believed Luckhurst was innocent and possibly covering up for someone who was still at large. The ritual killing angle troubled a number of people who eased their concerns by moving away from Pluckley.

Mutilator

Forty-one-year-old Francisco das Chagas Rodrigues de Brito, a bicycle mechanic, lived in an earth-floored shack in San José de Ribamar in Maranhão, Brazil. Police were called after neighbours complained of the dreadful smell. A search revealed the buried remains of two boys. He readily confessed to killing the two boys and admitted responsibility for eighteen other murders.

Investigators made connections between the discovery of human remains at Brito's house and a series of murders of boys in the states of Para and Maranh o between 1989 and 2003. The killings caused public outrage because the victims were sexually abused and there were reports that some had been decapitated and had their genitals cut off. There were rumours that the emasculated boys had featured in satanic rituals.

Brito was suspected of killing forty-two boys and, following his arrest in April 2004, he was charged with one killing, that of fifteen-year-old Jonathan Silva Vieira, who went missing in 2003. In October 2006 Brito went on trial in Maranh o for the murder of Vieira. This case was chosen because it was one in which the police had the most compelling evidence. In the event, Brito confessed to the murder on the first day of his trial.

When questioned by the police Brito had said he did not remember mutilating his victims because his mind had blanked out at the moment of killing. But in his defence in court, he told the jury that he had been sexually abused as a child by a man called Carlito. He explained that when he killed he did not see a boy before him but Carlito and gave vent to his anger. He said he could not remember how he had killed the boys but blamed their deaths on his reaction to his own ill-treatment. Of his home life he said, "I never knew what love was."

On 26 October 2006, the jury found Brito guilty of murder and he was sentenced to twenty years' imprisonment. With accusations of murdering dozens of other boys, further trials hang over him. This would make him Brazil's worst serial killer.

The nature of the serial killings, particularly with their overtones of sexual abuse and black magic, provoked Brazilian public opinion and there was criticism about the lack of action from the authorities. At least Brito's conviction, sixteen years after the first murder, was a positive step in resolving Brazil's series of satanic murders.

"I Love Satan"

A group of youths gathered at their favourite meeting place on 16 June 1984. They lounged around a gazebo in Aztakea Woods in Northport, New York State, playing heavy metal music. They were high on mescaline and arguing. Local residents complained about the noise to the police but there was no follow-up.

The first indication that something was amiss was when Gary Lauwers did not return home. On the teenage grapevine, there was talk about a murder having been committed. Little by little, worrying news came that the group ring-leader, Ricky Kasso, had taken friends to see a body. The police received an anonymous tip-off and, several days after the rowdy party in the woods, Gary Lauwers was found.

The teenager's body was discovered in a shallow trench. It was a gruesome sight, partly consumed by decomposition. It was later established that he had been stabbed many times, including his face, and that his eyeballs had been gouged out. Written on the nearby gazebo, at the teenagers' regular meeting place, were the prophetic words, "I love Satan".

This legend had been inscribed by Ricky Kasso who, together with his friends, was now urgently sought by the police. He and Jimmy Troiano were found sleeping in their car near the Northport Yacht Club on 4 July. Kasso pulled a knife when questioned by police. He was quickly overpowered and taken into custody, along with Troiano. The story that came out was that Kasso and Gary Lauwers were involved in a long-running feud over the alleged theft of some "angel dust". In a statement, Kasso admitted killing Lauwers while Troiano held him down. After signing the statement, he endorsed it with the words, "Gary Lauwers deserved everything I gave him".

Ricky Kasso invited trouble. At school, he was known as the "Acid King". He regularly took drugs and dealt in them. His first encounter with the law was in 1980 over stolen property and his drug-taking came to the attention of his parents. He befriended Jimmy Troiano who also used drugs and got into trouble over housebreaking offences.

Kasso's spare time was taken up with drug-enhanced reading of books on satanism in the quiet surroundings of Aztakea Woods. Both Kasso and Troiano got into trouble with the school authorities and, at different times, ended up in care for detoxification. They met with their friends at the gazebo in the woods and discussed the alleged theft of "Angel Dust". "Nobody steals from the Acid King," said Kasso, and a plot was hatched to make Lauwers pay. In April 1984, five members of the group drove to Amityville to see the house made famous by Ronald De Feo when he killed his family there. In a satanic ritual, they resolved that Lauwers should be killed.

Kasso had said that he would take his own life rather than go to prison. The seventeen-year-old satanist was as good as his word. Late on the day that he was arrested, he hanged himself in his police cell.

Lap-Dog Killer

Charles Riley lived in Terra Linda, near San Francisco, and attended high school there. He was an overweight teenager frequently mocked by his fellow students because of his size, lack of confidence and inability to acquire a girlfriend. The nineteen-year-old found compensation in collecting guns and he became a competent marksman. He also dealt in drugs, which earned him status.

Riley thought his luck had changed when he met Marlene Olive in 1974. She was aged fifteen at the time, precocious, a drug-user and interested in the occult. Riley fell for her in a big way and, to his pleasure and surprise, she agreed to date him. What ensued was no ordinary relationship between two young people but one in which Riley became her lapdog who was eager to do her bidding.

Marlene persuaded Riley to diet and reduce his weight and introduced him to her brand of mystic beliefs. An adopted child who had recently moved to California with her parents, she liked consorting with wayward boys and took drugs. She gave her parents a hard time and there was a bust-up when she stole her mother's credit card. Things went from bad to worse and she talked openly about the hatred she felt for her mother.

By this time, Riley was completely under Marlene's influence; she controlled him emotionally and sexually. For his part, he was pleased to have a girlfriend even though she subjected him to group sex and other erotic fantasies.

Riley thought Marlene was bluffing when she talked about killing her parents but she was making plans. The crisis point came after the unhappy pair were arrested for shoplifting and faced juvenile court. Marlene's parents tried to control her behaviour with sanctions and opposed the idea of her marrying Riley. Thwarted at every turn, Marlene asked Riley to kill her mother. On 21 June she said to him, "Get your gun. We've got to kill the bitch today."

Fuelled with drugs, Riley appeared at Marlene's house. She told him that she was going out with her father and while they were away, he was to kill her mother. Armed with a claw hammer, he approached Naomi Olive while she was sleeping and smashed her head in. For good measure, he also stabbed her. Jim Olive returned with his daughter who held back while Riley produced a pistol and emptied it into her father's body.

Riley and Marlene moved the bodies to a public barbecue area where they burned them. Having cleaned up the house, Marlene hit the shopping malls with her mother's credit card. After a week the police were informed that Naomi and Jim Olive appeared to be missing. Enquiries soon focussed on Marlene and Riley. He was very forthcoming, admitting he killed the couple because Marlene told him to. Marlene deserted Riley in his hour of need by shifting all blame on to him. As a juvenile, she was sent to a youth authority home, while Riley, now aged twenty-one, was put on trial. He was convicted on two counts of first-degree murder and sentenced to death. The sentence was later reduced to life imprisonment.

Initiation Rite

Two men walking in Salcey Forest, Northamptonshire, in the UK at Easter 1983 discovered two bodies lying in a shallow grave covered with leaves. The remains had been reduced to skeletons and had clearly been there some time. Dental records established their identities as Deborah Fallon and her fiancé, David Cox. Pathologists thought the deaths had occurred about a year previously.

Enquiries led to the Hell's Angels and to Michael Bardell, self-styled president of Lucifer's Outlaws, and Stephen Parkinson, described as his sergeant-at-arms. Fallon and Cox attended a meeting of the group in Northampton where Bardell said that, in order to impress the higher echelons of the movement, "... the chapter would have to prove themselves".

The young couple were earmarked for sacrifice and they were lured into the woods. Nineteen-year-old Fallon was handcuffed to a tree and strangled and Cox was subjected to a frenzied knife attack. Attempts to bury the bodies failed because the killers' spade broke. Bardell took colour photographs at the murder scene as proof of their actions.

Bardell and Parkinson were tried for murder at Northampton Crown Court in March 1984. The prosecution presented what was described as a terrifying and bizarre case. It hinged on the desire of the newly-formed Hell's Angels chapter called Lucifer's Outlaws to prove itself. The members began to build up an armoury of weapons and organized initiation ceremonies.

A witness said Bardell mentioned that one of the members had talked about where the armoury was stored. Shortly afterwards, he reported that Deborah Fallon and David Cox had been killed. In court, Bardell and Parkinson denied the killings. Bardell offered an alibi while Parkinson did not give evidence.

Questioned by the police, Parkinson admitted that they were both involved with the killing. He claimed that he was acting under duress and feared for his safety. In his summing-up Mr Justice Jupp said he was satisfied that Parkinson was under the influence of Bardell, although that did not excuse him.

The judge told the defendants, "You have been found guilty of two murders which were quite appalling. They were done entirely in cold blood ... were planned and ... carried out with appalling determination." He also believed an element of torture was involved in the way David Cox was murdered. The jury sentenced each man to life imprisonment with concurrent jail terms for conspiracy to murder.

God And The Devil

A shoe repairer by trade, Joseph Kallinger believed he could correct his obsessive urges by fitting wedges inside his footwear. By this means, he hoped to adjust the angle of his feet to harmonize with his brain.

Kallinger was a man with strange behaviour patterns. Initially, he was simply eccentric, filling his house in Philadelphia with all manner of junk which he thought would come in useful. In 1967, he moved to another house when his shoe-repairing business prospered and, at this time, he began to hallucinate, believing he received commands both from God and the Devil.

Fearing that he might be spied on, Kallinger started turning his home into a fortress. He put bars over the windows and kept vigil at night to fend off any intruders. In 1969, he moved to another house which he converted into a secret refuge. With the help of his family, he dug a twenty-foot hole in the basement. It was in this cellar that he began torturing his children by inflicting burns on them. In 1972, he received psychiatric counselling and returned to his family.

Throughout the 1970s, Kallinger hallucinated regularly. He believed God wanted him "to kill with a butcher's knife every man, woman and child and infant on the face of the earth". He began by enlisting the help of his twelve-year-old son to carry out robberies and theft but his urges soon gave way to murder.

On 7 July 1974, father and son abducted a boy from a recreation centre in Philadelphia, taking him to a disused factory where he was sexually mutilated and murdered. On 28 July, Kallinger took his fourteen-year-old son to the flooded basement of a derelict building. With his other son in attendance, he drowned Joey and reported him missing. Police suspicions hardened as soon as they heard that Kallinger had taken out $69,000 life insurance on the dead boy.

Charges were not proved and father and son continued to commit a series of break-ins, terrorizing house owners but not harming them. This changed on 8 January 1975 when the pair entered a house in Leonia, New Jersey, and tied up the occupants. Unsure what to do, they took a twenty-year-old woman and directed her to mutilate one of the male captives. When she refused, they killed her in a frenzy of stabbing.

The Kallingers were arrested nine days later and charged with kidnapping, robbery and assault. Joe was also charged with murder, while his son was sent for rehabilitation as a delinquent. Kallinger senior was tried for the lesser offences in September 1975 and despite claims that he was mentally incompetent, was convicted and sentenced to thirty years.

He was tried for murder in 1976, by which time his mind had descended into satanic fantasies. In court, he foamed at the mouth and chanted in an incomprehensible language. Defence experts said he was "totally crazy and psychotic". The jury inclined to the prosecution's view that he was an anti-social personality but not insane. He was found guilty and sentenced to forty-two years' imprisonment.

Flora Rheta Schreiber, a professor of criminal justice wrote a book about Kallinger, called *The Shoemaker*. She explored his early behaviour, his history of being abused and descent into sadism and murder.

Seeking Forgiveness

Jean-Claude Romand was a fantasist who pretended to be a busy doctor, attending meetings and medical conferences while in reality, he killed time sitting in cafés and hotel rooms. Rather than admit his secret life, he turned to murder.

A fire at the home of the Romand family in the French village of Prèvissin, near the Swiss border, on 11 January 1993 claimed three lives. Florence Romand and her two children died in the blaze and the only survivor was her husband, Jean-Claude.

Investigators discovered that the victims had not died in the fire; Mme Romand had been bludgeoned and her two children shot. Further drama ensued when a relative set out to inform Romand's parents of the tragedy, only to find the elderly couple dead in their house. They had been shot.

Suspicion focussed on "Dr" Jean-Claude Romand who was recovering from a coma after swallowing twenty Nembutal capsules. Although everyone thought he was a doctor working for the World Health Organization (WHO) in Geneva, he was a professional sham leading a double life. There was no Dr Romand listed in the medical directories and enquiries showed that while he had studied medicine at Lyon, he did not qualify.

Romand's story was that an intruder had killed his family and set fire to the house. During examination by psychiatrists, more details emerged of his incredible secret life. He made a practice of embezzling money from his friends and family to provide him with an income. He kept up a daily charade of taking his children to school before, supposedly, driving to his office at WHO headquarters, and returning home in the evening. He filled his days by hanging around in cafés and at filling stations. His more refined pretences involved attendance at medical conferences in other countries while he spent his time watching television in hotel rooms. On his return, he provided detailed accounts of his professional activities and even contrived to feign tiredness and jet lag.

"Dr" Romand's secret life started to unravel in 1992. A woman friend who had allowed him to invest some of her money asked to have it returned. He was already in difficult straits financially and his solution involved buying a silencer for the rifle he had borrowed from his father. He used this weapon to kill his wife and children and then his parents.

Around New Year 1993, he arranged to meet the woman to whom he owed money and attacked her with tear gas and a stun gun. She survived the assault, which he tried to explain away as the result of an alleged terminal illness. He walked away from this encounter, returned to his home, where his family lay dead, and set it on fire.

Romand denied the crimes at first but then made a confession. He was thought to have a narcissistic personality that prevented him distinguishing fantasy from reality. Rather than own up to all his pretences, he chose to kill his family. At his trial for murder he asked his dead family to forgive him. "I ask your forgiveness," he said, "Forgiveness for having destroyed your lives, forgiveness of having never told the truth." The bogus doctor was found guilty and sentenced to life imprisonment.

Angels Of Death

The Italian city of Verona acquired a reputation in the 1970s as the country's drug capital and a centre of right-wing extremism. Between 1977 and 1984, a string of grisly murders made the headlines.

A gypsy was burned to death in his caravan, followed by the murders of a homosexual, a prostitute, a hitchhiker and a priest. The victims were variously clubbed with a hammer, attacked with an axe or stabbed. The killing of a priest at Trento was particularly gruesome; a nail had been driven through his head and fixed to it was a wooden crucifix. There were also murders in public places, including the burning down of a pornographic cinema resulting in five deaths and a fire at a disco in which one person died and forty were injured.

After each incident those responsible circulated a leaflet, with the heading, "Ludwig", featured above Nazi insignia. The leaflets explained the reason for the latest murder and declared "We are the last of the Nazis ... Death will come to those who betray the true god" and finished with the words, "Gott mit uns" – God is with us.

Various explanations of the reference to Ludwig were offered and the most likely was a nineteenth-century writer,

Otto Ludwig, who preached that sinners should be clubbed to death.

The perpetrators of these outrages were caught red-handed in January 1984. Two men dressed in Pierrot costumes turned up at a disco in Mantua where 400 people were dancing and began pouring petrol on to the floor. Marco Furlan, aged twenty-five, and fellow student, Wolfgang Abel, aged twenty-six, were arrested. They said their stunt at the disco was a carnival joke.

Furlan and Abel were murderers and the authors of the "Ludwig" leaflets. The two men were students at Verona University and came from professional, middle-class backgrounds. They studied during the week and spent Saturday night killing people to break up the monotony of the weekend. One of their trademarks was to leave objects at each crime that were identified in their "Ludwig" leaflets, thereby authenticating their crimes.

The two young men, described by contemporaries as highly intelligent but strange, were put on trial in Verona to face charges of killing fifteen people. In keeping with "Ludwig's" philosophy, they targeted people who they chose to call sinners and who deserved to be eliminated. In practice, this meant some of the least advantaged members of society, like their first victim, a gypsy living in a caravan.

They were accused of acting as self-appointed "angels of death" in committing ritual murder. Furlan and Abel denied being "Ludwig" and both were judged to be "partially infirm of mind". They were convicted of killing nine people and were sentenced to thirty years' imprisonment.

Natural Born Killers

"Cut off from reality", "individual anarchism" and "passing ritualism", were some of the labels offered to describe the actions of two young people which resulted in six deaths on the streets of Paris in 1994. "Natural-born killers" was another epithet directed at twenty-two-year-old Audry Maupin and Florence Rey, his nineteen-year-old girlfriend. On 4 October

1994, armed with pump-action shotguns, the couple appeared at a police compound in Porte de Pantin in Paris. They held up two gendarmes and took their side arms before climbing into a taxi and directing the driver at gunpoint to take them to Place de la Nation.

What followed were moments of deadly drama. When they reached the Cours de Vincennes, the taxi driver drove his vehicle into a police car. He ran from his cab shouting to the two officers as he went. At this point Maupin opened fire, killing both officers and the taxi driver. The couple then hijacked a Renault 5 car and made off again, pursued by a police motorcyclist. They were blockaded in the Bois de Vincennes by police cars and began a second shoot out in which a police officer was killed. When the police returned the fire, Maupin was fatally wounded. Rey comforted him before surrendering. In the course of half an hour's violent mayhem, three police officers were killed, two taxi drivers were shot dead and Maupin also lost his life.

Maupin was a psychology student who held anarchistic and revolutionary views and Florence Rey was a first-year medical student who seemed to be in thrall to him. She told psychiatrists that she wanted to live up to Audry and impress him. They forsook their university work, acquired weapons and embarked on their own kind of revolution.

Rey was put on trial in September 1998. There was great public interest in this young woman and a desire to know what motivated her. The prosecutor said she had committed crimes that were described as gratuitous, absurd and irrational. Even though she had not fired any of the shots that killed five people, she was guilty with no extenuating circumstances.

Defence lawyers argued that Rey should not be made to pay for crimes committed by Maupin. Against this was the case made by lawyers representing the families of the three dead policemen who stressed that Rey did nothing to stop Maupin. She took an active part in the shooting and, "if she missed, it was because she was a bad shot". The passenger in the taxi commandeered by Maupin and Rey told the court that it was the girl who threatened to kill the driver and he described how she calmly knelt down to reload the shotgun.

Rey was found guilty of armed robbery, multiple murder, manslaughter, six attempted murders, theft of police weapons, abduction and criminal conspiracy. She was sentenced to twenty years in prison, less than the term demanded by prosecutors. Inevitably, perhaps, there were references in the popular press to "Bonnie and Clyde". The media interest in the trial had been intense but observers found it difficult to reconcile the image of the slim pale-faced girl in the dock with the uncompromisingly violent part she played in events that had claimed six lives.

A Malign Friendship

While driving home on the evening of 14 January 1994, Mohamed El-Sayed stopped his car at a "give way" sign in Bayswater, West London. A young man entered the car and threatened El-Sayed with a knife. He told him to drive on a short distance and stop. The youth then stabbed the driver in the throat and inflicted other wounds, leaving him dying behind the wheel.

Police enquiries made little headway until they received information that a student at Modes Study Centre in Oxford had confessed to murder. Nineteen-year-old Jamie Petrolini was taken to Paddington Green police station where he made a full confession, implicating his friend, Richard Elsey, and unveiling a world of fantasy heroics.

The two youths came from successful family backgrounds and they had received public school education. They met at Modes Study Centre where they formed what would later be called a "malign friendship". Their teachers regarded the pair as immature and Petrolini, in particular, was impressionable with an ambition to prove himself.

Elsey played the role of ringmaster, telling his new friend that he was an officer in the Parachute Regiment and spinning tales about his time in the SAS. He liked to talk about "slotting", denoting throat-cutting, a word he had picked up from reading books about SAS exploits in Iraq. One night in an Oxford pub, they became blood brothers, cutting their hands and allowing the blood to mix.

The scene was now set for Elsey to train for a mission. They gave each other fake names and officer status and tested their skills and nerve by climbing up to the jib of a tower building crane. The real test came within weeks of meeting each other when they decided to find a drug-dealer or pimp on the streets of London and kill him. This was to be Elsey's initiation into the SAS and forty-five-year-old Mohamed El-Sayed was their random victim.

Petrolini and Elsey were tried for murder at the Old Bailey in October 1994. They opted for what is called the "cut throat" defence, each blaming the other for what had happened. Petrolini drew a picture of his friend as a manipulator who had urged him to take a man's life. He pleaded manslaughter and diminished responsibility. Elsey said in court that he was shocked when Petrolini stabbed the car driver. He put the full blame for the killing on his friend's shoulders, claiming he was not even in the car at the time.

Ample evidence of their weird behaviour came out in court. Petrolini, who was nineteen on the day of the murder, described opening his birthday cards on the bus as they journeyed back to Oxford. The principal of Modes Study Centre said he feared the two students were "up to no good". Petrolini had taken to blacking his face with commando camouflage and running around Oxford at night. Elsey cut his hair short and told his friends he was going on special missions with the Paras.

At the end of the seventeen-day trial, the jury was out for five hours and returned guilty verdicts on both accused. Sentencing them to life imprisonment, Mr Justice Denison told them, "You created a world in which you both played out your fantasies. That obsession led to the brutal murder of a complete stranger . . ."

There were eerie parallels in this case with that of Nathan Leopold and Richard Loeb in Chicago in 1924. They killed a fourteen-year-old boy to find out what it was like to be a murderer. While Petrolini and Elsey drew their fantasies from military heroics, Leopold and Loeb were obsessed with the Nietzschean philosophy of superman.

Mission Ready

"Dr Crazy", as he was known by those who sold him weapons, lived in a fantasy world in which he was always armed and ready to go on a mission. He was obsessed with guns, kept survival gear in his vehicle and had a bomb wired up to the passenger seat. Fred Klenner, also known as Fritz, was in every sense armed and dangerous.

Fritz was the son of Dr Fred Klenner, an expert in vitamin therapy with a practice in Reidsville, North Carolina. It was the family's expectation that Fritz would become a doctor but when he failed to qualify, he told his father that he had passed the examinations and, henceforth, was referred to as "Young Dr Klenner".

He helped his father at his clinic at the weekends and in the early 1980s met Susie Newson Lynch. She was separated from her husband and, although she had custody of the children, there were legal problems about rights of access and growing bitterness between both sets of parents.

Old Dr Klenner died in 1984 and his clinic was closed down. Fritz spent his inheritance stocking up on guns and fitting out his Blazer station wagon with survival equipment and an explosive device. He was close to Susie and sympathized with her over the problems she was experiencing. Her parents were not keen about her association with Fritz whom they regarded as unbalanced. For his part, Fritz fuelled the flames of discontent by telling Susie her husband was involved in illegal activities.

Tragedy struck in July 1984 when Susie's mother-in-law and daughter were found shot dead at their home in Prospect, Kentucky. The talk was of a gangland killing but the police investigation made little headway. In the following March, Fritz and Susie moved in together and worked on each other's neuroses. He referred to her as his wife and, as a result, she became estranged from her family. Meanwhile, Fritz stocked up on military hardware and insisted that Susie's two boys wore combat uniforms.

Tragedy struck again in May 1985 with a triple murder in North Carolina at the home of Susie's grandmother. Her father, mother and grandmother were all killed in another mysterious shooting. Susie and Fritz were both questioned by the police and suspicion began to focus on Fritz when it was established he had been seen near the scene of the killings and that he was armed. Added to this was information he had imparted to a friend to the effect that he was involved in a CIA mission.

With many unanswered questions swirling around and a great deal of suspicion about his actions, Fritz and Susie, together with the two boys, took off in the Blazer heading for Greenboro. A police pursuit developed with Fritz firing at patrol cars with an Uzi machine gun. Three officers were wounded in the shoot-out before the Blazer came to a halt. Suddenly, there was a loud explosion and the vehicle disintegrated killing everyone in it.

That Fritz was preparing for war was borne out by the discoveries made at his home and the Klenner properties. Apart from 8,000 rounds of ammunition, investigators found numerous handguns, eight shotguns, two machine guns, two assault rifles and five semi-automatic rifles. In the course of his private campaign it looked as if "Dr Crazy" had taken the lives of nine people, including his own.

The Black Widow

Marie Audrey Hilley came from a family of textile workers in Alabama, USA. She married Frank Hilley in 1950 and worked as a secretary at a foundry in Anniston. Her husband died, aged forty-five, apparently of hepatitis, in 1975. His widow claimed $31,140 on his insurance and continued life as before.

When she started to spend rather ostentatiously, those who knew her circumstances thought perhaps she was spending beyond her means. At the same time changes in her personality were noticed; she developed a persecution complex, complaining about telephone harassment and reporting burglaries.

In 1979, Hilley's eighteen-year-old daughter, Carol, became ill, losing weight for no apparent reason. She underwent various medical tests but the cause of her wasting illness remained a mystery. It was only when Carol mentioned that her mother had been giving her injections that alarm bells began to sound. Analysis of a urine sample showed the presence of arsenic in the teenager's body and the source of her illness became evident.

The bodies of Frank Hilley and Marie's mother were exhumed and both found to contain arsenic. Marie was arrested and charged with the attempted murder of her daughter. But before proceedings could be started, she jumped bail and promptly disappeared.

At this point, she pulled off a remarkable deception that she perpetuated for four years. She went to New Hampshire where she re-married. With police searches for the bail jumper at their most intensive, she told her new husband that she needed to visit Houston in connection with the death of a relative. There she feigned her own death even to the extent of publishing an obituary. She then returned to New Hampshire in the guise of her twin sister, Teri Martin. But slowly, doubts began to creep into the minds of those she was trying to deceive and her stratagem unravelled. She was arrested in 1983.

Marie Hilley stood trial for murder at Calhoun County Circuit Court in May 1983. The prosecutor told the jury, "You're going to be looking at a cold, calculating and diabolical killer." Hilley denied injecting her daughter with poison but a fellow inmate told the court she had admitted to her that she poisoned both her husband and daughter. It was shown that Hilley had taken out life insurance on Carol a few months before she became sick.

Hilley amused herself while sitting in the dock by sketching the trial judge whom she portrayed as a monkey. The prosecutor said, "They tell me that the black widow spider mates and then kills its mate . . . That's what she reminds me of." Hilley was convicted of the first-degree murder of her husband and of the attempted murder of her daughter. She was sentenced to life imprisonment.

In June 1983, Marie Hilley entered the State Women's Prison in Alabama. Her appeal against conviction failed in 1985. She worked hard to secure lenient terms for herself, including day release from prison. On 19 February 1987 she walked out of the prison on a three-day pass. She did not return. She was found dead from hypothermia a week later. She was fifty-four years old.

As If In A Dream

On 29 July 1986, Robert Healey left a suicide note at his home in Stockport, Cheshire in the UK. It was addressed to his wife Greeba and read, "I cannot cope anymore." References were made to his inability to perform lovemaking adequately. After cancelling milk and newspaper deliveries and taking a pupil for a driving lesson, with echoes of a famous television programme, he faked his death by leaving his clothes on a beach at Prestatyn in North Wales. Ostensibly, he had walked into the sea and drowned. A note left for his mother said, "I might as well die now."

Fifteen days later the bodies of Healey's wife and stepdaughter were found in a shallow grave on farmland at Holywell in North Wales. Greeba had been bludgeoned to death and fifteen-year-old Maria asphyxiated. Two weeks after this grim discovery, Healey, who had been living in London under an assumed name, gave himself up to the police. There had been massive coverage of the deaths and the media played an important role in exposing the deception.

Healey admitted the killings but denied they had been premeditated. He said they occurred during a struggle. He produced a notebook in which he made various admissions, one of which was that Greeba, his second wife, had taunted him about his inadequate sexual performance. He went into the kitchen "as if in a dream" took up a rolling pin and battered her to death while she lay in bed. He said that when Maria ran into the room, he caught her by the throat to stop her struggling.

In fact, he had crushed the life out of her by putting pressure on her chest and throat. After the killing, he washed the rolling pin and restored it to its usual place in the kitchen. Then, he changed the bloodstained bed sheets and tidied up the house. He put the two bodies in his wife's car and drove to North Wales where he buried them in woodland.

Unknown to his second wife, Healey, who was a former petty-officer in the Royal Navy, had a conviction for child molestation. Greeba had answered a "lonely hearts" advertisement and made contact with him. Her friends advised her not to continue the liaison.

He was tried for murder at Liverpool Crown Court in March 1987. The scale of his charade was fully exposed as was the fact that before committing murder he had sexual intercourse with both his wife and their fifteen-year-old stepdaughter. He said when he killed them it was "like watching someone on TV".

It was given in evidence that a psychiatric assessment made when he was convicted of indecent exposure in 1982 suggested that he was getting back at women because his wife had left him for a second time.

Healey wept in court as the injuries sustained by his wife were described by counsel. Mr Justice McNeil commended the part played by the media in conjunction with the public and police in bringing him to justice. The jury returned a unanimous verdict of guilty. Healey was sentenced to life imprisonment and escorted, weeping, to the custody cells.

No Angel

When Patricia Allen and her two children, aged five and seven, disappeared from their home at Salcombe, Devon in the UK, late in May 1975, her husband John did not report them missing. He answered enquiries by saying that his wife had gone to live in America with another man after they had argued.

Devon and Cornwall police had their suspicions about Allen, one of whose forenames was "Angel", and from witnesses' statements a picture of marital discontent emerged. It was also significant that his wife had left her passport behind. Enquiries in the US about her supposed entry into the country produced negative responses. The police mounted a huge search operation in their efforts to find the missing trio, but to no avail.

Within two months of his wife's disappearance, Allen moved in with his lover, Eunice Yabsley, who had recently been widowed.

Despite his name, Allen had a far from angelic background. He was already married with two children when he wedded Patricia. He had lived with his first family in Surrey when he was found to be defrauding the company he worked for. His answer to this was to stage a fake suicide at Beachy Head. Later he reappeared and bigamously married Patricia. When his deception was discovered, he was given a suspended sentence for bigamy, theft and false pretences. Between 1974 and 1990 he served various terms in prison for fraud and deception.

In 1992, Eunice Yabsley published a book entitled, *Presumed Dead*, in which she recounted some of the background of her relationship with Allen. Her revelations proved pivotal in bringing him to justice. She recollected that he told her of his break-up with his wife and that she had left him. During their conversation, she noticed he had scratches on his arm extending from elbow to wrist.

Allen had been arrested in 1977 but the Director of Public Prosecutions ruled there were insufficient grounds to bring proceedings against him. But in the light of the new evidence and twenty-seven years after his family disappeared, Allen, aged sixty-eight, was charged with murder and sent for trial at Plymouth Crown Court.

He denied the charges and persisted with his story that his wife and children had gone to live in the US. The prosecution made out the case that Allen had eliminated his family in order to be free to join his lover. His wife disappeared first and he made attempts to get friends and relatives to look after his children. When these efforts failed, they too disappeared. The prosecutor said that nothing had been seen or heard of Allen's family – it was as if they had "disappeared off the face of the earth".

Allen was found guilty and sentenced to life imprisonment. Mr Justice Steele told him there was no possible explanation for the disappearance of his wife and children "other than you murdered them". Anthony John Angel Allen took his secrets with him to his prison cell while his wife's family expressed the hope that one day he would reveal what he had done with his victims' bodies.

"My Will Was Their Will"

Dr Fred Covell was a chiropractor in Brandon, Oregon, USA. He was married to Ebba and he had four children from a previous marriage. They lived in a spacious house that also accommodated Covell's invalid brother, Arthur, on the top floor. He had been confined to his bed since an accident had paralysed him.

On 3 September 1923, Dr Covell took a telephone call at his office from Arthur, urging him to return home quickly as "something terrible has happened to Ebba". Fred rushed home to find his wife dead. There were no obvious injuries but a post-mortem determined that her neck was broken.

Detectives thought she might have committed suicide as she was known to be depressed at times. The alternatives were accident or murder. They opted for murder and directed suspicion at Dr Covell for no better reason than his job called for a strong pair of hands. In a fast-moving scenario, Dr Covell, who strongly protested his innocence, was arrested and Ebba was duly buried.

The mystery of Ebba Covell's death was a big story locally and the gossips were soon at work. Suspicion strengthened around her husband and an independent criminologist, Luke S. May, was called in to assist with the investigation. Regarded by some as a veritable Sherlock Holmes, May enjoyed a reputation as a crime solver. He asked for Ebba's body to be exhumed and the first thing that was ascertained was that she had not died of a broken neck. That was a mistaken diagnosis. It was also noted that there were curious red blotches around her mouth.

Meanwhile, scrutiny of the arrangements in the Covell household revealed the extraordinary influence exerted by "Uncle Artie" from his upstairs room where he was confined to bed. He studied astrology and hypnotism and exerted a strong hold on those around him, particularly his nephew, sixteen-year-old Alton. Among his papers were coded instructions relating to twenty-nine potential murder victims. One of these was Ebba, earmarked in his diary to be eliminated on 3 September.

When he was questioned, Arthur Covell simply asked why he would want to kill anyone. He said that his coded plans were fictitious and helped him to escape from the boredom of being a cripple. The next person to be questioned was young Alton who was clearly under the influence of "Uncle Artie". He made a confession saying that, following his uncle's instructions, he had clamped an ammonia-soaked cloth over his stepmother's nose and mouth, thereby asphyxiating her. This accounted for the red marks found on her face.

Confronted with his nephew's admissions, Arthur made a written statement. He said that Alton and his sister were at all times under his control. "My will was their will," he said. He exonerated his brother from any involvement and said his reason for removing Ebba was because she impeded his complete control over the children. He instructed Alton how to commit murder without using violence.

At his trial, "Uncle Artie" pleaded not guilty, claiming he had only admitted the crime to spare his nephew. Perhaps believing his influence extended to the jury, he predicted, "The stars are in my favour, you'll see." It was a prophecy doomed to failure when he was found guilty and sentenced to death.

The crippled arch-manipulator who had appeared at his trial on a stretcher was strapped to a board to prepare him for his destiny with the gallows. His nephew suffered life imprisonment.

Scheming Wizard

"The Great Billik", as he billed himself, was a card-reader, seer and general all-round wizard. He sold charms and potions to the good citizens of Chicago at the turn of the nineteenth century, and decided to extend his wizardry by plotting murder.

Billik targeted his neighbour, Martin Vzral, who ran a successful milk-delivery business, with his Svengali-like talents of intimidation. Well versed in the art of preying on people's gullibility, he persuaded Vzral that he had an enemy who was out to destroy him. Billik offered to counteract this malign influence, who turned out to be a rival businessman, by using one of his potions against him.

Convinced that his enemy had been thwarted, Vzral was effusive in his thanks and pressed Billik to accept some payment. The wizard declined but he now had his victim firmly ensnared. Slowly and remorselessly Billik took control of Vzral's life, family and finances. He slept with his wife, turned his daughters into slaves, made his sons work for him and skimmed off all the business profits into his own account.

Inevitably, Vzral and his family slid into poverty as his assets were milked. Billik next instructed Mrs Vzral to insure the lives of her husband and daughters, which she did without question. At last, Martin Vzral began to rebel against his usurper but it was all too late and on 27 March 1905, he died and his life insurance found its way into Billik's account.

The relentless reduction of the Vzral family continued with the deaths of the four daughters over the next year and a half. What was left of the milk-delivery business was sold and Billik used some of the proceeds to pay for a holiday at Niagara Falls. When he returned to Chicago, it was to attend Mrs Vzral's funeral. Out of the nine original family members, only three were left.

The destruction of the Vzral family, witnessed by friends and neighbours, eventually led to finger-pointing in the direction of "The Great Billik". There were accusations of murder and a police investigation was started. Little headway was made due to lack of co-operation by the insurance companies and the reluctance of witnesses to give firm evidence. Nevertheless, Billik was tried and convicted of murder for which he was sentenced to death. There was a campaign to save his life and in January 1909, his sentence was commuted to life imprisonment. Sympathy for the Vzral family seemed to evaporate and the wizard served only a few years in prison before being released with a full pardon in 1917. His powers to influence the order of events seemed undiminished.

Psychic Detective

Myrna Joy Aken, aged eighteen, worked as a typist in an office in Durban, South Africa. On 20 October 1956, she left after work at about 6.00 p.m. and was seen to join a man, presumed to be her boyfriend, and drive off with him. She was not seen alive again.

Her parents called the police when she failed to return home and enquiries were made at her workplace. Colleagues had seen her leave with a man older than herself driving a Ford Anglia. She appeared to be a little depressed and friends thought that perhaps her social life was not going too well.

The police ran checks on Ford Anglia cars but after more than a week had passed, her parents became impatient at the lack of progress and decided to contact a psychic to see if he might help. Nelson Palmer had been successful in tracing missing persons and agreed to assist. He asked for some articles of clothing belonging to Myrna to aid his investigation.

The first conclusion Palmer came up with was to confirm the parents' worst fears that their daughter was dead. Then he determined where her body was. He described a location in the countryside outside the city where the body lay in a culvert and believed he could lead detectives to the spot.

A search party drove sixty miles out of Durban to the village of Umtwalumi and to a place in the roadside scrub where there was a culvert concealing a body. The naked, mutilated corpse was identified as the missing teenager. She had been shot in the head.

A breakthrough in the search for the driver of the Ford Anglia came when detectives traced such a car to a shop owner. He had loaned it to one of his employees who returned it the day after Myrna went missing. Thirty-three-year-old Clarence van Buuren was a neighbour of the Aken family. He seemed to have disappeared.

Surveillance was maintained on van Buuren's house and he was spotted on 11 October acting furtively outside his property. When challenged, he attempted to run off but was quickly seized and caught in the act of hiding a .22 calibre gun, which proved to be the murder weapon.

Van Buuren seemed to have had an unhappy life, he had been married three times and had a record for theft and forgery. He admitted knowing Myrna and said he saw her by chance when she left her office and asked her out for a drink. He said he unloaded some of his personal problems on her and then left her in the car while he went into a nearby hotel for a drink. When he returned, the car and Myrna were gone. He searched for the vehicle and found it in a nearby car park with Myrna lying dead on the back seat. Panicking, he drove out of town and dumped the body in the culvert.

It was not a story that was likely to find many believers and so it proved when he came to trial for murder in February 1957. He was found guilty and sentenced to death. Still protesting his innocence, he was hanged at Pretoria Central Prison on 10 June 1957. Apart from the implausibility of van Buuren's account of what had taken place, the most remarkable feature of the investigation was the part played by the psychic in locating the victim's body.

A Mother's Dream

At the end of the First World War, two ex-officers, Eric Tombe and Ernest Dyer, who were both in their twenties, formed a business partnership and started a motor business with money put up by Tombe. When this failed, they set up a second business and Dyer had grand ideas about motoring and horseracing.

After their initial failures, they ran a stud farm and racing stables called "The Welcomes" at Kenley in Surrey in the UK. Again, Tombe put up most of the money and Dyer moved into the farmhouse with his wife and children.

In April 1921, "The Welcomes" was destroyed by fire. No one was injured and Dyer was quick to lodge an insurance claim. Although the farmhouse had cost £3,000 to buy, he had insured it for four times that amount. The insurance company rejected the claim and Dyer did not pursue it further.

Dyer's ambitions began to outstrip his assets, despite borrowing money from Eric Tombe. When he forged his business partner's signature on a cheque, there was an argument. The relationship deteriorated rapidly and Tombe disappeared. He wrote to his parents on 17 April saying that he planned to visit them, but he never arrived.

Tombe's parents did all they could to locate their missing son and his father, a retired clergyman, began to learn for the first time about his son's business affairs and partnership with Eric Dyer. In due course, the Reverend Tombe visited "The Welcomes" but Dyer was not at home. Next, he made an appointment to see his son's bank manager. He discovered that Eric Tombe had given Dyer written power of attorney. The signature was a forgery and he learned that his son's once healthy account had been severely reduced.

By the time his double-dealing was discovered, Dyer had also disappeared. Then, on 16 November 1922 police went to a hotel in Scarborough to interview a Mr Fitzsimmons who was suspected of fraud. Fearful of arrest, Fitzsimmons put his hand in his pocket and withdrew a handgun. There was a struggle and Fitzsimmons, alias Dyer, was shot dead. His hotel room contained a wealth of incriminating evidence linking him to Eric Tombe.

The possibility of locating Tombe, now that Dyer was dead, looked remote. But then the missing man's mother began having recurrent dreams in which she saw her son's body lying at the bottom of a well. Extraordinary though it seemed, this phenomenon was reported to the police. It was known that there were several wells at "The Welcomes" and the police decided to inspect them. At the third attempt, they found a man's body.

Ten months after he had disappeared, Eric Tombe's body was recovered. He had been shot through the back of the head.

It was surmised that he had been killed by Dyer, probably after a quarrel over money, and his body thrown into the well. But for the extraordinary dreams of his mother, Tombe's body might never have been found.

The Art Of Murder

The railway station in the French town of Perpignon and its association with painter Salvador Dali were the unlikely inspiration for two horrific murders in the 1990s.

A few days before Christmas 1997, Mokhtaria Chaib, a sociology student at Perpignon University, spent the evening with her boyfriend in his city centre apartment. She left at around 11.00 p.m. to walk to her lodgings, a short distance away. Her naked body was found the next day with hideous injuries, which included amputation of her breasts and removal of the uterus. She had been killed with stab wounds to the head.

The killing had echoes of a previous unsolved murder in September 1995 when seventeen-year-old Tatiana Andujar disappeared after taking a similar route home from Perpignon railway station. Fears that a serial killer might be at work gripped the city in June 1998 when the mutilated body of twenty-two-year-old Marie-Hélène Gonzalez, last seen in Perpignon on 16 June, was found dead near a motorway.

What linked this latest killing to that of Mokhtaria Chaib was the similarity of the injuries. Gonzalez's head and hands had been severed, her vagina had been cut out and a number of abdominal organs had been excised. Police surgeons and pathologists noted the precision with which incisions had been made and their thoughts turned to a medical man as the possible murderer.

The strangest links were those made to the surrealist artist, Salvador Dali, who died in 1989. His association with Perpignon was well known and the square outside the railway station was named after him. He was particularly attracted to the station building, which, as railway stations go, was not especially distinctive. Indeed, he was so smitten with it that it featured in a number of his paintings. These were in his unmistakeably surreal style, but with bizarre sexual imagery.

Dali was said to loathe the sexuality of the female form and some of his paintings featured mutilated women's bodies as well as an obsession for unattached anuses, vaginas and breasts. His painting of the railway station at Perpignon showed an act of sodomy. The particular mutilations inflicted on Chaib and Gonzalez led investigators to think the killer might be imitating Dali's fantasies. This line of thought led to a murder suspect whose profile fitted the crimes. He was a Peruvian doctor who had practised in French hospitals but had his licence suspended. He was homosexual and known to the authorities for dealing in stolen passports and the theft of surgical instruments. He lived less than a mile from Perpignon railway station.

The doctor was arrested and questioned about the murder of Mokhtaria Chaib. There were no forensic traces linking him to the dead woman and, while he was in custody, Marie-Hélène Gonzalez was murdered. The Peruvian suspect was released and the Dali murders remain unsolved.

CHAPTER 8

Hold the Front Page!

There is nothing like a good murder story to sell newspapers. And a good story needs an eye-catching headline. The Victorians mastered this art and nowhere was the genre better demonstrated than during the 1870s in the Illustrated Police News. *This was a popular, high-circulation newspaper and a forerunner of the modern tabloids.*

The paper reported various types of criminal happenings and bizarre events with arresting headlines and, in an age before press photographs, used graphic artists' illustrations. Headlines contained two essential elements to connect with readers' interests. First was a reference to the nature of the crime and, all importantly, where it had taken place. This was usually preceded by an adjective to stimulate interest and convey a sense of outrage. Thus, in 1873, a "Dreadful Child Murder at Hull" was reported and, in 1876, a "Frightful Wife Murder in Bristol".

Crime reporting in newspapers continued to hold public interest in the age of television and radio and the advent of the internet has not diminished the appetite for written accounts of violence and murder. While the visual media make their own special impact, written accounts of events retain their power to hold the public imagination because they can delve into the minutiae that satisfy curiosity.

The template successfully developed by the Victorians has been honed to perfection by modern headline writers who can encapsulate the essence of a murder in two or three words. "Death of a Monster" was one of the tabloid headlines reporting the suicide of Fred West, the mass murderer, in 1995. The Yorkshire Ripper's justification for his crimes was reported in 1981 with the words "God Told Me To Kill Them".

References to places remain important, echoing Victorian practices when news of "The Whitechapel Murders" in London's East End preceded their attribution to Jack the Ripper. Thus, in modern times, "The Moors Murders" and "The Boston Strangler" will forever be associated with their location. These labels have acquired iconic status. But places need not be geographical entities; "The Bus Stop Stalker" and "Freeway Killer" also make descriptive headlines.

Any unusual facet of a murder is a godsend for crime reporters. Thus the killings perpetrated by Denis Rader, which remained unsolved for thirty years, were referred to as the "BTK Murders". This was an abbreviated reference to his methods – Bind, Torture and Kill. By the same process, Alfredo Galan became "The Playing Card Killer" and Alexander Pichushkin, "The Chessboard Killer".

Female murderers are often compared with ferocious stereotypes, so that Winnie Ruth Judd was referred to as "Tiger Woman" and the Papin sisters as "Les Diaboliques". Some headlines draw inspiration from, or comparison with, historical figures and events. Tillie Klimek was dubbed "The Polish Borgia" and Anatoly Onoprienko, the Eastern European serial killer, was described by the Ukrainian press as "The Terminator", a title with obvious Hollywood associations.

Some murderers make their own headlines, unwittingly. Rudolf Pleil, describing his activities, called himself "Der Beste Totmacher" – the death maker. Less dramatically, Carl Wanderer's appearance earned him the label, "Ragged Stranger". While von Braun Selz's antics, joking with newsmen at the graveside of his victim, inevitably earned him the name, "The Laughing Killer".

As long as newspapers are published, murder stories will continue to grab headlines, reflecting public interest in violent crime. Readers are drawn to savour the horror of bizarre deeds through front-page headlines whose writers tax their wit and imagination to produce the one-liners that sell newspapers. Thus, the revelation that Dr Harold Shipman tended to lose his patients after midday was greeted with a headline in the Guardian that echoed the title of one of Ernest Hemingway's books, Death in the Afternoon.

Bus Stop Stalker

Levi Bellfield's ploy was to follow buses late at night and target young women as they made their way home, for which he earned the name, "The Bus Stop Stalker".

Bellfield's first murder victim on 5 February 2003 was nineteen-year-old Marsha McDonnell whom he stalked when she alighted from a bus at Hampton in southwest London, a short distance from her home. She was bludgeoned with a hammer and died three days later.

In May 2004 "The Bus Stop Stalker" attacked Kate Sheedy and although he ran her over with his vehicle, she survived her injuries. Then, on 19 August 2004, Bellfield killed twenty-two-year-old Amelie Delagrange, a young French woman who had been in England only three months. She took a bus home after seeing friends but got off at the wrong stop. As she walked across Twickenham Green, Bellfield attacked her with a hammer and killed her.

Vehicles known to have been driven by Bellfield were reported as having been spotted at some of the attack locations. Aided by CCTV footage and information from the public, police were able to track his presence at the attack scenes.

Thirty-nine-year-old Bellfield, a former night-club bouncer, ran a wheel-clamping firm and he had access to a variety of vehicles. He also used many aliases to cover his movements. He took an arrogant approach when questioned by police and turned his back on detectives. A picture was built up of a predatory personality with a fixation for slim blonde women. He had a history of ill-treating his girlfriends and soon his hatred of women turned into violence. People who knew him described him variously as a "caveman" who "treated women like dogs". One acquaintance found magazines in which he had slashed the pages bearing photographs of beautiful models.

At his trial in February 2008, Bellfield behaved arrogantly in court. He made gestures to the victims' relatives, taunting them and mouthing obscenities. He showed no remorse for his actions and declined to appear in court to hear the sentence passed on him. The man whom criminal psychologists said was motivated by anger and erotomania was sentenced to life imprisonment. "Levi Spells Evil" was the headline in the *Sun* newspaper on 26 February 2008.

Detectives investigating the "Bus Stop Stalker" turned their attention to the unsolved murder of thirteen-year-old Amanda (Milly) Dowler who went missing on 21 March 2002 in Walton-on-Thames. Her remains were found at Yately Heath Woods in Hampshire in September. A possible link with Bellfield was made in 2005 when detectives found CCTV footage of a red Daewoo car near the place she was last seen. The car was also seen on the previous day driven by a man fitting Bellfield's description who approached another schoolgirl. The incident was reported at the time. However, the disappearance of Milly Dowler remains an unsolved crime.

Freeway Killer

William Bonin achieved the distinction of being the first convicted murderer in California to be executed by lethal injection. San Quentin Prison dispensed with its gas chamber in 1994, following a court ruling that it was too cruel a punishment. Bonin's last statement was to the effect that the death penalty sent the wrong message to the nation's youth. This was not a view shared by the families of his victims.

Over an eight-year period in the 1970s, forty-one boys and young men became victims of a homosexual rape murderer who roamed the highways of southern California. The victims, whose ages ranged between twelve and nineteen, were sexually abused, tortured and, in most cases, strangled. Their naked bodies were dumped by the roadside, which earned the murderer the name "The Freeway Killer".

There was a significant four-year break in the series of killings between 1974 and 1978. When the murders resumed, a victim of sexual assault in 1974 recognized characteristics in the new wave of attacks that matched his own experience. He had identified his attacker at the time as William Bonin who subsequently served a term in prison. In light of this information, police put Bonin under surveillance and arrested him on 11 June 1980.

Under questioning, Bonin admitted the killings and named several accomplices. Two nineteen-year-old youths turned States Evidence in return for lenient sentencing, while a third committed suicide in custody.

Bonin was put on trial in November 1981 when the court heard the full horror of his murderous activities. In all, he confessed to twenty-one murders during a reign of terror in which the bodies turned up at regular intervals. His trademark was strangulation, using his victim's T-shirt twisted to form a ligature around the neck. After he had finished his assault, in the words of the prosecutor, the bodies "were thrown like garbage along the streets and freeways".

The term "serial killer" had not yet entered the vocabulary when Bonin stood trial. Only later would it be realized that one of the characteristics that such killers shared was a troubled childhood. Bonin had been abused as a child and spent time in prison and mental institutions. After a period of service in Vietnam, he took work as a truck driver and set out on his murderous career.

He was found guilty of fourteen murders and sentenced to death. Bonin spent thirteen years on Death Row while appeal procedures were heard. He was reported as admitting that he would have carried on killing if he had not been captured. On 24 February 1996, he was put to death by lethal injection, only the third person to be executed in California since the death penalty was re-introduced in the state in 1977.

Relatives of some of Bonin's victims were pictured in press reports celebrating his death by drinking champagne. The mother of a fifteen-year-old boy murdered by Bonin hoped he would ". . . burn in hell".

The M50 Killer

Marie Wilks was travelling home to Warndon in Worcester in the UK on 18 June 1988 when she lost her way and ended up on the M50 in Gloucestershire. Then her car broke down and she stopped on the hard shoulder. Leaving her eleven-year-old sister and her thirteen-month-old baby in the car, she walked 500 yards to the nearest emergency telephone.

Twenty-two-year-old Marie was seven months pregnant. She had been to the Forest of Dean for the day to visit her husband who was taking part in a Territorial Army exercise. When the operator at the emergency call centre spoke to her, he heard a man's voice and the conversation went dead. The operator called the police who arrived to find Marie missing, the telephone handset dangling on its cord and two distressed children standing on the hard shoulder.

Marie was found two days later about two and a half miles away. Her body had been rolled down the motorway embankment. She had sustained a stab wound to her throat that severed the jugular vein, her jaw was fractured and there was bruising to the face.

The search began immediately for the "M50 Killer" and the police were particularly keen to talk to a man who several witnesses had seen pull over on to the hard shoulder at about the time Marie Wilks was telephoning for help. The man was described as in his twenties, sharp featured with distinctive blond crew-cut hair. He had been standing near his silver coloured car, which appeared to have broken down. An artist's impression of the man was circulated to the media.

There was no evidence that the victim had been sexually assaulted; the attack seemed motiveless. Scores of police officers searched for the murder weapon and a reconstruction of the murder was staged in the hope of stimulating responses from motorists using the M50 on the evening Marie met her death. The enquiry team received massive support from the public and over 400 callers telephoned about the artist's impression of the man wanted for questioning.

As a result of all this publicity, police made an arrest on 26 June. Thirty-six-year-old Eddie Browning was apprehended at the nightclub in South Wales where he worked as a bouncer. A former soldier in the Welsh Guards, Browning was married and had a young daughter. He had a reputation as being a bruiser and had served a prison sentence in the

1980s for aggravated burglary. His first marriage ended because he was violent and he had rowed with his second wife on the night of the murder. He got drunk, stormed out of the house and drove off with the intention of visiting a friend in Scotland.

Browning was tried for murder at Shrewsbury Crown Court in November 1989. Prosecutors painted a picture of a man with an aggressive streak who easily resorted to violence and bullying. After the argument with his wife, he left in a rage and, as Mr Justice Turner, put it, "you determined to reap violence when you spotted a lone, defenceless woman using the telephone by the side of the motorway."

The defence argued that the killing was not premeditated and that Browning had acted impulsively. The jury's unanimous guilty verdict was greeted with cheers and applause in the public gallery. Sentencing him, the judge said Browning remained "a dangerous man" and he would recommend that he be jailed for life and serve a minimum of twenty-five years. Reflecting the public response to the brutal killing of a vulnerable young woman the *Daily Express* ran the headline, "Cheers at life for M50 killer".

BTK = Bind, Torture And Kill

It sometimes takes a long time for justice to catch up with the ingenuity of the criminal mind. In the case of the BTK murderer, it would take thirty years.

During the 1970s a series of brutal killings created waves of fear in Wichita, Kansas. On 15 January 1974, while Joseph Otero was away from home, a murderer entered his house and strangled his wife and nine-year-old son. When Otero returned, he too was strangled, and in the basement, hung from a pike, was his eleven-year-old daughter.

When a man falsely confessed to the murders and the news was published in the *Wichita Eagle*, the paper received an anonymous telephone call from a man directing them to a book in the local library. Inside the book was a letter revealing details of the Otero murders that were known only to the police. Cryptic messages taunting the police and media were a feature of this killer's modus operandi.

During the next three years, other victims were killed in their homes in the Wichita area. A feature of the murders was that they stopped for a while and then began again with the same cat-and-mouse tactics. The killer gave himself a label, "BTK", meaning "bind, torture, kill". In one letter to the media he asked, "How many do I have to kill before I get my name in the paper or some national attention?"

When the messages stopped in 1980 and there was a lull in the violence, people cautiously began to wonder if the murders had ended. But, then, in 2004, the messages began again and the *Wichita Eagle* received a letter and photographs of a young woman who had been killed in 1986.

After three decades of murder and messages, the breakthrough came when one of the messages was sent on a computer disk. This was traced to a Lutheran Church in Wichita and suspicion fell on sixty-year-old Rader who was its president. A search of his home turned up files and photographs relating to some of the BTK victims and his DNA matched traces of semen found at some of the crime scenes. He was arrested in February 2004 and confessed to ten murders.

He said that he was driven by sexual fantasies and although he did not sexually assault his victims, he masturbated over their bodies. Rader had received a college education, held a regular job, helped the local Scouts and was an active church member. His job as a dogcatcher and enforcer of local byelaws gave him legitimate access to private premises. He was married with children, cared for his mother and seemed to be a regular family guy.

Rader was brought to trial in June 2005 when the enormity of his secret life was laid bare. In one of his messages to the media he had written, "I can't stop it so the monster goes on and it hurts me as well as society." He told the court how he trawled for victims and went out equipped with a "hit kit" which included ropes and housebreaking implements. He readily confessed to ten murders knowing that he would not face the death penalty if judged guilty because his crimes were committed before Kansas changed its law on capital punishment.

In August 2005, Denis Rader, the BTK murderer who had eluded capture for thirty years, finally faced punishment. He was given ten consecutive life sentences, totalling 175 years.

Playing Card Killer

A Spanish serial killer left his trademark playing card on the corpses of his victims. This trait, not surprisingly, won him the title of "The Playing Card Killer".

His first victim was Carlos Martin, a cleaner at Madrid's Barajas airport in 2003. His second victim was a twenty-eight-year-old man whom he shot dead as he waited for a night bus in the city centre. A playing card, the ace of cups (hearts), was left beside the body.

Ten days later Eduardo Salas, a student from Ecuador, was shot at pointblank range in a deserted street late at night. He survived his head wounds and in due course was able to give a brief description of his attacker. He described him as Spanish, aged about twenty-five and a tall man. A playing card, the two of cups, had been left at the scene of the shooting.

On 19 March 2003, the killer struck again, this time killing a man and seriously wounding his female companion. The couple were Romanian immigrants, who were shot in the back of the head and left for dead in the outskirts of Madrid. Playing cards were left at the scene of the shooting; three of cups for the injured woman and four of cups for the dead man.

Police believed the killer had timed his attack to coincide with a fireworks display in the city following a Champions League football game. The gunman had also been careful to pick up three spent cartridge cases. There were no witnesses and he disappeared without trace. The killer's modus operandi seemed to be that he kept in the shadows and appeared from behind his victims to shoot them in the back of the head. The attacks seemed to be random.

Madrid was reeling from the night-time shootings at a time when the city had experienced thirty lethal stabbings and shootings in the space of three months. A hundred and fifty police officers had been assigned to the hunt for the "Playing Card Killer".

Relief came in July 2003 when the killer surrendered to the police. He was twenty-six-year-old Alfredo Galan, a former soldier who had served with peacekeeping forces in the Balkans. He was reported to have told police that he wanted to know what it felt like to kill. Although he made a confession to the killings he later retracted it. He then tried to implicate others in the shootings, claiming he had sold them the gun that became the murder weapon.

Galan was tried for murder in March 2005 and the man whom psychiatrists labelled a "Human Predator" showed no remorse. According to police statements, he asked his victims to kneel before he shot them as he believed politeness was important. Galan was convicted of six murders and three attempted murders for which he received prison sentences totalling 142 years. His sentences will run concurrently, however, and under Spanish law he will serve no more than twenty years.

The Chessboard Murders

Nicknamed, "The Chessboard Murderer", the aim of the Russian serial killer, Alexander Pichushkin, appeared to be to outdo his country's most infamous killer in modern times, Andrei Chikatilo.

Chikatilo was convicted in 1902 of killing fifty-two people but his compatriot wanted to go for sixty-four, one for each square on his chessboard. Pichushkin, a supermarket worker, played chess under the trees at Bitsevsky Park in the southern part of Moscow. He targeted mostly elderly men and fellow chess players, starting to kill them off in 2000. He later bragged, "For me life without murder is like life without food for you."

His method was to entice his victims into a quiet part of the sprawling park and attack them from behind. Some of his victims were strangled and others were bludgeoned with a hammer. Their corpses were thrown into a sewage pit. Pichushkin's trail of death came to light in June 2006 with the discovery of the body of thirty-six-year-old Marina Moskalyova, a fellow supermarket worker. The dead woman had left a note in her apartment giving the name and telephone number of the man she was meeting. The police had incriminating CCTV footage that showed her in Pichushkin's company.

Having first tried denial, Pichushkin then boasted of killing sixty-three times with the ambition of making it sixty-four. Of his first murder he said, "It is like first love – it's unforgettable." He demanded that he should be charged with all the murders to which he had confessed. But the police were not able to find evidence to confirm his claim. They discovered forty bodies in a sewage pit, added to which were three victims who had been attacked but survived. A survivor identified him. One of his ploys was to ask his intended victim to join him in a drink of vodka to toast the memory of his dead dog. Once they were drunk and incapable, he killed them and it was an easy matter to throw the body into the pit.

Pichushkin was put on trial in Moscow in September 2007. He was charged with forty-eight murders and three attempted murders. Measured by his own standards this fell short both of the sixty-three killings he claimed and also the fifty-two murders committed by Chikatilo. He continued to delay matters by demanding a jury trial, unusual proceedings in Russia. On 29 October 2007 Pichushkin was found guilty and sentenced to life imprisonment. Asked if he understood the sentence, he replied, "I'm not deaf . . ." The thirty-three-year-old serial killer was destined to serve his term doing hard labour in a penal colony. Whether prison facilities include chessboards can only be speculated upon.

Tiger Woman

In the manner beloved of American newspaper coverage of crime in the 1930s, Winnie Ruth Judd came to be called "The Tiger Woman".

Winnie worked in a medical clinic in Phoenix, Arizona and, although married to Dr William Judd, she shared an apartment with a colleague, Agnes Le Roi and was friendly with another girl, Hedvig Samuelson.

Screams were heard coming from the apartment on 16 October 1931 and noises that might have been gunshots. Agnes Le Roi did not turn up for work the next morning and Winnie was late. Later that day Winnie arranged for a delivery company to call at the apartment to move a heavy trunk.

On 18 October, she travelled by train to Los Angeles and arrived with two trunks. She sought help from a porter to load her baggage into a car. While doing this, the porter noticed a dark fluid dripping from one of the trunks. He asked Winnie what was inside. She evaded the question and promptly drove off leaving the trunks behind. On closer examination, one trunk was found to contain the body of Agnes Le Roi and the other the dismembered corpse of Hedvig Samuelson.

Following a plea from her husband, Winnie gave herself up on 23 October. She surrendered to Los Angeles police at a funeral parlour. A letter she had written to her husband amounted to a confession. In it she claimed to have killed the two women in self-defence using a handgun and a bread-knife.

"The Tiger Woman" was put on trial for murder. She claimed to have had an accomplice, a Phoenix businessman, who helped her to cut up the bodies. Winnie's family members made much of the mental instability that they claimed ran in the family. Winnie played her part in this by shouting out in court that she wanted to throw herself out of the window.

Winnie Judd was sentenced to death but her histrionics won her a reprieve. The Governor of Arizona granted a stay of execution and ordered a sanity hearing. The result was that the death sentence was commuted to life imprisonment and Winnie was admitted to the State Hospital for the Insane.

She proved to be a resourceful, and at times, elusive prisoner. She contrived to make a dummy to simulate her sleeping presence in her cell bed and escaped. After a brief period of freedom, she returned to the State Hospital. Her next attempt involved obtaining a key and she let herself out. This too failed and in 1952 she tried again, and, spectacularly, once more in 1962 when she remained free for six years, living with a couple in California for whom she worked as a babysitter. In all, she absconded seven times.

Legal efforts seeking her extradition to California failed and she was sent back to Arizona, having been declared sane and fit to be imprisoned once more. Finally, in December 1971, her sentence was commuted and she regained her freedom to live in California. "The Tiger Woman" lived out her remaining days in the Sunshine State until the age of ninety-three. She died at Stockton, California, in October 1998.

Les Diaboliques

Twenty-eight-year-old Christine Papin and her twenty-one-year-old sister, Lea, worked as domestic servants in the home of a lawyer, René Lancelin, in Le Mans, France. On 2 February 1933, Lancelin arrived home from his office expecting to collect his wife and daughter and take them out to dinner. When he failed to get a response to his knock on the front door, he used a street telephone to call his wife but, again, there was no reply.

Returning to the house, Lancelin noticed that all the lights were out except for the attic room where the maids slept. He tried another vigorous knock on the front door and when that failed, he suspected something was wrong and called the police.

Officers arrived and broke in to the house. On the first floor landing they found the bodies of Madame Lancelin and her daughter. They had been grossly mutilated and the carpet and stairs were thick with blood. The two women had been bludgeoned, slashed and stabbed. Their faces had been disfigured and the eyes gouged out.

Moving to the top of the house, officers found the door to the maids' room locked. They broke the door open and found the Papin sisters naked and huddled together in a single bed. Christine made an immediate confession and her account of what had taken place went a long way to securing her conviction, and that of her sister, for murder.

The story was one of a trivial incident leading to an appalling reaction. She explained that her sister had damaged the electric iron and been fined for her clumsiness by Madame Lancelin. When the iron was next used, it blew the lighting fuse and Christine reported it was not possible to do the ironing. Believing that the Lancelins' daughter was going to strike her, she got in the first blow by leaping on her and scratching at her eyes. Lea joined in by attacking Madame Lancelin.

Taken by surprise, mother and daughter lay on the floor while Christine went down to the kitchen and returned with a hammer and a knife and ". . . with these," she said, "we attacked our mistresses." She added that she did not plan the crime or feel any hatred towards her victims.

The Papin sisters or "Les Diaboliques" as they were referred to in the press, were committed for trial at Le Mans against a background of intense public interest. It appeared that the two sisters were rather dull girls who did menial work in a household where they were generally well treated. But there was a strong undercurrent of petty criticism that was often delivered in written notes sent to the offenders by Madame Lancelin. Constant rebukes created feelings of persecution and the storm finally broke with the blown fuse.

A defence of insanity was put forward, but in a remarkably short trial, the jury rejected it. The Papins were found guilty and Christine, judged to be the instigator of the murders, was sentenced to death while Lea was to be imprisoned for ten years. In due course, Christine was reprieved and her sentence commuted to life imprisonment. She died four years after the murders in a mental institution.

The Polish Borgia

When Tillie Klimek developed the gift of prophesy the Polish community in which she lived in Chicago was suitably impressed. Steeped in superstitious beliefs, they marvelled at her powers, especially when she correctly forecast the death of her husband.

Tillie Mitkiewitz spent over twenty years of her married life slaving for her husband who had an aversion to work. When he died as she had predicted in January 1914, her friends stood in awe of her precognition while she collected the insurance money.

Within a month Tillie remarried and her new husband, John Ruskowski, was also the subject of her fatal predictions. In April 1920, she married a third time and was so certain of her forecast that she bought a coffin and stored it in the basement. Her prophesy was duly fulfilled when Frank Kutczyk was placed in the coffin which was so conveniently to hand.

Tillie's fourth husband was Anton Klimek, hitherto a healthy man, but who fell ill after the marriage. He complained of numbness in his legs but told friends that his wife was doing everything she could to help him. Tillie was nursing Anton at home and feeding him bowls of stew as his health continued to decline.

When Anton's brother insisted on calling a doctor, the physician suspected poisoning. This was confirmed in hospital when tests proved positive for arsenic. Suspicion fell on Tillie and, when questioned, neighbours were very forthcoming about her predictions and the unfortunate deaths of her previous husbands. In the nick of time, Tillie was arrested, while Anton survived after his stomach was pumped. Analysis of the stew confirmed the presence of arsenic. She confessed to poisoning him although she denied killing her former husbands. She said that one of her favourite meals was stew and explained the ease with which rat poison could be stirred into the mixture.

Tried for murder in March 1922 Tillie milked the publicity for all it was worth. The "Polish Borgia" as she was called in the newspapers seemed oblivious of the charges against her. Her confession was backed up by the evidence of poisoning in her exhumed husbands and led to her conviction. She declared in court that she would never stand on the gallows and her wish was granted when she was sentenced to life imprisonment.

Tillie Klimek was suspected of procuring the deaths of several other people in addition to her husbands, no doubt using a combination of her stew-making abilities and powers of prophesy. She died in 1936 at the age of seventy-one in Illinois' Women's Prison.

The Terminator

Nicknamed "The Terminator", Anatoly Onoprienko killed fifty-two people, ten of whom were children. The Ukranian serial killer boasted, "There is no better killer in the world than me."

Onoprienko was raised in an orphanage and his friends thought of him as quiet and generous. Some of them received gifts from the proceeds of robberies committed after the murders. Inevitably, doubts were raised about his sanity. He talked of being forced to kill and of being influenced by unknown powers and sinister forces.

On Christmas Eve 1995 the former sailor and forestry worker broke into a forester's home at Garmarnia. He killed the entire family with a sawn-off shotgun and set fire to their house. There followed a similar attack the next week when he wiped out a family at Bratkovychi, another massacre at Enerhodar and then a return to Bratkovychi. In less than a month, Onoprienko had destroyed four families, totalling twenty victims who were slaughtered by gun, knife and axe.

His reign of terror ended when a massive police manhunt located him at his girlfriend's house near Lviv. He seemed to have led an apparently normal life in between his orgies of killing, and shared some of the violence with an accomplice, Serge Rogozin. He was arrested after trying to shoot his way past the police.

During various interviews, Onoprienko showed not the slightest remorse, rather he gloried in what he had done. He compared his methods to an animal watching a sheep, commenting that he saw it as "a kind of experiment". He readily confessed to forty murders committed over a four-month period in 1995/96 and asked for another twelve, committed in 1989, to be taken into account.

Onoprienko was brought to trial in March 1999. Throughout the proceedings, he sat calmly in a metal cage in the courtroom at Zhytomyr, west of Kiev. This protected him from the threat of physical violence from enraged members of the public, many of whom demanded that he be tortured before being executed. The trial only came about after one of the judges made an appeal for extra funds in order to stage the proceedings.

Onoprienko's lawyer said his client fully admitted his guilt and the opinion of prosecution psychologists that he was sane was accepted. Although it was noted that he had spent time in a mental hospital before his arrest and had been treated for schizophrenia, at that time he was not thought to be a danger to the public. Defence counsel pleaded for leniency, arguing that the defendant as a child had been deprived of motherly love and lacked the care needed by a growing young person.

His confession placed him in the same hall of infamy as Andrei Chikatilo, the so-called "Rostov Ripper" who also killed fifty-two people. At the age of thirty-nine, Onoprienko was convicted of murder and sentenced to death. His accomplice, Sergei Rogozin, was sentenced to thirteen years' imprisonment.

The Death Maker

Rudolf Pleil was a former German soldier and policeman who claimed to have raped and killed fifty women in the aftermath of the Second World War. He described himself as "der beste Totmacher" (the best death maker) and, while in prison, wrote a parody of Hitler's *Mein Kampf,* consisting of a record of his sex murders, which he signed, "Rudolf Pleil, death maker (retired)".

Pleil's victims were female refugees crossing from East to West Germany. In his role as a police officer, he offered to escort them once they had crossed the border at which point he raped, robbed and killed them. He used various murder weapons, including knives, axes and hammers to kill and mutilate his victims. One of the women he attacked survived to tell the tale.

Charged with nine murders, Pleil appeared on trial at Brunswick in November 1950. He immediately took issue with the judge over the number of victims, claiming there were twenty-five, as if his honour was at stake. Twenty-six-year-old Pleil gave his evidence in a matter-of-fact manner, saying that his lust for murder had started when he was a boy and he tortured and killed a cat. He recorded his first murder of a human being in March 1946. He continually interrupted proceedings when the number of his murders was referred to. He insisted there were twenty-five victims and described in detail how he had raped and killed them. He reminded the court that he was the "best death maker".

In his version of *Mein Kampf*, Pleil stated that he wanted to be a professional executioner and had offered his services to the Russians. He related the satisfaction he gained by seeing a train carrying concentration camp inmates at the end of the war. Individuals who had died during the journey were transferred to a special wagon. Pleil described this grim spectacle as "my finest sexual experience".

A psychologist offered an explanation for Pleil's extraordinary behaviour, which he believed was related to his failure to have normal sexual intercourse. Appearing on trial with him were two accomplices accused of helping him commit some of the killings. Again Pleil was argumentative, saying that he broke with one of his helpers because he wanted to decapitate one of the victims. It seemed that Pleil decided this was going too far. In any case, he asserted his own right to kill because "it is dictated by my most innermost feelings".

After nineteen days of listening to the gruesome details of Pleil's murderous activities, the judge found him and his fellow defendants guilty. The judge described the trio as beasts and sounded a note of regret that the law in Germany would not allow him to apply the death penalty. Pleil's reaction was that he would not live behind bars for the remainder of his life. The man who was credited with saying, "Every man has his passion. Some prefer whist, I prefer killing people", hanged himself in his prison cell in February 1958.

Ragged Stranger

A war hero persuaded a stranger and a down-and-out to threaten him and his wife so that he could overpower the would-be assailant and, thereby, win his wife's admiration. The result, however, was that his wife and the stranger were shot dead.

Carl Wanderer, a man of German extraction, fought with American troops in Europe during the First World War. He returned home to Chicago in 1919 as a second lieutenant and was welcomed as a hero. Soon after his return, he married and the newlyweds went to live in the bride's family home until they could afford their own place.

On 21 June 1920, after returning home from an evening at the cinema, they were startled by a man in the shadows who warned them not to turn on the entry light. Suddenly, there were shots and Mrs Wanderer, who was several months pregnant, collapsed and died later from her wounds. Her husband shot and killed the stranger using his service revolver.

The dead man, "The Ragged Stranger", as he came to be called, was a down-and-out with just over three dollars in his pocket. Curiously, he was armed with a .45 Colt service revolver. While the public sympathized with Wanderer over the tragic loss of his wife, probing questions were being asked elsewhere.

The editor of *The Herald Examiner* thought it odd that the stranger, who was virtually penniless, should own a revolver costing at least ten dollars. It was less remarkable that Wanderer should be armed; he was, after all, an ex-officer and continued to carry his service weapon. Curiosity led to further investigation and the serial numbers on both weapons were checked. It seemed that the revolver used by "The Ragged Stranger" had been sold to a man who passed it on to Carl Wanderer's cousin and, subsequently, it was loaned to Wanderer himself.

The police lost no time in questioning Wanderer and searching his apartment. They found photographs of him posing with different girls and torn fragments of a letter written to one of them two weeks before his wife died. He expressed loving sentiments to a sixteen-year-old girl to whom he had proposed marriage.

Wanderer confessed to both killings. His scheme was to dupe an unfortunate whom he supplied with a gun to play the part of a hold-up man. Wanderer would then grapple with him and overcome him to win his wife's admiration. He found a down-and-out serviceman who was willing to accept this mission in return for a down payment of five dollars. With his wife tragically killed in a hold-up, Wanderer would be free to marry his teenage girlfriend.

The hero turned villain was tried for the murder of his wife and, to general astonishment, was given a prison sentence of twenty years. A campaign followed, demanding that he be tried for murdering the stranger. This commanded considerable public support and, at a second trial, he was convicted and sentenced to death.

One of the reasons Wanderer gave for the killing his wife was that he felt threatened by her pregnancy. He claimed that he was a secret homosexual. He was hanged on 19 March 1921 at Chicago's Cook County jail after giving a rendering of "Old Pal, Why Don't You Answer Me?"

The Laughing Killer

In December 1935, Ada Franch Rice, a wealthy fifty-eight-year-old, made the acquaintance of Ralph Jerome von Braun Selz in San Francisco. He was a ladies' man and used his youthful charm to escape with Ada to her cottage in the Santa Cruz Mountains.

When Ada disappeared from her usual haunts, she was reported missing. Then, in February the following year, the police picked up a man whom they suspected of having stolen a car. This was twenty-nine-year-old Selz who it seemed was very flush with money, despite being unemployed. Enquiries revealed that he had been cashing cheques in Ada Rice's name.

Under relentless police questioning over a period of several days, Selz cracked and made a confession. He said Ada's death had been an accident, the victim of a bizarre nocturnal encounter. His story was that one night, on entering the cottage in the mountains, he was surprised by an intruder. He grabbed a fire iron and lashed out in the darkness. When he put a light on he realized the intruder had escaped and he had accidentally killed Ada. He buried her body nearby.

Selz, with a team of police investigators and newsmen, went to a remote ridge in the Santa Cruz Mountains and pointed out where Ada was buried. As men with spades exhumed the body, Selz laughed and joked with the newsmen. "If you guys want a sensation," he said, "try hauling a corpse around in a car with the hoot owls hooting at night." At this point, he danced around the grave laughing like a man possessed. His final piece of repartee was to declare, "I'm going to Hollywood when I get through here."

In fact, he went on trial in March 1936 was convicted and sentenced to life imprisonment. Still laughing, he was taken to Chino State Prison from which he managed to escape in 1945. He was recaptured in Calgary, Canada, where he had joined up in the Canadian Military. Returned to the US, he was imprisoned at San Luis Obispo and, once again, contrived to escape.

Selz maintained his jocular approach to life, whether it was in or out of prison. In one of many petitions to the authorities he claimed that he had been put under duress when originally arrested in 1936 by being denied food while under questioning. This caused him to hallucinate and accounted for his weird behaviour.

"The Laughing Killer" gained parole in 1966 but was soon in trouble again over welfare fraud.

Düsseldorf Doubles Killer

Werner Boost was a sex murderer who preyed on courting couples in cars because they made him "see red". His technique, aided by an accomplice, was to kill, rob and rape in his campaign against what he called the curse of "sex horrors".

Thirty-one-year-old Werner Boost was the illegitimate son of an East German peasant family. In 1950, he moved to Düsseldorf where he was convicted of plundering metal from graveyards. He next began to wage a kind of vendetta against couples he saw sitting together in cars. This earned him his eventual title of the "Düsseldorf Doubles Killer".

His first attack was committed on 17 January 1953 when he shot dead a lawyer in his stationary car. He and his companion, Franz Lorbach, then beat up and robbed the passenger in the car. The next attack came in November 1955 when a young couple disappeared from a bar in the city and were later found dead in their car in a water-filled gravel pit.

In February 1956, another couple were reported missing and were later found in a village outside the city. They had been beaten and burned. A few months later, a courting couple in woods near Düsseldorf fought off two armed attackers and, in the following week, a forest ranger in the same area spotted a man shadowing a courting couple. The forester, who was armed, apprehended Werner Boost who put up no resistance.

The criminal investigation that followed achieved a break-through when Franz Lorbach made a confession. He told investigators that he had lived in fear of Boost who completely dominated him. They had experimented with drugs and injections of truth serum. Boost lived in a fantasy world, even manufacturing liquid cyanide with the intention of filling toy balloons with lethal gas to release into the cars of courting couples.

Boost was charged with murder and forensic ballistics showed that his gun had killed the lawyer shot in 1953. The investigation was then extended to cover a series of murders that had occurred in 1946 in Lower Saxony at a time when Boost was known to be living in the area. The enquiry was lengthy and it would be three years before Boost was finally judged and sentenced. He was given life imprisonment and his accomplice, Franz Lorbach, was jailed for six years.

Perhaps inevitably, the "Düsseldorf Doubles Killer" would be compared with the city's other infamous murderer, Peter Kürten, the so-called "Monster of Düsseldorf". Separated by a world war and the suspension of the death penalty in Germany, Boost lived while Kürten went to the guillotine.

Frying Pan Murder

A wealthy optometrist was found dead in his home with head wounds resulting from a domestic dispute with his wife. When the full story emerged, it appeared he had been beaten to death with a frying pan. What followed was naturally reported as "The Frying Pan Murder".

Dr John Bradford had built up a successful optical laboratory in Melbourne, Florida. He was widely respected and regarded as a man of mild temperament. He had been married to Priscilla for twenty-five years but the marriage came under strain when Priscilla became a strong advocate of the Women's Liberation Movement. She spent her time with two friends of similar outlook, Joyce Cummings and Janice Gould, and all three were avowed men-haters.

Early in 1980, Bradford began telling people that he feared for his life. Referring to Priscilla and her cohorts, he said, "I think they plan to kill me." On 28 March, police were called to the Bradfords' home where Dr Bradford lay on the kitchen floor battered to death. His wife explained that there had been a quarrel when her husband violently attacked her and she was forced to fight back in self-defence. She had been assisted by Cummings and Gould who, still in their swimming costumes, had come in from the pool when they heard the commotion.

This scenario was viewed with some suspicion, especially in view of John Bradford's well-documented fears. His body was cremated with what some regarded as indecent haste and the police continued their enquiries by questioning his family and colleagues. His laboratory staff suspected Priscilla's account of what had happened and her story was completely undermined by her daughter who had been present when her stepfather died. The teenage girl broke down when questioned and revealed the full horror of what was undoubtedly a murder.

Priscilla, aided and abetted by Cummings and Gould, had hatched a murder plot at a meeting in a Burger King restaurant. After other methods, including poison, shooting and cutting the car's brake hoses had either failed or been discounted, they opted to ambush Bradford at home in a staged domestic dispute.

On the day of the murder, with preparations calculated to a fine degree, Priscilla had her two henchwomen slap her about to produce a few bruises to authenticate the story of being assaulted by her husband. Cummings and Gould put on swimming costumes so they could more easily remove the blood that they rightly expected to flow. Priscilla's teenage daughter was told to take a shower so that she would not hear her stepfather's screams.

John Bradford stepped into a carefully prepared trap. When he entered the kitchen, he was felled with blows from a frying pan, which broke in the process, and other bludgeoning instruments including a kitchen stool and golf clubs. With Bradford on the verge of death, Priscilla called the police and told her daughter to start crying when they arrived. "I want real tears," she said.

The deadly trio of Priscilla, Cummings and Gould were charged with murder. The dead man's stepdaughter was granted immunity from prosecution as a state witness. In August 1980, having declared that she did not want to hear her daughter's testimony in court, Priscilla pleaded guilty to murdering her husband. All three women were convicted and sentenced to life imprisonment.

Thus "The Frying Pan Murder", a bizarre crime committed out of misplaced hatred and planned with ruthless efficiency, came to a conclusion with Priscilla still breathing defiance.

Bodies In The Barrel

An enquiry into missing persons in South Australia in 1999 led police to a disued building in Snowtown. There they made grim discoveries of what amounted to a murder factory where bodies had been dismembered and stored in barrels.

On 21 May 1999, investigators entered the vault of a disused bank and found decomposing human remains filling six large plastic barrels. There were eight bodies in the bank vault and two more were buried in a nearby backyard. Pathologists found evidence of death by strangulation and believed the killings had occurred between 1995 and 1999. Also unearthed at the crime scene were handcuffs, knives and rubber gloves. There was evidence that some of the victims had been tortured.

Exceptional forensic and police investigation established the identity of all the victims and led to the arrest of four murder suspects. Robert Wagner, John Bunting, Mark Haydon and James Vlassakis were arrested and charged with murder. In a sensational case that gripped Australia, it turned out that the victims were all friends and relatives of the four men.

Bunting and Wagner were known for their hatred of homosexuals, paedophiles and the disabled, having a view that "They need to be killed". Recordings made of the tortures inflicted on the victims were recovered from the bank vault. Victims were also compelled to repeat phrases on tape before they were killed so that their voices could be replayed later to maintain the pretence that they were still alive.

Vlassakis, aged nineteen at the time of the murders, admitted partial guilt and agreed to give evidence against the others. On 20 June 2001, he pleaded guilty to four murders and was sentenced to life imprisonment without parole for twenty-six years.

Bunting and Wagner went on trial in Adelaide in October 2002. In what the press described as the "Bodies in the Barrel" or the "Slice and Dice" case, the public, already shocked, were in for a courtroom account of torture, mutilation and cannibalism. The accused men pleaded not guilty.

Bunting was depicted as the ringleader of the gang of four who preyed on friends and neighbours with the intention of stealing from them. Theft turned to hatred and violence and they tortured and killed ten men and two women. Bunting had written down the agenda; "The routine of confession had to be got through. The grovelling . . . the screaming for mercy . . . the smashed teeth . . ."

Court proceedings were suspended at one point when a juror could not face the horror of what was being recounted. A description, made public after the trial, of an act of cannibalism on the part of Wagner was not for the squeamish. A piece of flesh was cut from the body of their last victim who had been strangled, and Wagner cooked it in a frying pan.

The trial, which lasted for eleven months, delivered its verdicts on 8 September 2003. Bunting was convicted of eleven counts of murder and Wagner of seven. Both men were sentenced to life imprisonment. In May 2005, their appeals against sentence were dismissed. The fourth man, Mark Haydon, was convicted of five counts of assisting in the commission of the crimes.

This extraordinary story of murder as a business fascinated and horrified at the same time. Twelve people were killed and their credit cards and state benefits were looted for a meagre A\$100,000. For Snowtown, the murders brought unwanted publicity in the form of tourists posing for photographs outside the building that housed the murder factory.

The Tombstone Murder

The murder committed in Stratford-on-Avon on the day local people celebrated Shakespeare's birthday in 1954, has never been solved.

Forty-five-year-old Olive Bennet was a state registered nurse and midwife. She had worked in various towns in Britain and in the 1950s was employed at a County Council Maternity Home at Tiddington, just outside Stratford.

On 23 April 1954, Bennet left the maternity home at around 8.10 p.m., telling a colleague she was going to Stratford and would be back later. She also said she was going to meet a friend. She was seen in several hotel bars that evening, including the Red House Hotel, and was observed standing outside at 11.45. That was the last time she was seen alive.

The following morning when the church gardener arrived at Holy Trinity Church to tidy up the graveyard, he spotted a pair of spectacles, a single shoe and part of a set of dentures lying on the ground. The gardener's keen eye also noted that one of the tombstones was missing. The police were notified.

Olive Bennet's body was found in the River Avon; she had been strangled. Half-buried in the silt was the missing tombstone from the churchyard. It bore the inscription, "Edward Adam. Died 1875. In the midst of life we are in death." The stone, which weighed fifty-six pounds, might have been thrown in after the body was dumped or, alternatively, it might have been attached by means of a long woollen scarf.

Enquiries into Olive Bennet's background revealed that she was not quite the reserved woman many believed her to be. There were suggestions that she might have had a secret lover. When she finished her nursing shift, she would appear in the evening with fresh make-up and smartly dressed ready to take the bus into Stratford. She often returned quite late in a taxi.

However, those who saw her there in hotel bars said that she was invariably alone, drinking sherry and chain-smoking. How she ended up in the graveyard at Holy Trinity Church was a mystery that the local police, even with the help of Detective Chief Superintendent Capstick from Scotland Yard, were unable to answer.

Stratford had been crowded with visitors on the day Bennet was murdered and there was talk of mysterious Americans who might have information about her and also a New Zealand man. Soldiers from nearby Long Marston camp also came under a degree of suspicion.

The police staged a reconstruction of Bennet's likely movements on the evening she was murdered and made appeals to the public for information. No useful leads came forward, although, five years after the murder, two women told police of an encounter they had with two servicemen in the graveyard at Holy Trinity Church. One of the soldiers was supposed to have said that he would throw one of them into the river and weigh her down with a tombstone.

Enquiries were apparently made at Long Marston camp but no action resulted. In November 1974, as part of a series of unsolved murders, the *News of the World* ran the story of "The Tombstone Murder" and offered £100,000 to any reader who could help solve the case. There were no takers. Intriguingly, John Capstick made no reference to Olive Bennet's murder in his memoirs. Perhaps that was because it was a case he could not solve.

The Little Old Lady Murders

A serial killer targeted elderly women in Mexico City during a three-year period beginning in 2003. More than thirty murders involving strangulation became known as "The

Little Old Lady Murders". The fact that the victims were frail, elderly people raised public concerns and put the police under pressure. Investigators were guided by witness sightings that described seeing a transvestite at the crime scenes.

The breakthrough in the investigation came on 25 January 2006 following the murder of eighty-two-year-old Ana Maria de los Reyes in her apartment. A man in the building saw a person leaving the scene and gave a detailed description enabling the police to arrest Juana Barraza, a single mother with three children.

Barraza admitted killing Mrs de los Reyes "from economic necessity", but denied the other killings. She was, nevertheless charged with ten murders and detectives thought a final tally might be twenty-seven.

In appearance, forty-eight-year-old Juana Barraza was of robust build, neatly dressed with dyed red hair. She had a rather unusual hobby; she was a female wrestler and an avid participant in Mexican masked wrestling called *lucha libra*. Her ringside name was La Dana del Silencio and she defined her style as "rudo to the core" that is a rule-breaker. She often attended wrestling events, organized small town meetings and sometimes participated in the ring wearing a pink outfit decorated with butterflies.

Barraza came from a poor family background and never learned to read or write. She was abandoned by her alcoholic mother at the age of twelve and brought up by a relative who abused her. Psychologists who questioned her believed she held strong resentment against her mother and sought to release her rage by killing defenceless old ladies. Barraza's fingerprints matched those found at ten murder scenes. She gained access to her victims by posing as a social worker or nurse, or offering to help with shopping and cleaning. Robbery was a factor in some of the killings.

In April 2008, Barraza was tried for the murders of sixteen elderly women. Defence attempts to have her declared mentally unfit to stand trial failed. She was convicted and sentenced to 759 years in prison. Her comment at the court's verdict was, "May God forgive you and not forget me."

Carbon Copy Killings

Two murders nine months apart, so similar that they were called the "Carbon Copy Killings", were separated by an apparently unrelated murder in Germany.

On 11 June 1960, a man's body was found in a ditch near the village of Baslow in Derbyshire in the UK. Sixty-year-old William Elliott had been savagely beaten and kicked to death. The lane where the body was discovered was recognized as a meeting venue for homosexuals. Elliott was a member of a gay group in nearby Chesterfield but despite appeals for information, there was no response. The dead man's car was found abandoned in Chesterfield, presumably driven there by the murderer.

In the following year, on 28 March, the body of forty-eight-year-old George Stubbs, a gay man, was found in almost the same location as the previous murder. He too had been savagely beaten and his car, as on the previous occasion, was found dumped in Chesterfield. The similarity of the two murders inspired press references to the "Carbon Copy Killings" and the police had little doubt they were looking for a double murderer.

When reports of the killings published in the British newspapers found their way to the British forces serving in Germany, the Commanding Officer of the base at Werden made a connection. The previous November, the brutal stabbing of a teenage German boy had led to co-operation between the British military authorities and the German police in the search for the killer. The Commanding Officer of the base at Werden called for a list of names of all military personnel not on duty on the day of the murder. One of the men free on that day was Private Michael Copeland. Twenty-one-year-old Copeland was a former miner and a powerfully-built man with a history of violent behaviour. When asked about the murder of the young German boy, he denied any involvement.

When Copeland was involved a short while later in a bar room brawl with local Germans, he was arrested and, in due course, dismissed from the army. The grounds for his discharge were that he was a psychopathic personality unsuited to military life. He returned to England and to his home town of Chesterfield.

Reading the press reports about the "Carbon Copy Killings" and the Chesterfield connection prompted the officer at Werden to contact the police in Derbyshire and tell them about Copeland. The ex-soldier had alibis for the days of the two murders in Chesterfield and denied any involvement in the killing of the German boy. Over a period of several months, Copeland was questioned and re-questioned. He spent time in a mental institution after attempting to commit suicide in 1962 and, when released, was embroiled in an assault that led to his arrest. Finally, over two years after the first Chesterfield murder, Copeland confessed to all three murders.

Copeland admitted he had a hatred of homosexuals and described the pleasure he derived from killing the two gay men. He had killed the German boy for no other reason than that he was aroused seeing him kissing his girlfriend. Michael Copeland appeared on trial at Birmingham Assizes in March 1965. He was found guilty of the three murders and sentenced to death. He escaped execution at a time when the death penalty was being discussed in Parliament. Hence, he was reprieved and sentenced to life imprisonment.

The Dracula Killer

The Dracula Killer began by torturing and killing animals and drinking their blood. Throughout his anguished life, Richard Chase was fascinated with blood, and fellow patients at the psychiatric institution where he spent some time in 1976 nicknamed him "Dracula".

After his release from psychiatric care, twenty-seven-year-old Chase lived with his mother in Sacramento, California. She ejected him from her home after he killed the family dog and he went to live in a rented apartment.

By now, Chase had graduated from animals to humans and on 29 December 1977, he shot and killed a man in the street using a pistol which he had recently acquired. On 23 January

1978, he committed a burglary and then moved to a nearby house where he shot dead the occupier, twenty-two-year-old Teresa Wallin. She was found by her husband when he returned home. The young woman had been shot in the head and eviscerated. Nearby was a yogurt pot containing blood. There was no evidence of burglary or robbery and the victim, who was three months pregnant, had not been raped.

Four days later, Evelyn Miroth, a single mother, and her six-year-old son were found shot dead in their home with her boyfriend, Danield Meredith, while a two-year-old boy, David Ferrara, whom they were looking after was missing. Miroth's body had been mutilated and two blood-stained knives were found on the floor. The bathtub was full of blood-stained water. The missing boy's body would be found two months later, gutted and headless, discarded in an alleyway.

Neighbourhood enquiries produced a report of a weird-looking man seen in the vicinity and a woman encountered him in a grocery store. He demanded that she give him a lift in her car. She recognized him as Richard Chase from the days when they attended the same school. Police headed for Chase's apartment and he opened the door to them. When he was searched, Danield Meredith's wallet was found in his back pocket.

The apartment was in a disgusting state and investigators found food blenders encrusted with blood and a box containing dog and cat collars. On one wall was a calendar with the date of Teresa Wallin's murder marked with the word "today". Forty-four other days were similarly marked. Under questioning, Chase was asked if he had committed the most recent murder. He admitted it and when asked why he had done it, he replied, "I did nothing wrong … I had to kill them to save my life." Asked to elaborate, he said, "I needed their blood."

The man whom newspapers now called "The Sacramento Vampire", was put on trial in San José in January 1979. There were real concerns that if he were found to be insane, Chase would be committed to a mental institution and at some time in the future would be freed. Chase testified in his own defence, admitting the killings and, as expected, pleading he was insane. There was clear evidence of premeditation in his crimes and psychiatric testimony was given describing him as paranoid and anti-social, but sane. The jury agreed and he was convicted of murder and sentenced to death.

Sent to San Quentin Penitentiary, Chase managed to accumulate a supply of anti-depressants prescribed on a daily prescription and, on 26 December 1980, took his own life.

Mad Butcher Of Kingsbury Run

A series of brutal murders between 1934 and 1938 turned Cleveland Ohio into a city of fear. Even the talents of legendary crime-buster Eliot Ness failed to solve the twelve grisly killings.

Kingsbury Run was a tract of wasteland in an industrial area on the edge of the city. It carried the railway lines to Pittsburgh, which in several places ran between steep embankments. The area was unkempt and strewn with litter and scruffy vegetation, which attracted hoboes and down-and-outs and also children seeking an adventure playground.

On 23 September 1935, two boys exploring this wasteland found two headless bodies lying among weeds in a clearing. The corpses were male, naked and evidently castrated. Police searches of the area turned up the missing genitalia where they had been thrown in the undergrowth. The severed heads were found planted in a railway embankment.

Post-mortem examination indicated that decapitation had been carried out with some skill and, possibly, while the victims were still alive. The younger of the two corpses, a man of around twenty-eight, was identified as Edward Andrassy, a petty criminal. With little firm evidence to guide it, the police investigation soon petered out.

Then, four months later, another mutilated corpse was found. The victim was soon identified as a local prostitute and again, dismemberment suggested some skilful knife work. "The Mad Butcher of Kingsbury Run" struck again on 6 June 1936 when boys playing in the area discovered an old pair of trousers and their curiosity was rewarded when the garment was found to be a wrapping for a severed head. The rest of the body lay close by. It was hoped to achieve identification by means of fingerprints and tattoos but neither produced results.

By now, the citizens of Cleveland were terrified by the horrors occurring on their doorstep. People were afraid and this was reflected in declining business for store-owners. Railway track inspectors felt vulnerable and would only work in teams. The police came in for criticism because of their inability to capture the "Mad Butcher". All that was known was that the killer selected his victims from the poorer members of the community, that both sexes were at risk and that males were castrated. A unifying factor in the murders was the killer's use of the knife, which suggested some practical knowledge of anatomy and butchery.

Eliot Ness, one of the so-called "Untouchables" who brought Al Capone to justice, was Cleveland's director of safety. He deployed unprecedented manpower in his attempts to solve the murders, but the killings went on, numbering at least twelve up to April 1938. The killing of a woman whose body was found on the shore of Lake Erie was the last, although five murders in Pittsburgh between 1939 and 1942 were also laid at the door of the "Mad Butcher".

In common with most of his victims, the murderer remained anonymous. It was rumoured that Eliot Ness had a secret suspect. This individual, believed to be Dr Francis Sweeney, initiated what amounted to a hate campaign against Ness, bombarding him with a stream of letters and postcards.

Sweeney was a practising physician in Cleveland and there is a well-documented record of his descent into alcoholism and mental illness. Crime writer James Jessen Badal comprehensively reviewed the evidence against Sweeney in his book on the murders published in 2001. Ness believed the doctor fitted the profile of the murderer and Badal thought his taunting of the authorities and obsessiveness conformed to our modern understanding of serial killers. It is fair to say though that the jury is still out on the identity of the "Mad Butcher".

Devil With Two Faces

"The Ogre of the Ardennes", as Michael Fourniret was called by the press, confessed to seven rape murders in France. He was aided by his wife, Monique Olivier, who procured his victims.

The deadly duo combined forces in 1987 when Fourniret was released from prison, having served a sentence for sexual assault. He advertised for a pen pal and Monique responded. They struck a deal whereby she would supply him with virgins to murder.

Fourniret was obsessed with the idea of virginity, claiming to have been traumatized when he discovered that his first wife betrayed him by not being a virgin bride. Their murder spree began in December 1987 when Monique stopped seventeen-year-old Isabella Lavike in Auxerre and asked for directions. The teenager responded by getting into Monique's vehicle to guide her. On the way, they stopped to pick up Fourniret, posing as a hitch-hiker. The girl was raped and murdered and her body thrown into a well. This modus operandi was successfully repeated with victims being variously strangled, shot and stabbed. Several of the bodies were buried in the grounds of Fourniret's house at Santou, near Sedan.

Monique was in thrall to the man she called "My Beast" and wrote to him saying, "It is with pleasure that I will execute your orders." Their exploits came to an end in 2003 following the attempted kidnapping of a seventeen-year-old girl in Belgium. The intended victim, bundled into the back of Fourniret's van, managed to break the binding around her wrists and escape.

Police identified the vehicle from the girl's description and found hair in it that matched the DNA of the girl who had been abducted and murdered earlier. First Monique confessed and then Fourniret. He showed no remorse and clearly believed himself to be a superior intellect. While in custody, he spent his time re-writing the works of some of France's classic authors.

The two were tried for murder at Charleville-Mézières. Fourniret demanded that the jurors should have been "virgins when they married". In court, lawyers described him as a "dangerous narcissistic pervert". The press had already called the duo a "Devil with two faces", a master and slave who raped and murdered at least seven girls aged between twelve and twenty-one over a twenty-year period. They were sentenced to life imprisonment following conviction at Charleville-Mézières in 2008.

The Easter Murder

A murderer taunted police by sending them coded messages that they could not decipher. He also left fingerprints at the crime scene, which were the only code detectives needed to catch him.

What became known as "The Easter Murder" occurred at Burnage near Manchester in the UK in April 1962. A neighbour noticed that the door to William Nelson's flat had been open for a couple of days and, fearing that something might have happened to him, called for help. The forty-eight-year-old railway telegraphist was found dead in his bed. His body was covered with bedclothes and, when these were drawn back, it was revealed that he had been severely bludgeoned about the head.

The pathologist determined that he had been struck nine times with a heavy implement probably while he lay asleep. There were some curious features at the crime scene. Apart from thumbprints on the bedhead, there were unusual blood patterns on the sheet and a clear palm print on the pillow. The person who left the handprint had distinctive lines on the palm, which when impressed with blood on the pillow formed an "E" shape.

William Nelson was an old soldier and it was surmised that he might have taken an old army mate back to his flat who robbed and killed him. Not much headway was made by detectives until 23 June when a letter was received at police headquarters in Manchester. This was written in code and referred to the murder of William Nelson. A few days later, another communication was received, comprising a detailed plan of "The flat of the late William Nelson". Clearly the murderer was playing a game with the police.

On 13 August, a man calling himself Frank and plainly drunk, dialled 999 and was put through to police HQ. He taunted officers with the boast, "I did it. Come and get me. . ." The call was traced to a phone booth at Manchester's Piccadilly Station and minutes later, the caller, Frank Goodman, was in custody.

His fingerprints were taken and found to match those left at the crime scene. Twenty-two-year-old Goodman, an unemployed fitter, said he met Nelson in a pub and the old soldier took him back to his flat. Goodman admitted killing him. He also decoded his message, which amounted to another confession to attempted murder. Two weeks before he killed Nelson, he attacked a man on a train, robbed him and threw him out of the carriage. The victim of this attack was Dennis Cronin who had ended up in hospital with severe head injuries.

A search of Goodman's home yielded the murder weapon, which proved to be a long, heavy threaded bolt. It was this implement that had left the unusual bloodstains at the scene of William Nelson's murder. The palm print with its "E" shape impression proved to be a virtual signature as far as Goodman was concerned.

He was charged with murder and appeared at Manchester Crown Court in December 1962. He pleaded not guilty to capital murder but guilty to murder. The distinction lay in changes in the law abolishing the death penalty for most types of murder but the ultimate penalty still applied for capital murder which included killing in the furtherance of theft.

The hearing lasted two minutes and Goodman was sentenced to life imprisonment. The charge of attempted murder was not pursued. Dennis Cronin died of his injuries three years after he had been attacked.

Wedding Night Killer

Basil Laitner was a wealthy solicitor and his wife, Avril, was a medical practitioner. Basil and Avril Laitner celebrated the marriage of their eldest daughter on 24 October 1983 with a reception held in a marquee at their home in Dore, Sheffield, in the UK.

Just hours after the guests had left, the Laitners and their son Richard were stabbed to death. Their eighteen-year-old daughter, Nicola, was raped but otherwise unharmed and was able to give police a description of her attacker. He was a man already known to the police who had escaped custody while attending Selby magistrates court a month previously.

Arthur Hutchinson was charged with alleged offences of rape and theft. During the course of his escape at Selby he had cut himself. This was to prove significant for detectives investigating the murders at Sheffield. Hutchinson had a rare blood group and blood of the same type was found on the bed in the room where Nicola had been assaulted. Also, his palm print was found on a champagne bottle in the wedding reception marquee and, if further evidence was needed of his presence in the house, it was provided by his teeth. He had taken a bite out of a piece of cheese in the Laitner's refrigerator, leaving an identifiable dental impression.

Forty-three-year-old Hutchinson was a man with a colourful lifestyle. One of a family of eight born in Durham, he had worked as a trainee miner, farm labourer and as an entertainer at circuses and fairgrounds. He had been married twice and had a record of offences involving indecent assault and theft. His life was that of a petty criminal and he was known as a man with a strong sexual appetite.

He tried to evade capture after the murders by keeping on the move, travelling from one northern town to another. He also changed his hairstyle to alter his appearance. The police finally caught up with him at Hartlepool where he was arrested on 5 November 1983. He commented to officers, "I should have stayed in my fox-hole, shouldn't I?" He denied being at the Laitner's house and denied the killings.

"The Wedding Night Killer", as he had been called by the press, was sent for trial at Durham Crown Court in September 1984. He told a fanciful story, relating that he had met Nicola Laitner in a public house in Sheffield two nights before the murders. She invited him back to the house after the wedding reception and he alleged that she willingly responded to his sexual advances. He left at about 11.00 p.m. but returned later because he had left his coat behind. On entering the house, he said he was attacked by Nicola wielding a knife who explained that her parents had been killed by intruders.

Defence counsel claimed that Hutchinson lied repeatedly because he thought it would protect his innocence. Nicola Laitner denied that she had invited him to her home. She said she heard her mother's screams and then the intruder came into her bedroom and said, "Scream and you're dead." He ordered her downstairs and into the marquee where he handcuffed her and committed rape.

The jury took four hours to consider their verdict and decided unanimously that Hutchinson was guilty on all charges. The man in the dock showed no emotion on hearing the verdict. Mr Justice McNeill told him that he was, ". . . arrogant, manipulative, had a self-centred attitude towards life, and a severe personality disorder which is not amenable to any form of treatment." He sentenced him to life imprisonment and recommended that he should serve at least eighteen years.

The apparently lenient sentence provoked fierce headlines in the tabloid press. The *Sun* led with, "Only 18 Years! Storm as wedding massacre monster gets soft sentence." The Chairman of the Police Federation described the sentence as "far too low for the atrocious crimes committed". One question that was not resolved was Hutchinson's motive. It was suggested that he acted as he did against a wealthy family because he was an individual who had struggled and achieved very little in his life.

". . . Beyond Good And Evil"

The "Night Stalker" terrorized Los Angeles in 1985, leaving a trail of rape and murder in his wake. His calling card was a scrawled satanic symbol left at the crime scene, denoting that he was a devil worshipper.

In six months, this man had murdered thirteen times and raped eleven other victims. The killer chose suburban locations close to main roads and struck at night when his victims were asleep; a modus operandi that earned him the title of "Night Stalker". He gained entry to apartments through unlocked windows or insecure doors. He countered any possible resistance by killing male occupants before sexually assaulting their female partners.

The stalker's killing methods were brutal, including, throat-cutting, multiple stabbing, shooting and mutilation. A number of victims survived and told police of a black-clad intruder with a gaunt face and rotten teeth. He frequently made reference to the devil and told one victim to, "Swear upon Satan that you won't scream for help."

Fearful citizens began to arm themselves, buying guard-dogs and installing surveillance equipment. Perhaps because of increased security, the "Night Stalker" travelled to San Francisco in August 1985 and continued his killing there. He kept on the move and attacked a woman in her apartment in a small township south of Los Angeles and shot her partner. By a stroke of luck, his assault victim spotted him leaving the area in a rusting orange-coloured Toyota car.

Identification of this car proved to be the undoing of the "Night Stalker". It was found abandoned and detectives were able to get fingerprints from it. Within hours, the serial killer was identified from police records as twenty-five-year-old Richard Ramirez. Mug-shots of the stalker soon appeared on television screens and in newspaper reports.

On 31 August, Ramirez was spotted by an alert member of the public in a liquor store in a Los Angeles suburb. A hue and cry ensued and the killer was chased through streets and gardens before being overpowered by a construction worker. When the police arrived, Ramirez, fearing for his life, asked them, "Save me before they kill me." He was arrested and taken away as an angry mob bayed for blood. He also said to the officer who arrested him, "Shoot me, man – kill me. I don't deserve to live."

It took four years before the judicial system was ready to put Ramirez on trial. In September 1989, he smirked and sneered at the testimony given by some of his victims. He appeared before the court showing his palm on which was marked an inverted pentagram, his symbol of devil worship, and, at times, shouting, "Heil Satan".

On 20 September, Ramirez was found guilty on various counts; thirteen murders and numerous felonies including rape, sodomy and burglary. Before being sentenced, he told the judge, "I am beyond your experience. I am beyond good and evil, legions of the night breed – repeat not the errors of the Night Prowler and show no mercy." He received twelve death sentences and life sentences of imprisonment of over a hundred years. He joined the other death row inmates in California's penal system where no death sentence has been carried out for nearly twenty years. Meanwhile, the "Night Stalker" receives offers of marriage from women who admire his sweet nature.

The Diabolical Lovers

A Belgian couple, Peter Uwe Schmitt and Aurore Martin, conspired to murder each other's spouses and collect the insurance money.

Their diabolical pact began to unravel with the death in 1995 of Marc Van Beers, Martin's husband. While the couple were on honeymoon in Corsica, their car went off the road and into a deep ravine, killing Van Beers, while Martin miraculously survived. She claimed to have been thrown clear of the vehicle moments before it plunged into the ravine.

Martin moved quickly to cash in insurance worth £400,000. Her insistence that her husband's body be cremated raised suspicions. Examination of the body showed that he had been bludgeoned to death before the car went over the ravine. It also appeared that insurance documents had been forged.

Investigators discovered that Schmitt, who was Martin's lover, had lost his wife in remarkably similar circumstances in 1992. A few months after they were married, Ursula Deschamps lost her life when her car plunged into a canal and she was drowned. Her husband Peter had a remarkable escape when he swam free from the sinking car.

His claim was not without suspicion, chiefly on account of the fact that his clothes were remarkably dry. Schmitt was charged with involuntary homicide and he served two months of a suspended sentence. Meanwhile, he scooped £280,000 from his late wife's insurance and went to live with his lover, Aurore Martin, in Florida.

The couple, known in the US as the "honeymoon killers", were extradited to Belgium in 1998. They protested their innocence. They were tried for the murder of Marc Van Beers at a hearing in Brussels. Prosecutors contended that Schmitt was in Corsica at the same time as Aurore and Marc and that he paid to have Van Beers beaten up.

But for Aurore's insistence on a cremation, they might have got away with this crime. When the circumstances of Schmitt's wife's untimely death became known, comparisons were inevitable. In both cases, separated by three years, the spouse was murdered and the body placed in a car. The first sank beneath the water of a canal and the second disappeared over a ravine. And, in both instances, the passenger had a miraculous escape from death.

With insurance payouts totalling hundreds of thousands of pounds, Schmitt and Martin, "the Diabolical Lovers", went off to live in America and lead a life of luxury. Schmitt had been married a few months when he disposed of his wife, and Martin was on honeymoon when her husband was eliminated. Schmitt, aged thirty-one, was sentenced to twenty years imprisonment and Martin, one year older, was jailed for fifteen years.

Granite Woman And Lover Boy

Ruth Snyder and Henry Judd Gray created sensational headlines in the New York newspapers in 1927 as their trial for murder progressed. They were referred to as "The Granite Woman" and "Lover Boy".

Thirty-two-year-old Ruth Snyder was trapped in an unhappy marriage to Albert Snyder, thirteen years her senior and a dull, if successful man. Ruth yearned for excitement and her chance came when she met Henry Judd Gray in New

York. He was a corset salesman and, like Ruth, was unhappily married.

Ruth and Judd met clandestinely in hotel rooms for nearly two years. This was not quite the life she wanted so she hatched a plan whereby she would be both rich and free of marital encumbrance. Her idea was to insure her husband for a large sum and then murder him.

Judd was, to say the least, apprehensive about the scheme and he turned to drink to ease the pressure Ruth put him under. But she nagged him constantly and when he declined to co-operate she tried her hand at poisoning husband Albert. She failed in these attempts, so kept up the pressure on Judd to fulfil her wishes. "What are you trying to do?" he asked. "Kill the poor guy," replied Ruth.

Finally, his resolve broke and he agreed to eliminate Albert Snyder whom Ruth had insured for $96,000. On 19 March 1927, fortified with generous doses of whisky, Judd entered the Snyder household and waited in the dark until Ruth and Albert returned from a party. While Albert, the worse for drink, retired for the night, Ruth and Judd engaged in love-making in the spare room where she had thoughtfully laid out the implements of murder, including a heavy sash-weight, chloroform and picture wire.

Once they had sated their sexual appetites, Ruth took Judd into the bedroom where her husband lay sleeping. Taking the sash weight, Judd smashed it down on Albert's head. He was only stunned and began shouting and struggling with his attacker. Ruth responded by hitting him again with the sash weight. Still he did not succumb, so the chloroform and picture wire were brought into use, and he finally expired.

The deadly duo faked a robbery and Ruth was bound and gagged which was how she was found when the alarm was raised next morning. She told police she had been attacked by a prowler and several items had been stolen. When these same articles were found hidden about the house, suspicions started to form. Judd Gray's name was recorded in her address book. When the police used the ploy that he had been arrested, Ruth was tricked into a confession.

Under questioning, Ruth said that they had plotted to kill her husband but that she had not struck a single blow. Weak-kneed Judd admitted his part in the plot and said, "She told me what to do and I did it."

The pair were put on trial in New York in April 1927 and it turned out to be a major attraction. Many celebrities of the day took seats in the public gallery and the press were well represented. "The Granite Woman", as she was now called, attempted to shift blame on to "Lover Boy". Judd's defence played the hapless male card. The poor man was drawn into the spider's web, weakened by her passionate entreaties. The jury took an hour and a half to bring in a guilty verdict and Snyder and Gray were sentenced to death.

Their appeals were dismissed and while waiting on Death Row, each wrote an autobiography. Ruth Snyder received over 160 offers of marriage from men who clearly wished to bring some excitement into their lives. "Lover Boy" and "The Granite Woman" were executed within a few minutes of each other at Sing Sing Prison on 12 January 1928. The last act in a bizarre case came in the form of a photograph taken of Ruth as she died in the electric chair. This was the work of a newspaper reporter who secretly recorded her moment of death using a camera strapped to his ankle. This was published on the front page of the *New York Daily News* under the headline, "Dead!"

The Tourist From Hell

John Martin Scripps was an international criminal and opportunist who travelled the world's airways in search of human prey, earning him the name, "The Tourist From Hell".

Scripps was jailed for drug offences in the UK in 1987 and 1991 and, on both occasions, managed to abscond from custody. While in Albany Prison on the Isle of Wight he learned the butchery trade and acquired skills that he put to use when he later graduated to serial killing.

In early March 1995, Scripps was staying in Singapore where he befriended a visiting South African, Gerard Lowe, and offered to share a hotel room. As others would find to their cost, Lowe was charmed by the tall, smiling Englishman, and agreed to his proposal to save money.

The next morning, the hotel security guard observed Scripps leaving the hotel carrying a heavy suitcase. Scripps returned, minus the bag, to check out, explaining that Lowe had left earlier. Two days later, dismembered body parts appeared in the sea near Clifford Pier. Scars enabled police to identify the victim as thirty-three-year-old Gerard Lowe and they learned that he had been staying at a hotel in a shared room. It also appeared that large sums of money had been withdrawn from his account using his credit card.

An alert was put out for the smiling Englishman who had travelled to Thailand and was foolish enough to return to Singapore on 19 March when he fell into the arms of waiting police. His luggage contained a stun-gun, hand-cuffs, a hammer and numerous knives. Also in his possession were passports and credit cards belonging to a Canadian mother and son, Sheila and Darin Dalmude.

The Dalmudes had travelled on the same flight as Scripps to Bangkok on 11 March. Their dismembered remains were found in the Phuket area later the same month.

Once in custody, the full extent of Scripps's criminal activities became evident. In addition to murders committed in Thailand and Singapore, he was believed to have killed a British tourist in Mexico in 1994. His criminal career spanned thirteen years and three continents. He used his mild-mannered charm to offer friendship to people he met on his travels and then resorted to brutal murder to plunder their bank accounts.

Scripps was tried in Singapore in November 1995 for the murder of Gerard Lowe. He admitted killing the South African but claimed he did so out of anger when the man who was his room-mate made a homosexual advance. After he murdered Lowe with hammer blows to the head, he used his victim's credit card to draw cash and, among other purchases, bought a ticket to a symphony concert.

The "Tourist from Hell" was found guilty and sentenced to death. Scripps appealed against the sentence but then withdrew it. In February he instructed his lawyer not to appeal for clemency. He said he was "impatient" for the execution to proceed and was angry that the legal formalities were so protracted. On 19 April 1996, his wish was granted when he was hanged at Changi Prison, the first Briton to be executed for murder in Singapore.

The Poisoner From Windy Nook

After the fourth unexpected death with which she had been associated, sixty-six-year-old Mary Wilson joked with the undertaker and suggested he might quote her a wholesale price for funerals.

Red-haired Mary Wilson lived at Windy Nook, near Felling in County Durham, in the UK. In her younger days, she had been in service to a local family and married the son. An avid reader of popular romantic magazines, she also yearned for money.

Growing tired of her husband after forty-three years of marriage she had taken a lover, a man who lodged with her employer. Within a few months, both he and her husband died, seemingly of natural causes. The doctor who examined them suspected nothing sinister. They were elderly and the fact that the two deaths had occurred close together merited no more than passing comment. Mary Wilson benefited from the deaths to the tune of less than fifty pounds.

In 1957, she met a retired estate agent, seventy-five-year-old Oliver Leonard, whom she persuaded to move in with her. They were married in September and, two weeks later, Leonard became ill with breathing problems and died. Again, nothing unusual was suspected and Mary collected another fifty pounds.

Her next move was to approach Ernest Wilson, a retired engineer, who was looking for a housekeeper. In no time at all, Mary was hired, moved in with Wilson and marriage followed. At the wedding reception, she joked with the caterer about saving any leftover cakes as "they will come in handy for the funeral". Two weeks later Ernest Wilson was dead, supposedly of cardiac failure.

When the undertaker called to measure his body for a coffin, Mary, still in jocular mood, said that as she had put so much work his way, he might consider giving her a wholesale price.

Post-mortem examinations were carried out on both Leonard and Wilson. In neither case was death from natural causes confirmed. What was found was that both had died of phosphorus poisoning. Mary Wilson was charged with murder.

At her trial, prosecution expert witnesses expressed the view that rat or beetle poison containing phosphorus had been administered, most likely in tea. Countering this was a suggestion that the two men had been taking pills to stimulate their sex drive, which had the effect of hastening their demise. This produced laughter in court.

Mary Wilson came to trial in 1958 at a time when the death penalty had been revised under the provisions of the Homicide Act, 1957. The death sentence was retained in five classes of capital murder and in cases where a person had twice committed murder. She did not give evidence and the jury returned guilty verdicts. She avoided a death sentence on account of her age and was sentenced to life imprisonment. She died in prison four years later.

Following her trial, inquests were carried out on the death of her former husband and that of her one-time lover. In both cases, phosphorus poisoning was confirmed as the cause of death, thereby bringing the Poisoner from Windy Nook's tally of victims to four.

CHAPTER 9

Contract and Conspiracy

The idea of contract murders originated in the US during the 1930s in the gangland world of Murder Inc. When the mob bosses wanted to eliminate someone who was a threat or a rival, or who had simply outlived their usefulness, a contract was issued to a middleman or broker who hired the hit man. This arrangement meant that the puppet master was completely insulated from the eventual killing. Murder management of this kind ensured that very few gangland killings were ever solved.

The concept of the contracted or hired killer readily translated into the general domain, especially for those with wealth and power. If the gangland bosses could hire people to do their killing for them, why not others who saw murder as a convenient way of solving problems and eliminating those who stood in their way?

Dr Karl Menninger, the eminent US psychiatrist, put it succinctly in the context of capital punishment when he wrote that if the state can justify hiring someone to do its killing why shouldn't powerful people do the same?

The hired killer is usually a person who is a stranger to his targeted victim and operates to a preconceived plan dispassionately and with ruthless efficiency. The victim, perceiving no threat or danger, is caught off-guard. The killer strikes, is meticulous about not leaving traces and disappears.

In what might be called the domestic sector, as opposed to the world of organized crime, the desire to eliminate an unwanted wife, husband or lover may reach a point where hiring a contract killer is seen as a favourable option. Among the advantages are that the hirer keeps their hands clean and may feel this lessens the guilt. In such plans, the middleman is often dispensed with and the contract agreed directly between procurer and operator. The exchange of the necessary co-ordinates to identify the victim and a down-payment are all that is required. This strategy, though, can lead to bungled results as Elizabeth Duncan discovered in 1958 when she hired two young men to kill her daughter-in-law. The plot began to unravel when she defaulted on payment.

Payment was not a problem for billionaire property developer, Hisham Talaat Mousafa, who wished to dispose of his girlfriend. He paid $2 million to one of his employees in 2008 to kill his former lover. The scheme foundered on the inexperience of the hitman and a trial which led directly to his pay-master.

Hired killers acting as part of a conspiracy acquire greater protection. Where a powerful organization, such as a government, is involved, the contract comes with benefits. Organization and planning resources are there to ensure a successful outcome. The unsolved murder of Georgi Markov in London in 1978 was achieved by a combination of sophisticated technique and toxic agent. Echoes of his death were apparent in the fatal poisoning of Alexander Litvinenko, again in London, in 2006, using Polonium 210 as the lethal agent. In both cases, dissidents of East European regimes were eliminated by means that indicated the kind of expertise and resources only available to governments.

The same criteria applied to the unsolved killing of the popular British broadcaster, Jill Dando, in 1999. She was gunned down on her own doorstep with a single custom-made bullet in an execution-style killing. Her murder suggested sophisticated planning beyond the scope of a mere stalker. There is a likelihood that all these murders will remain unsolved as the high-level conspirators enjoy the same protection as Murder Inc.

Conspiracy and cover-up go together, as alleged in the Vatican murder in 1998 when the commander of the Swiss Guard was shot dead. A similar fate awaited Dr Gerald Bull, inventor of the supergun, when he visited Belgium in 1990, and the mysterious death of God's Banker, Roberto Calvi, in London in 1982 is blurred by ambiguity.

One reason why conspiracy theories take root is that only organizations or governments with international scope can reach

out to finger their targets in distant places. Even when compelling
evidence is available, as in the poisoning of Alexander Litvinenko,
high-level denial disarms further enquiry. The truth will emerge in
the jurisdiction of future generations.

Mother's Boy

Elizabeth Duncan, to all outward purposes, was a prim, caring
mother in her fifties. She doted on her son, Frank, a twenty-
nine-year-old lawyer. He was Mama's little boy and she did
not want him to leave home. She told him that if he married
"some girl" she would get rid of her.

When Frank met attractive Olga Kupezyk, who worked
in Santa Barbara, California as a hospital nurse, his mother
took an instant dislike to the young woman. For months, she
harassed Olga with threatening telephone calls and told her,
"I will kill you before you ever marry my son." Despite this,
marry they did but Frank was too scared to tell his mother.
When she found out, she heightened the war of nerves to the
extent that Olga was forced to change her address twice.

Duncan even paid a window-cleaner to pose as Frank
and seek an annulment of the marriage. When this failed,
she resumed her threatening telephone calls, pursuing Olga
wherever she moved. She told her daughter-in-law, "If you
don't leave him alone, I'll kill you."

Following this unequivocal threat, Duncan began shopping
around for a contract killer. She approached a Mexican café
owner for help on the grounds that her son had given the lady
legal representation to fight an immigration case. Esperanza
Esquirel thought she knew "two boys" who might be able to help.

Duncan met the two young men, both in their early
twenties, at the café to discuss strategy and terms. They were
unemployed and willing to consider her proposition to dispose
of Olga. They agreed a contract of $6,000 to kill her and
Duncan warned them, "You better watch out, she's a pretty
strong girl."

On 17 November 1958, the hired killers appeared at Olga's
apartment where they kidnapped the seven months pregnant

nurse and drove out to the mountains some thirty miles from Santa Barbara. They bludgeoned her into unconsciousness and buried her, possibly alive, in a roadside culvert.

When the contract killers demanded payment, Duncan told them she had run out of funds but gave them a few hundred dollars. In the meantime, Olga was reported missing and the investigative trail soon led to Duncan. When questioned, she claimed that the Mexicans were blackmailing her and threatening her life.

The two killers, Moya and Balonado, were arrested and a confession was soon on the table. They admitted taking turns in strangling and hitting Olga with a rock for, as Duncan had predicted, the young woman put up fierce resistance. They put her body in a culvert and directed investigators where to find it. They also detailed their difficulties in extracting payment from Duncan.

Elizabeth Duncan and her two hired killers were tried for murder. They were convicted and sentenced to death. After all appeals were exhausted they died in the gas chamber at San Quentin Prison on 8 August 1962. Duncan protested her innocence and her last words were, "Where is Frank?"

"Knives Have Been Sharpened"

The arrest in 2008 of forty-nine-year-old Hisham Talaat Mousafa caused a stir when he was charged in connection with the death of a popular Lebanese singer. Thirty-year-old Susanne Tamin rose to stardom in Lebanon in 1996 after she appeared on a TV talent show. But with fame came troubles after she separated from her husband/manager and became embroiled in legal disputes.

Tamin and Mousafa, who was married, became lovers but when their relationship began to fracture, she tried to escape by travelling first to London and then to Dubai. Ironically, her last hit song, was called, "Lovers". It was in Dubai that she met her death in July 2008. Her body was found in her apartment where she had died from multiple stab wounds and a cut throat.

Investigators discovered that Tamin had been trailed to

Dubai by Mohsen el-Sukkary, a former Egyptian security officer who worked at one of Mousafa's Cairo hotels. It was claimed that El-Sukkary had followed the singer to her apartment and gained admittance by posing as a representative of the building's owners.

Mousafa denied any involvement but was accused of participating in murder by inciting and assisting El-Sukkary. Transcripts of phone calls allegedly made by Mousafa were published in the Egyptian media, in one of which he directed El-Sukkary, "OK, let's finish with this." Mousafa was stripped of his immunity from prosecution as a member of the National Democratic Party and committed for trial.

Although the murder was committed in Dubai, the trial was held in Egypt, which does not permit extradition of its citizens. While in custody awaiting trial, Mousafa wrote to a Cairo newspaper complaining that he was being pursued by people who envied his success. "Knives have been sharpened," he wrote.

The trial proved controversial when the judge imposed an order prohibiting reporting and banning the public from proceedings. This followed publication of pictures of the murder victim as she was found lying dead in her apartment.

The prosecution argued that Mousafa had paid El-Sukkary to kill his lover. Evidence supporting the charge came from CCTV footage at the crime scene and recordings of telephone conversations. There was also linking DNA evidence from the hit man's blood-stained clothing discarded in a nearby rubbish bin.

The guilty verdict delivered by the court and pronouncement of death sentences on both men was received with shock and surprise by the Egyptian public, which had grown used to the idea that wealthy individuals could contrive to be unaccountable.

The Umbrella Murder

"I've got a horrible suspicion that this has got something to do with something that happened today . . ." Thus did Georgi Markov explain to his wife the illness that had struck him down. On 7 September 1978, while walking to his work at BBC Bush House in London, Markov felt a sharp jab in his right leg. Turning round, he saw a man with an umbrella who apologised in a foreign accent and hailed a taxi. Four days later Markov died at St James Hospital, Balham.

Following the incident on Waterloo Bridge, the Bulgarian broadcaster completed his shift and returned home about 10:30. In the early hours of the following morning, he experienced vomiting, had a high temperature and flu-like symptoms. By the time he reached hospital, his red cell blood count was 33,000 per ml, the highest doctors there had seen.

Markov was the victim of what became known as "The Umbrella Murder". At the coroner's inquest, expert evidence was given that a tiny platinum pellet measuring 1.52mm had been recovered from his leg. This was the vehicle for implanting a lethal dose of ricin, a little understood and rare poison, into his body. Experts in bacteriological warfare said that ricin, extracted from castor oil seeds, was one of the five most toxic substances known. One thousandth of a gram was enough to kill an adult.

Knowledge of Markov's background as an anti-Communist dissident was taken into account as a possible motive for murder. Information about ricin and its toxic properties was kept by defence establishments in Britain and the US. In 1970, the World Health Organisation had warned about the dangers of ricin as a possible warfare agent. It was agreed that manufacturing the platinum pellet implanted in the victim's leg would have required special skills. Somewhat chillingly, it was noted that a similar attack had been made on a Bulgarian defector in Paris who had survived.

The coroner's inquest brought in a verdict of unlawful killing. Meanwhile, the newspapers hummed with stories of cold-war killings and international espionage. Scotland Yard made no progress in finding the attacker and the taxi-driver who allegedly took the killer away from the scene did not respond to calls for information. The Bulgarian Embassy in London simply stated that they had no knowledge about the attacks in London and Paris.

In 1991, a story surfaced that the disgraced Bulgarian dictator, Todov Zhivkov, would be charged with Markov's murder following the overthrow of the Communist state. There were reports that key files had gone missing and Scotland Yard officers went to Sofia to assist enquiries. The following year, a former Bulgarian general was jailed for destroying documents.

In 1993, an ex-KGB man visiting London was questioned by police. He was said to have known that the Bulgarians had requested technical assistance from the KGB in 1978. After a flurry of stories about the continuing cold-war legacy, the news died away again. In 1997 Scotland Yard said that the case was still open. The identity of Georgi Markov's assassin remains a mystery but in June 2008 Scotland Yard detectives travelled to Bulgaria in an attempt to solve the case before Bulgaria's thirty-year statute of limitations expired.

Polonium Trail

The death in London of Alexander Litvinenko in 2006 from a rare poison brought back memories of *The Umbrella Murder* carried out twenty-eight years previously.

Litvinenko, a former KGB officer, defected in 2000 and came to live in London. He was apparently working on a story about Anna Politkovskaya, the Russian journalist and critic of President Putin, who was shot dead in Moscow in October 2006. On 1 November, Litvinenko met two Russians in a London hotel and later the same day talked to an Italian academic about Politkovskaya at a sushi bar.

After this meeting, Litvinenko felt unwell and came to believe that he had been poisoned. He was taken to hospital and guards were placed outside his room. He was jaundiced, lost his hair and declined rapidly. Initial thoughts that he had been poisoned with thallium gave way to the view that he had ingested a radioactive substance. Photographs of the dying man lying in his hospital bed were published in the national press. Hours before he died on 23 November, Polonium 210 was discovered in his urine.

Toxicologists said that small amounts of Polonium 210 were to be found in the natural environment but larger amounts would be needed to create a fatal dose for a human being. This indicated a man-made source and the use of sophisticated technology. Traces of radiation were detected at Litvinenko's home as well as at the hotel and sushi bar that he had visited. What had been viewed as an unexplained death now took a more sinister turn and there was talk of a political assassination.

Theories on the motive abounded, ranging from self-administered poison to embarrass the Russian government to an act of state terrorism to eliminate a critic. In December 2006, Scotland Yard announced that Litvinenko's death was being treated as a murder enquiry.

Toxicologists described Polonium 210 as a designer poison pill created by nanotechnology. It is colourless, odourless and transparent. Ingestion of the poison, probably in liquid form, leads to irreparable damage to the body's organs and bone marrow. The substance emits alpha radiation, which is not detected by airport security scanners. As the investigation proceeded, traces of Polonium 210 were found in a trail from Moscow to London, including a British Airways plane that had brought the suspected hit man to London.

Andrei Lugovoi, a former KGB agent, was one of the businessmen Litvinenko met in London. The Foreign Office requested his extradition from Russia. The Director of Public Prosecutions believed the evidence was sufficient to bring a charge of murder. In May 2007, the Russian authorities refused and there were some tense diplomatic exchanges between the two countries.

The facts were that a murder had occurred on British soil involving poisoning with a dangerous substance. Three thousand scientists and health officials worked on the follow up to Litvinenko's death. Over 700 people were tested for radiation and seventeen were found to be contaminated. The circumstances of Litvinenko's death remain unsolved.

A Signature Bullet

Described as the nation's favourite television broadcaster, Jill Dando was shot dead on the doorstep of her London home on 26 April 1999. Her murder was a high-profile crime and the chilling manner in which it was carried out shocked the public.

The thirty-seven-year-old presenter of BBC television's *Crimewatch* programme returned to her home in Fulham, London, after shopping locally. She was killed with a single shot fired at close range to the head. The close discharge of the weapon muffled the noise of the shot but eyewitnesses saw a man running down the street after the incident.

The silent nature of the shooting, the custom-made bullet fired from a smooth-bore weapon in an execution-style killing led to speculation about the perpetrator's motive. The weapon was never recovered but the spent cartridge case found at the crime scene indicated a 9mm semi-automatic handgun firing a "signature" bullet. This led to suggestions that Jill Dando might have been murdered in an underworld revenge attack as the result of one of the crime probes which she pursued on television. Other theories were that she was killed by a lone stalker or by a politically-motivated hit man.

Rewards were offered for information that would lead to the killer and, just over a year after the murder, the police arrested an unemployed man who lived less than half a mile from Dando's home. He was forty-seven-year-old Barry George, a man with a history of personality disorder. He was a fantasist who had learned to use weapons at a gun club.

The evidence linking George to the shooting consisted of a minute particle of firearm residue lodged on his coat, which was similar to forensic traces found on the victim. This piece of evidence was controversial and remained so throughout Barry George's trial and re-trial.

Pleading his innocence, he was tried at the Old Bailey in 2001. The particle of firearm residue was crucial to the prosecution case, especially as eyewitnesses who had seen a man running in the street after the shooting did not pick out George on an identity parade. Doubts were voiced about his ability to carry out an execution-style killing using a customized weapon. Nevertheless, on 2 July 2001, by a majority verdict, he was found guilty and sentenced to life imprisonment.

While there might have been satisfaction in some quarters that the killer of a high-profile personality had been brought to justice, there were concerns elsewhere about the safety of the verdict. George's appeal was heard in August 2002 and dismissed. A commentator at the time remarked that it was a prosecution in which there was no murder weapon, no witness to the shooting, no confession and no motive.

Consistently claiming his innocence, George won the right to a retrial. This took place at the Old Bailey in June 2008. The jury was told that he was a man fascinated with guns and in the habit of stalking local women. During questioning by the police he had made no secret of his fantasies which included pretending to be a member of the SAS and using the names of various personalities.

It was acknowledged that George had a personality disorder and he also suffered from epilepsy. He was supported in court by a clinical psychologist who helped him to understand the proceedings. When the judge rejected the case for the forensic evidence based on the gunshot particle, the prosecution argued on the basis of circumstantial evidence. After deliberating for two days, the jury brought in a not guilty verdict and after eight years in prison, Barry George was a free man. That re-ignited the question, "Who killed Jill Dando?" One of the theories was that a Serbian hit man was sent to London to exact revenge for the NATO bombing of the Radio Television Serbia building in Belgrade on 23 April 1999.

Murder In The Vatican

Five shots were fired in the Vatican on 4 May 1998, but no one heard them apart from the victims. Captain Alois Esterman, Commander of the Swiss Guard, and his wife, Gladys Meza Romero, were shot dead. A third fatality was Lance-Corporal Cedric Tornay who had also been shot.

The Vatican semi-official daily, *L'Osservatore Romano*,

published a report of the shootings on its front page. Pope John Paul II wrote a letter of condolence to Captain Esterman's parents. The official line was that Tornay, in a "fit of madness", shot Esterman and his wife and then committed suicide. His motive was that his superior had denied him the award of a medal to which he was entitled. Tornay left a letter for his mother which mentioned the refusal to give him the medal.

This quick explanation led to a great deal of comment and controversy. Conspiracy theories abounded. There were suggestions that Esterman had been killed as part of a power struggle inside the Vatican and that evidence had been tampered with. One theory had it that Tornay was made a victim by conspirators who killed him and placed his body in the Esterman's apartment to stage a double-murder followed by a suicide.

Stories circulated that Tornay was gay and in a relationship with Esterman. This led to opposition to Esterman's appointment as head of the hundred-strong corps of Swiss Guards. He was told to reject Tornay whose response was one of revenge. Other theories were that Esterman had worked for the Stasi, East Germany's secret intelligence service, and had been caught up in the murky world of spying. For good measure, there were allegations about rivalries and bullying in the Swiss Guard barracks. One thing that all these theories had in common was a lack of corroborating evidence.

The Vatican report in February 1999 mentioned that Tornay had a cyst on the brain that affected his behaviour. Tornay, a Swiss national, had been buried in Martigny. His mother had already shed doubt on the authenticity of the letter she received from her son in which he said he had been refused his medal, the only thing he really wanted. In 2002, Tornay's mother released details of a new post-mortem carried out in Lausanne. This recorded that there was no cyst on the brain and claimed that he had not committed suicide. He had been killed by a 7mm bullet, not the usual calibre issued to the Swiss Guards. This inspired newspaper headlines proclaiming, "Not suicide but assassination".

There was a flurry of books building on some of the theories about the three deaths. Then, in 2005, lawyers acting for Tornay's mother petitioned the Swiss courts to open a murder enquiry. Despite the Vatican's efforts to close the case, the events of 4 May 1998 remain open to explanation.

Supergun

As he stepped out of the lift to walk to his sixth-floor apartment on the evening of 22 March 1990, Dr Gerald Bull was shot dead. An assassin fired five bullets into the back of his head. No one at 28 Avenue François Folie in Brussels heard the shots. The assassin was never caught.

Bull's body was found by a woman friend visiting him that evening for dinner. When the news broke, there was a flurry of diplomatic activity and excitement among the intelligence agencies of several countries. Dr Bull, a Canadian engineer and innovator, was the controversial designer of a supergun with an immense range.

Within weeks of Bull's death, British newspapers were full of stories about parts for a supergun manufactured by British firms and destined to be shipped to Iraq. Metal tubes had been loaded aboard a freighter at Tees Dock for shipment to the port of Qasr in Iraq. HM Customs and MI6 were involved in enquiries and documents were seized from the engineering companies that had manufactured the tubes. Some experts believed these were components for a 40-metre gun barrel, while Iraqi sources said they were simply pipes for the petro-chemical industry.

The House of Commons staged an ill-tempered debate on the issue and there were claims, counter-claims, denials and conspiracy theories. The undeniable fact was that an acknowledged designer in the field of artillery development had been gunned down by an assassin using a 7.65mm pistol.

Bull was a brilliant, if controversial figure. He was the youngest person ever to receive a doctorate from Toronto University and for ten years he worked on armaments research funded by Canada and the US. He had set up a test firing facility in Barbados to launch rocket-driven projectiles into space. This was of enormous military significance and, if theory could be put into practice, offered a cost-effective way of launching satellites.

In 1967, government funding dried up, so Bull established his own Science Research Corporation in the US. He was irritated by what he believed was a rejection of his ideas by western governments and turned his attention to South America, South Africa, China and Iraq. He developed the GS howitzer, a gun with a range of 40 km (25 miles) for South Africa.

When plans for a supergun emerged, with orders from Iraq, alarm bells began to ring in several countries. With a projected range of 1,000 km (620 miles), a supergun located in Iraq would bring Israel, Saudi Arabia and Turkey within range.

It was believed that Dr Bull had been warned that Mossad, the Israelis' secret intelligence service, wanted to kill him. An Egyptian nuclear scientist had been mysteriously murdered in Paris in 1980 and Israel had made it plain that they would not stand back and allow Iraq to develop nuclear and long-range weapons. For its part, Mossad suggested that Dr Bull had been killed by the Iraqis when they discovered his CIA connections.

"This Somewhat Strange Story"

On 18 June 1982 a man met an untimely end suspended from a rope under Blackfriars Bridge, London.

Sixty-two-year-old Roberto Calvi was found by a postman on his way to work at 7.30 a.m. He had been suspended by his neck with a metre-length of rope. His pockets were filled with stones and bricks weighing 5 kg (11 lb). His passport and a wallet containing £7,000 in different currencies were intact. A post-mortem concluded that Calvi had died of asphyxiation by hanging.

Enquiries into the dramatic death of God's Banker, as he was known, revealed the complex inner workings of the international banking system. Many murky secrets were uncovered and unsolved mysteries pinpointed. Calvi had had close financial ties with the Vatican and, the day before he died, he was stripped of his powers as head of Banco Ambrosiano.

The bank crashed in 1982 with debts of over £700 million ($1.3 billion). There were allegations of fraudulent dealings and Calvi was under investigation in Italy for false accounting and exchange control violations.

The inquest into Calvi's death, held in London in July 1982, concluded that he had killed himself. This verdict did not quell the speculation about the man and what had led up to his death. It was known that he had connections with the Sicilian banker, Michele Sindona, who had been convicted of fraud in the US. It was Sindona who had introduced Calvi to the intricacies of financial manipulation.

Members of Calvi's family were not satisfied with the inquest verdict. They believed he had been murdered to prevent him from revealing the identity of major players in the banking underworld. In March 1983, a second inquest was held into Calvi's death during which witnesses spoke about plots to kill him. It was believed that he had been trying to set up a deal to repay Banco Ambrosiano's debts. The second inquest recorded an open verdict in what Lord Chief Justice Lane described as, "This somewhat strange story."

For the next few years, Calvi's name was rarely out of the news. The Prime Minister of Italy, Bettino Craxi, suggested in 1984 that the banker's death might be connected with criminals operating within the banned P2 Masonic lodge. In 1989 a court in Milan ruled that Calvi's death was murder. In 1992, Calvi's family commissioned a forensic report confirming their belief that he had been murdered.

In June 1998, an Italian judge ordered the exhumation of Calvi's body to establish whether the cause of death was suicide or murder. There were hopes that fingernail scrapings might help determine whether Calvi had loaded his pockets with bricks. In 2002, investigators in Italy recovered a safety deposit box in the Milan branch of Banco Ambrosiano that contained documents possibly shedding new light on the affair.

In July 2003, it was reported that Italian prosecutors had concluded Calvi was murdered and suspected the involvement of four people. Their belief was that Calvi was killed by the Mafia for mishandling its money. The four were put on trial in Rome in March 2004 when new evidence was put forward seeking to show that Calvi was involved in laundering treasury bonds stolen by the Mafia in 1982.

In June 2007, the Court in Rome decided there was insufficient evidence to convict those accused and they were all acquitted. The prosecution reconstruction of Calvi's death was that he had been lured from his London home and strangled before being taken by boat to Blackfriars' Bridge where his body was suspended. This scenario was rejected by the judges.

More than twenty years after the event the mystery of Roberto Calvi's death remains. Commenting on the affair, Licio Gelli, the former master of the P-2 lodge, said, "It is not up to us to deliver judgments. Only God will be able to tell the truth."

". . . Cold, Calculating And Evil . . ."

A retired businesswoman and property owner hired a contract killer to eliminate the woman she saw as a rival for the affection of the man she loved.

Fifty-seven-year-old Kathleen Calhaem lived at Cheddar in Somerset in the UK and harboured an obsessive love for her solicitor, Kenneth Pigot. She became jealous of the wife of Pigot's best friend, fellow solicitor, Hugh Rendell. Pigot and Shirley Rendell were involved in a long-standing affair. Calhaem saw Shirley Rendell as a rival and resorted to following Pigot and spying on him. She wanted to move in with him but he rejected this approach.

In October 1982, Calhaem hired a private detective to follow Pigot and report on his activities. The man she selected for this task was Julian Zajac, a twenty-nine-year-old foundry worker from Avonmouth, Bristol. In his spare time, under the name Julian Jones, Zajac ran a detective agency which he called Eagle Investigations.

In due course, Calhaem told Zajac that she wanted him to get rid of Shirley Rendell. She agreed to pay him £10,000; half the money up-front and the remainder after the task was completed. On 23 February 1983, Zajac stole a car from his employer and drove to the Rendell home at Yatton. He had prepared the way by telephoning first to make sure that Shirley Rendell's husband was not at home. He sat outside the house in the car drinking vodka to steady his nerves. Then, claiming to be delivering a package, he gained entry to the house.

Armed with a shotgun, knife and hammer, he attacked Shirley Rendell, clubbing her with the hammer and then stabbing her in the throat. Zajac was arrested after a mutual acquaintance came forward to tell the police that he had tried to enlist his help as an accomplice. Later, Zajac told him that he had attacked Shirley Rendell.

Zajac was tried for murder at Birmingham Crown Court in September 1983. He admitted going to the Rendell home but said his intention was to commit robbery. He said he lost his head when Shirley Rendell put up resistance and tried to reassure her that his only motive was robbery. He hit her with the hammer, then panicked and stabbed her through the throat. Zajac said he was sorry for what he had done and would assist the police in bringing a prosecution against the woman who hired him. Of Kathleen Calhaem he said, "I feel she is such an evil person . . . she made me feel like a schoolboy." Mr Justice Stephen Brown passed down a life sentence.

Calhaem was tried at Winchester Crown Court in January 1984. She denied the charge. Zajac was the chief prosecution witness and he clearly implicated Calhaem who had paid him to carry out the killing. She did not give evidence. Described as "cold, calculating and evil", the jury took four hours to decide that she was guilty of hiring a man to commit murder on her behalf. She was sentenced to life imprisonment.

A Yellow Jaguar

The murder victim was given a distinctive yellow car as a means of identifying her as the target for the gunman who killed her.

Alan Palliko, a former police officer in Los Angeles, created a macho image for himself. He was dedicated to physical fitness, had a succession of girlfriends and loved cars and guns. He vowed that he would make his first million by the time he reached the age of thirty-five.

He married Katherine Drummond in 1964 but the marriage was soon under strain due to his constant philandering. In August 1965, Katherine was badly injured in a hit-and-run incident and, a few months later, she was attacked by Palliko while she sat in her car. He attempted to strangle her and passers-by heard him say, "I'm going to kill you". When his assault created too much public attention, he ran off. Katherine decided not to press charges but she asked for a divorce.

Around this time, Palliko was in a renewed relationship with Sandra Stockton, whom he had married in 1960 and subsequently divorced. On the evening of 11 December 1966, Sandra's husband, Henry Stockton, was shot dead in his home by intruders as he watched television. Questions began to be asked when it was discovered that Sandra was his main beneficiary and stood to gain a substantial sum from the insurance pay-out.

Officers investigating the murder found that Sandra had bought a .22 calibre pistol earlier in the year and enquiries led to Alan Palliko. As the murder investigation dragged on, Palliko became the owner of The Grand Duke bar in Burbank and he moved in to a luxury apartment nearby. He also acquired a new girlfriend, Judy Davis, a swimming pool instructor, whom he married in March 1968. The marriage was full of tension from the very beginning and was destined to be shortlived.

On 18 April, Palliko leased a yellow Jaguar car for Judy's use and, two days later, his bride of six weeks died a violent death in her distinctively coloured car. Judy Palliko was shot dead at the wheel of her stationary car close to their apartment. She had been beaten about the head with a gun butt and shot twice; she died in hospital.

Palliko confided to a friend who was employed in his bar that he had committed murder. "Do you remember Sandra Stockton?" he asked, "I killed her husband." He was arrested at The Grand Duke on 30 April 1968 and charged with the murder of Henry Stockton and Judy Palliko. Investigators found an arsenal of weapons in his apartment.

Palliko and Sandra were tried for murder in November 1968 when the prosecution argued that Sandra's husband had been killed for his money. Sandra had taken out insurance on his life two weeks before he was murdered. It was brought out in evidence that Palliko had insured Judy shortly before they were married with the intention of setting her up for murder. The purpose behind giving her the yellow Jaguar to drive was to mark her out as a murder target.

Palliko denied killing his wife, saying that he had been set up. While the evidence was mainly circumstantial, the case was persuasively argued by Vincent Bugliosi, the celebrated prosecutor. Palliko and Sandra Stockton were convicted of murdering Judy and of attempting to murder his former wife, Katherine. He was sentenced to death and Sandra to life imprisonment. The scheming would-be millionaire made three attempts to escape from prison and in 1972 his death sentence was commuted to life.

"Someone Has Just Shot My Husband"

The day before he died, a murder victim placed a personal ad in his local newspaper that was intended to quell rumours that his marriage was breaking up and denying gossip about fraud and theft.

Around midnight on 26 November 1991, fifty-one-year-old retired banker, Terry Daddow, was shot dead when he answered the front doorbell at his cottage in Northiam, Sussex in the UK. After a significant delay, his wife Jean called the emergency services. "Someone has just shot my husband," she told the operator.

Detectives thought the scenario had the hallmarks of a killing carried out by a hired hit man. House-to-house enquiries established that no one had seen the gunman although many had heard the shotgun fired in the still of the night. Those who noted the time, recorded the blast fifteen minutes before Jean Daddow had called 999.

Jean Daddow appeared tearfully in television interviews appealing for information that would help the police find the killer of her husband. Meanwhile, investigators were looking into the background of Terry and Jean. Local gossip followed two paths; one was that Terry was an alcoholic wife-beater and the other that Jean had forsaken her husband for a string of lovers.

The financial affairs of the Daddows offered some interesting background. Terry had been involved in a financial scandal at the bank concerning his handling of customers' accounts for personal gain. He was asked to retire after twenty years' service.

Some time before her husband's death, Jean had begun to transfer their joint assets into a large number of bank and building society accounts. Part of this financial overhaul involved Terry making a new will leaving everything to Jean and nothing to the children from his previous marriage.

In her role as grieving widow, Jean suggested that her husband's killer was a jealous husband or boyfriend taking action as a result on one of his affairs. By now, suspicion was hardening around Jean and investigators began to look into her family background. She had a twenty-three-year-old son from her first marriage to Roger Blackman, who appeared to have connections in the criminal underworld. The police were looking for a professional hit man and so a new line of enquiry opened up.

It seemed that Blackman had dealings with a former soldier, Robert Bell, who owed him money. Bell promptly disappeared to the US but returned when he realized the game was up. He was arrested and readily confessed to accepting £12,000 in a plot to murder Terry Daddow. He claimed he lacked the courage to kill in cold blood and that, although he was present on the night of the shooting, it was Blackman who fired the fatal shot. He claimed that Jean Daddow was the arch schemer behind the plot.

The deadly trio were tried at Hove Crown Court in February 1993. Jean Daddow played the grieving widow card but to little effect and she and Blackman were convicted of conspiracy to murder. Bell was convicted of murder and conspiracy to murder for which he was sentenced to life imprisonment. Daddow and Blackman were each sentenced to eighteen years.

Hit Squad

Part-time special constable Nisha Patel-Nasri, aged twenty-nine, was stabbed to death outside her home at Wembley, north London in the UK late on the night of 11 May 2006. Neighbours found her at around midnight dressed only in her nightclothes lying in a pool of blood. She had been stabbed in the groin and died later in hospital. Detectives thought she had gone outside carrying a torch to investigate a disturbance and had been attacked by a would-be intruder.

The dead woman's husband, thirty-four-year-old Fadi Nasri, made a televised appeal for information that would help the murder enquiry. He had been away from home on the night in question playing snooker. In honour of her work as a special constable, three police motorcycles led mourners at her funeral.

As the murder investigation proceeded, more was learned about the background of the bereaved husband and the state of his marriage. It seemed that Nisha wanted a child and was disappointed at the amount of time Fadi spent away from home. She worked hard running a hairdressing business and was a more than equal money-earner.

Fadi drove a stylish car and ran a limousine business, which he claimed earned more than £150,000 a year. He was recognized as a big spender and, in fact, had large debts. He was also leading a double life running an escort agency and he kept a Lithuanian prostitute as his mistress. After Nisha's death, he sold the marital home and moved in with his mistress.

The first breakthrough in the investigation came in September when a kitchen knife, believed to be the murder weapon, was found in a drain near the Nasris' home. Mobile phone records led detectives to two men who Nasri claimed were business associates. These were Rodger Leslie and Jason Jones; the former was a drug dealer and the latter a bouncer. Both men were arrested in December 2006 and Nasri followed in January 2007. All three were charged with murder.

They appeared on trial at the Old Bailey in May 2008. The prosecution argued that Nasri arranged the murder and employed hit men to do the killing while he was away playing snooker. He provided them with keys to his house and a knife taken from his own kitchen. There appeared to have been a dummy run several days before the murder took place when Nisha Patel-Nasri confronted strangers armed with a knife at her front door.

Mobile phone records linked the three men and CCTV of a getaway car pointed detectives to Leslie and Jones. Nasri denied having his wife killed so that he could claim on her insurance and continue his extra-marital affair. On 28 May after deliberating for twenty-six hours, the jury found all three defendants guilty of murder. Sentencing was announced in June; Nasri, Leslie and Jones all received life sentences.

Death Of A Lawyer

Maître Jacques Perrot, a French lawyer with friends in high places, was shot dead in Paris on 27 December 1985. His violent death and its aftermath raised many questions that have never been satisfactorily answered.

Successful in his own right, Perrot added lustre to his career by marrying Darie Boutboul, a beautiful and talented woman, who achieved celebrity as France's premier female jockey in April 1982. Perrot was also an amateur jockey and horseracing was a feature of the couple's lives.

Darie's family background could at best be described as unusual. Her father, Dr Robert Boutboul, was supposed to have died in an air crash in 1970 and her life was managed by her mother, Elisabeth Boutboul, a trained lawyer with a manipulative personality.

Shortly before he was gunned down on the stairs leading from his parents' apartment, Perrot made some discoveries about his in-laws. First was that Darie's father was still alive and living in retirement and, second, that Madame Boutboul had been disbarred from legal practice following a disciplinary hearing into a currency swindle involving one of her clients.

Perrot's murder shocked France, not least because the dead man was a personal friend of Laurent Fabius, the Prime Minister. It later emerged that Fabius had asked Perrot for his help in investigating racehorse scandals. More personal details followed with news that Perrot was seeking a divorce from Darie and had arranged to meet his mother-in-law on the evening that he was killed. She did not turn up.

Within days of the shooting, and to the amazement of the French public, Dr Boutboul was reunited with his family in an outpouring of emotion before television news cameras. Mme Boutboul, who appeared to be stage-managing the occasion, said that her son-in-law had been murdered because he had uncovered a scandal, the details of which she could not divulge. She did, though, drop a heavy hint when she said she didn't want to end up like Robert Calvi.

This was a reference to the man known as "God's banker" who was found hanging under Blackfriars Bridge in London in June 1982 (*see page 233*). He had been chairman of Banco Ambrosiano which collapsed with huge debts. Scandal swirled around Calvi's death and the possible involvement of the Italian P2 lodge. Initially, it was believed that Calvi had committed suicide but in 2002 after a long enquiry, it was thought he had been murdered.

Mme Boutboul continued to make controversial statements and it seemed that her son-in-law had unearthed some unsavoury facts about her misuse of client's money. In 1994 she was found guilty of complicity in Perrot's death and given a fifteen-year prison sentence. The mystery of her husband's feigned death and resurrection and the precise motive for her son-in-law's murder have not so far been adequately explained.

"Red Elvis"

The death of Dean Reed, an American pop singer, in Berlin during the Cold War remains an unexplained mystery.

The body of forty-seven-year-old Dean Reed was recovered from the Zeuthner See, a lake in East Berlin, on the morning of

16 June 1986. He had apparently drowned and East German news media spoke of a "tragic accident".

The singer was a controversial figure. He had lived in the East for fourteen years and his songs were very popular in the eastern bloc countries. While he was highly regarded east of the Berlin wall, he was a hate figure for many Americans who regarded him as a defector and referred to him as "Red Elvis".

In the 1960s, Reed spent time in South America where he embraced Marxist doctrines. He was passionate about his beliefs and took out newspaper advertisements urging readers to write to President John Kennedy and Soviet leader Nikito Kruschev demanding an end to nuclear testing. This led to his expulsion from Peru and subsequently from Chile where he publicly insulted the Stars and Stripes flag in a protest against the war in Vietnam. His campaigning for world peace did not endear him to Americans who despised him as a "Commy lover".

In 1972 Reed moved to East Berlin where he was welcomed and he married Renate Blume, an actress. He rented a villa at Snoeckwitz and it was in the nearby lake that he was found, apparently drowned, inside his car. The East German authorities were coy about the precise cause of death but ruled out foul play. His friends were not so sure. His manager, a Denver businesswoman, expressed the opinion that he had been murdered because he had talked about returning to the US. This would have made him a double defector and a loss to the East who saw him as a propaganda asset.

A *Sunday Times* correspondent was in Berlin at the time of Reed's death on an assignment to interview him for the newspaper. He learned from Renate Blume-Reed that her husband had been taken into hospital on the day that he died. Doctors thought he had a viral infection; he was feeling ill and perspiring. The news was that he would be kept in hospital for a few days while tests were carried out. According to later reports, he was already dead.

Reed's death seemed to make minimal impact on the American authorities and there were rumours that he had committed suicide. There were also suggestions of a cover-up and no comprehensive post-mortem report was made public. Some of his friends said that the Russians were making life uncomfortable for him and he had admitted to being fearful of what might happen.

Six weeks before he died, Reed featured in an interview on CBS' "60 Minutes" in which he defended the building of the Berlin Wall. For a short time in the late 1970s, he had worked for the East German intelligence service, STASI. No enquiries into his death were made by the US authorities and speculation remained that one of the international intelligence agencies had put out a contract on him.

Dressed Up

The mysterious death of an Australian government scientist in 1963 had many curious and unexplained features. One of these was that although his body was naked when discovered, someone had carefully arranged his clothes over it to make it appear as if he was dressed.

Two youngsters stumbled across the body of a man by a riverside path in Sydney when they were out walking on New Year's Day. They were uncertain whether the man was drunk or dead. The police were called to the scene and quickly discovered a second body, that of a woman wearing a dress pulled up exposing her thighs.

The man was identified as Dr Gilbert Bogle and the woman as Margaret Chandler. Neither body showed any marks of violence and post-mortems revealed no signs of organic disease. Cause of death was recorded as cardiac failure.

Enquiries showed that the couple had been to a New Year's party. Both were married and Bogle went to the party on his own, as his wife was looking after their baby. While there, he met Margaret Chandler and her husband, and when the gathering broke up at around 4 a.m., it was decided that Bogle would drive Margaret home, leaving Mr Chandler to make his own way. They drove down to Lance Cove River and parked the car at a spot about a hundred yards from where their bodies were discovered.

There was speculation that the couple were drunk and had sexual intercourse during which one of them became unconscious through asphyxia precipitated by alcoholic intoxication. This theory did not hold up too well in light of the post-mortem finding that there was no alcohol in their blood.

In view of Dr Bogle's work as a government scientist, further speculation focussed on secret research of military importance and the angle that he had been killed by enemy agents using an undetectable poison. The inquest held in March 1963 learned that every available test had been applied to determine the precise cause of death but with no positive outcome. The coroner concluded that the deaths had resulted from acute circulatory failure with an unknown cause.

A story surfaced in 1970 that Margaret Chandler's husband had received a number of telephone calls from an individual who told him that Bogle had been targeted by international conspirators and that Mrs Chandler was killed for no other reason than that she was in the wrong place at the wrong time.

A more straightforward theory was that the couple had overdosed on LSD at the New Year's party and subsequently suffered cardiac arrest. This suggestion surfaced in 1977 after Bogle's former lover, Margaret Fowler, died. She was not allowed to give evidence at the inquest in 1963 because it was thought she would say that Bogle used LSD as an aphrodisiac. Theorists proposed that she might have followed the couple after the New Year party and tidied up the scene when she found them in compromising circumstances.

Murder Or Suicide

The mysterious death of Uwe Barschel, a prominent German politician, in a hotel room in Switzerland in 1987 resulted in a scandal at the time and the cause of death remains unresolved.

Forty-three-year-old Barschel was a high-flyer in political circles and was premier of the state of Schleswig-Holstein. He was also a controversial figure who attracted publicity including allegations of using devious methods to discredit opponents.

In September 1987, Barschel resigned his premiership as a result of allegations made against him, which he denied but for which he was due to face a parliamentary enquiry. After resigning, he took his wife for a short holiday and, on returning, travelled alone to Geneva by train.

Barschel checked in at the Beau-Rivage hotel and was found in his room twenty-four hours later. His body was discovered in the bath, fully dressed except for a jacket, and lying partly submerged but with his head above water. Post-mortem examination determined that he had a weak heart and traces of anti-depressant drugs were found in his blood. These findings led to the suggestion that he had committed suicide, although that conclusion was not officially endorsed.

The dead politician's family believed he had been murdered. There was talk that he met two men when he arrived at Geneva railway station, one of whom was supposed to be Robert Roloff. Barschel had told his wife that this man had evidence which would clear his name. A counter suggestion was that Roloff did not exist other than as a cover masking his intention to commit suicide and giving him a reason to travel to Geneva.

Uwe Barschel's funeral service at Lübeck Cathedral on 27 October 1987 was attended by over 2,500 people, including Chancellor Helmut Kohl. A great deal of soul-searching ensued and the prevailing public view was that he had been murdered.

The controversy over his death rumbled on with no satisfactory conclusion being reached. In April 1997, a report was published by investigators, which the media described as a "whodunit with a cast of thousands". There were allegations about changing the course of justice and talk of a cover-up.

A new line of enquiry began to open up, suggesting that, in addition to dirty tricks in internal political affairs, Barschel was involved with international arms deals. It was alleged that he was involved in the Iran-Contra affair. Witnesses claimed to have seen a photograph of Barschel together with Colonel Oliver North and an East German Stasi agent. This was backed up by reports of trips made by Barschel to East European destinations.

What happened in the Geneva hotel room has never been fully explained and the cause of Barschel's death has not been proved. Suggestions that there was another person present at the time of death fuelled further speculation about a killing by foreign agents.

Grand' Terre

The conviction of an elderly French farmer for the murder of the Drummond family in 1952 sparked off a spate of conspiracy theories.

Sir Jack Drummond, aged sixty-one, was an internationally recognized biochemist. In the summer of 1952 he was on holiday in southern France with his wife and eleven-year-old daughter. He pulled off the road near Lurs on 4 August and camped for the night by the riverside.

The following morning, thirty-four-year-old Gustave Dominici, who lived with his father in a nearby farm called La Grand' Terre, discovered a girl's body in the field. Her head had been crushed with a rifle butt and she was found some distance from the campsite where her parents lay dead from gunshot wounds.

It appeared that Sir Jack and Lady Drummond had been shot first and that their daughter had run away, only to be caught by the murderer who clubbed her to death. The murder weapon, a US army carbine, was found nearby in the river.

Once the identity of the murder victims was established, the local police called up reinforcements to examine the crime scene and question witnesses. The murder of an English family on a touring holiday in France quickly made it to newspaper front pages.

Investigators suspected that the Dominici family knew more about the deaths than they were prepared to admit. Gustave had divulged that the Drummonds' daughter was still alive when he found her but said he was too scared to fetch help. He was charged with failing to help a dying person and sent to prison.

The Dominicis were a close-knit family. Seventy-five-year-old Gaston had nine children and nineteen grandchildren. The farm was run by Gustave and the old man tended his goats. The police were receiving mixed messages from the occupants of Grand' Terre farm and inconsistencies began to appear in their recollection of events. It was Gustave who finally blew the whistle by declaring that his father had committed the murders.

Eventually, the old man admitted the killings when he said he was caught spying on Lady Drummond as she undressed. Her husband appeared on the scene to deal with the "Peeping Tom" and there was a struggle, in the course of which the Drummonds were shot dead. Dominici changed his story several times and made numerous confessions. Finally, in November 1954, he was tried for murder at Digne Asssizes and convicted on a majority verdict. He received the death sentence, which was subsequently commuted to life imprisonment. In 1960, he was freed on the orders of the French President and he died in 1965.

For many commentators, the murder of the Drummonds remained a mystery. There was a suggestion that the killings were part of a wider plot and that the Dominicis were caught up in a bigger game plan. A French historian writing about the case in 2002 put forward the theory that Sir Jack Drummond had been a spy and his presence in France soon after the ending of the Second World War involved an espionage mission related to chemical weapons. According to this account, Sir Jack Drummond had been to France on three previous occasions after the war finished and the presence of a chemical factory nearby was noted.

A further development of the conspiracy angle emerged in 2007 with the notion that Sir Jack Drummond was drawn in to the post-war machinations of the agrochemical and pharmaceutical industries. One theory suggested he was spying for the British government and had planned to meet someone who would pass on secret intelligence, all in the context of cold war politics.

Many questions about the murders remain unanswered. Local people said there were strangers in the Lurs area on the night of the shooting whose presence was unaccounted for.

Also, it has been alleged that Sir Jack Drummond attended a meeting with a former French Resistance fighter two days before he was killed. Post-mortem findings on the murder victims were supposed to have indicated that two different weapons were used. And so the speculation continues.

What is certain is that old man Gaston Dominici, cast in the role of voyeur and killer, took many secrets with him to the grave.

CSI Stockholm

The Prime Minister of Sweden, Olof Palme, and his wife Lisbet visited the Grand Cinema in Sveavägen in central Stockholm on the evening of 28 February 1986. They left the cinema just after 11 p.m. and were walking down the street when a man came up behind them and fired two shots at close range. Palme was fatally wounded with a shot in the back and his wife suffered a minor injury.

Apart from the shocking death of its Prime Minister in a busy street, Sweden had to come to terms with a bungled investigation, a controversial trial and unhelpful witnesses. The police failed to secure the crime scene adequately. It took a long time for reinforcements to reach the crime scene and no road checkpoints were set up. Several witnesses, including Lisbet Palme, saw a man running down the street after the shooting.

There was snow on the pavement at the time of the murder and it was a passer-by who, several days later, found two spent .357mm copper-tipped bullets. The type of gun that fired them was never identified and no murder weapon was ever recovered.

The prelude to the shooting was that Palme had stood down his bodyguard detail at midday because he intended to spend the rest of the day at home. In the afternoon, he decided to take his wife to the cinema to see a comedy, *The Brothers Mozart*. He queued for tickets along with other Stockholm filmgoers. He and his wife left at the end of the film just after 11 p.m. and by 11.21 he was dead.

Two theories emerged concerning the motive behind the murder. The Kurdish Workers' Party (PKK) had an active group in Sweden and its members had been branded as terrorists by the government. Their leader had also been refused political asylum in the country. An alternative theory was simply that Palme had been shot at random by a disturbed individual unaware of his victim's identity.

Christer Pettersson, a forty-two-year-old, alcoholic, drug-user and convicted criminal fitted the random killing scenario. He had been seen in the vicinity on the night of the shooting and his alibi did not add up. He was questioned by the police and strenuously denied he was the killer. Pettersson was put under surveillance and, in December 1988, he was detained as a suspect. One witness claimed to have identified him as the man running from the scene.

Pettersson was put on trial in Stockholm in June 1989. Much of the prosecution's case was circumstantial. It depended heavily on the evidence of Lisbet Palme who identified Pettersson after watching a video of a police identity parade. Mrs Palme proved to be a difficult witness, initially declining to go into the witness box. In the event, she did confront the accused man and identified him. Asked if she was sure, she answered, "Yes".

Four witnesses changed their pre-trial statements, weakening the prosecution case, and critics said that Mrs Palme's evidence was worthless. Pettersson made a confident denial, "I did not kill Olof Palme," he told the court. His declaration of innocence conformed to public opinion, for in a pre-trial poll carried out by the Swedish Institute of Opinion, only 18 per cent thought he was guilty.

After deliberating for seventeen days, the jury delivered a guilty verdict and Pettersson was sentenced to life imprisonment. The verdict did not calm public unease and doubts continued to surface.

In October 1989, the High Court of Appeal, by a unanimous decision, overturned the conviction and Pettersson was released from Kvonoberg Prison. The police handling of the murder investigation was criticized as was the judicial process in a case where no murder weapon had been found, there was no clear motive and the identification evidence was unreliable.

Further twists to the story emerged as time progressed. In 1991 there was a suggestion that an unnamed former French legionnaire was involved in a right-wing extremist plot to kill Palme. In 1997 came news of an alleged plot to assassinate King Carl Gustaf XVI, which had gone awry when Palme was shot by mistake. And, finally, Pettersson, who had steadfastly denied the killing, allegedly claimed in 2001 to be the murderer after all. The truth of this died with Pettersson in 2007.

Demands With Menace

The murder of a leading heart surgeon in Sydney in 1991 shocked Australia. It was a crime that had overtones of extortion related to traffic in human organs for transplantation.

Dr Victor Chang became an icon to Australians when he carried out life-saving surgery on a fourteen-year-old girl. He was a greatly respected figure and a pioneer in heart transplant surgery. He inaugurated a national transplant programme at a leading Sydney hospital and carried out hundreds of transplant operations with a high survival rate.

Born in Shanghai to Australian-Chinese parents, Chang set out his ambition to be a doctor early on. Once established, he quickly made his professional mark and in the 1990s was at the peak of his career, travelling widely to carry out life-saving surgery. He lived with his British-born wife and three children in Sydney and, despite his success, kept a modest social profile.

Early in the morning of 4 July 1991, Dr Chang left his home driving his Mercedes and heading for St Vincent's Hospital. During his journey, he telephoned his wife and reported nothing untoward. Shortly afterwards he turned off the main road in the suburb of Mosman and drove into a side street following a minor collision with another car. Witnesses later said they saw him standing by his car apparently arguing with two young men. One of them pulled a gun and fired two shots into Dr Chang's head before fleeing from the scene in their car.

The murder of the fifty-four-year-old doctor led to a huge manhunt for his killers and after ten days of intensive investigation, the police arrested two suspects. They were both Malaysians; a thirty-four-year-old chef, Philip Lim Choon Tee, and forty-nine-year-old Liew Chiew Seng. Initial reaction was that the murder was related to Chinese Triad activity, a group which ran drug, gambling and prostitution in Sydney's underworld.

Another theory lay in Dr Chang's well-known opposition to the trade in body organs harvested in China for transplantation into wealthy patients. He was especially vocal about the practice of taking kidneys from prisoners executed in China.

When Lim and Seng were put on trial in Sydney in October 1992, they both pleaded guilty to murder and it seemed that their crime began as one of extortion. They apparently conspired to demand three million Australian dollars from the Chang family. Aided by a third man, Stanley No, they visited Chang's house intending to threaten him but gave up when they saw he had company. Their plan, it was argued by the prosecution, was to abduct Dr Chang and demand money with menaces. When he refused, after they had driven him off the road on 4 July, Liew produced a gun and fired the fatal shots.

The two men, described in court as amateur desperadoes, were found guilty of murder and sentenced to life imprisonment.

CHAPTER 10

Mixed Media

The written and published word have played a leading role in defining the history of crime. Printed accounts of the execution of criminals accompanied by stark illustrations of hanged felons were a source of public information throughout the nineteenth century. They also served as a reminder to the general populace that crime does not pay. As the printed word evolved and was augmented by other media, especially the visual dimension of film and television, so opportunities arose for graphic reporting of events. The new developments also brought scope for the exercise of criminal ingenuity.

Death sometimes imitates art and such was the case when Konrad Beck contrived a murder in a locked room in his Berlin apartment. He had stolen the idea from a novel he had been reading. The mystery was solved when investigators found a copy of the book in his flat, which conveniently fell open to the page providing the solution. Krystian Bala had a different idea. He committed his murder first and then wrote a fictionalized account of it in a novel. And Snowy Rowles gleaned his ideas about disposing of his victim's body in Australia's outback after reading a story about a fictional crime.

Murderers are chiefly motivated by passion or enmity and know full well who their victim will be. But where the objective is the calculated business of gain, it may be necessary to seek out victims. One of the means of doing this is by advertising. Part of Elfriede Blauensteiner's strategy was to find elderly men to kill and fleece them of their savings by advertising for gullible companions in the newspapers. Here was an echo of an earlier example established by

Martha Beck and Raymond Fernandez and their exploitation of Lonely Hearts Club advertisements in 1940s America.

Words can also entrap, for example, when a policeman lay dying from gunshot wounds in a London street and wrote the name of his killer in his notebook. Or when Ghislaine Marshal, mortally wounded in a knife attack in her flat in the south of France, scrawled her attacker's name on a door using her own blood.

New media present new opportunities for law enforcement. Thus wireless was used in 1910 to pinpoint the arrest of Dr Crippen and television has been successfully used to acquire public information about crimes and criminals. Programmes such as the BBC's "Crimewatch" and 20th Century Fox's "America's Most Wanted" have played a significant role. In the US, John List and William Hewlett, both fugitives from justice, were caught due to public responses to television appeals for information.

One of the great debates of modern times has been about the possible effect of movie films and, later, of television, on impressionable minds and leading to criminality. In 1952, when a young man shot and killed a policeman on a warehouse roof in south London, the question asked was whether his actions were influenced by having watched a gangster film depicting gun violence.

While sociologists debated what they saw as the issues, they were overtaken by rapid developments in the media industries. The cinema had the power to show violent images to paying audiences but television and, in due course, video, brought the culture of violence into every home. The proliferation of brutal and sadistic scenes combined with a lessening of moral inhibitions, rendered the debate virtually meaningless.

A watershed occurred in 1971 with the cinema screening of Stanley Kubrick's film, "A Clockwork Orange", based on the novel by Anthony Burgess. The film, which showed disaffected young men committing gang rape, was highly controversial and accusations followed that it glamorized violence. As a result, the film was withdrawn from distribution the following year.

While Kubrick's film was graphic, it was simply ahead of its time and complaints about film violence have become muted as images have become more explicit. In modern cinema and television, gritty realism is everything. Films such as "The Silence

*of the Lambs", "Natural Born Killers" and "Nightmare on Elm
Street", entertained and horrified their audiences. They also entered
the psyche of some individuals who went beyond the threshold of
entertainment and into the realm of personality deviation. Thus
Peter Moore explained that he killed for pleasure and lay the
blame on a character in the horror film, "Friday the Thirteenth".
Similarly, incidents in the film, "Copycat" were said to have been
emulated in the Zakrzewski murders in Paris in 1996.*

*The internet has further extended the range of media that can
be exploited by those seeking publicity and self-promotion. A
particular phenomenon has been the use of the internet by mass
murderers to justify their acts of destruction and promote their
brand of personal beliefs. In 2007, Pekka-Eric Auvinen killed nine
people after he had posted a hate-filled manifesto on YouTube. In
the same year, Cho Heng Hui killed thirty-two people and sent his
revenge credo to NBC news in New York. In 2008, Matti Juhani
Saari killed ten people, having declared on YouTube that, "the
whole of life is pain". Between them these three killers destroyed the
lives of fifty-one people.*

*There is a strong literary tradition among the murdering
fraternity including Thomas Griffiths Wainewright and Pierre
François Lacenaire. The French murderer won over many
sympathizers with his soul-baring memoirs written in his prison
cell. Karl Hau wrote two books while serving his term of life
imprisonment. Hirasawa, the Tokyo poisoner and Jacques Mesrine,
France's Public Enemy Number One, also wrote books detailing
their lives and crimes.*

*Pre-eminent among the ranks of those who have developed
literary careers following convictions for killing are Dr William
Minor and Stephen Wayne Anderson. Minor was judged insane
in 1872 after killing a man and spent thirty-eight years in an
asylum where he became an acclaimed lexicographer of the English
language. While Anderson, who was executed in the US in 2002
after spending twenty-two years on Death Row, was an award-
winning poet and playwright. In their different ways, perhaps, both
men showed that the pen is mightier than the sword, although in
both cases, their weapon of choice was a handgun.*

Inspired Reader

Death imitated art when a novelist's ingenious murder scenario was adopted by a man who wanted to eliminate his family in order to remarry.

Konrad Beck made a living in Berlin in the 1880s as a general dealer buying and selling second-hand goods. On a November day in 1881, appearing somewhat flustered, he approached a police officer in the street to say that he could not open the door to his apartment. The key did not work and the door seemed to be bolted on the inside.

Beck's concern was for his wife and five children who he believed must be inside. He was convinced something was wrong. The combined forces of the landlord and a carpenter succeeded in taking the door down and allowing access to the flat. They were greeted by the macabre spectacle of Mrs Beck hanging from a hook in the ceiling.

The children were not in evidence so a search was made of all the rooms and cupboards. They were found in a cupboard in the hallway. The five children, ranging in age from four to twelve years, were hanging from hooks like rabbits in a butcher's shop. They had all been strangled.

Observant detectives noted that both Frau Beck and her children looked undernourished and were dressed in shabby threadbare clothes. By contrast, Konrad Beck appeared to be fit and healthy. The immediate interpretation of the deaths was that Frau Beck had killed her children and then hanged herself after first bolting the front door.

Detectives decided to probe a little into the background of the Beck family. They learned from neighbours that Frau Renate Beck was always short of money and sometimes asked them for old clothes and even food. Konrad Beck spent a great deal of time away from home and when he was there he seemed to spend his time sitting around reading books.

Further enquiries established that Beck was spending a lot of time with another woman and helping her pay the rent. This went some way to explaining why he kept his own family short of food and clothing. But mysteries remained and one of these was that the door had been bolted on the inside. The obvious answer was that Renate Beck had secured the door to prevent any intrusion while she killed her children.

The door bolt was found to be exceptionally well-oiled and moved freely when operated. While detectives found that curious, they made further searches of the apartment and looked at the titles of some of Beck's books. They flipped through the pages of the volumes in the hope that they might find letters or other documents. When a book called *Nena Sahib* by John Ratcliffe was taken from the shelf, the pages fell open at a particular spot.

There, detectives found the solution to the conundrum of the bolted door in a story explaining the death of a man in a room secured from the inside. In the fictional account, a small hole was found in the doorframe next to the bolt, making it possible to pass a wire through and operate the bolt from the outside.

No doubt with some excitement, detectives investigating the deaths of the Beck family members took a close look at the doorframe. They found a tiny hole blocked with wax that made it possible with a wire or loop of some kind to slide the bolt across from the outside.

Confronted with these revelations, Konrad Beck confessed that his lover had insisted on marriage and as he could not bear to lose her, he eliminated his own family. Beck was tried for murder and found guilty by a unanimous verdict. The forty-year-old reader of detective stories who wanted to please his lover paid with his life. He was executed on 4 December 1881.

Novel Twist

The body of Dariusz Janiszewski, a thirty-five-year-old businessman, was discovered by fishermen in the River Odva in Warsaw in December 2000. He had been missing for over a month and his corpse bore clear evidence of having been beaten and tortured.

Scene of crime investigators noted that the dead man had been trussed up with a single piece of rope in such a way that he might have strangled himself. Pathologists were not certain if he had died in this way or whether he had drowned.

The enquiry into Janiszewski's brutal death made little headway and it was closed in May 2001. The case remained closed for five years until the publication of a novel called *Amok* written by a pulp fiction author, Krystian Bala, when the contents came to the attention of the policeman leading the murder enquiry. The book's storyline concerned a group of sadists discussing a murder, the details of which were practically identical to that of Janiszewski.

When the police were alerted to the evident similarities between the murder under investigation and a fictional killing, Bala was questioned. He was released because of lack of evidence and there the matter might have rested but for an astute piece of police work. Officers reviewing the case noted that Janiszewski's mobile phone had not been retrieved from the crime scene. His service provider co-operated fully by tracing his SIM card. It seemed that the phone had been bought from an internet auction site within days of Janiszewski being reported missing. The seller was Krystian Bala.

Bala was arrested in September 2005. He denied any knowledge of the killing but a search of his apartment told a different story. Information stored on his computer referred to Janiszewski and the dead man's telephone card had been used to make calls to Bala's friends.

Bala was a philosophy graduate, married and father of a ten-year-old son. He separated from his wife in 1999 and she had been meeting Janiszewski. This liaison appeared to have inspired pathological jealousy in Bala who was described as a control freak. In his novel, Bala described the murder of a young woman, tied up in the same manner as Janiszewski and stabbed to death. The murder weapon, in an echo of the fate of Janiszewski's mobile phone, was auctioned on an internet site.

In April 2006 Bala made a confession but declined to sign it on the grounds that he had not been well. He was put on trial in September 2007. Psychologists referred to his high IQ and described him as a narcissist who craved attention. Evidence was also given that he had physically abused his wife. When they separated, he plagued her with e-mail messages and tried to keep track of any partners she might have. Bala said that he included the circumstances of Janiszewski's murder in his novel by reading the details reported in the media.

Bala was convicted on circumstantial evidence and sentenced to twenty-five years imprisonment. The judge said the evidence showed he planned and orchestrated the crime. This was a case in which art, in the form of Bala's novel, imitated life or, more correctly, death.

Fiction Becomes Fact

Dromedary, a camel-breeding station in Western Australia, was the unlikely venue for a discussion about committing the perfect murder. In October 1929, Arthur William Upfield, a writer of detective fiction, stopped at Dromedary and joined a group of men gathered around the campfire. One of the topics in the conversation that ensued was Upfield's crime-writing career and the concept of the perfect murder. The novelist offered a small prize to anyone who could provide him with a scenario for the perfect crime.

One of those present who took a particular interest in the discussion was Snowy Rowles, a young man from Perth. However, the prize went to the station manager whose suggestion was to shoot the victim in the back of the head, burn the corpse together with an animal carcass to disguise the remains and sieve what was left for any metal fragments. This storyline was used by Upfield in his novel, *The Sands of Windee*, published in 1932, by which time the impressionable young man at the campfire soirée, Snowy Rowles, was on trial for murder. After the meeting at Dromedary, Upfield had recommended Rowles for a job with a fencing business working at Mount Magnet.

Around the end of 1930, the police in Western Australia were searching for a man who was reported missing. Leslie John Brown had last been seen in the company of Snowy Rowles earlier in the year. Rowles was interviewed and said that he had worked with Brown who he believed had moved to the north of the territory. The police persisted in their enquiries and investigated reports that human remains had been found in the bush.

At a deserted encampment known as 183 Mile Gate, they found evidence of three campfires. Careful sifting of the ashes revealed bone fragments, some shirt buttons, a gold ring and false teeth. Rowles was questioned again about Brown's disappearance and, when Upfield's book was published, the similarity between his fictional crime and the discoveries made in the bush seemed curious, to say the least. Upfield confirmed that Rowles had been present when the idea of the perfect murder was discussed.

Snowy Rowles was tried at Perth for the murder of Leslie Brown. Much of the evidence was circumstantial in view of the fact that there was no victim's body. Unfortunately for him, Rowles failed to carry out every detail of the perfect murder plan. Had he done so, he might never have been convicted. He claimed in court that he could not be found guilty of a crime that had not been committed. But those fragments that survived the fire in the bush told a different story – the gold ring and false teeth were positively identified as belonging to the missing man. Taken together, this was sufficient to deliver a guilty verdict and Rowles was sentenced to death. He was hanged at Fremantle Prison.

Shocking Death In The Bath

A novel that described the death of someone in the bath when a radio connected to the electricity supply was thrown into the water provided a plan for a murder in real life.

On 11 June 1967, police were called to an apartment in Toronto following a report by Terence Milligan that his wife had died in the bath. Officers found nineteen-year-old Jane dead, sitting in about twelve inches of water with her back to the taps. A mains radio with its electric lead connected to a socket in the living room lay immersed in the water.

Milligan appeared remarkably calm in the tragic circumstances of his young wife's death. They had been married less than a year. He laid great emphasis on her habit of placing the radio on the edge of the bath. Suspicion began to form when it emerged that he stood to gain a considerable sum from her insurance. Added to which was the statement by neighbours that the couple were heard engaging in a noisy argument on the day Jane Milligan died.

The pathologist reported that death had probably been caused by asphyxia resulting from electrocution. Examination of the dead woman's organs told a different story, though, indicating that drowning rather than electrocution had been the cause of death. Milligan's behaviour continued to excite suspicion when it was learned that he had frequently referred to his wife's habit of using the radio in the bathroom in conversations with workmates.

The police decided to search a little deeper into Terence Milligan's background and made an interesting discovery at his uncle's farm on Prince Edward Island, which he visited after his wife's death. There they found a copy of a book called *The Doomsters*, which told the story of a person killed when a radio connected to the electricity supply was thrown into the bath.

At the inquest into Jane Milligan's death on 27 July 1967 a verdict was reached of "Homicide at the hands of her husband". Terence Milligan was arrested and charged with non-capital murder.

The bathtub had been removed from the Milligans' apartment and taken to police headquarters where various tests were carried out. Crucially, it was shown that it was not possible to balance the radio on the edge of the bath as alleged. Accidental drowning was ruled out by an experiment in which a volunteer sat in the bath in twelve inches of water with her back to the taps in the position in which Jane Milligan was found. In that position, drowning by accident would have been impossible.

At Terence Milligan's trial in May 1968, the prosecution made a powerful case to the effect that he drowned his wife and then simulated accidental electrocution. When he was first questioned by the police, he said he touched his wife when he found her to see if she was still alive. In that case, said the detective, he must have received an electric shock. Milligan's response was that he must have disconnected the radio from the mains electricity supply first.

Milligan was convicted of non-capital murder and sentenced to life imprisonment.

The Black Widow

"Widow, sixty-four ... would like to share the quiet autumn of her life with a widower." Lonely hearts responded to this advertisement in Austrian newspapers in their droves. Among the replies was one from Alois Pichler, a seventy-six-year-old retired post office worker. He had a house and savings, and after altering his will in favour of Elfriede Blauensteiner, died of a heart attack in November 1995.

The dead man's relatives were suspicious of the circumstances and a post-mortem revealed there was more to his death than a failing heart. It seemed that he had also been poisoned. The trail inevitably lead to Blauensteiner who had been caring for him. At first she denied any involvement, but enquiries uncovered a series of deaths of elderly men, including her husband.

Following sustained questioning in January 1996, she confessed to two murders and then to a further three. The police thought there might be many more. She told detectives that, following her childhood upbringing in poor circumstances, her aim in life was to become rich. In 1986, she developed her strategy, drawing men into her web with promises of all-round caring companionship. Her advertisement in the "Lonely Hearts" pages tempted lonely old men, whom she accepted after carefully scrutinizing their bank balances. Then she slowly but surely disposed of her clients by dosing them with diabetic medication, which fatally reduced their blood sugar level without raising suspicion.

Blauensteiner benefited from numerous bequests and, at the time of her arrest, was thought to be worth £6 million. She also had a full social life, appearing in furs and jewellery at the roulette and blackjack tables in Vienna's Casino.

"The Black Widow", as she was called by the Austrian press, was tried for murder at Krems in February 1997. Her three-week trial turned into something of a pantomime; clutching a gold crucifix she declared that only God could judge her. She warned journalists, "If there's a vampire among you, he will turn you into a heap of ashes."

The press had a field day reporting on The Black Widow's excesses. She had confessed to five murders, commenting to detectives that they deserved to die. The public, while feasting on the details, cast its mind back to the 1980s when Waltraud Wagner was convicted in an Austrian court over the deaths of thirty-nine hospital patients. Many questions were asked about the attitudes and responsibilities in the care of old people.

The Black Widow was not without supporters, though, and her trial was twice interrupted by bomb scares. Finally, on 7 March 1997, Blauensteiner was convicted of murder and sentenced to life imprisonment. And, in a final bizarre twist, it was noted that she had donated the body of her third husband, Friedrich Döcker, who died in 1995, to medical science. His remains were preserved in a tank of formaldehyde in Vienna's Anatomical Institute.

Look What I've Done Sweetheart

Martha Beck and Raymond Fernandez, two individuals looking for romance, met through a Lonely Hearts Club and formed a deadly duo.

Thirty-one-year-old Martha Beck was obese and emotionally unstable, possibly as a result of being abused as a teenager. She qualified as a nurse and in the 1940s worked at a home for disabled children in Florida. She was sexually overactive and entered into several disastrous relationships.

In December 1947, Martha responded to a Lonely Hearts Club advertisement placed by Raymond Fernandez, a thirty-seven-year-old charmer who preyed on vulnerable women. He believed he had hypnotic powers that compelled women to fall in love with him. The two misfits met and began an amorous partnership.

Martha quickly recognized that her new partner's ability to charm the opposite sex could be turned to advantage. Their hunting ground for potential victims was the Lonely Hearts Clubs. Initially, the idea was that Fernandez would woo lonely women with the promise of affection and Beck would help him fleece them of their savings.

Swindling elderly women led to more sinister approaches involving murders. In December 1948, the deadly duo tricked New York widow, Janet Fay, into marriage with Fernandez and, at a stroke, withdrew all her savings. Not content with this, they killed Janet Fay with a hammer and hid her body in a trunk. This was placed in the cellar of a house they had rented.

The murderers moved on to Michigan in search of another victim and made the acquaintance of forty-one-year-old Delphine Downing who had a two-year-old daughter. They shot Delphine and Beck drowned her child in the bathtub, calling Fernandez and saying, "Oh come and look what I've done, sweetheart."

After burying the bodies in the cellar, they went off to the cinema. They had a surprise when they returned and found the police waiting for them. The murder of Janet Fay had been discovered and the New York police alerted their colleagues in Michigan. Beck and Fernandez pleaded guilty to double murder, probably believing they would be spared the death penalty as Michigan had no capital punishment. In the event, despite resisting extradition to New York, they ended up on trial for the murder of Janet Fay.

The trial lasted forty-four days and Beck's account of her love life with Fernandez provided the newspapers with sensational headlines. They were found guilty of first-degree murder and sentenced to death. While being held at Sing Sing prison, they exchanged notes with each other and generally managed to make a spectacle of themselves.

While the couple were known to have claimed three murder victims, they were suspected of a dozen further killings. On the eve of execution, Beck sent a note to Fernandez expressing her undying love for him and was granted a final request to have her hair curled before facing the electric chair. On 8 March

1951, the Lonely Hearts Murderers were electrocuted. In the wake of the trial, regulation was passed to prevent participants in Lonely Hearts Clubs being so easily targeted by swindlers.

". . . Reside With Us"

George Nichols and Alfred Lester, an enterprising pair of ex-convicts, devised a murder-for-profit plan by advertising for victims in an Australian newspaper.

The Parramatta River Murders caused a stir in Sydney in 1872 when bodies began turning up from their watery graves. On 12 March, John Bridger was found floating in the river. The former wardroom steward from HMS *Rosario* had been discharged from the navy a few days before he was found dead. He had suffered severe head wounds and his body had been weighted with a large stone tied to his feet.

A week later, a second body was found by a fisherman near Five Dock Bay. It too had been weighted with a heavy stone and bore evidence of wounds to the head. This victim, William Walker, was a newly arrived immigrant from England. His killers had made two mistakes, however, leaving his personal papers on the body and attempting to sell his watch.

Within forty-eight hours of finding Walker's body, George Nichols and Alfred Lester were in police custody. A letter found in the dead man's pocket signed by George Nichols, offered him the post of clerk advertised in the local newspaper. He was offered a salary of thirty shillings a week and the menacing message, "you will reside with us".

It seemed that Nichols had placed two advertisements in the 4 March 1872 edition of the *Sydney Morning Herald*, to which he had received two hundred replies. He was identified by the newspaper office clerk who took down the wording of his advertisement. He was also identified by a boatman who had seen him in the company of John Bridger, the first murder victim.

Nichols and Lester had criminal records and had only recently been released from prison following convictions for acting under false pretences. Nichols was the mastermind;

an intelligent man who spoke several languages and made effective use of aliases. Lester had sought refuge in Australia after he had embezzled money from his employer in England.

The two men were tried for murder at Sydney's Central Criminal court. The evidence against them was circumstantial. Several witnesses had seen them with Walker at Blow's Hotel where his trunk was deposited for safe keeping. The pair were also seen on the harbour front when they returned from a night-time trip up the Parramatta River when, according to Nichols, they had caught several fish.

Justice was swift in the 1870s and the jury deliberated for a mere thirty minutes before finding the defendants guilty. The pair in the dock wilted on hearing the verdict and four policemen were required to keep them upright to hear Mr Justice Hargreaves pass sentence. Condemning them to death, he referred melodramatically to the time "when the dark waters of ocean and river shall give up their coffined millions to the voice of God".

Nichols, aged thirty, and Lester, aged twenty, fulfilled their appointment with the hangman at Darlinghurst Gaol on 18 June 1872.

"Here's My Marker"

The kidnapper and murderer of a priest buried his victim on a sandy beach, marking the spot with a scarf, so that he could report the discovery as his "civic duty".

On the night of 2 August 1921, a man wearing driving goggles to protect his identity, appeared at the priest's house next to the Church of the Holy Angels at Colma near San Francisco. The man asked the housekeeper if she would fetch the priest as he needed his services to attend a dying man. Father Patrick E. Heslin responded to the summons and he drove off into the night with the stranger. He was not seen alive again.

When sixty-year-old Father Heslin failed to return home, his housekeeper notified the church authorities and the police were alerted. Within a few days, the Church received a typewritten ransom note demanding $6,500. A huge search was under way to locate the missing priest when a second ransom note was received. This repeated the earlier demand for money and the note read, "Fate has made me do this," adding, with emphasis, "the father is not yet DEAD."

On 10 August, the Archbishop received an unexpected visitor who told him he thought he knew where the missing priest was. He related his claim to the police telling them that Father Heslin had a man who fried flapjacks watching over him. This seemingly mad utterance made sense when someone recalled a seaside advertisement at Salada Beach which showed a man tossing flapjacks over a camp fire. The eccentric individual who had imparted this information was William A. Hightower. He was something of a Walter Mitty character who had worked at mostly menial jobs but claimed to be an inventor.

Hightower went with the police and a search team armed with shovels to Salada Beach. He directed them to a particular area in the sand. Pointing to a black scarf, he said, "Here's my marker". They found the body of Father Heslin who had been beaten and shot.

Clearly knowing too much for his own good, Hightower was charged with murder. A search of the room he had been using in a San Francisco hotel produced the typewriter on which he had written the ransom notes. Further enquiries established that he had pawned the .45 revolver used to shoot the priest.

There was great public outrage at the violent death of Father Heslin and demands for his killer to face the death penalty. Hightower was sent for trial and found guilty of murder. His sentence was life imprisonment at San Quentin where he worked in the kitchens, having once been a baker, and produced a newsletter written in his quirky style.

Questions about his sanity were lost in the storm of protest over the killing of a priest lured from his home on what he believed to be an errand of mercy. Hightower came from a poor background and his dreams of making money from his inventions never materialized. His motive for murder was financial gain.

"I Got His Identity Card And Name"

A police officer dying in the street after being shot recorded the name and address of the murderer in his notebook before expiring.

On 13 February 1948, PC Nathaniel Edgar was working in plain clothes as part of a drive to curb a spate of housebreaking incidents in the Southgate area of London. He had been following a suspect in the vicinity of Wades Hill. At around 8 p.m. he stopped and questioned a man who responded by drawing a revolver and firing three shots at the policeman.

Local residents found the wounded constable lying in the street and called for help. A patrol car arrived at the scene. Edgar told them, "The man was by the door. I got his identity card and name. He shot me in the legs with three shots. The pocket book is in my inside pocket." In it the dying PC had recorded the details "M or (Mr) Thomas Donald, 247 Cambridge Road, Enfield, BEAH 257/2." He became unconscious and died in hospital later that night of the wounds he had received in his right upper leg.

The police had no difficulty identifying Donald Thomas, an army deserter who had been on the wanted list since October 1947. He was not at his home in Enfield but was located at lodgings in Clapham. Being a deserter had made him wary and he spotted the police when they arrived in a wireless car. But he was not quick enough to evade their tackles when they burst into his room and he attempted to pull a gun from under a pillow.

The man was quickly overpowered and dispossessed of his loaded pistol. "That gun's full up and they were all for you," he told the arresting officer. A search of his room produced several rounds of ammunition, a truncheon and a book entitled *Shooting to Live with the One-Hand Gun*. This was an instruction book written by two army commandos on the use of the pistol by security forces. Bullets test-fired from Thomas's Luger pistol matched those found in the dead policeman's body.

Thomas had left school at the age of fourteen and was

generally regarded as a bright boy. He fell into bad habits and spent time at an approved school before being called up for military service in January 1945. He deserted within two weeks and spent two years on the run before the military police caught up with him. After a period of detention, he deserted again.

He was tried for the murder of PC Edgar at the Old Bailey in April 1949 and found guilty. He was sentenced to death but escaped the hangman's clutches because the death penalty was suspended for five years following a vote on capital punishment in the House of Commons. Thomas was therefore given a sentence of life imprisonment. As Sir Harold Scott, Commissioner of the Metropolitan Police, put it, this decision was, "viewed with critical feelings by police officers".

"Omar Killed Me"

When Ghislaine Marshal, a wealthy widow, was fatally stabbed in her apartment in Nice, in France, she managed to write the name of her murderer on a door using her own blood. She died around midday on 23 June 1991, leaving a clue that proved to be not as straightforward as it seemed.

Sixty-three-year-old Madame Marshal lived in a luxury apartment with a swimming pool in the grounds. Her daily routine was to take a walk in the garden in the morning and then settle down in her home to solve the newspaper crossword. This routine was a clue in itself.

On the day she was murdered, Madame Marshal, despite being stabbed, dragged herself to the boiler room in the basement. There, on the back of the door, using her finger and the blood from her wounds, she wrote, "Omar m'a tuer" – Omar killed me. Omar Raddad was the part-time gardener and he had been working at a nearby villa on the day of her death.

Raddad denied committing the crime and gave a detailed, timed account of his movements. Police put the time of death at between 12.00 and 12.30 p.m. when, according to his account, Raddad was riding his moped home for lunch. This was not corroborated, but he was seen when he returned an hour later to continue working in the garden. At about 1.30 p.m. he spoke to the owner of the property where he was working who found him to be his usual self. He was generally regarded as a good worker and had no criminal record.

The key to the murder was the message on the door accusing Omar of murder. But herein lay an enigma, because the words as written contained a fundamental spelling error. "Omar m'a tuer" is grammatically incorrect and should have been written as "Omar m'a tué". Experts pondering the message, asked would Madame Marshal, an avid crossword fan, have made such a fundamental mistake?

The question produced many theories. One camp argued that Madame Marshal was forced to accuse Omar by her attacker and she left a clue in the spelling error. Another school of thought was that she simply made the error in her dying moments. Mystery was heightened when the maid told police that her employer received a telephone call on the eve of her death and that she was given the next day off.

The police investigation was faulty from start to finish. Madame Marshal's handbag from which money had been stolen was not tested for fingerprints, her body was cremated prematurely and there were inaccuracies about the time of death in official reports. Comparisons were made with the bungling film detective, Inspector Clouseau.

Omar Raddad was charged with murder and appeared on trial in January 1994. He denied the charge. A strong defence was mounted on his behalf by Maître Jacques Verges. The evidence against the Moroccan gardener was circumstantial, apart from the accusatory message, which the prosecution claimed was "absolute proof of his guilt". On 2 February, Omar Raddad was found guilty and sent to prison for a term of eighteen years.

He served only four years of this sentence, being pardoned in 1998, following high-level intervention by the French and Moroccan governments. Raddad demanded a retrial to clear his name.

From Information Received

An anonymous letter sent to the police, followed by a public guarantee of protection for the sender, led to the arrest of a murder suspect.

The Cameo Cinema in Liverpool in the UK was the scene of a fatal shooting on the evening of 19 March 1949. About 9.30 p.m., a masked man armed with a revolver burst into the manager's office where Leonard Thomas and John Catterall were counting the takings. Six shots were fired which brought the box-office cashier running to the office together with the doorman. They were pushed aside by the masked gunman who told them to stand back. He was wielding a gun menacingly, so it was no time for bravery. They followed his instructions and he fled down the emergency stairs and out into the street.

The two men who had been quietly counting the money lay on the floor mortally wounded and the takings were missing. Unaware of the drama being enacted behind the scenes, the cinema audience continued to watch the evening film.

After an investigation lasting six months, the police were no nearer solving the Cameo Cinema murders when a breakthrough came by chance. An anonymously written letter was received offering information to the police in exchange for guaranteed protection. A further stipulation was that acceptance of the terms should be confirmed by an acknowledgment published in the *Liverpool Echo*. The police complied by inserting a notice in the paper which stated, "Letter received. Promise definitely given."

The outcome was the arrest of twenty-seven-year-old George Kelly, a small-time Merseyside gangster, and his accomplice, George Connolly, also in his twenties. They were charged jointly with the murder of Leonard Thomas. Connolly's part in the fatal shooting was to keep watch in the street outside the cinema while Kelly committed robbery. In the event, as soon as he heard shots being fired, he ran off in panic.

The two men were tried at Liverpool Assizes in January 1950. Legal history was made when Rose Heilbrun KC led the defence on behalf of Kelly. This was the first occasion in a British court when a woman led in a murder case. After a trial lasting thirteen days, the jury could not agree and a verdict was not possible.

A re-trial was ordered which took place in the following month when the two defendants were tried separately. Kelly was again represented by Rose Heilbrun but, on this occasion, the jury returned a guilty verdict. Mr Justice Cassels sentenced Kelly to death. No evidence was offered against Connolly on the murder charge and, following the judge's direction, the jury found him not guilty. He had pleaded guilty to conspiring with Kelly to carry out the robbery at the Cameo Cinema and of stealing fifty pounds. For these convictions he was sentenced to two years' imprisonment.

George Kelly was executed at Walton Prison on 28 March 1950, just a year after the cinema murders. Fifty-three years later, in an extraordinary turn of events, his conviction was judged a miscarriage of justice. The case was referred to the Criminal Cases Review Commission in 2003 and, on appeal, three judges decided that George Kelly was an innocent man.

Central to the appeal was information which came to light in police files in 1991 when a researcher found a statement, not disclosed at the original trial, in which another man confessed to the crime. In light of this new evidence the convictions of both Kelly and George Connolly were overturned.

Both men had consistently protested their innocence during their trial for the murders at the Cameo Cinema. Connolly died in 1997 without knowing that he had been exonerated.

A Dead Man Speaks

Joseph Williams, tried and acquitted of murder, gloated about how he had cheated the hangman and made a confession that remained a secret until his death twelve years later.

On 21 May 1939, Walter Dinivan, a wealthy retired businessman, was found unconscious and badly injured at his home at Branksome, Bournemouth in the UK. He died the next day in hospital from severe head wounds. It appeared that he had been attacked with a hammer and an attempt had also been made to strangle him.

Examination of the crime scene revealed no signs of forced entry to the house, suggesting that Dinivan knew his attacker. The safe in the drawing room had been emptied and a watch and rings taken from the dead man. The crime scene was a treasure trove of clues. On a side table were a bottle of beer and two glasses, one of which bore a thumb print. On the floor was a paper bag which might have been used to wrap a hammer and a number of cigarette butts were strewn about.

Regular visitors to the house had their fingerprints checked but no match was found with the impression on the beer glass, Local enquiries were fruitful, with reports that Dinivan had a friend who called on him, it was believed with the intention of borrowing money. The visitor was sixty-nine-year-old Joseph Williams who had a reputation for pleading poverty but, since Dinivan's death, seemed to have come into some money.

Williams, a former soldier, was out of work and lived a squalid life. When questioned, he admitted calling on Dinivan a few days before he died and borrowing five pounds. He explained his recent free spending as the result of a win on the horses.

The murder investigation focussed on the cigarette butts found at the crime scene and the possibility of testing saliva traces for blood-grouping. It was discovered that the smoker had a rare blood group shared by just three per cent of the population.

Williams was the prime suspect and, by devious means, detectives collected a cigarette butt he had discarded in a pub and sent it for laboratory testing. Williams, it seemed, belonged to the same three per cent as the smoker at the crime scene. A search of his home produced a supply of paper bags identical to the one found near Dinivan's body. When Williams' thumb print matched that on the beer glass, the police lost no time in charging him with the murder.

When he appeared on trial at Dorset Assizes Williams loudly and aggressively maintained his innocence but a conviction on forensic evidence seemed assured. But to the consternation of the police and prosecution, the jury found him not guilty and he walked free.

Twelve years later, Williams died of natural causes and the following day, his confession to murder was published in a national newspaper. He was interviewed by a journalist on the day of his acquittal. Over a whisky he toasted ". . . the hangman who had been cheated of a victim" and made a full confession which had remained secret until his death.

"Forgive Me . . ."

Besotted with his love for another man's wife, William Pettit took her life away with a dagger inscribed with the words, "I cut my way."

Pettit, a twenty-seven-year-old labourer from Eltham in south London, lodged with Mr and Mrs Brown. René Brown was old enough to be his mother but he believed he was in love with her. He had a history of violent behaviour and convictions for petty crime. When his attentions towards René Brown became a nuisance, he was told to leave their house. In his anger, he broke one of the windows.

Some time later, in mid-September 1963, a woman's body was found in a field near Chislehurst in Kent. Identified as René Brown, wife of a civil servant with her home in Eltham, she had been killed with a single knife thrust to the heart.

At the Coroner's inquest, Mr Brown stated that he knew who had killed his wife and named William Pettit. He also said that he was consulting a medium with a view to establishing Pettit's whereabouts. The police had other ideas and made history by having the missing man's description and photograph broadcast on television. Pettit thereby contributed a footnote in the annals of crime.

The television transmission was preceded by a great deal of soul-searching as to the ethics involved. The appeal for information came after the national news and before a magic show. A detailed description of Pettit was given, stating his height, sallow complexion and dark brown bushy hair. His clothes were described and nothing was left out regarding his appearance, including his sunken cheeks and cleft chin. The transmission, delivered with gravitas by John Snagge, and accompanied by a photograph of the wanted man, produced a huge response. There were hundreds of calls from viewers who claimed to have seen Pettit. All of this was backed up by massive coverage in the press.

Most of the sightings of the wanted man came from people in the London area and, indeed, that was where he was eventually found – to be precise, in the City of London. He lay dead in a bombed building near Cannon Street. The identity card in his pocket confirmed his name. Next to his body was a scribbled note, reading, "Forgive me for what I have done. I could have gone on living with Mr and Mrs Brown but not without Mrs Brown. I love her. I love her. I love her."

A post-mortem revealed that Pettit was suffering from an advanced form of tuberculosis. That is what may have killed him and death was given as probably due to natural causes. The pathologist estimated that he had died between four and six weeks prior to the discovery of his body. That implied he was already dead before the groundbreaking media appeal was launched to find the wanted man.

Fairplay

What might have been a perfect murder was foiled by an anonymous letter to the police urging them to look more closely into the recent death of a local man. Having been alerted, they called in detectives from Scotland Yard to help their enquiries and set about finding a poisoner.

Forty-four-year-old Arthur Major, a lorry driver, lived with his wife Ethel and their fourteen-year-old son at Kirkby-on-Bain in Lincolnshire. Neighbours regarded them as an odd couple. Ethel was unpopular and known for being difficult, while her husband spent a great deal of time in the pub.

On 22 May 1934, Ethel called on the local doctor to tell him that her husband had collapsed with a fit and, two days later, reported that he had died. A death certificate was issued giving epilepsy as the cause of death. Preparations were made for Arthur Major's funeral.

Then, on 26 May, police at Horncastle received a letter signed, "Fairplay", which drew their attention to the recent death. The anonymous writer raised several questions, one of which was why had Arthur Major complained about the bad taste of his food and thrown it out to the neighbour's dog which later died?

The police were used to receiving occasional cranky or malicious letters but they acted on "Fairplay's" warning and the coroner ordered the funeral of Arthur Major to be stopped. The corpse of the dog referred to had been buried in the garden and was exhumed for post-mortem examination. An autopsy was also carried out on Mr Major. Both dog and man were shown to have strychnine in their bodies.

Scotland Yard officers were called in to lead the investigation into what was now a murder case. Detectives interviewed Ethel Major and learned something of the strained relationship with her husband who had published a notice in the local paper saying that he was not responsible for his wife's debts.

During the interview, Mrs Major was at great pains to impress on the officers that her husband's last meal consisted of corned beef, a product she would never buy herself. It later emerged that she had sent her son to buy a tin. She did not appear to be grief-stricken over her loss. The next question was to find the source of the strychnine.

Tom Brown, Ethel's father, was a former gamekeeper. He said he had a small supply of strychnine that he kept in a box of which he had the only key. When he thought about it, though, he remembered there had been another key that was lost. A search of Ethel's home produced the second key, which she kept in her purse.

Ethel Major was tried for murder at Lincoln Assizes in November 1935. She pleaded not guilty and was defended by Sir Norman Birkett. Her defence was based on mitigating circumstances involving her abusive husband who she believed was seeing another woman. She did not give evidence.

The jury found her guilty but made a strong recommendation to mercy. She was sentenced to death and the jury's recommendation was not followed. Ethel Major was executed on 19 December 1935. The identity of the letter writer who precipitated the police investigation was never established.

"I Cannot Live Without You . . ."

Forty-seven-year-old Cecil Maltby had inherited his father's tailoring business which he ran from a shop near Regent's Park, London. His world had begun to disintegrate when he became bankrupt and his wife and child lived apart from him. He also took to drink but his prospects possibly looked brighter when Alice Middleton moved in with him to share the accommodation above the shop in 1922.

Mrs Middleton was the wife of an officer in the merchant navy and it was her custom to live in lodgings when he was away at sea for a long time. With her husband in the Far East, she went to live with Cecil Maltby. As he had lost interest in his business, he was free to entertain her, which he did by taking her to race meetings.

Alice Middleton was not seen after 15 August and, when her husband returned from his seafaring in December, he was confronted with the situation that his wife had gone missing. He reported her disappearance to the police and, in due course, officers came knocking at Mr Maltby's door.

Maltby would not allow the officers to enter but shouted down from an upstairs window. He said that Alice Middleton had left him and he did not know where she was. This dialogue in the street attracted the attention of neighbours, especially when Maltby's house was put under surveillance. The story reached the newspapers and public curiosity continued to grow. The man under scrutiny made occasional appearances at an upstairs window but he declined to come down.

The stalemate was broken after a week when a magistrate's order was granted, allowing the premises to be entered on health grounds. On 10 January 1923, medical health officials escorted by armed police officers approached the house.

Watched by a crowd of spectators, officers simultaneously broke their way into the front and rear of the premises.

The raiding parties were greeted by the sound of a gunshot coming from the first-floor bedroom. Breaking down the door, they found Cecil Maltby lying on the bed mortally wounded by a shot he had fired through his mouth. Further revelations came when officers searched the premises and made a grisly discovery in the kitchen. In the bath, wrapped in a sheet and covered with a board, was the decomposing body of Alice Middleton.

On the body was a note, "In memory of darling Pat, who committed suicide on 24 August 1922, 8.30 a.m." Nailed to the bedroom door was another note, "In memory of Alice H. Middleton", recording her suicide and asking, ". . . why did you do it? . . . I cannot live without you", and signed, "Cecil Maltby". Other letters were found in different parts of the house. One of these indicated that she planned to shoot herself and there was a struggle over the gun, which she succeeded in using against herself.

Maltby wrote, "I put Mrs Middleton in the bath, and have not liked to part with the dear soul." Medical examiners confirmed that she had died from three shots entering her body from behind. The coroner's inquest returned a verdict of murder and of suicide against Maltby.

". . . Take Three Paces Forward"

When two young robbers murdered an elderly, reclusive farmer who was rumoured to be wealthy, they came away with a few pounds and a couple of watches. What they had missed, lying on their victim's desk, were written instructions on how to reach his savings; "From the stone doorposts of the pigsty, take three paces forward. Go three feet down", read the note. The problem for the robbers was that it was written in Spanish.

William Rowe was an elderly bachelor who lived on his own at Nanjarrow Farm in Cornwall in the UK. He lived frugally, rarely went out and was not keen to admit people to his farmhouse. He was respected as an astute cattle dealer and local gossip had it that he was a wealthy man.

The rumours reached the ears of Russell Pascoe and Dennis Whitty, both in their twenties, who lived locally. In the summer of 1960, they chose a day when Rowe made one of his rare outings to Truro, and broke into his farmhouse. They found money salted away in old jars and tins and came away with £250. The police had their suspicions about who was responsible but could not bring charges as the evidence was insufficient.

In August 1963, William Rowe suffered another break-in, this time with fatal consequences. When a cattle dealer visited the farm he found the old man lying dead in a corner of the yard. He had been severely battered and the house ransacked. Contents of cupboards and drawers were strewn about on the floor and mattresses had been torn apart in an obvious search.

Suspecting that the attackers were local, the police focussed again on Pascoe and Whitty. It was not long before their enquiries produced results. Pascoe had parted from his wife and child and gone to live with Whitty in a caravan and with the company of three girls.

The girls had been threatened to keep their mouths shut but under police questioning, the truth emerged. Pascoe and Whitty said they were going to do a job and armed themselves with a knife and a crowbar. When they returned, they said they had killed the farmer. Confronted with these admissions, each blamed the other.

Their story was that they thought Rowe was absent from home and when they arrived and found lights on, they resorted to a ruse to get him to unlock the door. On the pretext that a plane had crashed nearby, they asked to use the telephone. Rowe did not have a telephone but he opened the door to give them directions to the nearest call box. As soon as he appeared on the doorstep, he was clubbed with a crowbar. The pair ransacked the house in their hunt for money and found next to nothing. Having bludgeoned the old man, they finished him off with stab wounds to the chest and neck.

Pascoe and Whitty were charged with murder and sent for trial. Much of the evidence involved expert medical testimony as to which weapon, the crowbar or the knife, had caused the fatal injuries. Pascoe had armed himself on the night of the attack with a crowbar while Whitty had the knife. In any event, as the law stood, if the two had acted together, each was equally guilty. This was the view of the jury, which returned a guilty verdict. Both men were sentenced to death; Pascoe was hanged at Bristol and Whitty at Winchester.

After the trial, it emerged that William Rowe, probably prompted by the first robbery, had carefully hidden his money. But among the papers on his desk was a note written in Spanish, giving details of where to find his treasure. He had also left another clue in the form of a *Teach Yourself* Spanish book. When his instructions were followed, a safe buried in concrete came to light, which contained £1,500. The wily farmer had protected his savings but at the cost of his life.

The Alias Man

The chance recognition of a face seen on "America's Most Wanted" television programme revealed the alias of a man sought as a murder suspect.

Thirty-five-year-old Rosalyn Goodman disappeared during a hiking trip to the Great Smoky Mountain Park in the US in 1984. She left home in Memphis, Tennessee, driving her Volkswagen car on 23 September. She was heading for a popular scenic spot called Cades Cove where she intended to spend a few days before returning home.

When Rosalyn failed to return from her trip and did not call home, she was reported missing. The police asked for information from the public that might enable them to reconstruct her movements. There were reports that she had been seen with a man in the vicinity of Cades Cove at the end of September.

Three months later, deer hunters found a partly concealed body near a cabin at Cades Cove. The body had been reduced to a skeleton and there was evidence that it had been attacked by animals but no other obvious signs of violence. There was no identity on the body and initial examination showed that the remains were of a female aged around thirty. The possibility that the body was that of Rosalyn Goodman was confirmed by dental evidence.

Forensic examination failed to establish with certainty how the woman had died, although death by strangulation was strongly suspected. Her car was found in a parking lot near Cades Cove and it had evidently been thoroughly cleaned both inside and out. With no forensic traces to help them, investigators once again appealed to the public for information.

Four years elapsed with no progress in the investigation of Rosalyn's death but then, in June 1988, the breakthrough came due to the alertness of an FBI agent. While watching the television programme, "America's Most Wanted", in Knoxville, the agent saw a face on screen that he recognized. The programme featured William Hewlett who was wanted for rape and assault in two states. While recognizing the face, the agent knew the man by another name. He made the connection to Harry Steven Mercer who was wanted for questioning by the FBI in connection with the Cades Cove investigation.

At that time, the FBI did not realize that Hewlett and Mercer were the same individual. Forty-four-year-old Hewlett and his wife were an itinerant couple who worked in the restaurant trade. They moved from place to place and it was believed they had been seen in the Cades Cove area in September 1984. Investigators were keen to interview them.

Hewlett/Mercer had form as a bank robber and he was wanted for sexual assault. While on several "most wanted" lists, he had managed to avoid arrest by constantly keeping on the move. He liked to think of himself and his wife as a kind of latterday Bonnie and Clyde.

Eventually, Hewlett, a man with many aliases, was traced to Gulfport, Mississippi, where he was arrested. He confessed to raping and strangling Rosalyn Goodman, a crime for which he was tried, convicted and given a life sentence.

"Crimewatch" Points The Way

Fleeing to another continent, changing his name and adopting a new lifestyle did not prevent the British forces of justice catching up with a rapist and murderer.

On the evening of 14 March 2003, seventeen-year-old Hannah Foster was returning home in Southampton in the UK when she was abducted. Her parents reported her missing and, two days later, her body was found in bushes by the roadside in the West End of the city. She had been raped and strangled. DNA on her clothing offered some prospect of identifying her murderer. The young woman had made an emergency 999 call on the evening she disappeared but the call was cut off.

On 17 March, the victim's handbag and mobile phone were found at a recycling plant in Portsmouth. They had been discarded in a bottle bank. On 26 March, the murder featured on the BBC television programme, "Crimewatch". An appeal was made for information that might help crime investigators. One of those who responded was an employee at a food supplier in Southampton. He reported his suspicions regarding a man named Kohli who drove a sandwich delivery van for the firm.

Kohli was not at his home but an examination of his van revealed possibly incriminating forensic traces. Using the latest technology for automatic number plate recognition and analysing the dead girl's mobile phone data enabled investigators to place both Kohli and the victim on the motorway between Southampton and Portsmouth on 15 March.

It was evident that Kohli had taken evasive action and it was discovered that he had left Heathrow airport on a flight to India on 18 March. He had tried to borrow money to buy a plane ticket from a friend saying he wanted to visit his mother who was ill. When the friend declined, he approached his father-in-law who lent him the money.

An arrest warrant for Maninder Pal Singh Kohli was issued on 13 April 2003 and the tortuous process began of locating him and bringing him back to Britain. Hannah Foster's parents travelled to India and helped to generate public interest in their quest for justice. Intense media coverage resulted in the location of Kohli who was living in West Bengal under an assumed name. Having deserted his wife and family in Britain he had married an Indian girl as part of the new life he planned to lead.

On 15 July 2004, Kohli was taken into custody by Indian police and the slow business of extraditing him to Britain began. It would take over three years. A month after he was arrested, Kohli appeared on Indian television and admitted that he had killed Hannah Foster. "I did it. I raped her. I strangled her . . ." he said. He later withdrew his confession.

He was finally extradited to Britain on 28 July 2007. His DNA was shown to match that found on the victim's clothing. Kohli was tried at Winchester Crown Court in October 2008. The prosecution case was that he had accosted his victim, forced her into his van and later raped her. He strangled her to avoid being identified as a rapist, dumped her body and returned home to his family.

Kohli's bizarre defence was that he had been set up by the supervisor at his workplace and forced into sexual relations with a woman who happened to be Hannah Foster. The jury convicted the forty-one-year-old deliveryman of murder and he was sentenced to life imprisonment. Mr Justice Keith told him, "It took a long time for you to be brought to justice, but the law finally caught up with you . . . you took her life so she would not be able to point the finger of guilt at you."

Case Of The Yellow String Bag

A replica knitted yellow string bag proved to be an inspired piece of lateral thinking by a detective, which solved a murder case.

Forty-eight-year-old Dagmar Peters, a lady of modest means, lived on her own in a hut at Kingsdown in Kent in the UK. Her elderly mother lived nearby. On 31 October 1946, Peters' body was found at a place called Labour-in-vain Hill on the Downs close to the A20 Maidstone to London road. She had been strangled. It was evident that she had been killed elsewhere and then dragged to the place where she was found.

It was learned that she was in the habit of visiting her brother in London by hitching lifts on the A20. Her mother mentioned that when she left home she had with her a brown attaché case and a yellow string bag. Both items were missing.

The pathological condition of the body indicated that she had remained in a seated position for some time after she was killed. Everything pointed to a roadside pick-up that had gone wrong. Police began the task of checking vehicles using the A20.

Chief Inspector Robert Fabian took charge of the investigation. He had an idea that the missing string bag held the key to the case. He learnt that the bag had been knitted by Dagmar Peters' sister-in-law. Would she make another one, asked Fabian? A new, distinctive yellow string bag was made and photographs of it were published in the press.

The photograph of the bag brought an immediate response from a fifteen-year-old boy who said he had found a bag like it in Clare Park Lake three days after Peters' body was discovered. He had given it away and the bag passed through several pairs of hands before it was retrieved. Forensic examination revealed traces of hair similar to that of the murder victim.

Detectives guessed that the bag had been thrown into a stream which fed through a culvert under a factory and into Clare Park Lake. Narrowing their search, they found fragments of the missing attaché case. The next focus was the factory, which had taken a recent delivery of bricks from a supplier in Cambridge. With the instinct for which he was renowned, Fabian now homed in on the driver.

The company supplying the bricks said the driver for that particular delivery was Sydney Sinclair who had since left their employ. His real name was Harold Hagger, a man with several convictions including assault. He confessed to strangling Dagmar Peters, who he alleged had tried to steal his wallet. He didn't mean to kill her he said, he just pulled her scarf too tight around her neck.

The man with a string of convictions had been trapped by a string bag. Hagger was found guilty and sentenced to death. He was hanged at Wandsworth on 18 March 1947.

". . . It Looks Like Murder"

A nineteen-year-old literary poseur called a Sunday newspaper to report his discovery of a body. He believed he had uncovered a murder and wanted payment to tell the story. His written account proved to be a confession.

Forty-eight-year-old Mabel Tattershaw was married with two daughters. Her husband worked away from home. To help the family budget, she took in lodgers. On 2 August 1951, Mabel watched a film showing at the Roxy Cinema in Nottingham. She found herself sitting next to a young man who chatted her up. They agreed to meet the next day and he took her to a quiet spot in Sherwood Vale.

Later that day the *News of the World* received a telephone call from Herbert Mills to report his discovery of a woman's body. ". . . It looks like murder," he said. The newspaper alerted the police and the body was found in a quiet wooded area. The dead woman, later identified as Mabel Tattershaw, had been bludgeoned and strangled.

Mills was questioned and he gave an account of finding the body and reading poetry before he called the newspaper. He explained his literary aspirations and how walking in Sherwood Vale inspired his poetic imagination. Once he had left the police station, he was free to talk to the press. He made several statements for which he requested payment.

On 24 August, following an interview with a journalist, he made a remarkable confession. This was handwritten and took an hour to complete. He began by stating that he had considered the possibility of committing the perfect murder. When he found himself in the cinema sat next to Mabel Tattershaw, whom he claimed responded to his approaches, he saw the possibility of putting his theory into practice.

His assignation with the middle-aged lady who was conceivably flattered by the young man's attention, was easy. He led her to a quiet corner in the woods and carried out his experiment. He wrote that, "The strangling itself was quite easily accomplished."

Mills was charged with murder and put on trial at Nottingham Assizes in November 1951. The defence offered on his behalf was that he had stumbled across the body when he was walking in the woods and saw an opportunity to make some money and gain public recognition by inventing stories for the newspapers. However, the forensic evidence irrefutably linked him to his victim. There had been transfers of contact evidence, including hair and fibres. Most incriminating were the fibres from Mills' suit which had been retrieved from beneath the victim's fingernails.

Mills was found guilty and sentenced to death. He responded by smiling at both the judge and the jury. Ironically, Shelley, whose poetry Mills claimed to have read at the crime scene, wrote the line, "I met Murder on the way . . .". He also met the hangman, Albert Pierrepoint, who despatched him on the gallows at Lincoln on 11 December 1951.

The Man In Black

Peter Moore ran a small chain of cinemas in north Wales, working as a businessman by day and turning into a monster at night. He bought a combat knife to celebrate his forty-ninth birthday and used it to kill a retired railway worker outside his home at Anglesey in September 1995. Henry Roberts was stabbed fourteen times.

His second victim was Keith Randles, a night security guard at a road works site. The man begged for his life and asked Moore why he was attacking him, "I just said, 'Fun'," he later told detectives. After stabbing Randles fourteen times, he drove home but returned to the scene to retrieve his bow tie, which had come adrift during the attack.

Two other killings followed, accompanied by multiple stabbing. Moore had lived with his mother at Kinmel Bay and the neighbours regarded him as "a nice lad" who preferred to stay at home. He later told detectives that his mother's death in 1994 and the loss of family pets had turned him into a serial killer. He said, "Death literally seemed to start following me around."

When detectives searched his home they found a collection of sex toys, handcuffs, gags, vibrators and military style clothing. His bedtime reading included a book about the world's most evil men.

Moore was put on trial for murder at Mold Crown Court in

November 1996. He denied all the charges and claimed that the killings had been carried out by a man he called Jason who was a character in the horror film, "Friday the Thirteenth".

A sadistic homosexual who killed four men in the space of three months in 1995, Moore was believed to have carried out around fifty assaults over a period of twenty years. What started as domination and humiliation escalated into violence and murder, possibly triggered by the loss of his mother. Following his arrest he was asked if killing gave him pleasure. "Yes," he replied, "there was a certain enjoyment from it . . . it was a job well done."

When he sat in the dock Moore wore a black shirt. This was commented on by the prosecutor. "Black was his uniform and he was the man in black, with black thoughts and the blackest of deeds," he said.

Peter Moore was found guilty on all four counts of murder. Mr Justice Kay told him that, "not one of the victims had done you the slightest bit of harm. It was killing for killing's sake." He reminded him of his admission to police officers that he did it for fun. He had shown no remorse and in passing sentence, the judge said, "I consider you to be as dangerous a man as it is possible to find." He sentenced Moore to four life sentences.

Hollywood Role Model

David Gonzalez sought fame by emulating the crimes of a fictional character. During the course of three days in September 2004, twenty-five-year-old Gonzalez committed four murders and attempted two other killings in the UK. On 15 September, he murdered a man in Worthing, Sussex and, two days later, killed a couple in Highgate, north London, in a savage knife attack. On the same day he killed a pub landlord, also in north London.

Gonzalez's attacks were fuelled by drugs and his desire to become a famous serial killer. His role model was Freddy Krueger who played the part of an undead serial killer in the Hollywood horror film, "Nightmare on Elm Street". On screen, Krueger was depicted as a demonic figure with a disfigured face who slaughtered for pleasure.

Gonzalez confessed to the killings and said, "I just want to get locked up." He had a history of mental health problems but had not previously threatened violence. After his arrest, he was referred to Broadmoor maximum security psychiatric hospital where he attempted to commit suicide by biting himself to death.

Sent for trial at the Old Bailey in March 2006, Gonzalez was described by the prosecution as a cold, callous individual. It was suggested that he was manipulative and had tried to convince psychiatrists that he heard voices that commanded him to kill. The case argued by the prosecution was that he was a psychopathic individual whose inhibitions were reduced by drugs and alcohol.

The defence case was that Gonzalez was guilty of manslaughter and not murder. The contention was that he was driven to kill at random because of mental illness. The jury rejected this proposition and found him guilty of murder. He was sentenced to life imprisonment.

"Burn, Baby, Burn"

Jean Powell, Glyn Powell and Bernadette McNeilly – a gang led by a woman who called herself "Chucky", after the evil doll in the film, "Child's Play", held a sixteen-year-old girl captive for six days. During that time, they subjected her to humiliation and torture before setting fire to her and leaving her for dead in woodlands near Stockport, Lancashire in the UK.

Powell and McNeilly lived in Moston, Manchester, in a rundown community that was riven with theft and drugs. The two women, known locally as "The Witches", were interested in the occult and they drew young people into a world of sex, drugs and crime.

Suzanne Capper, aged sixteen, did not like school. She came to know the Powell family and looked after their children. It was said of Jean Powell that she could manipulate anyone and Suzanne was scared of her. Crisis point was reached when

Suzanne was supposed to have stolen a coat from one of the women and tried to arrange a sex session with a wealthy Arab. The two "Witches" decided to exact revenge on the teenager.

In December 1992 Suzanne was taken captive and held in two different houses for six days. She was gagged and blindfolded, stripped and beaten. Her hair was cut off, she was injected with drugs and scrubbed savagely with disinfectant. Music, with the words, "I'm Chucky, wanna play?" was played continuously to Suzanne through headphones.

The two "Witches" were strong personalities and they drew in others to engage in their sadistic activities, including seventeen-year-old Anthony Dudson. On 14 December, Suzanne was put in the boot of a car and driven fifteen miles to Compsall near Stockport. She was pushed down a slope from the roadside into woodland, doused with petrol and set alight.

Her attackers confidently expected Suzanne to die quickly. On the way home, they stopped to buy soft drinks and on reaching home went to bed with McNeilly singing, "Burn, baby, burn". Despite suffering burns covering seventy-five per cent of her body, Suzanne managed to stagger back to the road where she encountered some workmen who called for help. She was taken to hospital and before she lapsed into a coma was able to give detectives the names of her attackers. Suzanne Capper died on 18 December.

When the police visited Powell and McNeilly they laughed and joked as they were arrested. All those involved denied everything, but Anthony Dudson had pangs of conscience and began to talk. Slowly the whole sordid story emerged and police found the torture room where Suzanne had been held in McNeilly's house.

At Manchester Crown Court in December 1993 six people were tried for various offences, ranging from murder to false imprisonment and committing grievous bodily harm. During the twenty-two days of the trial, jurors wept as they heard the details of Suzanne Capper's horrifying ordeal. The jury deliberated for ten hours before giving their verdicts. Mr Justice Potts said, "This was as appalling a murder as it is possible to imagine."

He sentenced Jean Powell, aged twenty-six, her husband, Glyn Powell, aged twenty-nine, and Bernadette McNeilly, aged twenty-four, to life imprisonment. Anthony Dudson was ordered to be detained during Her Majesty's Pleasure. Two other men received custodial sentences.

A sordid footnote to a tale of unbelievable horror was that demand for the film, "Child's Play", described as an adult black comedy, were boosted.

Wired For Sound

Possibly the first live broadcast of a murder trial took place in Canada in the 1890s when a young Englishman was on trial for his life.

Two young men, Frederick Benwell and Reginald Birchall, left Liverpool in February 1890 on board the liner *Britannic* heading for New York. The two men discussed a scheme whereby they would enter into a partnership to run a stock farm in Ontario, Canada. Benwell handed over £500 for his share of the deal.

On 21 February, two farmers discovered a body in a swampy field near Princeton, Ontario. The frozen corpse was identified as Frederick Benwell by Birchall who saw his photograph in a newspaper report. Benwell had died from a gunshot wound in the head.

Enquiries revealed that Birchall had been running a moneymaking scheme which involved selling shares in non-existent Canadian farms. One of his clients was another passenger who had travelled on the *Britannic*, Douglas Pelly, a British emigrant embarking on a farm-pupil scheme operated to encourage colonization.

It appeared that while Birchall and Benwell went off together to look at a prospective farm, Pelly stayed behind at Niagara Falls. Birchall returned alone, explaining that the farm was no good and Benwell had opted out of the arrangement. According to Pelly's account, Birchall made an attempt on his life by pushing him on a narrow bridge over the Niagara River.

Birchall was arrested and charged with Benwell's murder.

The case created great public interest not least because of the adverse publicity felt by many Canadians that immigrants were being lured to their country and exploited by money-grabbing go-betweens.

With Birchall in custody awaiting trial, a storm of unprecedented press activity began to brew. Birchall's character was blackened and he was characterized as a diabolical schemer preying on vulnerable young people wanting to create new lives for themselves. Local entrepreneurs of a different kind cashed in on Birchall's notoriety by staging waxwork representations of the murder scene for public consumption. Meanwhile, the man awaiting trial put pen to paper and wrote an autobiography.

Reginald Birchall was tried at Woodstock and the proceedings attracted an almost manic response from the press. Reporters descended on the court in great numbers and leading newspapers went to extraordinary lengths to gather news. London newspapers telegraphed reports to England by trans-Atlantic cable, the details arriving in London minutes after the event in Canada. To satisfy local demand, the courtroom was wired for sound so that members of the public could make a telephone call and listen in on the trial as it progressed.

The prosecution set out to prove that Birchall had been in Princeton and produced witnesses who claimed to have seen him there and had heard the sound of gunfire. The evidence against him was entirely circumstantial and his defence counsel made an impassioned plea on his behalf. This failed to sway the jury, which delivered a guilty verdict and sentence of death was pronounced by the judge. He was hanged on 14 November 1890 in a bungled execution whereby he was strangled because the executioner decided to use an unorthodox noose, which failed to dislocate the neck.

Such was the interest in the case that a Toronto publisher quickly brought out an account of the Benwell murder, entitled *Swamp of Death*, promising a full description of Birchall's last days and execution. Thus was the public's interest catered for at a cost of 30 cents a copy.

Media Mania

Lyle and Erik Menendez, sons of a wealthy Beverly Hills family, were accused of killing their parents in order to acquire their fortune. After many twists and turns, which captivated the American public for several months, the brothers were eventually found guilty, after twice being tried for murder.

On 20 August 1989, death stalked the home of Jose and Kitty Menendez at Elm Drive, Beverly Hills, California. While they were watching television, two men armed with twelve-gauge shotguns entered the house and killed them both. Jose was hit five times and Kitty received ten shotgun wounds. The killers picked up the expended cartridge cases and left as they came, unseen.

The dead couple's sons, Lyle and Erik, had been out for the evening and returned home just before midnight. They found the driveway gate open and the front door unlocked and then discovered their murdered parents. Lyle made a 911 call sobbing, "Somebody shot and killed my parents."

Forty-five-year-old Jose Menendez had made a successful career in the video entertainment business and was thought to be worth around $14 million. There were suggestions that he and his wife had been killed by the Mafia, but then suspicion began to focus on his two sons. The police noted that the young men seemed to show little concern about the search for their parents' killers.

Little by little, the brothers' alibi began to unravel and Lyle indulged in a spending spree. They denied any knowledge of the killings but in March 1990 were arrested and charged with murder. No murder weapons were recovered and the evidence against them was circumstantial. They were held in custody at Los Angeles County Jail to await trial.

Speculation about the brothers was rife. One theory was that they knew the identity of the murderers but were too afraid to tell. Another angle was that Erik had made a confession recorded on tape by a therapist he had consulted. Erik had also apparently written a film script in which the leading character discovered that he stood to inherit a large sum of money from his parents, so he murdered them.

What the media called "Menendez Mania" gripped America in October 1993 when the two brothers were put on trial. The proceedings were broadcast live on Court TV and people camped overnight outside the courtroom in the hope of getting a seat in the public gallery. While the Los Angeles District Attorney's Office received calls offering advice that would secure convictions, Lyle Menendez enjoyed letters of love and sympathy.

A month before the trial began, the defence strategy became known. It would be based on a notion of self-defence in that the brothers shot their parents after their father threatened to kill them because of his fear that they would expose the years of sexual abuse they had experienced at his hands. A few days before the trial began, a legal ruling admitted the evidence of the tape-recording made of Erik Menendez's hitherto confidential session with a therapist. After months of denial came an admission that the brothers had indeed killed their parents. The argument offered was that they shot their mother to prevent her suffering any further from their father's infidelity. There was no mention of sexual abuse or of fear for their own lives.

Public opinion was polarized and this was reflected in the outcome of the trial. Separate juries considered the case against each brother and, in proceedings that had lasted six months, both juries were deadlocked.

The second trial began in October 1995. The judge ruled out live television broadcasts and the proceedings were heard by only one jury. The defence pleaded the sexual abuse argument and contended that the brothers killed out of fear. The prosecution maintained that they shot their parents in order to gain their father's fortune.

The jury's verdict was that Lyle and Erik Menendez were guilty of murder. The verdict noted special circumstances that potentially carried the death penalty. A sentencing hearing in April 1996 rejected the death penalty argument and the brothers were sentenced to life imprisonment without parole.

The verdict came six and a half years after the murders and

the irony was that José Menendez's fortune was consumed by the legal fees incurred in the defence of his sons.

"I Am Going To Be Famous"

A delivery van driver in London who wanted to become a new Jack the Ripper was convicted of killing two women whose bodies were never found.

Xiao Mei Guo, a twenty-nine-year-old illegal immigrant, sold DVDs on the streets of London's East End. She went missing at the end of August 2007. CCTV images recorded on cameras at Whitechapel Tube Station showed her talking to a man identified as forty-seven-year-old Derek Brown. A further link to Brown was made in the following month when twenty-four-year-old Bonnie Barrett, a Whitechapel prostitute, went missing. Brown was known to be one of her clients.

Weeks before these women disappeared, Brown had told a friend, "You will hear of me. I am going to be famous." Brown was a known sex offender who had been identified by various rape victims over ten or more years. He had been convicted of rape at Preston, his home town, in 1989.

When he was questioned by the police, Brown admitted knowing Xiao Mei Guo, with whom he had regular sex. A search of his flat at Rotherhithe in southeast London turned up receipts for an assortment of equipment bought at a DIY store. This included a saw, rubber gloves, plastic sheeting and cleaning materials.

From the state of the flat, with its stripped walls and recently taken-up carpet, it was clear that a clean-up operation was under way. Traces of blood were found on the walls and ceiling and there was evidence of bloodstains in the bath.

Books found in Brown's flat included accounts of activities of serial killers such as Peter Sutcliffe, the Yorkshire Ripper, and Dennis Nilsen. Police believed Brown wanted to emulate Jack the Ripper, which was why he chose Whitechapel as his killing ground. If he killed women in that area, he knew the link to the Ripper would inevitably be made and he would gain the notoriety he was looking for. Detectives believed he had only just started his killing spree.

Brown was sent for trial at the Old Bailey in September 2008. The prosecution said that his victims lived on the edge of society and represented soft targets for a man who thought their disappearance from the streets would not be noted. On 3 October, Brown was found guilty of murder and sentenced to life imprisonment.

Police believed that Brown might have killed before and unsolved cases were being reviewed. The man who wanted to be compared with the serial killer who terrorized Whitechapel in 1888 was granted his wish with a newspaper headline that read, "Killer wanted to be Jack the Ripper".

"You Next!"

When Margaret Backhouse started her car on 9 April 1984, there was an explosion and, although severely injured, she survived. An investigation found that a pipe bomb loaded with shotgun pellets had been hidden under the driver's seat and wired up to the car's ignition.

The explosion occurred at the farm in Widden Hill in the Cotswolds in the UK where Graham and Margaret Backhouse lived. Backhouse told the police that he had found a sheep's head on his land with a note reading, "You next." He had also complained about receiving threatening telephone calls. The police advised him to tighten up his security and make sure he kept his vehicles locked. An alarm was installed in his home, which was linked to the police station.

On 30 April, the alarm sounded and police arrived at Widden Hill where they found the body of Colyn Bedale-Taylor in the farmhouse. He had been shot twice in the chest with a shotgun. Graham Backhouse was found lying on the floor of the study with knife wounds to his face and chest. His wife was still in hospital recovering from the injuries caused by the car explosion.

Colyn Bedale-Taylor, aged sixty-three, was a retired engineer and neighbour of the Backhouses. According to Graham Backhouse, his neighbour had confessed to planting the bomb and he shot him when Bedale-Taylor attacked him with a knife.

The forensic evidence did not add up. For a start, Bedale-Taylor would surely have dropped the knife when he was shot. Secondly, the knife had his initials, CBT, scratched into its surface but this was uncharacteristic because none of the many tools used by Bedale-Taylor, a keen furniture restorer, was similarly marked. The indications were that the knife had been placed in his hand.

Enquiries revealed that Graham Backhouse was in financial difficulties and needed £100,000 to pay off his debts and secure his business. Significantly, he had taken out two life insurance policies on his wife, equivalent to that amount.

Backhouse was arrested and charged with the murder of Bedale-Taylor and the attempted murder of his wife. He was tried at Bristol Crown Court in February 1985 where the prosecution made its case that he had hatched a plot to kill his wife to claim on the insurance and to put the blame on his neighbour. Backhouse denied attempting to murder his wife and claimed he killed his neighbour in self-defence.

Forensic evidence made it clear from an examination of bloodstains at the scene of the killing that the knife had been put into the hand of the dead man. The inference was that Backhouse had used the knife to slash his own face in a simulated attack. The self-inflicted scars were evident on his face when he appeared in court.

Backhouse had worked out his murderous scheme early in 1984, beginning with the stories about threats to his life. This was a prelude to the bomb planted in his wife's car which he would claim was intended for him. Once that part of the scheme unravelled, he decided to make a scapegoat of his neighbour inviting him to his home for coffee and a chat. He literally had his victim in his sights when he produced a shotgun and killed him.

Apparently, Graham Backhouse had ambitions to write detective stories but that was another plot that failed. The trial jury found him guilty of both charges on a majority verdict. Mr Justice Stuart-Smith told him, "You are a devious and wicked man" as he sentenced the would-be writer to life imprisonment.

Enough Rope

An amateur filmmaker, who fixated on images of young women in dire predicaments, enticed a girl into his studio where she was hanged while the camera recorded her death agonies.

Forty-nine-year-old Geoffrey Jones lived in Hall Green, Birmingham in the UK. He made films with grisly content, featuring young women in distress, lying under the wheels of a bus or about to be crushed by a train. The girls wore tight, form-fitting clothes and acted as suitably terror-stricken maidens. The films were viewed at private showings and distributed through a video network.

Jones advertised for models by means of cards displayed in newsagents' shop windows. In April 1985, he placed an ad reading, "Wanted – Young Lady for part-time modelling. Experience not necessary." Contact details were included. Seventeen-year-old Marion Terry was unemployed after leaving school and thought the ad offered a money-earning opportunity. The going rate was £2 an hour.

Marion went to Jones' house where he had an upstairs room fitted out as a studio. He had written the script for a film to be called "Enough Rope", the central feature of which was the death of a young woman by hanging. Marion was to be cast in that role.

What happened next would be the subject of a later reconstruction, but Jones appeared at a friend's home and told her he had taken an overdose of aspirin tablets to kill himself. He mentioned that there was a dead body in his house.

The full details of the filming session that took place in Geoffrey Jones's studio emerged at his trial for murder at Birmingham Crown Court in April 1986. The prosecutor gave a graphic reconstruction of the way in which Marion Terry had met her death.

Jones explained what he wanted, indicating a noose hanging from the ceiling of the studio, underneath which was a chair.

When Marion was directed to stand on the chair and place the noose around her neck, she rebelled. He forced her to comply and then pulled the chair away. As she dangled from the ceiling, the camera recorded the event.

It was argued on Jones' behalf that the mock hanging went tragically wrong and Marion died by accident. His attempts to resuscitate her failed and, in a state of distress, he went to a friend's house where he explained what had happened. The prosecutor dismissed this account, maintaining that Jones was sexually inadequate and derived pleasure from visualizing young women in life-threatening situations. His ultimate fantasy was to hang a young girl.

Jones was found guilty of murder and sentenced to life imprisonment. He made no response when asked if he had anything to say. One of the mysteries is what happened to the film that Jones was making. Detectives believed that he did record his victim's dying moments on film but it was never recovered.

Natural Selector

In a tragedy reminiscent of the Dunblane and Columbine massacres, eighteen-year-old Pekka-Eric Auvinen went on a killing spree in a school in Finland. On the morning of 7 November 2007, he shot dead eight students and the head teacher before turning the gun on himself.

A witness to the tragedy at Jokela High School in a small town near Helsinki said that Auvinen moved systematically down the school corridors, opening doors and firing at the occupants of classrooms. He appeared to be acting without emotion. "He was not laughing: his face was a blank," said a fellow student.

Hours before the killings, Auvinen had posted a video on YouTube with the title, "Sturmgeist 89" (Stormspirit). It showed him pointing a handgun at the screen and was accompanied by a "manifesto" in which he described himself as a "natural selector". He declared, "I will eliminate all who I see as unfit, disgraces of human race and failures of natural selection." He added, "I am so full of hate and I love it."

The eighteen-year-old student had joined a gun club in Helsinki earlier in the year and used his membership to obtain a gun licence and then bought a handgun and ammunition. During the shooting tragedy, he fired his .22 weapon sixty-six times and had hundreds of rounds of ammunition with him.

Comparisons were made with the massacre at Dunblane in Scotland in 1996 and the Columbine school killings in Colorado in 1999. More specifically, attention was drawn to the shooting earlier in 2007 at Virginia Tech in the US when Cho Heng Hui killed thirty-two students. Attention was drawn to Finland's murder rate, which at twenty-eight per 100,000 is the highest in Western Europe, and also to its gun ownership. In a country of 5.3 million, there are fifty-six privately-owned firearms for every 100 citizens.

Pekka-Eric Auvinen was described as a solitary youth with few friends who was lonely and angry. He came from a comfortable home and in his manifesto said, "Don't blame anyone else for my actions ... Don't blame my parents or my friends ..." It appeared that the young man had been influenced by the Columbine massacre and was committed to controversial ecological views in which not all human beings were deemed fit to survive.

Act Of Revenge

Just after 7 a.m. on 18 April 2007, shots were heard in a dormitory at Virginia Tech in Blacksburg, USA. Two students were found dead and there was a trail of bloody footprints in the corridor but no apparent gunman.

At 9.40 a.m. a reign of terror was unleashed on students in another building on the campus. A gunman wielding two handguns went from classroom to classroom firing at students attending lectures. Panic ensued as students tried to escape through windows or tended their injured colleagues. The gunman fired repeatedly, discharging 200 shots and re-loading his weapons, without uttering a word. Finally, with thirty-two dead, including both students and teachers, the gunman put one of the weapons to his head and killed himself.

Between the two shooting phases, twenty-three-year-old Cho Heng Hui mailed a video package to NBC News in New York. It contained his chilling manifesto in which he declared he would kill himself but he was going to take others with him.

Cho was a student at Virginia Tech where he shared a room with five others. His behaviour had been the subject of concern since 2005. One of his lecturers raised concerns about his obsession with violence and unwillingness to communicate. He rarely spoke and, when he did, it was often in whispers. He shunned contact and seemed angry and depressed.

Cho had been born in South Korea and moved to the US with his parents in 1992. His father ran a dry-cleaning business and he attended the local school where, apparently, he was bullied. He studied English at Virginia Tech where tutors worried about the violence underlying his plays and essays. In one of his plays, he described the wishes of three students to kill a sadistic teacher.

In his manifesto, he ranted about the evils of materialism and the snobbery and debauchery of his fellow students. He planned his revenge carefully. In February, he bought a Walther P22 pistol and the following month he acquired a Glock semi-automatic. These were the weapons that he used to such devastating effect.

The 25,000 students and 10,000 staff at Virginia Tech were shocked at the tragedy that had unfolded on their campus. The wider American public were equally appalled and minds immediately went back to the Columbine massacre in 1999 when two teenagers shot dead thirteen people. American gun ownership was again re-examined with the customary analysis of statistics; 200 million guns in private ownership, 300,000 gun-related assaults annually and around 30,000 deaths.

Commenting on Cho Heng Hui, Boston-based criminologist Jack Levin said his acts were revenge against people he believed were persecuting him.

"... Life Is War ..."

Finland experienced its second classroom massacre in less than a year when a trainee chef opened fire on his classmates in September 2008, killing ten of them.

Twenty-two-year-old Matti Juhani Saari turned up at the school in Kauhajoki on the morning of 23 September carrying a bag which contained a handgun, ammunition and explosives. Pulling a balaclava over his head, he produced a .22 pistol and entered a classroom where students were sitting an examination. Calmly and without warning, he began firing, moving from room to room. In the space of an hour and a half, he shot dead ten students, fatally wounded another and set off numerous fire-bombs. At around 12.30, he put the gun to his head and killed himself.

In an eerie reminder of the classroom massacre carried out in November 2007 by Pekka-Eric Auvinen (*see page 298*), Saari had posted a video on YouTube showing him at a shooting range, pointing a weapon at the camera and saying, "You will die next." He added that his hobbies were computers, guns, sex and beer and had commented that the "whole of life is war and whole life is pain".

It transpired that Saari had been questioned by the police about his video but he was not detained and was permitted to keep his .22 calibre pistol for which he had a gun licence. He had broken no laws. The next day, he took eleven lives, including his own.

As before, the shocked people of Finland questioned their country's gun culture. Youngsters from the age of fifteen years have the right to seek a firearms permit providing they have their parents' permission. Hunting and target shooting are national pastimes and Finland has one of the highest levels of gun ownership in the world.

People who knew Saari described him as ". . . one of us – quiet but not a hermit". Police believed he had been planning his day of violence for several weeks, posting videos showing him firing a handgun.

Sociologists looked for deeper meaning and referred to the tendency of some parents to leave their children on their own. While this breeds self-sufficiency, it may also encourage an excess of individualism. It has been suggested that where young men become over-introspective, they have a tendency to turn to violence rather than discussion. Saari's obsession with song lyrics such as "... you will fight alone in your personal war", suggests a degree of fatalism.

In the wake of the fatal shootings, Finland's interior minister promised to give police greater powers to question applications for gun licences. Meanwhile, the shocked community of Kauhajoki received a visit from their Prime Minister on 24 September to share a national day of mourning. He told reporters that he was very critical of gun ownership.

A Man Of Many Words

Dr William C. Minor was a wealthy American Civil War surgeon who came to London in 1871 on a cultural visit. It was a visit that was to end in tragedy, for in the early hours of 17 February 1872, Minor shot dead a man he believed was an intruder.

George Merrett worked at a Lambeth brewery and was on his way to work when he was pursued in the street by a gunman who shot and killed him. The gunman did not flee. He was still holding his smoking revolver when the police arrived. Dr Minor explained that it was an accident; he had shot the wrong person after someone broke into his room.

William Chester Minor was an American citizen holding medical qualifications and a commission in the US Army. He was a cultured man who had a liking for the seamier side of life, frequenting bars, music halls and brothels. It was also discovered that he had a history of mental illness and had been diagnosed in the US as suffering from monomania. He spent some time in an asylum and, on his release, took passage to England.

At his trial in April 1872 for the murder of George Merrett, his defence was one of insanity. The judge applied the McNaghten Rules and the judgment was that thirty-two-year-old Dr Minor was innocent of murder although he had unquestionably killed a man. He was sentenced to be detained at the Asylum for the Criminally Insane at Broadmoor.

The prisoner was allowed to buy books and his cell soon turned into a library. Feeling deep remorse for his act of violence that had widowed a mother and six children, he contacted Eliza Merrett through the US Embassy. She accepted his sincerity and asked if she could see him. It was unprecedented for a prisoner to be allowed a visit from a relative of his victim. But permission was granted and Eliza offered to obtain books for him.

Then, an event occurred which completely changed Minor's life in prison. He responded to a call he had read from the editor of the Oxford English Dictionary, Dr James Murray, for contributions to this great editorial task. In 1880 Minor wrote to the editor offering his services and, over the next thirty years, he read countless books and refined tens of thousands of contributions to the dictionary.

All Murray knew about his most diligent contributor was that he lived in Crowthorne, Berkshire. When he first visited in January 1891 he was astonished to find that Minor was confined to an asylum. The two men became friends and as Minor's health began to fade, Murray campaigned for him to be repatriated. Winston Churchill, Home Secretary, granted this request in 1910. Thus, after thirty-eight years at Broadmoor, Minor returned to the USA where he died, aged eighty-five, on 26 March 1920.

The full story of the murderer who turned lexicographer was told by Simon Winchester in his bestselling book, *The Surgeon of Crowthorne*, published in 1998.

"The Executed Ones"

Stephen Wayne Anderson was a murderer with a passion for eating who went on to distinguish himself as a poet and playwright.

On the night of 26 May 1980 Anderson broke into a house in Bloomington, California. He was intent on robbery and cut the telephone line before checking each room of the house. The house was owned by eighty-one-year-old Elizabeth Lyman, a retired music teacher, who screamed at the presence of an intruder in her bedroom. Anderson responded by shooting her in the face.

As she lay bleeding to death, Anderson busied himself making a meal of noodles and sat down to eat it while watching television. A neighbour, sensing that something was wrong, called the police who interrupted his meal by arresting him.

Anderson was a man with form. He had been imprisoned in 1971 and 1973 on burglary charges and, while serving time in Utah State Prison, he had murdered a fellow inmate. When on the run from prison in 1979, he became involved in contract killings and at the time he killed Elizabeth Lyman, he was a fugitive from justice.

He was tried for murder in San Bernardino County and convicted on 24 July 1981. He was sentenced to die by lethal injection at San Quentin Prison. As Anderson put it later, "I was passing through California when I shot someone during a bungled burglary, and found myself a permanent resident."

Anderson spent his time in prison constructively, writing poetry and plays, which gained wide recognition. His published work won him two Pen awards for prison writing and his *Doing Time* was taken as an example of the way creativity can mellow even the most callous mind.

He spent twenty-two years on Death Row and his poetry, particularly *Conversations with the Dead*, seemed to reflect his remorse for those he had killed, whose lives were stolen away by his actions. Anderson did not deny killing Elizabeth Lyman; "I was very wrong," he told his trial jury.

His supporters believed that the abuse he suffered at the hands of his father had not been properly presented in court. There were also questions raised over the quality of the defence provided for him by the state. Criticism was directed at his attorney, now deceased, who was described variously as incompetent and lacking in integrity. The bigger question was whether capital prisoners received fair representation.

Writers' groups and human rights activists fought long and hard to win clemency for Anderson but his final appeal was turned down by the Governor of California in January 2002. It seemed that the condemned man had a hearty appetite on his last day, consuming toasted sandwiches and large quantities of cottage cheese and ice cream.

One of Anderson's poems referred to the "executed ones" whose ranks he joined at 12.30 a.m. on 29 January 2002, following death by lethal injection.

"Here You Go!"

A popular novelist was shot dead in a public park in New York by a man who believed a character in one of the writer's novels represented a slur against his sister.

Forty-four-year-old David Graham Phillips wrote under the pen name of John Graham, and made his reputation in America with novels that exposed political corruption and attitudes towards women. He lived in New York and it was part of his daily morning routine to walk in Gramercy Park, Manhattan.

On 23 January 1911, as he took his customary stroll in the park he was suddenly confronted by a man who appeared from behind some bushes menacingly waving a pistol at him. Shouting, "Here you go!" he fired five shots at Phillips who fell dying to the ground. As passers-by gathered at the scene, the gunman put the gun to his head and exclaimed, "Here I go" before pulling the trigger. In the space of a few minutes, victim and murderer lay dead and dying together on the ground.

The novelist lay mortally wounded for several hours before dying. His final words, worthy of a novel, were, "I can fight one bullet, but not five." One of Phillip's best-known novels was *Susan Lenox: Her Fall and Rise*, published after his death, which told the story of a country girl who resorted to prostitution and later became a successful actress. The reason he lost his life was that a character in another novel, *The Fashionable Adventures of Joshua Craig*, inspired a murderous impulse in one of his readers. That reader was Fitzhugh Coyle Goldsborough, a neurotic, spoiled young man of twenty-one who was from a wealthy Philadelphia family. He was a man with little inclination to work or follow a profession whose days were spent reading novels and idolizing his socialite sister.

In fact, Goldsborough was captivated by his elder sister to the point of madness. He guarded her with a neurotic jealousy, refusing to allow her to be criticised in any way, even by her father. He had a fiery temper and a reputation for throwing punches at people he thought were critical of his idol.

One of the characters in Phillips' novel was a self-centred girl who moved in the higher flights of society. It was an unflattering portrait of a spoilt personality, which Goldsborough took as a slur against his sister. The insult, as he saw it, preyed on his mind and he decided to take revenge on the author. In a moment's madness, a man of little substance but full of jealous hatred terminated the promising life of the writer and destroyed himself in the process.

Murder In Disguise

Greed inspired a cunning scheme to gain an inheritance but when plan A failed, plan B was murder. Wearing a disguise, the killer used a pretence to lure his victim into the shadows and shot her dead.

Karl Hau was a handsome young German who wanted to follow a career in law. He also aspired to be rich and when he met Lina Molitor in Baden-Baden in 1901 he was as much attracted to her beauty as he was to her widowed mother's wealth. When his proposal of marriage to Lina was vetoed by her mother, the couple eloped. After Lina attempted to commit suicide, her mother relented and allowed them to marry. Mr and Mrs Hau moved to Washington DC where Karl took up his legal studies.

In October 1906, Frau Molitor, who suffered from a heart condition, received a mysterious telegram from Paris asking her to come at once as her daughter, Olga, who was visiting the city with Lina and Karl, was very ill. The old lady made hasty travel plans only to find on her arrival in Paris that Olga was perfectly well. It was not clear who had sent the telegram. Frau Molitor returned to Baden-Baden with Olga and the Haus moved on to London.

During the evening of 6 November, Frau Molitor was again the recipient of an urgent message. On this occasion she was asked to call at her local post office where an important message from Paris awaited her. She hurried down Kaiser-Wilhelm Strasse, accompanied by Olga, and when they reached a poorly lit section of the street, a shot rang out and Frau Molitor died where she fell with a bullet in her heart. Olga noticed a man in a long overcoat running down the street.

Karl Hau became the immediate focus of suspicion, especially in the knowledge that he stood to gain financially from his mother-in-law's death. He had absconded to London but was arrested and returned to Germany. He admitted being the sender of the messages to Frau Molitor but denied killing her.

He was charged with murder but before he appeared on trial at Karlsruhe, his wife, Lina, committed suicide. Hau proved to have a murky past. He had contracted venereal disease in his teenage years while travelling around the world, and enjoyed a succession of mistresses. His lavish lifestyle meant that he was constantly in need of funds and Frau Molitor had generously provided him with an income during his legal studies in America.

Hau's trial began on 17 July 1907 amid scenes of great public disorder in which the police had to be supported by two infantry companies. Inside the court, there was a stark reminder of the reason for the trial; on a bench stood a glass jar containing the heart of the late Frau Molitor.

Hau opted to defend himself. He admitted sending the mysterious telegram summoning his mother-in-law to Paris and indeed admitted everything else, including being dressed in disguise in Baden-Baden on the evening of the shooting. But he denied the murder. The only reason he offered for his actions was that he was secretly in love with Olga, his wife's sister. He even managed to imply that she committed the murder.

The jury returned a guilty verdict and the judge sentenced him to death. By now, public opinion had swung in his favour and troops with fixed bayonets helped to keep order outside the court. His sentence was commuted to life imprisonment and he served seventeen years before being pardoned by the Grand Duke of Baden in 1924.

Hau wrote two books, *Death Sentence* and *Life Sentence*, which shed no light at all on his actions or predicament. A leading psychiatrist suggested that he was schizophrenic and possibly suffering mental disorientation due to his having contracted venereal disease. On 4 February 1926, he was found dying in the ruins of Hadrian's Villa near Rome. He had taken poison.

Lethal Immunity

The mass murder of twelve bank employees in 1948 by a Japanese artist has never been fully explained. Sadamichi Hirasawa would have hanged for the crime but for a Japanese law. Instead, he became a celebrity and spent the rest of his life in prison while conspiracy theories and allegations of a cover-up swirled around him.

On 26 January 1948, just before the Teikoku branch of the Imperial Bank in Tokyo closed, a man identifying himself as a health official appeared at the main entrance. He presented the acting manager with his business card, which identified him as "Dr Jiro Yamaguchi". He explained that owing to an outbreak of dysentery in the district he had been instructed to immunize the bank staff as a preventive measure.

Sixteen employees of the bank obediently lined up to receive their medication. The doctor gave each one a pill to swallow and then distributed a number of small cups into which he dispensed a small quantity of liquid. Within seconds of drinking this potion, the bank employees collapsed where they stood. Ten died immediately, two lingered a while before dying and four survived later in hospital. "Dr Yamaguchi" escaped with over 200,000 yen in cash and cheques.

The mass killing had been accomplished using cyanide and the police quickly discovered that "Dr Yamaguchi" had carried out a dress rehearsal, aimed at perfecting his technique, a week earlier at another bank. There were no ill effects on that occasion. It also became known that a similar immunization session had been carried out at a bank the previous year administered, according to his business card, by Dr Shigeru Matsui.

Dr Matsui was a respected physician and it was believed that his business card had been fraudulently used. The Japanese custom of exchanging cards provided the key to "Dr Yamaguchi's" identity. It was thought possible that Dr Matsui had met the mystery man at some point and therefore his identity would be found among the many cards retained by Dr Matsui.

By a painstaking process of elimination, the police narrowed the field to one man, fifty-year-old Sadamichi Hirasawa, an artist whom Dr Matsui remembered meeting two months before the bank murders. Survivors of the bank poisoning recalled the visiting health official as a middle-aged man with greying hair, a mole on his left cheek and a scar under his chin. Hirasawa matched this description.

Following his arrest, Hirasawa made a confession, which he later withdrew. Post-war Japan was controlled by the American Occupying Forces and it was against this background that in December 1948, Hirasawa was tried for murder, found guilty and sentenced to death by hanging. His execution did not proceed and, on appeal, was reduced to life imprisonment. The grounds for this decision lay in Japanese law which did not permit a citizen to participate in his own destruction and judicial hanging was a process that relied on the weight of the individual when suspended to break the spinal cord.

Hirasawa's appeal against conviction was rejected in 1955 and he remained in Sendai Prison where he spent his time painting and writing his autobiography, *My Will: The Teikoku Bank Case*. He became an iconic figure in Japan, with many people believing he was innocent of the bank murders and had been made a scapegoat due to the failure of the authorities to find the real murderer.

A "Save Hirasawa Committee" was set up, calling for justice. There were claims that the Japanese and American governments had colluded to cover up wartime atrocities. In particular, links were made to military assassination squads using cyanide to eliminate enemy leaders. There was talk of experiments using human guinea pigs to test killing methods and of the agents being held under arrest after the war to protect their secrets. The real murderer responsible for the Tokyo bank killings was said to have been a Japanese officer in one of these units.

Meanwhile, Hirasawa served out his time until his death in 1987 at the age of ninety-five. During his thirty-two years on Death Row no government justice minister was prepared to authorize his execution, suggesting to his supporters that they did not believe he was guilty. The Teikoku Bank Murders remains one of Japan's most enduring crime mysteries.

Dangerous When He Smiles

Jacques Mesrine was a scheming and ruthless career criminal who terrorized Paris with his daring bank raids in the 1970s. He earned the title of "Public Enemy Number One" and operated with style. After his arrest in 1977, he offered detectives champagne and told them he could not be held. He escaped from prison while serving a sentence for robbery, kidnap and attempted murder by scaling the walls of Santé Prison. This was one of his several high-profile escapes.

Mesrine spent his childhood in German-occupied France during the Second World War and was conscripted into the army in 1956. He served in Algeria and was decorated for bravery. Once demobilized, he found civilian life tame and resorted to crime. He started with petty crime in the 1960s but soon graduated to grand schemes.

His special skills lay in bank robberies and his technique was to strike and move on. He became an internationally sought criminal in North and South America in the late 1960s. He was imprisoned in Canada for a failed attempt to kidnap a wealthy industrialist, but as he was to do on several other occasions, he staged a sensational prison escape in 1972.

He returned to France in 1973 and continued his pattern of daring robberies. In 1978 he robbed the casino at Deauville. Wearing a disguise he held up the cashier who was astute enough to sound the alarm, which brought police officers swarming around the casino. In the resultant shoot-out, Mesrine was wounded but still made good his escape.

Wanted posters were put up around Paris bearing an image of Mesrine sporting his trademark moustache and the warning, "He is dangerous when he smiles". He was a man of ruthless cunning with a criminally adventurous spirit. After his military service, he trained as an architect and while in prison wrote his memoirs, *The Death Instinct*. This account of his life detailed his various crimes, which, by his tally, included thirty-nine murders.

Mesrine's daring antics infuriated the police. Even when he was captured, he contrived to escape and in 1978 hired a light aircraft to buzz the prison, where his girlfriend was being held, in a threatened rescue attempt. Police Commissaire Robert Broussard regarded him as the most dangerous man in France, a description he fulfilled by planning to kidnap the judge who had sentenced him to prison.

But Mesrine's daring and taunting adventures went too far and the police finally took their revenge. On 2 November 1979, France's most wanted man was ambushed in a Paris street as he walked to his car. Marksmen from a special anti-gang unit gunned him down using high velocity ammunition. The officers returned to their base and toasted their success with champagne and the congratulations of the President of France ringing in their ears.

After a criminal career in France lasting seven years, forty-three-year-old Mesrine was dead, but his demise, or the manner of it, did not meet with universal approval. For some, he was a kind of larger-than-life Robin Hood character whose raison d'être was to defy authority. More significantly, though, came claims in 2002 that Mesrine had, in effect, been assassinated when police riddled his car with bullets without offering him the chance to surrender. The police finally got their man but Mesrine, as usual, stole the headlines.

Journey To Purgatory

Having paid his debt to society for committing murder, Johann (Jack) Unterweger emerged from prison a reformed character. He used his time wisely, educating himself and training to be a writer. When he regained his freedom in 1990, the prison governor proclaimed that it would be difficult to find a prisoner so well prepared for freedom.

Unterweger had strangled an eighteen-year-old prostitute in Vienna in December 1974, for which he received a life sentence. He used his fifteen years behind bars to good effect, developing a talent for writing which brought him to the notice of the literary and artistic world. He wrote poetry, children's stories and published an autobiography. The man on the inside was lionized by those on the outside who campaigned for his freedom.

Within months of walking through the prison gates a free man, he strangled a prostitute in Prague while he was in the city doing research. The next month, two prostitutes disappeared in Graz. Their bodies were discovered in January 1991. The Austrian police suspected Unterweger and took him in for questioning. He smooth-talked his way clear, denying any involvement in eight unsolved murders in Graz and Vienna.

As suspicion hardened against him, Austrian police issued a warrant for his arrest in February 1991. But, by then, he had flown to the USA via Switzerland. He planned to do research in Los Angeles on his favourite topic, the twilight world of the red-light district.

In April 1991, Irene Rodriguez travelled to Los Angeles from El Paso. Her body was found in a business car park in Hollenbeck. She had been strangled. On 19 June, the body of Shannon Exley, a prostitute, was found on vacant ground near a Scouts Centre in Los Angeles. A trio of murders was completed with the discovery of Sherri Long's body at Malibu on 11 July. In each case, the victim had been strangled with her bra.

Detectives in LA realized they were looking for a single murderer, a conclusion supported by the evidence provided in each murder by the bra which had been formed into a strangler's noose. Meanwhile, Unterweger was using his time attempting to interview film stars in Malibu before returning to Austria. Once again, he was questioned by the police in Vienna and, despite his denials, the evidence against him began to mount up. It was time to return to the USA.

In February 1992, he was detained in Miami for a breach of entry regulations; he had failed to mention that he had a criminal record. US detectives contacted their counterparts in Austria and established a detailed diary of his movements, tying up dates and places.

On 28 May, Unterweger was extradited from the USA to Austria. It would take nearly two years to bring him to court, but in April 1994 he faced eleven charges of murder; seven in Austria, one in the Czech Republic and three in the USA.

The jury returned guilty verdicts on nine counts of murder, including the three in the USA. For the second time in his life, Jack Unterweger was sentenced to life imprisonment. What would later be seen as a prophesy was a poster that had been designed to promote a film about his life, based on his book, *Purgatory*. He posed for a photograph with a noose around his neck.

Six hours after he had been convicted of murder, forty-three-year-old Unterweger took his own life in his cell beneath the courtroom at Graz. He hanged himself with the drawstring from his jogging trousers.

Poet, Artist And Poisoner

Thomas Griffiths Wainewright was a man of considerable intellect but flawed personality. He was an accomplished artist and writer and also an effective poisoner. Oscar Wilde captured these talents in his essay on Wainewright, *Pen, Pencil and Poison*.

Wainewright was born in 1794 and his mother died shortly after bringing him into the world. He also lost his father at an early age and the boy was brought up first by his grandfather and then his uncle. He showed promise as an artist at school but dreamed of being a soldier.

After an unfulfilling spell as a guardsman, he left the army and developed his talents as an artist and writer. He exhibited his work at the Royal Academy and published essays under pseudonyms. During this period of his life he cut a figure as a bit of a dandy and mixed with contemporary men of letters such as Thomas de Quincey, William Hazlitt and Charles Lamb.

He also incurred debts and, having tried the pen and the pencil, he next resorted to poison. In 1829, he poisoned his uncle with strychnine to gain possession of his house. The following year, he poisoned his wife's mother, Mrs Abercrombie, and then set his sights on his sister-in-law, twenty-year-old Helen Abercrombie. Before fatally poisoning her, he insured her life for £18,000.

Wainewright's attempt to claim on the insurance was met with suspicion and the companies refused to pay out. He took them to court and lost. Still in debt, he resorted to forgery and on returning to England in 1837 from a visit to France, was arrested.

Despite pleading guilty to some of the charges, he was convicted and sentenced to transportation to Van Dieman's Land. While in Newgate prison, he was visited by various friends and acquaintances. One of them chastised him for poisoning Helen Abercrombie. His response was to shrug off the criticism saying, "Yes, it was a dreadful thing to do, but she had very thick ankles."

Along with 300 other convicts, he was shipped to Van Dieman's Land complaining bitterly that "the companion of poets and artists" was assigned to mix with "country bumpkins". He took up painting again in 1840 but, by then, he was a man on his own after his wife and son emigrated to America and he lost contact with them.

In 1844, he made an eloquent application to the Lieutenant-Governor in Van Dieman's Land for a ticket of leave which was refused. He died, aged fifty, three years later.

CHAPTER 11

Solved and Unsolved

Some murders seem forever destined to remain unsolved while others that appear to have been solved, unravel with time as other explanations emerge. Even the most intractable cases have some feature that might provide a key to unlock the mystery although, very often, they just seem to tantalize investigators. The killing of Robert Workman, for instance, shot dead on his own doorstep in 2004 offered very little crime scene evidence and no suspects. There was, though, an intriguing telephone call that has never been traced. And in the case of Hugh Chevis' death in 1931, which gave partridges a bad name when he dined on a bird laced with strychnine, again there was a mysterious message in a telegram, seemingly rejoicing in his death, whose sender was never traced.

A murder investigation may produce a strong suspect but with insufficient evidence to succeed in the trial courts. When Helen Jewett fell victim to an axe murderer in New York in 1836, suspicion was directed against Richard P. Robinson. He faced powerful circumstantial evidence that placed him at the scene of the crime and all but put the murder weapon in his hand. To general disbelief, he secured a not guilty verdict. Consequently, Helen Jewett's murder remains unsolved.

Some murder cases considered solved at the time, reappear at a later date with sufficient doubt to be returned to the unsolved category. One such is the conviction of Dr Crippen in 1910 for murdering his wife in London. Over ninety years later, new evidence has been adduced to suggest that the human remains believed to be those of his wife, belonged to another, unknown individual.

Scientific advances, particularly in the field of DNA technology, make possible the re-examination of forensic evidence stored by the police or gleaned from other sources. This was the background to developments in the Crippen case and the grounds on which his descendants are seeking a pardon.

Pressure from campaigning groups and families of victims or murder suspects, where an injustice is perceived, may persuade the legal authorities to re-open a once-closed case. The body of Albert De Salvo, self-confessed "Boston Stranger" and murderer of thirteen women, was exhumed in 2001. He died in prison in 1973 and was believed to have made a false confession. Comparison of DNA taken from his exhumed body was compared with that of traces found on the last murder victim. The result showed that whatever De Salvo may have said, he was not the "Boston Strangler". This left the uncomfortable conclusion that the real murderer got away with the crimes and that the case is far from being closed.

Similarly, the hoped-for solution of the "Bible John" murders in Glasgow in the late 1960s failed to materialize with the exhumation of the body of a man regarded as a strong suspect. Comparison of the suspect DNA with traces found on the last victim did not match, so the three murders remain unsolved.

The Black Dahlia murder in 1947 is probably America's most notorious unsolved murder case. Various suspects have been named over the years but none has been confirmed. In 2003, a former detective named his father as the likely killer using new information. And the Zodiac Murders in San Francisco in the late 1960s, with the enigmatic messages left by the killer, have defied all attempts at resolution. Again, a re-examination of the available evidence in 2007 has been used in an attempt to provide an answer. Like the infamous Jack the Ripper murders in 1888, high-profile unsolved killings taunt those of an inquisitive persuasion to find answers.

There are a few notable cases whose status changes at the whim of the chief suspect, when previous denials turn into confessions of guilt. In a world where things are not always as they seem, reverses happen and court verdicts are turned on their heads. Tony Mancini won an outstanding not guilty verdict when he was tried for the murder of Violette Kaye in 1934. And, forty-two years later, what had been an unsolved case acquired a different status when he made a confession to murder. Harold Loughans took rather less time, a mere twenty years, to confess to the crime for which he had been judged not guilty in 1943.

The converse of this is when a blameless individual who has been wrongly punished for a crime he did not commit, is re-judged and given back his innocence. Such were the circumstances that overtook Stefan Kisko when his conviction was quashed in 1992 after he had spent sixteen years in prison.

The judicial process is sufficiently robust to absorb these reversals aided, as it was in the Kisko case, by advances in forensic technology. It shows that with the passage of time, a self-correcting process can set the innocent free and call to account some guilty fugitives. Such are the dynamics of solved and unsolved crimes.

A Killing At "Cock House"

Lieutenant-Colonel Robert Workman, known to his friends by his middle name, Riley, was shot dead on his doorstep on 7 January 2004. Several residents of the peaceful Hertfordshire village of Furneux Pelham in the UK heard a noise at around 8 p.m., which sounded like a car backfiring. His body was found sprawled on the doorstep of his cottage early the next morning by his daily care worker.

It was only when the eighty-three-year-old man's body was moved for transit to the mortuary that it was realized he had been shot. He had been killed with a blast from a 12-bore shotgun fired from close range. Death would have been instantaneous.

At about 5 a.m., and before the body was found, an unidentified caller dialled 999 from a public phone box in the neighbouring village of Braughing. The caller asked for an ambulance to be sent to "Holly Hock Cottage" at Furneux. The ambulance operator sought clarification by asking the caller to spell out the destination. He responded by incorrectly giving the house name as "Hollycock" and also misspelled Furneux. Colonel Workman's cottage had been renamed, Cock House, twenty-four years previously. The identity of this mystery caller was never established.

Colonel Workman had a record of military service going back to the days when he was ADC to Field-Marshal Slim. Since retirement, he had run an antiques business and, following his wife's death in 2003, lived quietly as a widower.

Firearms specialists determined that the shotgun ammunition used to commit the murder was not widely available. It was the largest type of shot available and ordinarily used to kill deer. Profilers assisting the police believed the Colonel may have been the victim of a deep-seated and long-held grudge. They discounted the idea of a hitman on the grounds that he had chosen an unusual type of weapon.

Researches into the dead man's background in December 2004 revealed that he had something of a secret past inasmuch as he had visited London's gay scene during the 1950s. This led to speculation about his sexual orientation and provided a possible motive for his killing. The police believed the killer lived locally, and offered a £10,000 reward for information.

Attempts to analyse the taped conversation between the mystery caller and the ambulance service produced a number of theories. One such was that the shooting was a mistake and the person involved was simply trying to summon assistance. The voice was described as mature and probably of a person in the age range of fifty to sixty. It was significant that he directed the ambulance to "Holly Hock Cottage", a name that had long been redundant.

Failure to identify the mystery caller was reminiscent of the Wallace Case in 1931 when a telephone message sent William Wallace on a wild goose chase in Liverpool.

"Hooray, Hooray, Hooray!"

The "Case of The Poisoned Partridge" was a mystery worthy of the attention of Arthur Conan Doyle and his famous sleuth, Sherlock Holmes. It remains unsolved.

On 20 June 1931 Lieutenant Hugh Chevis and his wife, Frances, sat down to dinner in their army quarters at Blackdown Camp, Surrey. Mrs Chevis had ordered a brace of partridges for the meal which was prepared by their cook, Mrs Yeomans, and served by the officer's batman.

Chevis was fond of game and, no doubt, looking forward to eating the partridge, which had been served with potatoes, peas and bread sauce. But, after one mouthful, he found the bird not to his liking. He complained about the taste and asked his wife to sample it. She agreed that it tasted "ghastly". Disgruntled at the turn of events, Chevis told his batman to destroy both birds. The remains were thrown into the fire in the kitchen range.

Shortly afterwards, Chevis became ill, with vomiting and suffering convulsions. Mrs Chevis sent for the doctor who arrived quickly and found the sick man saturated in perspiration and lying on the floor with his back unnaturally arched. The doctor recognized the classic symptoms of strychnine poisoning. Meanwhile, Mrs Chevis began to feel ill and the doctor drove both of his patients to hospital. While Frances began to recover, her husband's condition worsened and his breathing stopped. He was declared dead after several hours of respiration failed to revive him.

Analysis of the dead man's stomach contents confirmed that he had died of strychnine poisoning. The mystery of how the partridges had become contaminated was pursued by the Surrey police. They checked with the butcher who supplied the birds and still had partridges in his cold store; they were uncontaminated. That left the possibility that the partridges had been interfered with during the time that elapsed between delivery and consumption by the Chevis'. In an age before universal refrigeration, it was common to keep food in a mesh-covered meat safe. In the case of the Chevis's this was fixed to the outside of their hut and very accessible.

An open verdict was returned by the Coroner's inquest, although few doubted that Hugh Chevis had been murdered. On the day of his funeral, his father, Sir William Chevis, a distinguished former judge in India, received a telegram; it read simply "Hooray, Hooray, Hooray". The message had been sent from Dublin and the sender complied with the post clerk's request to write his name and address on the back of the form. He wrote – "J. Hartigan, Hibernian". The Hibernian was a hotel in Dawson Street, Dublin.

This message of hatred was maliciously cruel and it was followed five days later by a letter, also from "J. Hartigan" saying, "It is a mystery they will never solve." Efforts to trace the sender produced no result and this essential part of the poisoning and its aftermath remains a mystery.

There was much speculation as to the motive behind such a murder. In view of the malicious postcard sent to Sir William Chevis, it has been suggested that killing his son was revenge by someone who had a grievance against the former judge.

An alternative theory was that Chevis was accidentally poisoned by strychnine that had been ingested by the partridges when they had fed on contaminated berries. Strychnine was readily available at the time for use as rat poison and might conceivably have been employed by a farmer for that purpose. If that was the case, the explanation for the telegram was that it was sent out of malice at the news of Hugh Chevis' death. If the poisoning was deliberate, there was ample precedence for its effectiveness in the murder committed in the 1890s by Dr Thomas Neill Cream.

Poisoned Ale

"I have removed him as I might a weed from the garden," was the chilling message sent after a cleverly contrived death by poison.

Doctor W.H. Wilson was dining with his family at their Philadelphia home on a warm summer's evening in June 1908. The sultry weather reminded the doctor that he had been sent a bottle of special ale, which was in the kitchen. He poured the ale and remarked on its taste before becoming dizzy and collapsing. He was rushed to hospital but died soon afterwards.

Attention focussed on the bottle of ale, which proved to have been laced with cyanide. Wilson had received a letter purporting to have been sent by a brewery company as part of a campaign to inform physicians about their new health-giving product. A bottle of ale was brought to his home by special delivery.

Police enquiries established that the letter was a forgery and that the brewery company was not marketing a new product. The delivery company's employee said a man brought a package to the office and paid for it to be delivered to Dr Wilson's address. It appeared that someone had targeted Wilson, forging the letter to disarm any suspicions, and doctoring, labelling and re-capping the bottle of ale which would be the means of killing him.

An investigation into Wilson's background produced a few surprises. To start with, he was not a qualified doctor, although he was known to everyone as "Doc". His neighbours regarded him as a pleasant person who gave no offence, although there was some mystery about the exact nature of his business. It was observed that callers tended to be mostly women and frequently well-to-do. Little by little, it emerged that "Doc" Wilson ran an abortion clinic.

Wilson's death captured the newspaper headlines and much speculation ensued. His practice as an abortionist demanded secrecy and also provided a possible motive for someone wishing to kill him. A patient may have wanted to exact some kind of revenge or a husband might have discovered a guilty secret. With this in mind, the coroner took charge of Wilson's case records.

One of the theories about the mystery came into focus when the coroner received a letter from "An outraged husband and father", stating that his wife had died as the result of treatment administered by Dr Wilson. The letter continued, "I have removed him as I might a weed from the garden," adding, ". . . let those who live by poison die by poison."

That this letter had been sent by the poisoner was strengthened by the knowledge that it was posted the day after Wilson's death and made a reference to poison, and cyanide in particular, which had not been made public.

The sender of the letter, and presumed murderer, was never traced and never identified.

". . . A Bad Business"

The discovery of an axe-murder victim's body in a smoke-filled room shocked New York in 1836 and created great excitement when the murder suspect was put on trial.

Twenty-three-year-old Helen Jewett was a lady with a certain reputation of whom it was reported that, "she had seduced more young men than any (woman) known to police records". She entertained a string of lovers in what some writers liked to call the city's demi-monde. In 1834, she met Richard P. Robinson who worked as a clerk and enjoyed the status of a man about town.

Robinson, described as frequenting every *maison de plaisir* (pleasure house), added Helen to his retinue of female conquests. They endured a stormy relationship and she became jealous of his other lady friends. Matters came to a head when she surprised him courting one of his lovers and a fight broke out between the two women.

Robinson tried to keep his distance from Helen but she pursued him with entreaties to take her back. He relented but toyed with her feelings by sending anonymous letters criticising her morals. After another major quarrel, he told her he would not see her again.

A year passed and then, in October 1835, they met by chance and Helen discovered that he was intending to marry another woman. She used all her wiles to coax him back, including a threat to expose his attempt to poison one of his former girlfriends who had died in mysterious circumstances.

Early in the following year, Robinson's marriage plans fell into disarray when his bride-to-be reacted unfavourably to his colourful past. Whether or not Helen had any part in this was not clear but she took the blame.

Once again, she tried to patch things up between them and Robinson responded with a curt note saying, "Keep quiet until I come on Saturday night." During the late evening of 11 April 1836, the proprietress of the establishment where Helen lodged, along with other *filles de joie*, admitted Robinson who said he was visiting Helen.

Around 11 p.m., the couple asked for a bottle of champagne to be sent up to their room. All was quiet until the small hours when the girl occupying a nearby room heard noises. Opening her door a fraction, she saw a cloaked figure disappearing down the stairs. As this was not an uncommon occurrence in a house where ladies and their consorts came and went during the night, she returned to her room.

At about 3 a.m. there was consternation at the discovery of thick black smoke coming from Helen's room. An inspection quickly established that Helen lay dead by her bed, her head split open by an ugly wound. A fire had been started, apparently with the intention of burning her body.

Her assailant had clearly escaped through the back yard of the house, leaving behind his cloak as he scaled a fence and dropping a bloodstained axe. Robinson was immediately suspected and police went to his lodgings where they found him in a deep sleep. When told that Helen had been murdered, he replied, "This is a bad business."

A coroner's inquest concluded that Helen had been murdered "by the hand of Richard P. Robinson". The editor of the *New York Herald* managed to sneak a visit to the murder scene and viewed Helen's body before it was removed. He described "a beautiful female corpse – that surpassed the finest statue of antiquity".

Robinson appeared on trial in June 1836. He denied murder and provided an alibi witness in the form of a late-night grocer who said he had been in his shop at the time of the murder. The bloodstained axe retrieved from the scene was shown to be a tool kept at Robinson's place of work and the discarded cloak was identified as belonging to him.

The jury retired for less than thirty minutes and to everyone's amazement returned a not guilty verdict. This seemed to meet with public approval and Robinson went to Texas where he ran a saloon and later moved to Louisville where he died in 1855.

Helen Jewett's fate was to be exhumed from her grave so that her skeleton could be used for medical teaching. Her murderer was never officially identified and one of Robinson's friends made the degrading remark that, "It is no crime to kill a whore."

Cut-Out Fugitive

Twenty-two-year-old Lindsay Ann Hawker was a newly graduated teacher from Coventry in the UK who had been working in Japan for several months. She taught at the Nova English School in Ichikawa, a suburb of Tokyo.

On 28 March 2007 the young woman was reported missing by the friend with whom she shared a flat in Funabashi, about a mile from her work. Police activity centred on an apartment in Ichikawa where it was believed Lindsay Hawker had been giving private language lessons.

Police searched a fourth-floor apartment belonging to twenty-eight-year-old Tatsuya Ichihashi who was described as an acquaintance of the missing woman. They found her handbag and clothes in the apartment, while an examination of the balcony turned up the startling discovery of a body in a bath. Only one hand was evident, the bath having been filled with sand to conceal the naked body of a young woman.

Neighbours told investigators that they had heard scraping noises coming from the fourth-floor flat several days previously, presumably created by the bath being dragged out onto the balcony. While the police were talking to local residents, Ichihashi was preparing his getaway. He took his chance to disappear in a taxi and, in his haste, dropped a rucksack containing clothes and money. He was in such a rush that he had no time to put on either shoes or socks.

A nationwide search was mounted to locate Ichihashi. He was described as a loner, a university graduate who did not need to work as he was supported by well-off parents. He regularly attended a gym and was proficient in martial arts.

Investigators questioned the dead woman's friends and family in their efforts to establish her movements. There were reports that she was romantically attached to Ichihashi, but these were denied. It appeared that he met her in a café on 24 March and asked her to give him private English lessons. Apparently he followed her for several days. This was borne out by an internet message she sent to a friend in England voicing concern about "a strange man" who had been following her. It was assumed that Ichihashi either tricked or persuaded her to visit him at his apartment.

Post-mortem examination established that the dead woman had been bound and gagged before being strangled. She had also been badly beaten and her hair had been cut off possibly as some kind of trophy.

A warrant was issued for Ichihashi's arrest for abandoning a body. Despite numerous alleged sightings, he avoided capture. In October 2008, there was speculation, denied by the police, that the man they suspected of murdering Lindsay Hawker had committed suicide.

The murder of a young English woman in Japan inevitably drew comparison with the death of Lucie Blackman in 2000. Her body was found buried in a shallow grave on a beach. In December 2008, Joji Obara was convicted of abduction, mutilation and abandoning a body.

In March 2009, Japanese police, in their efforts to find Ichihashi, used a novel method to stimulate public information. They placed life-size photographic cut-outs of the wanted man at strategic intervals around the crime location. This paid off a few months later in November, when an alert member of the public spotted Ichihashi in Osaka. He was arrested and taken into police custody to be questioned as the prime murder suspect.

"Hysteria Solves Nothing"

"The Boston Strangler" set off an unprecedented reign of terror, raping and murdering thirteen women in a little under two years. He claimed his first victim on 14 June 1962. She was fifty-five-year-old Anna Slesers, a divorcee who lived alone in an apartment in the Back Bay area of the city. She was found lying partly unclothed on the floor near the bathroom. She had been strangled with the cord of her housecoat, which was tied in a neat bow under her chin. She had also been left with her legs spread apart following sexual assault.

This first killing established a pattern that was to be repeated twelve times. Boston became a city of fear with women afraid to walk the streets and the police under pressure to find the murderer. Their cause was not helped by having to deal with a string of false confessions. Investigators called on forensic psychiatrists to help them compile a profile of the killer and files of known sex offenders were searched for possible suspects.

But still the killing went on. Using an established technique, the strangler talked his way into the homes of women living on their own. Once he had gained admission, rape and strangulation followed, with the ligature tied in a characteristic bow, and the victim's legs spread. Part of the psychological profile was that the strangler was consumed with hatred for his mother.

The Boston Herald reminded its readers that "Hysteria solves nothing" but this was of little help to a city paralysed by fear. Investigators explored every avenue, calling on the help of Dr James Brussel, the distinguished psychologist, and Peter Hurkos, a Dutch psychic detective.

In January 1964, there was a break in the sequence of murders and hopes rose that, perhaps, the killer had given up. But, on 27 October, the strangler struck again but in a manner that would lead to his identification. He attacked a young woman in her home and, departing from his modus operandi, left her unharmed. He threatened her with a knife and tied her up but, then, inexplicably, apologised and left her.

This survivor of the Boston Strangler's attack was able to give the police a full description of her assailant and he was quickly identified as Albert De Salvo. He was a man with a police record and questioning soon established that he needed psychiatric help. He was admitted to the Bridgewater Mental Institute in Cambridge, Massachusetts and, it was there in 1965 that he confessed to thirteen murders. As soon as his photograph was published in the press, a number of women came forward with their accounts of being sexually assaulted by him.

De Salvo had a troubled family background and was an early offender. He served with US forces in Germany in the 1950s where he married a local girl. They returned to live in Boston but the marriage was soon under strain due to his insatiable sexual appetite. He found satisfaction by committing sexual assaults and rape.

Despite his confession, there was no corroborating evidence of murder. In consequence, De Salvo was never tried for the crimes of the Boston Strangler. He was convicted only of earlier robberies and sexual offences for which he was sentenced to life imprisonment in 1966. He was confined at Walpole State Prison, Massachusetts where on 26 November 1973, he was found dead in his cell, having been stabbed through the heart by a fellow prisoner.

In 2001, De Salvo's body was exhumed for the purpose of taking DNA samples to compare with DNA found on the last of the Boston Strangler's victims killed in January 1964. This followed doubts voiced about De Salvo's confession. The findings were that the DNA found on the victim belonged neither to her nor De Salvo. His family pointed out inconsistencies in his taped confession to the 1964 murder compared to the autopsy report.

This led to the conclusion that De Salvo certainly did not commit the January 1964 murder and it was possible he confessed to the Strangler's crimes in order to gain public attention. If that was his purpose, he achieved his ambition, while the real Boston Strangler remained unidentified and at liberty.

"Bible John"

Police investigators of a twenty-five-year-old murder mystery hoped to use DNA evidence to unveil the identity of "Bible John".

Between February 1968 and October 1969, three young women were murdered in Glasgow, UK. What they had in common was that they loved dancing and fell victim to a Bible-quoting killer.

Bible John's first victim was twenty-five-year-old Patricia Docker who was found dead in a doorway near Carmichael Street on 22 February 1968. She had been strangled. The second victim was Jemima MacDonald whose body was found in a derelict building in Mackeith Street on 16 August 1969. She too had been strangled.

Witnesses who had seen Jemima at the Barrowlands Ballroom on the night she was murdered in the company of a man aged about thirty-five came forward. An artist's impression of the man based on their description was widely circulated.

It was the third murder that provided the clue that defined the murderer as "Bible John". On 30 October 1969, Helen Puttock and her sister enjoyed the dancing at Barrowlands. They had made a pact to stay together throughout the evening. During the dancing, they met two men, both of whom were called John. It became clear as conversation progressed that one of them was attracted to Helen and wished to be alone with her.

When the dancehall closed at around midnight, the two women climbed into a taxi with John who said he would take them home. The other John waited for a bus. Breaking their pre-arranged pact, Helen's sister was dropped off, leaving Helen and John to travel together. They left the taxi at Earl Road. Helen Puttock's body was found the following day in a nearby tenement. She had been strangled.

Helen's sister was able to provide a detailed account of their encounter with "Bible John", including his biblical references to the immorality of married women visiting dance halls and the evils of adultery. An artist's impression of "Bible John" was published in Scottish newspapers, and information was sought from the public.

Despite huge publicity and a far-ranging manhunt, "Bible John" remained uncaught. Other murders occurred which led to the possibility that he had resumed killing, and in 1980, there were suggestions that he and the Yorkshire Ripper were the same person. While there were some common elements in these comparisons, there was no firm connection.

In 1995 a possible breakthrough in the investigation came when the author of a book called *The Power of Blood*, put forward a possible identity for "Bible John". The suspect was John Irvine McInnes who had been interviewed at the time of the murders but no action was taken against him. He had committed suicide in 1980.

With a possible new lead to pursue, Strathclyde Police were given authority to exhume the body of McInnes. The intention was to take a sample of his DNA and compare it with stains found on the clothing of the third murder victim. There was local public concern at the turn of events but Strathclyde Police said that the murder enquiry was not closed and they were bound to follow up new evidence.

After laboratory investigations lasting five months, a report submitted to the Lord Advocate made it clear that the forensic evidence did not identify John McInnes as "Bible John".

"Evil Incarnate"

The tortured and mutilated body of Elizabeth Short was found on waste ground in the Crenshaw district of Los Angeles on 15 January 1947. The body had been cut in two at the waist and drained of blood. Multiple stab wounds and cigarette burns were evidence of the torture that the killer had inflicted.

Twenty-two-year-old Elizabeth Short, known as the "Black Dahlia" on account of her liking for tight-fitting black dresses, dreamed of being a Hollywood star. The reality was that when her love affairs brought no happiness, she took to drinking and slid into a promiscuous lifestyle. The "Black Dahlia" became something of an icon. James Ellroy wrote a novel based on her murder, while Goth rocker, Marilyn Manson, painted pictures of her and Robert de Niro starred in the film, *True Confessions*.

Ten days after the murder, a cardboard box was found with a note attached bearing a message made from letters cut from a newspaper. The note read, "Here are Dahlia's belongings. Letter to follow." The box contained Elizabeth Short's birth certificate, address book and social security card. There were pages missing from the address book and all the items in the box reeked of gasoline. The inference was that this was an attempt to destroy any fingerprints. The logical assumption was that the sender of these personal possessions was involved with the murder.

America's most notorious murder case remained unsolved, despite dozens of confessions. In 1991, a Los Angeles detective commented, "We have a lot of people offering up their fathers and various relatives as the murderer." One of these was a Californian woman who recalled repressed memories from forty years previously. She named her father, who was killed in a car crash in 1962, as the possible murderer.

In 1994, another candidate was put forward by writer John Gilmore, who argued a persuasive case naming Jack Anderson Wilson. A former soldier, Wilson died in a hotel fire in San Francisco two years after Elizabeth Short was murdered.

A claim to have solved the twentieth century's most baffling case was made in 2003 in a book by Steve Hodel, sensationally naming his father as the murderer. The author of this theory was a former Los Angeles police detective who began to research the case after his father's death. In the course of dealing with the affairs of Dr George Hodel, his son found a photograph album which contained a picture of Elizabeth Short.

This discovery prompted a detailed look into his father's background. Before training as a doctor, George Hodel had been a crime reporter in Los Angeles. He had led an unconventional life, mixing with the celebrities of the day but also enjoying a sleazy existence.

Steve Hodel painted an extraordinary picture of his father as a sadistic misogynist who committed incest with his daughter. Dr Hodel had been on the police list of suspects in 1947 because he had the surgical skills that had been demonstrated by the murderer in severing the victim's body. The doctor had possibly committed other murders in Los Angeles and eluded suspicion by virtue of his connections with the police.

Dr Hodel deserted his first wife in 1949 and went to live in Hawaii where he spent the next forty years. Of his father, Steve Hodel said, "My journey's end revealed to me a father who was evil incarnate . . ." His revelations did not convince everyone and, for some, the search for the killer of the "Black Dahlia" continues.

"I've Got To Kill"

An unknown serial killer stalked the San Francisco Bay area in the 1960s, committing five murders and taunting the police with cryptic messages and telephone calls.

Two teenagers were killed on 20 December 1968 while out on their first date. They had been sitting in their car when they were confronted by a gunman. He shot them dead when they attempted to run away. On 5 July 1969, a gunman attacked another couple in their car, killing the girl and wounding her escort. Later that night, a man called the police and said he wanted to report a double murder. He told them where to find the victims. He added, "I also killed those kids last year."

On 1 August, the *San Francisco Chronicle* received the first letter from the killer. It was signed with a crossed-circle and included a message containing eight lines of arcane symbols. The killer struck again on 27 September when he stabbed two students who were in their parked cars. The man survived and was able to describe his hooded attacker. The killer later telephoned the police saying simply, "I'm the one that did it."

On 11 October, taxi driver Paul Stine picked up a fare in central San Francisco. A man put a gun to his head, there was a brief struggle and a shot was fired. Before leaving the scene, the gunman tore off a piece of the driver's shirt. Onlookers gathered at the scene and the man walked calmly away as the cab driver lay dying in the driver's seat. Four days later, the local newspaper editor received a letter bearing the symbol of a crossed circle. Accompanying the letter was a piece of material torn from a bloodstained shirt.

The murder of Paul Stine was the so-called Zodiac killer's last but, although the killings stopped, the messages continued. His letters and threats made chilling forecasts about targeting school children. In one communication he wrote that he would be reborn in Paradise and all those he had killed would become his slaves.

"This is the Zodiac speaking" was one of his opening lines and he observed that he liked killing "because it is so much fun." There were numerous cryptic messages, some with drawings and maps and others in plain language. Experts in calligraphy, cryptography and astrology minutely examined the steady barrage of letters in the hope of gleaning some useful clues.

Ten days after the last murder, a man claiming to be the Zodiac killer called the Oakland Police Department and offered to give himself up provided he was defended by a well-known attorney. Melvin Belli, a high-profile criminal lawyer, accepted the challenge and received a number of phone calls from a man who complained of headaches and said, "I've got to kill."

What might have been a promising contact was broken off, but in 1971 the Zodiac killer began writing to the newspapers again claiming he had collected more "slaves". This phase continued until 1974 with more threats and the claim that he had killed thirty-seven times. Analysis of homicide patterns in the USA suggested that the Zodiac killer might have killed forty victims at locations forming a large letter "Z" when plotted on a map covering several states.

Contact with the Zodiac killer petered out and police believed that he might have died. In 2007, a film was produced based on the lives of those involved in attempts to trace the killer. Chief among them was Robert Graysmith, a writer who had chronicled the quest for the Zodiac killer for thirty years.

Inevitably, comparisons were made between the Zodiac killer and Jack the Ripper, two unidentified serial killers, who were separated by time and continents. A trait they shared, however, was to write letters containing menacing threats and taunts.

"Yes, I'm The Man . . ."

In 1934, the seaside town of Brighton in the UK experienced two trunk murders in the space of a month.

On 17 June 1934, staff at Brighton railway station became concerned over the smell associated with a trunk deposited at the left luggage office. Police were called and the trunk was opened to reveal the headless, legless body of a woman. The discovery created sensational newspaper headlines but, despite intensive enquiries, the identity of the dead woman was never established nor was the mystery of her murder solved.

Among the many people interviewed at the time was twenty-six-year-old Tony Mancini who worked as a waiter at the Skylark Café in Brighton. A parallel line of enquiry was to check on missing persons in the hope of identifying the woman found in the trunk. When it became known that Violette Kaye who had disappeared on 10 May, had been living with Mancini, the investigation took on fresh impetus.

Forty-two-year-old Violette Kaye was a former dancer who had become a prostitute and formed a liaison with Mancini. They lived together at various addresses in Brighton and after an argument at the Skylark Café on 10 May, Kaye disappeared. Mancini said she had gone to Paris.

Soon afterwards, Mancini changed lodgings and moved into a room in Kemp Street, near the Railway station. A friend helped him with his belongings, which included a very heavy trunk. After being questioned by police, Mancini took flight to London and was not present when officers entered his room at Kemp Street.

There, on 15 July, they found a trunk, which contained the decomposing body of Violette Kaye. Thus, enquiries into Trunk Crime No. 1 led to the discovery of Trunk Crime No. 2. Two days later, Mancini was arrested; he said, "Yes, I'm the man – I didn't murder her though." Post-mortem examination indicated that Kaye had been killed with blows to the head inflicted with a hammer.

Tony Mancini, whose real name was Lois England, was charged with murder. His explanation of Kaye's death was that he had returned to their rooms one day in May and found her lying dead on the bed. He panicked at what he had discovered, and its implications, and concealed her body in a trunk. He pointed out that because of her calling, Violette Kaye entertained many men in her room. Asked why he had not contacted the police, he said that a man who has previous convictions would not get a fair deal.

Mancini was tried at Lewes Crown Court in December 1934 where he was defended by Norman Birkett. Counsel played on the panic that overwhelmed Mancini when he found the body and decided to conceal it. He pointed out that concealment of a body did not necessarily amount to murder. Birkett's argument based on a chain reaction of panic, concealment and lies persuaded the jury, and Mancini walked away a free man after the court acquitted him. Forty-two years later he confessed in a Sunday newspaper that he had murdered Violette Kaye. The first Trunk Murder remained unsolved.

Getting A Grip

A man with a mutilated right hand, tried and acquitted of murder by strangulation, later confessed to the crime.

Rose Ada Robinson was a sixty-three-year-old widow who managed the John Barleycorn public house in Portsmouth. She had been in business there for forty years and was in the habit of keeping the takings on the premises. When the pub closed on 28 November 1943, she took the money out of the cash till, put it in her handbag and retired to her bedroom.

The following morning, she was found dead in her room and the takings, amounting to £450, were missing. Police found a broken window on the ground floor, which had allowed an intruder access. Rose Robinson had been strangled and there was evidence of a struggle. No fingerprints had been found at the scene and the only trace left by the attacker was a small black button found beneath the broken ground floor window.

Known criminals in the area were questioned but no suspects emerged. The murder enquiry was faltering when two alert detectives in Waterloo Road, London, picked up a man who was behaving furtively. When questioned, he volunteered the information that he was wanted "for more serious" things.

The man was Harold Loughans and he had a great deal of guilt that he wanted to get off his chest. The police just allowed him to incriminate himself and dig an even larger hole to fall into. He admitted killing a woman in Portsmouth and said it so preyed on his mind that he committed other crimes as a diversion. The problem with his story about killing Rose Robinson was that his right hand was mutilated and four of the fingers were just stubs. There were, though, various fibres on his clothing, which linked him to the crime in Portsmouth.

During preliminary hearings, Loughans changed his tune and now claimed that the police had distorted what he had told them and protested his innocence. He was tried at Winchester Crown Court in March 1944 when three witnesses came forward saying that they had seen Loughans in London on the night of the murder. The jury could not agree a verdict and a retrial was ordered.

This took place two weeks later at the Old Bailey when defence counsel called Sir Bernard Spilsbury as an expert witness. The pathologist testified that he had examined Loughans's mutilated hand and did not believe he had sufficient gripping power to enable him to strangle anyone. Faced with this new testimony and the alibi, which the police had been unable to shake, the jury found Loughans not guilty.

Loughans was in and out of prison with convictions for other crimes but twenty years after he had been acquitted of the Portsmouth murder, he sued the prosecutor, J. D. Casswell, for libel, on the grounds that the barrister had suggested he was lucky to have been acquitted. The libel case went to court in 1963 and Loughans lost. In effect, the jury in a civil case had overturned the verdict in a criminal trial but, as the law stood, Loughans could not be tried again.

In a final twist, three months after losing the libel case, Loughans talked to a Sunday newspaper and signed a confession to murder. He claimed he had not long to live and wanted to set the record straight. He died at the age of sixty-nine two years later.

Veil Of Silence

The investigation into the murder of Sophie Toscan du Plantier in her holiday home in Ireland was re-opened over a decade after her mysterious death.

The thirty-nine-year-old French television producer was married to Daniel Toscan du Plantier, a distinguished figure in the French cinema world. She was found battered to death on 23 December 1996 at her home in Schull, West Cork. She had been spending a few days on her own before returning to France to celebrate the New Year with her husband. She had booked her flight ticket and spoken to him a few hours before meeting a violent death.

Her body was found inside the gateway of her home. She was dressed in nightwear, suggesting she had opened the door to a late caller. She had been battered to death with a concrete block, which lay close to the body. Crime scene investigators found hair and blood in her fingernails, possibly originating from her attacker.

The local community was shocked by the violent death of one of its wealthy visitors. The area had seen an influx of celebrity figures seeking a tranquil place to live and the beautiful natural environment attracted filmmakers and movie stars.

The Gardai organized a man hunt to track the killer who had acted with such brutality. It appeared that a struggle had occurred at the du Plantier's home and that Sophie had broken free and run out of the house. She was attacked with a metal implement, possibly a hatchet, and her fingers were broken as she tried to fend off the attack. Cruelly injured, she was dealt a death blow from a heavy concrete block smashed over her head.

A characteristic of the murder investigation was lack of information. A newspaper correspondent was reported as saying, ". . . You sometimes think you're dealing with an affair of state because everyone is so secret." It was acknowledged that the dead woman, who was well-connected in French social circles, was a private person not courting publicity. Locals in Schull saw her as gentle and friendly. After her death, family and friends refrained from responding to questions from the media.

The veil of silence, of course, did not stem the rumours, which ranged from sexual indiscretions to criminal links in the world of filmmaking. In the immediate aftermath of the murder, the Gardai appealed to the local community for anyone who might have information to contribute about the possible identity of the murderer to come forward.

There was speculation that Sophie du Plantier knew her attacker and admitted him to her house. When detectives searched the premises, they found two wine glasses on the kitchen sink. Another curious feature of the crime scene was that, although the murder had occurred outside the house, both front and back doors were latched shut.

Following pressure from du Plantier's family, a French judge in 2008 ordered the exhumation of her body from the cemetery at Mauvezin in south west France. The hope was that forensic traces on the body might yield DNA leading to the murderer. The Gardai, who had come under heavy criticism for their perceived failures, made their files available to a new French-led investigation team.

SOS Unanswered

Twenty-eight-year-old Julie Ward was a keen amateur photographer. Her brutal murder in a Kenyan wildlife reserve in 1988 remains unsolved.

The young woman had been in Africa for three months when she left Nairobi on 2 September heading for the Masai Mara game park. She was accompanied by a marine biologist friend and they were driving a Suzuki jeep. When the vehicle broke down they decided that her friend would make his way back to Nairobi and return with a necessary spare part. Meanwhile, Julie managed to fix the jeep and decided to drive back to Nairobi on her own.

When she did not reappear, alarm bells started to sound, and after her father failed to contact her by telephone on 10 September, Julie was reported missing. John Ward flew out to Kenya and organized a search for his daughter. Her abandoned jeep was located three days later bogged down in the Sand River. The distress call letters, SOS, were visible on the vehicle's roof where they had been marked out with mud.

The search continued and, at a place called Keekovok, Julie Ward's remains were found; she had been hacked and burned.

Her father believed she had been kidnapped and murdered but the Kenyan authorities suggested she had been attacked by wild animals.

The dead woman's remains were returned to Britain for forensic examination. Pathologists concluded that she had been killed with a machete. An inquest into Julie's death was held in Nairobi in August 1989. The Kenyan pathologist said his report confirming that she had been killed with a machete had been altered by his superiors. Clearly there had been mistakes in procedure, but in October, the Kenyan government acknowledged there had been foul play.

John Ward was determined to keep up the pressure to establish the truth of what had happened to his daughter. In 1990 Scotland Yard detectives travelled to Kenya to carry out further enquiries. Witnesses were re-interviewed and the evidence re-examined. At one of the huts at the park rangers' camp at Makari, investigators found traces of hair which matched that of the dead woman.

The two rangers who used the hut were Peter Metui Kipeen and Jonah Tajeu Magiroi. They explained that they had found Julie after her vehicle became bogged down. There were suspicions that she had been taken hostage and probably raped. A possible scenario was that the two men panicked when they realized a massive search for her was under way, so they killed her and hacked the body to pieces to suggest an attack by wild animals.

Kipeen and Magiroi were tried for murder at Nairobi in February 1992. In acrimonious proceedings, the police were accused of a cover-up and the Scotland Yard detectives were criticized for pressurizing witnesses. The outcome was that the two accused were acquitted.

John Ward pursued his quest with gritty determination and, in March 1993, the Kenyan government agreed to re-open the case. In April 2004, an inquest held in Britain re-examined the case after the failure of the Kenyan authorities to establish who had murdered Julie Ward. The pathologist acting for the Kenyan government admitted signing false post-mortem reports in accordance with the official line which was to treat the death as an accident and not as a murder. There were rumours that a highly placed Kenyan citizen had been involved in the young woman's death and a cover-up was instigated to protect him.

In 2005, Kenya once more re-opened the investigation and, in 2008, John Ward offered a cash reward for information leading to the arrest and conviction of the murderer. In the twenty years since his daughter's death, he is reported to have spent a million pounds in his attempt to solve the case. He remained optimistic that new information would help find those responsible.

Rush Hour Killing

The driver of a sports car was killed with two bullets to the head in central London during the morning rush hour on 9 November 1970. A great deal was known about the dead man but his murderer has never been found.

A young woman cycling to work noticed a red TR5 sports car parked at an odd angle in South Carriage Road near the Albert Hall with its engine still running. Looking through the windscreen, she saw a man slumped over the steering wheel and fetched help.

Unfortunately, in a crime scene blunder, the police moved the car before it could be forensically examined. Consequently, the circumstances in which the driver was shot were unclear. What was certain was that he had been killed with two shots from a small calibre weapon fired at close range.

The dead man was identified as forty-eight-year-old Andre Mizelas, a well-respected Mayfair hairdresser. His movements on that fateful morning were easily reconstructed. He left his home close to Kensington High Street at around 9 a.m., saying goodbye to Betty Warburton, his partner, and climbing into his red sports car. His route took him through Knightsbridge towards his hairdressing salon in Grafton Street. He stopped his car for some reason in South Carriage Road. As the rush hour traffic swirled around him, an unknown gunman shot him dead. No one saw the assailant nor heard the sound of gunfire.

In partnership with his brother, Bernard, Mizelas had set up a hairdressing business, trading as Andre Bernard, with twenty salons and a distinguished list of clients. Despite his relative celebrity status, Mizelas did not mix socially with the Mayfair set. He liked boxing and often attended bouts at the Albert Hall. He was prosperous, owning a town house in Kensington and a holiday home in Portugal, happy in his relationships and, as far as anyone knew, without enemies.

The police questioned many of his friends and business associates without establishing any leads. Reconstructing the crime proved difficult as Mizelas's car had been moved prematurely and many would-be helpers had left their fingerprints on it. The nature of the fatal shots also posed intriguing questions. It appeared that the two killing bullets had entered the driver's left temple, travelling from front to rear. This suggested the gunman fired from inside the car and pre-supposes that Mizelas had stopped to pick up a passenger.

Four years after the shooting, and with the killer uncaught, a theory emerged that Andre Mizelas had been killed by a hit man for some obscure reason. There was talk of a man of Mediterranean appearance wearing blue clothing and sunshades who had been seen in the vicinity of the shooting by several motorists. An identikit picture was issued but the individual was never traced. An ITV "Police Five Special" programme on the shooting favoured the theory that Mizelas knew his killer and stopped his car to pick him up.

A development of this theory was the idea that the killer was a woman whose attentions Mizelas had scorned. As a successful hair stylist, he was acquainted with many women and those close to him said he had a quick temper. Perhaps a confrontation in the car got out of hand, ending in violence. That is as good as any other explanation of this unsolved murder.

"Bandits, Bandits!"

On the evening of 24 May 1957, seventy-five-year-old Countess Teresa Lubinska, alighted from a tube train at Gloucester Road on her way home from a visit to friends in

Ealing. A few minutes later, she lay dying from stab wounds in the lift. Her last words were, "Bandits, bandits . . . I was on the platform and I was stabbed." She had sustained five stab wounds, two of which penetrated her heart. She died before reaching hospital.

The police ruled out robbery as a motive because the Countess was still wearing her jewellery. Her attackers were presumed to have escaped by way of the emergency staircase. Appeals for witnesses to come forward produced no response.

Teresa Lubinska had lived through the Russian Revolution, the German invasion of Poland and survived the horrors of Ravensbruck. Her husband had been killed during the 1917 Revolution and she became strongly anti-Communist and was a staunch Catholic. As an exiled member of the Polish nobility in London, she used every opportunity to criticize the Communist rulers of her homeland.

Over a thousand mourners attended her funeral and detectives mingled with them in the hope of gleaning useful information. For the most part, her friends believed she had been killed because she was an embarrassment to the Polish Communist regime.

Detective Chief Inspector John du Rose and police colleagues staged an experiment at Gloucester Road tube station to test their theory about the attacker's escape route. They proved that someone running up the stairway could beat the lift by several seconds. Their theory was that the Countess was stabbed while on the platform and collapsed into the lift, which arrived at street level after the attacker had made good his escape.

After an investigation that lasted four years and involved thousands of interviews, detectives concluded that the Countess's murder was a mugging that went wrong. The murder weapon, described as a penknife with a two-inch blade, hardly sounded like an assassin's weapon of choice.

The key to the mystery probably lay in the dead woman's character. She was known to hate bad manners and discourteous behaviour and she was also outspoken. It is possible that she was jostled by someone when she got off the tube train and gave him a piece of her mind. In the confrontation that ensued, this individual threatened her with a penknife, possibly demanding money. Resistance would have been in her nature and she paid a grim price. It was a sad end for the woman who had been described as "The Angel of Ravensbruck".

Not One More!

In 2005, Amnesty International estimated the number of women murdered since 1993 in the Mexican city of Ciudad Juarez as 370.

During that time, young women had been systematically raped, beaten and murdered in and around Ciudad Juarez, which is situated close to the US border. Because of its proximity to the USA, the city had become a centre for migrant workers employed in the sweatshops making cheap goods for export. The city's population of around one million, doubled with the influx of low-paid workers, as well as drug-dealers, shady businessmen and criminals.

The first victim in what was to become a series of serial killings was Alma Chaviva Farel. She had been beaten, raped and strangled and her body dumped on waste ground. Other victims, usually aged between eleven and thirty-five followed, and were variously stabbed, beaten, strangled and burned. By the end of 1993, there were nineteen such murders. Not all the victims were identified.

Public outrage focused on corrupt policing and confessions extracted by torture from innocent suspects. The official explanation was that a serial killer was at large. What initially appeared as a breakthrough came in 1994 with the arrest of Abdul Latif Sharif. He was a man with a chequered history of violence towards women, including rape and assault in the USA. He plea-bargained his way out of charges and, in May 1994, crossed the border into Mexico and settled in Ciudad Juarez.

Sharif was accused of rape in 1995 and allegedly made a confession. He was tried for rape and murder, found guilty and sentenced to thirty years imprisonment. Although he was named as the Juarez serial killer, the murders continued unabated, with nineteen victims in 1995. The police admitted that hundreds of people, mostly women, had disappeared in less than a year.

The FBI were called in to review the murders in 1999. In May of that year it was reported that nearly 200 women had been murdered over a ten-year period. Experts in serial killing and criminologists from the USA and Canada pooled their knowledge and concluded that two or three serial killers were at work. As a footnote to their deliberations, a mass grave was found in December 1999 containing nine corpses, three of which were identified as US citizens.

Further mass graves were found in 2001 and 2002 and the body count seemed endless. New suspects were charged and their lawyers received death threats. Various motives for the killings were suggested. These included the idea that the women were used as drug mules and executed by gangs when they had completed their tasks; that the women were murdered by organ harvesters; and that the killings were attributable to a satanic cult.

In February 2004, Jane Fonda, the Hollywood film actress, led a protest in Ciudad Juarez demanding action against the murderers. Their demand was *Ni Una Mas* – not one more. Allegations implying that the police, apart from being inept, were either involved in the killings or covering up for the perpetrators were rife. The police investigation was riddled with incompetence; many victims remained unidentified, others were misidentified. DNA evidence was botched, files were destroyed, suspects were framed and innocent people were tortured into making confessions. And still the killing went on, leading to the conclusion that a powerful cartel existed that exploited young women for its own ends and which was protected by a combination of drug barons and political and business interests.

"Started With A Bang . . ."

The murder of Joseph Bowne Elwell, the "Wizard of Whist", in his home while he sat reading his mail has been an abiding mystery for over eighty years.

Forty-seven-year-old Elwell was an acknowledged expert at cards and had written books on the subject of playing bridge. His expertise had earned him a good living and he enjoyed a stylish life in his three-storey house in New York. He was divorced and devoted to female companionship for which he had a specially furnished bedroom.

During the evening of 10 June 1920, he dined out with friends and went to the theatre, returning home at around 2.30 a.m. When his housekeeper arrived for work at 8.10 a.m., she was startled to see her employer, dressed in pyjamas and sitting in a chair in the living room. More distressing was the bullet wound in his forehead between the eyes. Elwell was still breathing and an ambulance was called. He died later in hospital.

The circumstances of the shooting were odd. Elwell was sitting with a letter on his lap and unopened mail lying on the floor. The mail had been delivered at 7.10 a.m., an hour before his housekeeper arrived. A .45 calibre bullet was found on a table where it had landed after passing through Elwell's head and ricocheting from a wall. A spent cartridge case lay on the floor. Detectives examining the entry and exit wounds reasoned that the killer had fired from a crouching position.

There were no fingerprints left at the crime scene, no sign of a struggle and nothing was missing. Nor was there a murder weapon. The indications were that the murderer had been admitted to the house by Elwell and was therefore someone he knew. Working on this premise, detectives began questioning his staff, friends and family.

This proved to be quite a task particularly in light of the number of female acquaintances in Elwell's life. He kept a card index of names and addresses relating to over fifty ladies, some married, many of whom had visited his home. There were rumours about jealous husbands and lovers, of mystery spies and fashionable matrons mad with lust, but no real suspects.

There were no clues in the letters which Elwell had received on the morning he was shot and no witnesses to the arrival at his door of his killer. All that was left was speculation and, on that score, the New York newspapers had a feast. The renowned crime writer, Jonathan Goodman, in his book on the unsolved murder, wrote that it was a case "... which started with a bang heard only by the culprit and the victim", and "ended with a whimper".

Death Of A Twitcher

Dr Helen Davidson, a popular fifty-four-year-old doctor with a practice in Amersham, Buckinghamshire in the UK, was bludgeoned to death while bird-watching. Her murder remains unsolved but there are pointers as to the identity of the killer.

Dr Davidson was last seen alive at 3.15 p.m. on 9 November 1966. She drove her blue Hillman Minx along the Amersham to Beaconsfield Road and parked in a lay-by at Hodgemoor Wood. She locked her car with her handbag inside and, equipped with binoculars and accompanied by her dog, walked about a mile into the Forestry Commission Reserve.

The alarm was raised when she failed to return home. A search was mounted and her car was soon located. Searchers then found her body in the woods. She had been bludgeoned to death and, in an act of callous brutality, her killer had stamped her head into the ground. Her dog kept watch over her body during the night.

Police questioned walkers who had been in the vicinity but no one had seen Helen Davidson. They checked on known sexual offenders and made enquiries about mental patients. A theory that surfaced fairly quickly was that, perhaps, the doctor, using her binoculars, had observed a pair of lovers who did not wish to be seen. She was fully clothed when discovered and there were no other injuries apart from those to the head. Investigators were convinced the murderer was a local man familiar with the woods.

Motive was a key issue. Robbery was ruled out as the dead woman was still wearing her jewellery, there were no signs that a struggle had taken place and no suggestion of sexual attack. The murder weapon appeared to be a tree branch picked up at random. A new approach was the possibility of a revenge attack by a former patient. No progress was made with any of these lines of enquiry.

In 1974, the *News of the World* published an account of the unsolved murder and offered a reward of £100,000 for information leading to the arrest of the killer. There were developments at around this time involving a suspect who had once lived in Amersham and had emigrated to Australia after Dr Davidson's death. This unnamed man returned to the UK in 1979 and came to the attention of the police through a motoring offence.

His reaction to being questioned was to rebuke the officers for not using their time to greater effect by finding the killer of Dr Davidson. This was an unusual response, especially bearing in mind that he was referring to an event that had occurred thirteen years previously. In November 1980, he was taken into custody and questioned about the Davidson murder. He was released without charge and subsequently told a newspaper that he was a medium and was willing to help the police in that capacity.

In February 1986, the man, who it transpired was a former patient of Dr Davidson, was interviewed by a local journalist and made some enigmatic references to her death. Crime writers, Bernard Taylor and Stephen Knight, in their account of the case in 1987, speculated that Dr Davidson had come across a flasher in the woods, a person she knew who killed her to protect his identity.

Peoples' Heroine

The execution in Singapore of Flor Contemplacion, a Filipino housemaid convicted of double murder, created a storm of protest in 1995 and bitter disagreement between two governments.

Forty-two-year-old Flor Contemplacion worked as a maid in the Huang household in Singapore. She was one among 60,000 Filipinos employed in the city state. In 1991, she was accused of drowning her employer's four-year-old son and of strangling a fellow maid, Delia Maga. She apparently confessed to these crimes in letters written to family and friends.

Put on trial and found guilty of murder, Contemplacion was sentenced to death. On the day of her execution at Changi Prison, 17 March 1995, hundreds of protesters assembled outside the Singapore embassy in Manila. They chanted the minutes down to the time of execution and then erupted in furious outrage.

When Flor Contemplacion's body was returned to the Philippines, Amelita Ramos, the President's wife, was among the mourners gathered to witness her return. She spoke of the President's regret that his pleas on behalf of the nation to Singapore for a stay of execution had not been heeded. Human rights groups described Singapore as tyrannical and the Catholic Church condemned the disregard of mercy.

The stage was set for irritable exchanges between the two governments and their respective ambassadors were recalled. The President of the Philippines, Fidel Ramos, threatened to break off diplomatic relations if an enquiry he had set up found that Contemplacion had been unjustly treated and executed. In the meantime, Filipinos intending to work in Singapore as maids were banned from travelling.

In April 1995, a commission of enquiry into the circumstances of Contemplacion's trial convened in Manila to consider the evidence and deliver their own verdict. A new autopsy was carried out on Delia Maga and a pathologist gave it as his opinion that the injuries she had suffered resulted from a fierce struggle. In his view, Contemplacion was not strong enough to have overpowered Maga. In other words, she was innocent of the charge of murder. Suggestions gained ground that the Huang family's son died of drowning in the bath during an epileptic attack and that family members killed Maga who they held responsible for his care. Guilt for both deaths was then shifted onto Contemplacion.

The Singapore authorities rejected the notion that the maid was innocent, especially in light of her confession, and declared that it was a "totally absurd" suggestion. They refused to re-open the case but in an attempt to defuse the situation, put forward the idea that forensic experts from Britain and the USA should examine any new evidence.

Recriminations continued to fly backwards and forwards and there were reports about squabbles involving family members and production companies over television and film rights to Contemplacion's story. Singapore continued to occupy the moral high ground by claiming its stance on crime was the foundation of a peaceful society. In her own country, Flor Contemplacion has come to be regarded as a heroine of the people.

"A Skilled Killer"

A late-night summons from an unidentified caller asking for a doctor's help led to the murder of Dr Richard Castillo. The caller has never been formally identified and the murder remains unsolved.

Seventy-two-year-old Dr Castillo was a highly respected doctor, working in a medical practice in Chelsea in London. On Sunday 7 May 1961, he had been out walking his dog and returned home to be greeted by his daughter with the information that there was a caller on the telephone seeking help. Dr Castillo took the call from a man called Allenby who said his wife was ill. It was after 11 p.m. but the doctor said he would visit the sick person. He got into his car and drove across the River Thames to Albert Bridge Road, looking for 3 Albert Studios.

Albert Studios was a quiet, dark passage and it was there, at about 11.40 p.m. that an artist living at number two heard someone knocking at the house next door. There was no reply because the occupants had moved out earlier in the day. Then, the neighbour heard voices and someone in distress outside in the street. He went outside and encountered Dr Castillo who had been attacked and had collapsed unconscious on the ground. He was dead before the police arrived.

Alarmed that her husband had not returned home by 2 a.m., Mrs Castillo called Dr David Craig, a colleague in the medical practice. She explained that her husband had gone out to answer an emergency call at Albert Studios and Dr Craig said he would go there immediately. When he arrived, he found police officers standing around the body of his fellow doctor. Castillo had been killed with two knife thrusts, one in the abdomen and the other through the ribs and directly into the heart. Dr Craig's estimation was that "The knife was put in in a skilled fashion . . . A skilled killer . . .", he said. The murderer escaped without leaving a trace and the murder weapon was never found.

On the face of it, the murder appeared to be motiveless. Dr Castillo, who was born in Malta, had moved to England in 1921 and practised as a doctor in Chelsea since 1922. He was popular and highly respected, particularly for his willingness to answer out-of-hours calls from his patients. When he was called out on the last night of his life, he believed he was to see a Mrs Allenby, one of his colleague's patients, at 3 Albert Studios. But the house was unoccupied and the previous tenants were not Mr and Mrs Allenby.

The curious nature of the telephone call, luring the doctor into a dark corner of London late at night, led to the idea that he had been targeted. The Coroner summarized the few known facts at the inquest; the caller knew the doctor's habits sufficiently to understand that he would respond to a call for help and the killing ground had been ideally chosen as a place of ambush.

There was speculation that Dr Castillo had stumbled on some clandestine espionage activity involving foreign agents for which he had to be silenced. The phenomenon of the apparently motiveless murder inevitably gives rise to such theorizing. The London *Evening News* ran a story that the doctor was murdered by someone he knew and who had been interviewed by the police. This man allegedly killed out of jealousy but was able to furnish a plausible alibi, which inhibited any further investigation.

". . . His Heart's Blood"

When Dr Harvey Burdell, a wealthy New York dentist, was murdered in his consulting room, the chief suspects were drawn from the odd assortment of lodgers who rented rooms in the building he owned.

Forty-six-year-old Dr Burdell had built up a lucrative dental practice but his professional standing was tainted by a quarrelsome nature and a reputation for swindling. He owned a mansion in New York at 31 Bond Street and worked from his consulting room on the first floor. He sub-let ten of his rooms, providing him with healthy rents.

On 29 January 1857, the tall bearded figure of Dr Burdell was seen entering the mansion at around 10.45 p.m. The following morning, the dentist was found dead in his consulting room. He had been repeatedly stabbed, with knife thrusts in his neck, chest and abdomen. The room was heavily bloodstained, suggesting there had been a struggle.

There were no indications of forced entry and the police naturally concentrated their enquiries on the various tenants in the mansion. No one had heard any noise or disturbance, possibly because it had been a stormy night. Suspicion fell on Emma Cunningham, a lady in her late thirties, who appeared to have a special relationship with Burdell. She claimed to be his wife, although the legality of an alleged marriage was unclear.

What was not questioned was that Emma Cunningham acted for Burdell by supervising the letting of his rented rooms. Two considerations that weighed against her were that she had been overheard making threats against the dentist to the effect that she would "have his heart's blood". And secondly, she was left-handed, a characteristic which she apparently shared with his murderer.

Among the other boarders questioned were John J. Eckel, a dealer in animal hides, and George V. Snodgrass, the effeminate son of a preacher who had a penchant for wearing female undergarments. These two joined Emma Cunningham in a trip downtown where they were held pending the inquest into Dr Burdell's death.

The evidence presented at the inquest by sundry maids and boarders from the Bond Street mansion can best be described as exotic and confusing. Threats allegedly issued by Emma Cunningham were repeated and there was conflicting evidence about her relationship with the dentist. Despite the lack of hard evidence, she, together with Eckel and Snodgrass, were charged with involvement in the murder and committed for trial. At this point, Cunningham lodged a claim for part of the dead man's estate, on the grounds that they were secretly married.

The trial collapsed in farce when Cunningham declared that she was pregnant and was given a not guilty verdict. Her doctor reported that she was not pregnant and that she had offered him money to buy a baby for her. She was charged with fraud and the case against Eckel and Snodgrass was dropped. Completely undaunted, Emma Cunningham rented out her imposter child to P. T. Barnum's circus where people could view the "Bogus Burdell Baby".

The contents of Burdell's mansion were sold by auction to help pay his debts. The blood-soaked carpet from his consulting room was a sought-after item. The nearest anyone came to solving the murder lay in a confession made by a man called Lewis who was executed in New York for a different murder. The likelihood is that Burdell, with his reputation for being quarrelsome, was killed by one of his creditors.

CHAPTER 12

Mysteries of the Missing

Thousands of people go missing every year. The reasons are many and varied including loss of memory, mental aberration, illness or a desire for anonymity. Happily, only a fraction of those who disappear do so permanently. The great majority are found or reappear of their own volition. But some will have encountered foul play, either turning up dead or never being discovered.

People who go missing from a conventional home environment are quickly reported. But some individuals, such as prostitutes and others who follow a lone existence, are particularly at risk from serial killers and their disappearance may go unreported. Some of British killer Fred West's victims were young women who had disappeared twenty years before their buried remains were found. The UK Missing Persons Bureau was set up in 1994 to co-ordinate information. Statistics show that the largest group of missing persons are young people under the age of eighteen.

Among the mysterious high-profile disappearances in the UK that are unsolved are Lord Lucan, wanted for murder in 1974; Victor Grayson, a former Socialist MP, who vanished in 1920, and Suzy Lamplugh, the young estate agent who went missing, presumed murdered, in 1986. Others achieve resolution through confession or chance discovery. James Camb, for instance, admitted pushing the body of Gay Gibson through a ship porthole and out into the ocean in 1948. She was never seen again and he was punished as her murderer. Jim Lowell disposed of his victim's body in a shallow grave in rural Maine, USA, in 1870, but her remains resurfaced three years later to haunt him.

Max Haines, the veteran Canadian crime writer, has commented to the effect that murderers cannot just put the corpse out with the rubbish and walk away. As discussed earlier in Chapter Two: "Parts and Parcels" (page 10), one solution open to the murderer is to dismember the victim's body and dispose of it piecemeal. This is a tedious procedure calling for stamina and determination, whereas the easy option is to leave the corpse where it falls and make good an escape. While this may be an appealing strategy, it is one which usually provides crime scene investigators with a wealth of forensic evidence. Transfer of contact traces and telltale fingerprints and DNA are inherently dangerous to the perpetrator.

Consequently, some murderers opt for a form of disposal that is intended to make sure the victim simply vanishes. An out-of-sight, out-of-mind policy, this is often based on the misconception that no body means no murder. But, as generations of criminals have discovered to their cost, that is not the case. John Haigh, the infamous "acid bath murderer" in the late 1940s, made that fatal calculation and paid for it on the gallows.

Earth, fire and water are consuming elements that offer possible disposal routes for unwanted corpses. But each has it drawbacks. Shallow graves may be visible to the trained eye or be unearthed by animals, and water has an inconvenient habit of giving up its dead. Fire is not necessarily all-consuming as the French murderers, Dr Marcel Petiot and Henri Landru, discovered when combustion residues revealed charred bones and teeth. Martin Ryan, though, with his access to an industrial incinerator, boasted that he knew how to dispose of a body. No traces of his missing wife's body were found in 1990 despite intensive sieving of the incinerator's ashes.

Some murderers have an urge to keep their victims close to hand. Dennis Nilsen, who killed fifteen young men in London in the late 1970s, buried some remains in his back garden but kept others under the floorboards. Using a similar strategy in the 1950s, John Christie, the killer at 10 Rillington Place, walled up some of his victims in the kitchen.

The combination of time and chance can produce surprises. It was forty-two years after she went missing in 1919 that Mamie Stewart's body was found by cavers in an airshaft in the Gower

Peninsula, Wales. While her murderer was identified, he escaped retribution by dying a natural death.

Ingenious methods have been employed by murderers to remove the mortal remains of their victims' existence. Everything has been tried, from cannibalism to feeding body parts to animals. The Hosein Brothers in 1968 fed the remains of their kidnap victim to the pigs at Rook's Farm in Herefordshire. No traces were ever found and the brothers' conviction was proof that murder does not require the evidence of a body. Equally effective, but unproven, was the disposal of Urban Napoleon Stanger who disappeared from London's East End in 1831 never to be seen again. It was widely believed that his fate was to be turned into meat pies.

Lost At Sea

A ship's steward was convicted of murdering a passenger and pushing the body out of a porthole and into the sea. Although it was a suspicious death with no body, it led to a life sentence.

Twenty-one-year-old Gay Gibson, an actress, boarded the liner, *Durban Castle*, at Cape Town on 10 October 1947. She joined a number of mostly elderly first-class passengers for the voyage to England.

A week later, when the liner was sailing off the coast of West Africa, Gay Gibson was reported missing from her cabin. She was presumed to have gone overboard. The captain turned round and made a search. When this proved unsuccessful in locating the young woman, he resumed his course to England.

Ship's officers examined the cabin occupied by the missing passenger. The porthole was open and it was noted that the bed sheets were crumpled and stained. It was also noted that, during the early hours of 18 October, the cabin call-button had been pushed. The call was answered by James Camb, a deck steward. It was forbidden for crew members to fraternize with passengers and Camb denied entering Gibson's cabin. He was examined by the ship's doctor and scratches were evident on his forearms. Camb was relieved of his duties and handed over to the police when the ship docked in Southampton.

After changing his story several times, Camb admitted that

he had been in Gibson's cabin. He claimed she consented to having sex and, during intercourse, she had a seizure. When his attempts to revive her failed and believing that she was dead, he pushed her body out of the porthole.

Camb was charged with murder and appeared on trial at Winchester Assizes in March 1948. The prosecution case against him was that he had raped and strangled the young woman before throwing her out of the porthole. With no body, much of the evidence was necessarily circumstantial. He repeated his claim that they had consensual sex and that he panicked when she appeared to be dead.

The jury returned with a verdict of guilty after forty-five minutes. Asked if he had anything to say, Camb reminded the court that he had pleaded not guilty, ". . . and I repeat that statement now." Mr Justice Hilbery then pronounced sentence of death by hanging. While Parliament was debating the abolition of capital punishment, executions were suspended. Camb was reprieved and given a life sentence. He was released on parole in 1959 and, in 1971, served a term of imprisonment following a conviction for sexual offences. He was released in 1978 and died the following year.

While there was no doubt that Camb had pushed Gay Gibson's body through the cabin porthole and into the sea, it was not certain that he had murdered her. An alternative explanation of her death is that she suffered heart failure during vigorous sexual intercourse. However, it is rare for a twenty-one-year-old to die of heart failure during sex. In the 1940s, well before the age of permissiveness, this was not an argument that could be thoroughly aired in court.

"Don't Murder Me!"

A mother's dream about the circumstances of her missing daughter's murder turned into reality three years later. The people of Lewiston, Maine in the US, had several reasons for remembering the events which occurred on the weekend of 11 and 12 June 1870. The circus came to town, the Central Hall burned down and Lizzie Lowell disappeared.

Jim and Lizzie Lowell were married but lived apart, following a domestic upset. Jim was a teamster and Lizzie worked as live-in help at the home of Mrs Sophronia Blood. After supper on 12 June, Jim called for Lizzie to take her out on a summer's evening drive.

When Lizzie had not returned by 10 p.m., Mrs Blood assumed that she was staying the night with her husband. The next morning, she saw Jim and he told her that he had returned Lizzie to her home the previous evening. He added that she had probably gone off with some "damned circus fellow". And, there Lizzie's disappearance rested until her mother, Sarah Burton, turned up in Lewiston. She confronted Jim Lowell who repeated his story that Lizzie had gone off with another man. Sarah Burton's next call was to speak with Mrs Blood who showed her two letters supposedly written by Lizzie and received two weeks after she went missing.

Sarah Burton returned home and related to a friend a dream that she'd had around the time her daughter went missing. In her dream, she saw Jim and Lizzie together and then Lizzie was on the ground with her husband threatening her and she was pleading, "Don't murder me." The following morning, Sarah Burton made a written record of her dream, little knowing the important part it would play in subsequent events.

In 1872, Jim Lowell re-married and went to live in Lawrence, Massachusetts. Then, in the following year, a farmer clearing a plot of land he had bought near Lewiston, made a discovery. He stumbled across a shallow grave containing a skeleton. The remains were headless but the clothing, which was still intact, identified them as Lizzie Lowell.

A coroner's enquiry returned a verdict of murder against a person or persons unknown. Two days later, Jim Lowell was arrested and charged with murder. On the day he returned to Lewiston, the local newspaper published the text of the dream that Sarah Burton had recorded three years previously. This resulted in a surge of public hostility towards Jim Lowell.

He was put on trial and faced largely circumstantial evidence. It was sufficient to persuade the jury to return a guilty verdict and Lowell was convicted of first-degree murder. Sentence of death followed, but the legal statutes of Maine required a year to pass before the sentence was carried out. Time passed and the sentence was reduced to life imprisonment.

Turning Up The Heat

What might have been a perfect murder, involving the complete destruction of the victim's body in a hospital incinerator, unravelled when the murderer lost his nerve.

Lynda Ryan was reported missing from her home in Barry, South Wales, by her sister on 6 July 1990. Her husband, Martin Ryan, said he saw her on 28 June in the company of two men at a pub in Barry. He told police he believed Lynda was having an affair and he went to the pub to reason with her. He implored her to return home with him but she declined. That was the last time he saw her.

Ryan had a history of convictions for minor offences but he appeared genuinely upset at his wife's disappearance. This was borne out by a search of their home which turned up a letter he had written to Lynda expressing his love for her and asking for a chance to make up their differences.

Police enquiries led them to one of the men who had been in the pub. He readily admitted having had a sexual liaison with Lynda Ryan and related the incident in which she was confronted by her husband. He slapped her and began shouting. Detectives learned from Lynda's employer, a department store in Barry, that she had called in sick on 29 June. A subsequent call was received from Martin Ryan asking if his wife had reported for work.

At this point, Martin Ryan disappeared, thereby prompting detectives to take a closer look at his background. He worked as a porter at Llandough Hospital in Barry where his duties included operating the hospital incinerator. This piece of equipment became the focus of attention when it was reported that the hospital had been permeated by an unpleasant smell emanating from the incinerator. Suspicions began to build as a result of a 999 call made on the night Lynda Ryan went missing. Residents next to the hospital heard screams coming from the grounds at about midnight. The police responded but nothing unusual was found.

The search was now on to find Martin Ryan who had been sighted in Manchester, Oxford and London. He was located at a pub but avoided capture by leaping out of a window as a result of which he broke his ankle. He was admitted to hospital for treatment under a false name.

Meanwhile, the ashes in the Barry hospital incinerator were sifted for possible human remains but without success. On 9 August, having returned to Cardiff, Ryan decided to surrender to the police and was charged with murdering his wife, even though her body had not been found. He was put on trial at Cardiff Crown Court in April 1991.

The prosecution case was that he believed Lynda was having an affair and confronted her at the pub. He went home and took a knife from the kitchen and returned to the pub where Lynda agreed to leave with him. They drove to Llandough Hospital where they had an argument and he stabbed her. He then pushed her body into the incinerator which he stoked with extra fuel to increase the burning temperature. A witness who knew Ryan recalled how he had once bragged that he knew how to dispose of a body if the need arose.

In Ryan's defence, an expert witness testified that he was in a depressed state as a result of the breakdown of his marriage and personality failings which impaired his sense of responsibility. The jury took the view that Ryan was fully accountable for his actions and found him guilty and he was sentenced to life imprisonment.

Murder By Accident

A murder without a body was solved by DNA evidence that came to light two years after the victim's disappearance. Her body was never found but her lover was successfully prosecuted for her murder.

Thirty-year-old Anne Marie Fahey worked as scheduling secretary for Thomas Carper, Governor of Delaware. She was last in her office at Wilmington on 27 June 1996. When she failed to make contact with her friends and family, they became concerned about her safety.

A check on her apartment revealed nothing amiss, although she seemed to have left with her keys but did not take her purse. When her sister read Anne Marie's diary, she found some surprising entries referring to secret meetings with someone called TC. Immediate thoughts were that this might be Tom Carper but then letters were found indicating that TC was Thomas Capano, a prominent Wilmington lawyer.

It appeared that Anne Marie and Thomas Capano had been seeing each other for many months. Forty-nine-year-old Capano worked in a successful law practice and moved in the highest political and social circles. He was also married, although currently separated from his wife.

When the police interviewed Capano, he admitted having an affair with Anne Marie. He said he had dinner with her a few days previously and he drove her home. He said their affair was over and advised officers, somewhat ungraciously, that Anne Marie was an unpredictable person, adding that she was depressed, anorexic and suicidal. He denied any involvement in her disappearance. A search of Capano's mansion revealed small traces of blood on a closet. Without a body, there was no possibility of a DNA match. There were also signs of cleaning activity, redecorating and replacement of carpets in the house.

The FBI was called in to help with the investigation, which lasted for two years before there was a breakthrough with DNA. In the meantime, investigators pieced together some potentially incriminating evidence from Capano's younger brother who said that he had been asked for help. Capano told him that he was being blackmailed and feared for his life. He said he might have to kill the blackmailer and needed money and a gun. He also asked to borrow his brother's boat.

The two men loaded a refrigerator into the boat and cruised out some sixty miles into the Atlantic. They cut the engines and dropped the refrigerator over the side. It floated, despite Capano's efforts to sink it by shooting holes in it. Finally, the refrigerator was pulled back to the boat. Capano opened it and dragged out a body which he then heaved over the side into the sea.

On 17 November 1997, Thomas Capano was charged with first-degree murder. By a stroke of good fortune, investigators found that Anne Marie had been a blood donor and that a blood sample existed. DNA testing showed that her blood matched the traces found in Capano's home.

Capano went on trial in December 1998. After two years of denial, he finally made some admissions. He claimed that Anne Marie had died accidentally when another girlfriend confronted them in his house. She was armed and threatened to take her own life. The gun discharged accidentally and Anne Marie was fatally shot. The woman in question denied being in the house.

Capano gave evidence on his own behalf, attacking the testimony of other witnesses, abusing the prosecutor and trying to manipulate the proceedings. The judge threatened him with "draconian sanctions" if he did not curb his outbursts.

The jury returned a guilty verdict, which was greeted with cheers outside the courtroom. In a forthright summation, Judge William Lee Swain described Capano as angry, sinister and malignant. On 17 January 1999, he was sentenced to death but this was reduced to life imprisonment by the Delaware Supreme Court in 2006. The conviction was upheld again in 2008.

Killer Landlord

Twenty-two-year-old Helen McCourt left work early on 9 February 1988 to return to her home in Billinge, near St Helens in Lancashire in the UK, to get ready for a date with her boyfriend. Her journey from Liverpool by train and bus was reconstructed and it was known that she left the bus at the stop close to her home at about 5.40 p.m. Her mother became concerned when she did not return home and, later in the evening, called the police.

Helen was regarded as a reliable, level-headed girl with no reason to absent herself from home and none of her friends could shed any light on her whereabouts. After leaving the bus near her home, her short walk took her past the George and Dragon public house. Detectives decided to question the landlord to see if he had any information that might help them.

Ian Simms proved evasive and barely co-operative in talking to detectives, who noted that he had what appeared to be scratch marks on his neck. Officers discovered that Helen McCourt had recently worked behind the bar at his pub and their interest in the landlord intensified when they learned of an incident that occurred two evenings before Helen went missing. On 7 February, one of Helen's friends had become involved in an argument with Ian Simms and Helen had joined in. Asked about the marks on his neck, he explained that his wife had attacked him after she learned he had spent the night with his mistress. His wife denied this had happened.

While appeals were made on television for information that might help police enquiries, detectives began searching Simms's car and property. In the boot of his car, they found a muddy spade and also a broken sapphire and opal earring, which was identified as Helen's. The fastener belonging to the earring was found on the carpet of the bedroom used by Simms at the George and Dragon. Most significantly, a smudged bloody fingerprint was discovered on the bedroom doorframe. Simms, who admitted nothing, was arrested on suspicion of murder.

Local searches continued to turn up evidence. Bloodstained men's clothing was found on a waste tip at Warrington and the missing girl's bloodstained garments were retrieved from a bin liner near Irlam, together with a knotted piece of electric flex. These items provided significant trace evidence, but despite searches for possible gravesites, there was still no body.

Clinching evidence linking Simms to the missing girl came with DNA testing. Blood on Simms's clothing matched Helen's DNA profile using samples provided by her parents. Simms was tried for murder at Liverpool Crown Court in February 1989. He pleaded not guilty and claimed that he had been framed by someone who stole his clothes, killed Helen while he was asleep and disposed of her body. The prosecution case rested on the DNA evidence which the jury found convincing. Simms was convicted and sentenced to life imprisonment. The body of Helen McCourt has never been found despite direct appeals made by her mother to her convicted killer.

". . . Unremitting Malevolence"

Eighty-two-year-old Irene Silverman, widow of a multi-millionaire mortgage broker, lived in an elegant town house in Manhattan, New York, that was furnished with antiques. The five-storey mansion was divided into apartments, which she let to wealthy clientele.

Silverman entertained guests to dinner on 4 July 1998, and was seen the following morning by her maid whom she asked to walk her dog. When the maid returned to the mansion, Irene Silverman was not there and she was never seen again. The police were called and their initial searches gave no indication of any struggle having taken place inside the house. Next, they questioned people who knew the missing woman, including some of her tenants.

Suspicion centred on a young man using the name, Manny Guerin, who had also disappeared. Enquiries revealed that Guerin was twenty-three-year-old Kenneth Kimes who, together with his mother, was in police custody suspected of stealing a car. Kimes and his mother, sixty-four-year-old Sante, had been arrested on the evening of 5 July.

Further enquiries revealed that Kimes, mother and son, were on the FBI's most wanted list for questioning in connection with murder, fraud and theft in several states. The pair had a record of suspect dealings going back to the 1970s and Sante had served a three-year prison sentence in 1985 for theft and ill-treatment of Mexican immigrants.

Sante was the widow of a wealthy Californian property dealer and owned several houses. She and her son lived a life of luxury and young Kenneth had been looked after by nannies and schooled by private tutors. He had bonded very closely with his mother.

When the pair were arrested, Sante was found in possession

of a forged document whereby Irene Silverman transferred ownership of her home to her. Detectives also found a 9mm handgun, hypodermic syringes and drugs in her car. What was not found was any forensic trace evidence linking the Kimes to Mrs Silverman's disappearance nor were there any witnesses.

The pair were put on trial for murder in New York in 2000. They appeared together on the *60 Minutes* television news programme during the pre-trial hearings. They held hands and whispered to each other like a couple of lovers. An investigation that had taken nearly two years revealed details of an elaborate plan to take possession of Irene Silverman's home valued at $8 million, which involved Kenneth moving into one of her rented apartments.

With no body and practically no forensic evidence, the prosecution's case was circumstantial. The trial lasted three months and the Kimes' lawyer argued simply that there was no body, no witnesses and no proof of murder. Sante staged several interviews during the court proceedings, declaring her innocence and demanding to talk to reporters. The prosecutor described Sante as the brains of the operation – she gave the instructions and Kenneth carried them out.

On 19 May 2000, the jury found mother and son guilty of murdering Irene Silverman. The judge sentenced Sante to 120 years to life in prison and Kenneth to 126 years. Judge Rena Uviller described Sante as a "sociopath ... of unremitting malevolence" and Kenneth as a "vacuous dupe" who had turned into a "remorseless predator".

The Billionaire Boys' Club

A dozen or so young men who met at prep school shared a dream about becoming rich. They formed a group known as the Billionaire Boys' Club with the aim of achieving their dream. Unfortunately, the riches turned to ashes and, in due course, to murder.

This group of young men, comprising sons of a number of wealthy Los Angeles families, was led by Joe Hunt. He ran an organization that combined cult, business and social activities. With funds at their disposal, they set out to compound their riches by persuading family and friends to invest in commodities trading ventures.

By 1983, Hunt, at the age of twenty-four, was managing millions of dollars worth of funds on behalf of eighty investors. His initial success meant that he and his friends could live a lavish lifestyle. They operated from condominiums in West Wilshire Boulevard, Beverly Hills, drove expensive cars, dined in the most fashionable restaurants and, generally, assumed an arrogant disregard for anyone who might seek to curb their appetites.

These good times were achieved by running classic Ponzi or Pyramid selling schemes; keeping existing investors sweet by giving them generous returns funded with monies provided by new investors. But, by 1984, the wheels began to fall off this get-rich-quick vehicle when funds started to run short.

Matters came to a head with the disappearance of a former artist and journalist, Ronald Levin. He went missing in June 1984 having reportedly cheated Joe Hunt and his fellow Billionaire Boys out of $4 million in commissions owed to them.

Hunt was desperate to raise money and there was speculation that he resorted to murder to do so. Forty-two-year-old Levin, reputedly a friend of Hollywood stars, was a flamboyant con man who posed in whatever professional capacity suited his purpose at the time. He lived in a luxury home and had the uncanny knack of vanishing when creditors or lawsuits loomed on the horizon.

Despite the lack of a body, Hunt was charged with killing Levin. Also implicated was James Pittman, Hunt's bodyguard. The allegation was made that they shot Levin and buried his body in woods at Soledad Canyon, north of Los Angeles. Hunt was supposed to have boasted to his fellow club members that he had "knocked off" Ron Levin.

Joe Hunt was tried for murder at Santa Monica in February 1987. While the victim's body had not been found, there were reports that he had been sighted after he was supposed to be dead. Hunt protested his innocence and his defence attorney argued that Levin had deliberately dropped out of view in order to escape prosecution over fraudulent business deals. Nevertheless, Hunt was found guilty and sentenced to life imprisonment. After lengthy criminal proceedings, James Pittman pleaded guilty to being an accessory.

In a subsequent development in Hunt's colourful life, he and three other club members, were tried for the murder of a former Iranian government official, Hedayat Eslaminia. He was the wealthy father of one of the Billionaire Boys and the charge was that he had been murdered in order to gain access to his fortune. Hunt represented himself at the trial and secured an acquittal because of a hung jury.

While Hunt was serving his prison term, filmmakers were busy making a series based on his life and two books were published featuring the Billionaire Boys' Club. Perhaps the most significant outcome was the suggestion that the film about Hunt inspired the brothers, Lyle and Erik Menendez (*see page 292*) , to murder their parents for money in 1989. They shot them as they watched television in their Beverly Hills home and were found guilty in 1996 after a previous trial had ended in deadlock.

Framed?

Next to the murder in the locked room, murders without a body present some of the greatest crime mysteries. Such a case occurred in France in 1924, resulting in a controversy that remains unsolved. Guillaume Seznec was a sawmill owner with a business in Brittany and, in May 1923, he left on a trip to Paris with his friend Pierre Quemeneur, a fellow businessman and local councillor.

The pair were driving to meet a man called Boudjema Gherdi to discuss the sale of a hundred Cadillac cars left behind by the American forces after the First World War. During the journey to Paris, their car repeatedly broke down and, according to Seznec, his travelling companion decided to complete the trip by train. Quemeneur did not arrive in Paris and was never seen again.

A month after his disappearance, Quemeneur's suitcase was found at Le Havre. Among its contents was a document in which he apparently promised to sell his land to Seznec. In 1924, Seznec was tried for murder, despite the absence of a body. The case against him was that the car dealer, Gherdi, did not exist and that Seznec had eliminated Quemeneur in order to take possession of his land. The accused man pleaded his innocence of any wrongdoing but the court found him guilty and he was sentenced to hard labour for life in the French penal colony at Guyana, South America.

Seznec was a model prisoner and at the end of the Second World War he was granted a presidential pardon. He returned to France a broken man where he died at the age of seventy-five in 1954. His family, incensed at the perceived injustice, campaigned to clear his name and pressured the judicial system to admit that a mistake had been made.

In the intervening years, a great deal of new information had become available. It was shown that Gherdi, far from being a figment of Seznec's imagination, was a police informer. He had been working for Inspector Pierre Bonny, a man with an unenviable record. He was dismissed from the police service for falsifying evidence and, during the German occupation of France in the Second World War, joined the Gestapo. He was shot by firing squad in 1945. It was alleged that prior to execution, he confessed to helping convict an innocent man.

A former resistance worker confirmed that Gherdi collaborated with the Gestapo and in 1993, an elderly witness who had testified at Seznec's trial in 1924 retracted her evidence, claiming she had been coerced by the police.

In 2005, Seznec's family succeeded in gaining a retrial at which it was hoped the original verdict would be overturned. The decision was greeted with wide public approval. One of the issues was whether the police had framed Seznec in 1923 to cover up a racket involving the sale of US vehicles. Despite the new evidence and powerful arguments regarding a miscarriage of justice, the judges upheld the original ruling made eighty-two years previously. They maintained the new arguments were insufficient to overturn the guilty verdict. The mystery of the murder with no body persists and the French legal system refused to accept that a mistake had been made.

Beware The Red Chair!

A red armchair became literally a seat of murder and featured prominently in a courtroom re-enactment of the crime.

On 28 March 1944 Jeanne de Sigoyer, the twenty-five-year-old estranged wife of the self-styled Marquis de Sigoyer, visited her husband at his Paris house. She was politely received by her husband and his lover, Irène Lebeau.

Invited into the library, she sat is a solidly made red plush upholstered chair. De Sigoyer asked her if she was the mistress of a mutual friend. She replied, "I won't tell you." With a smile, he produced a piece of cord from his pocket and playfully placed it around her neck. His mood changed dramatically as he pulled the cord tight and braced his knee against the back of the chair to throttle his wife. She struggled but soon slumped back lifeless in the chair.

Within a few months of the murder Paris was liberated from the German occupation and de Sigoyer was denounced as a collaborator and put into prison. He was a man with pretensions and a murky background. He assumed the title of Marquis and modelled his appearance on Emperor Napoleon III. He had been certified as insane in 1938 but escaped from the asylum and went into hiding. During the war years, he returned to Paris and made a fortune on the black market.

Jeanne de Sigoyer had been reported missing and searches for her had been unsuccessful. Meanwhile, from the confines of his cell, de Sigoyer wrote a letter to Irène Lebeau intended to ensure that she kept quiet about what she knew. He told her to "beware of the red chair". As prison correspondence was censured, this veiled threat was picked up and a search was made of de Sigoyer's house. Under the floor of the wine cellar, they found Jeanne's body.

As a result of these developments, Irène Lebeau came forward and made a statement in which she said she had been present when de Sigoyer murdered his wife and that he had threatened her to remain silent. De Sigoyer was tried for murder in Paris in December 1946 and the infamous red armchair occupied a prominent place as a crime exhibit.

Lebeau was charged as an accomplice and gave a graphic account of the murder. De Sigoyer challenged her story, claiming that the two women had quarrelled over their affections for him and that Irène had fatally shot his wife. He challenged the court to examine the body for the bullet. The judge ordered the corpse to be X-rayed and the trial proceeded with the defence seeking to show that it would have been impossible to strangle a person sitting in the red chair.

A re-enactment was staged in the court with a volunteer occupying the red chair to test the claim that the back of the chair was too low to permit strangulation in the manner described. The prosecution countered this by saying it was simply a matter of technique. When the result of the X-ray examination made it clear there was no bullet in the victim's body, de Sigoyer's fate was sealed. He was found guilty and sentenced to death while Irène was acquitted.

Change Of Ownership

Urban Napoleon Stanger came to England with his wife in the 1880s and settled in Whitechapel. He was an industrious man and was soon running a successful bakery. His wife, Elizabeth, who from all accounts was rather a plain lady with a passion for jewellery and colourful clothing, became the subject of much rumour-mongering and the main item of gossip among friends and neighbours was that she nagged her husband.

Stanger employed a maid and an errand boy and a young apprentice called Christian Zengler. A friend who lived locally, Franz Stumm, often helped out at the bakery. Stumm was married but was rumoured to be on more than friendly terms with Mrs Stanger.

On 13 November 1881, customers noticed that Stanger was not at his shop. His wife answered enquiries, saying he had gone to Germany on urgent business. Christian Zengler mentioned that he had seen Stanger late on the night he disappeared standing outside the shop with three other men, one of whom was Stumm.

Elizabeth Stanger seemed unconcerned by her husband's absence and, with daily assistance from Stumm, the bakery business ran smoothly enough. Stumm was obviously getting his feet under the table and he took up permanent residence. On Sundays, he was observed walking arm-in-arm with Mrs Stanger.

Events at the bakery fed the gossips and soon people were whispering that Stanger had been murdered and his corpse turned into meat pies by his wife. Crowds gathered outside the bakery; tongues wagged and fingers were pointed. Rumour reached fever pitch when the sign over the shop proclaiming its ownership by U.N. Stanger was changed to F.F. Stumm.

In April 1882, a notice was published by an enquiry agent offering a reward for information regarding the whereabouts of Mr Stanger who, as it was phrased, "had mysteriously disappeared".

A few months later, in October, in an unexpected development, Elizabeth Stanger was arrested on fraud charges initiated by the executors of her husband's will. It became known that he left everything to his wife but with the stipulation that she should not remarry.

She and Stumm were sent for trial on fraud charges. Mrs Stanger did her best to blacken her husband's name and claimed that after a quarrel he left the house and she had not seen him since. She said that Stumm had been a good friend and lent them money.

Charges against Elizabeth Stanger were dropped and her unpopularity was such that she was hissed by members of the public present in the courtroom. Stumm was found guilty of forgery and sentenced to ten years' penal servitude. The good citizens of Whitechapel were of the strong belief that Mrs Stanger had murdered her husband and that Stumm helped her dispose of his body.

CHAPTER 13

Motive, Method and Opportunity

*The three cardinal requisites of murder – Why? How? And When?,
broadly translate into motive, method and opportunity. Together,
they form the murderer's modus operandi.*

*A key element in the investigation of crime is motive. F. Tennyson
Jesse in her book,* Murder and its Motives, *published in 1924 set
out six classic motives – elimination, gain, revenge, jealousy, lust
and conviction.*

*A few murders that appear to be lacking in discernible motive
are popularly termed motiveless. Some serial killings fit into this
category because they seem to be devoid of purpose. In truth, they
are usually the result of predatory instinct – simply killing for the
pleasure it gives, which is a kind of motive. The explanation for the
crimes committed by, for example, Peter Sutcliffe, Jeffery Dahmer,
Dennis Nilsen and Jack Unterweger, properly lie in the realms of
forensic psychiatry. And there is also Sybrand van Schoor, who
unashamedly killed burglars in the belief that he was acting in the
public interest. He exterminated them as if they were vermin.*

*The How of murder, the method of exercising the intention to kill,
includes an ever-increasing list of death-dealing implements and
agents. Again, there is a menu of classic methods characterized by
the deadly effect they have on the human body. Shooting, stabbing,
strangulation and bludgeoning are probably the most popular.
Poisoning, drowning and burning are not far behind, to which
may be added murder by neglect and death by vehicular impact.
Implements of choice include everything from axes to pitchforks,
while the list of poisons grows with every drug brought to the
market that may be administered as an overdose.*

The When of murder, that is, choosing the right moment, seizing or creating an opportunity, may involve premeditation or impulse. Poisoning usually involves careful planning, selecting the right opportunity based on the routines of the victim. These help to determine the time and place.

Other murders may be entirely opportune, a moment being picked when the victim is off-guard and a preformed intention to kill is put into effect. Murders committed in the heat of passion or provocation may have little regard for opportunity – they just happen. In a surge of lethal violence the nearest weapon may be a knife from the kitchen drawer or the poker from the fireplace.

These are the actions that constitute a murderer's modus operandi and become a signature for a particular crime. Unravelling that signature is the task of the detective and forensic expert.

The majority of murders fall within the classic definitions of motive. Gain is a powerful motivator, and those tempted to enrich themselves at others' expense frequently resort to poison. Henri Girard, for example, used ingenious methods including lethal bacteria. While Lydia Sherman was more conventional, using arsenic as her death-dealing agent.

Revenge is another powerful motivator that takes many forms. Daniel Sickles simply walked out onto a Washington street and shot the man whom he believed had stolen his wife's affections. Anna Fort, on the other hand, took her time, choosing poison mushrooms as her weapon and using an accomplice to create opportunities to strike down her victims.

Many murders are difficult to categorize or understand. Flora Haskell might have taken her crippled son's life as an act of mercy killing. And two Kurdish brothers hired a gang to destroy a young woman in a so-called "honour killing". While Steven Wright, the Suffolk serial killer, murdered five prostitutes with no apparent sexual motive, leaving their bodies unmarked. And Brendan Harris and Herbert Ryan were members of a gang that attacked and killed a young woman in a public park because they did not like the way she dressed.

Motives for killing seem to be deeply ingrained in the human psyche and will continue to shape the thinking of those whose minds turn to murder. Methods will evolve, guided by ingenuity *and innovation. Opportunity will remain just that – dependent, as ever, on chance or the co-ordinates of time and place.*

"I Love Louis . . ."

Sybrand Lodeweikus van Schoor, a South African security investigator and former police officer found an effective way of dealing with burglars – he shot and killed them.

Van Schoor was a police dog handler for twelve years and when he retired from the service in 1980 he set up a security company in East London specializing in responding to alarms installed in business premises. He was frequently called out in the small hours of the morning to answer silent alarms which, while they alerted him, left the burglars unaware that they had been detected. He lay in wait and shot them before they could escape.

In the beginning, Van Schoor shot and immobilized his victims but his methods evolved into killing them with deadly force. During three years' activity, he shot sixty-four people, killing forty-one of them. Businessmen paid him significant fees to keep their offices and factories safe and, if anything, the system encouraged his vigilante methods. Inquests on his dead victims invariably resulted in verdicts of justifiable homicide.

When he was brought to account in 1992, public opinion was divided on how to view his actions. Louis, as he was popularly known, appeared to have been encouraged by the system that effectively gave him the nod when he questioned the effects of what he was doing. The law said that certain offenders might be shot if life was in danger. Van Schoor interpreted that as a green light to kill any burglar he caught on premises he was committed to defend. His methods were publicly approved of by many East London citizens who put "I love Louis" stickers on their car windscreens.

The fact that Louis' victims were all black was noted at the time. Some believed the justice system was too lax when arrested felons were given bail and promptly absconded to carry out their next robbery. In a man like Van Schoor, this inspired the view that shooting criminals caught red-handed was the surest way of dealing with the problem.

Forty-year-old Van Schoor was an imposing man, tall, well-built and with a fine beard. While he was viewed as a monster by some, he was a hero to others and a criminologist testified at his trial in an attempt to clarify his motives. There was a suggestion that the law encouraged him in his ambition to eradicate criminals, leaving him bewildered when the system turned against him.

An expert who examined him did not see him as a psychopath nor a particularly brutal person. He saw it as his right to shoot to kill, almost a duty to those who hired him. But his record showed a trend towards increasing violence and, towards the end of his career as a burglar investigator, he was using nine shots to kill. The man who some saw as an inherently good person who had been encouraged by the system to become a mass killer was found guilty of seven murders and sentenced to twenty years imprisonment.

Gentleman Girard

Henri Girard was a gentleman charmer who experimented with bacterial cultures.

Forty-six-year-old Girard was a man of means who liked to entertain his friends lavishly while discussing art, literature, music and the finer things of life. His suave manner, which worked on both sexes, earned him the name "Gentleman Girard".

He worked as an insurance agent in Montreuil-sous-Bois, near Paris, and indulged his interest in science and especially bacteriology. In 1909 he met Louis Pernotte, an insurance broker and man of modest wealth, who was completely swept up by Girard's charm. Pernotte granted his new friend power of attorney and had his life insured for 300,000 francs. Despite the fact that he had a wife and children, Pernotte's instructions were, that in the event of his death, the insurance was to be paid to Girard.

In August 1912, Pernotte and his family went on holiday and they became ill with what appeared to be typhoid. On returning to Paris to convalesce, Pernotte received daily visits from his friend, Girard. Claiming to have some medical knowledge, he offered to treat Pernotte with injections, which he carried out in the presence of Mme Pernotte whom he reassured with the words, "Notice, madam, that it is quite definitely your own syringe. You observe that I have nothing in my hands."

Louis Pernotte died on 1 December from a cardiac embolism. Girard lost no time in collecting the insurance and also informed Mme Pernotte that she owed him 200,000 francs.

In the years that followed, two of Girard's acquaintances became ill after taking out life insurance policies. One was sick with typhoid fever but survived and the other also survived after a bout of food poisoning.

Girard served in the French army during the First World War and was based with a transport unit in Paris. This enabled him to continue with his bacteriology experiments for which he bought quantities of typhoid cultures from wholesale chemists.

In April 1918, Girard met Madame Monin who had been widowed as a result of the war. He advised her to take out life insurance. They met socially and, during an encounter at his apartment, Girard offered her a glass of wine. When Mme Monin left, she made it no further than the Metro where she collapsed and died.

Girard came under suspicion and he was arrested on 21 August. A search of his apartment revealed his interest in bacteriology. There were culture dishes of typhoid bacilli and other toxic agents and evidence that he had been experimenting with poisonous fungi. An entry in his diary around the time of Louis Pernotte's death read, "Poisons; prepare bottle, tubes, rubber gloves; buy microbe books." Another entry for May 1917 read, "Mimiche Dinner – mushrooms".

When arrested, Girard declared, "Yes, I have always been unhappy, no one has ever tried to understand me: I will always be misunderstood – abnormal, as I have been called – and for all that I am good, with a very warm heart." The investigation into "Gentleman Girard's" crimes lasted three years but, in May 1921, before he faced trial at the Paris Assizes, he committed suicide, thereby depriving the guillotine of a probable victim. It was reported that he made a full confession.

". . . We're Alive With Rats"

Death from poisoning was always lurking in the shadows when Lydia Sherman was around.

Sherman married Edward Struck in the 1840s and they lived in New York where they brought up six children. When Struck was accused of neglecting his duties as a police officer he was discharged from the service and quickly slid into depression. With six children to bring up, a sick husband and little income, life for Lydia was tough so she decided to lighten the burden by disposing of Edward. In 1864 she bought some arsenic, explaining to the pharmacist, ". . . we're alive with rats!" Edward died after a short illness and cause of death was given as consumption. In quick succession over the next two years, her children, aged between nine months and eighteen years, all died of illnesses variously described as fever, typhoid and bronchitis. Their mother appeared appropriately grief-stricken, collected on the insurance and no questions were asked.

In 1868, she met and married a wealthy farmer, Dennis Harlbut, and moved to New Haven, Connecticut. The widow Lydia had been recommended to work for him as housekeeper but within a few days they were married and within months, he was dead. She acquired her late husband's farm and monetary assets.

Her next move was to secure employment as housekeeper to Horatio Nelson Sherman and his two children. In no time at all she became Mrs Sherman. Shortly afterwards, one-year-old Frank died, followed by his sixteen-year-old sister, Ada. As if this was not tragedy enough, Horatio also became ill in May 1871, complaining of burning pains in his stomach.

The doctor was called and Sherman said he was having "one of his turns". Lydia had been dosing him with medicine administered in cups of chocolate. Dr Beardsley became suspicious, especially in light of the deaths of the two children.

He called in a second opinion but Sherman's illness remained a mystery until he died on 12 May.

The doctor required a post-mortem and arsenic was found in Horatio Sherman's body. This discovery prompted the exhumation of the bodies of the two children and, again, arsenic was found. A further line of investigation led to the exhumation of Dennis Harlbut's body, which it was no surprise to learn was riddled with arsenic.

Lydia Sherman was charged with the murder of her third husband and sent for trial in April 1872. She claimed to be innocent and her defence was that she lacked motive. The evidence of arsenic poisoning in his case was irrefutable but it was also known that he had bought poison to kill off rats. Lydia's previous history and the trail of death that seemed to follow her made suicide an unlikely cause of her husband's demise.

She was found guilty of second-degree murder and sentenced to life imprisonment. She made a confession, owning up to eleven murders and, of her first husband, Edward Struck, she said that she "put him out of the way". Lydia Sherman served her sentence in Wethersfield Prison where she died on 16 May 1878.

"... You Must Die"

Philip Barton Key was the famous son of a famous father. Key senior wrote *The Star Spangled Banner*. His son was District Attorney for the District of Columbia, Washington, USA.

On 27 February 1859, Philip Barton Key was walking down Monroe Place near Lafayette Square when he stopped to wave at someone in the upper windows of one of the houses. The residence belonged to Congressman Daniel Sickles who, at that moment, was digesting reports about his wife's infidelity with Key.

Enraged at the idea of the man who had cuckolded him standing outside his house, Sickles rushed downstairs and out into the street. He pursued Key and confronted him in Madison Avenue, where, gun in hand, he accused him of dishonourable conduct and said "... you must die".

Key tried to evade his accuser by dodging behind a tree, pleading, "Don't shoot." Sickles was not listening. Blinded with rage he fired at Key and missed. His second shot struck home and his victim fell to the ground. He then emptied his weapon into Key until the gun jammed. This was a very public incident witnessed by several bystanders. The mortally wounded Key was carried to the National Club where he died before medical assistance could be given.

Daniel Sickles was arraigned for murder in April 1859. The Congressman had discovered what everyone else seemed to know, which was that his wife was having a passionate affair with Key. His discovery had prompted him to consider the idea of challenging Key to a duel but he was overtaken by events.

At his trial in Washington City Hall, Robert Ould, Key's successor as District Attorney, led the prosecution and emphasized the particularly heinous nature of Sickle's act which had been committed on the Sabbath. Eyewitnesses testified to the deliberate nature of the shooting. For the defence, it was argued that Sickles had simply exercised his moral right as a husband by slaying the man who dared to defile his marriage bed. There were numerous biblical references and quotes from both Old and New Testaments about charity and retribution.

The thrust of the defence was that Sickles had experienced such provocation as to unbalance his mind in a way that exculpated his crime. The jury were inclined to agree. After an hour's recess, they returned a verdict of not guilty. The acquittal received a mixed reception. Many Washingtonians were shocked that such a cold-blooded public killing was judged to be without guilt.

Sickles' wife, Teresa, who had told the court what a wicked woman she had been, was destroyed by the consequences of her infidelity and died eight years later. The Congressman's career was in tatters, although he achieved some recognition as a Union General in the Civil War.

Death Cap

Three deaths by poisoning using death cap mushrooms led investigators to unveil a plan for deadly revenge. The method was inspired by a religious sect.

In February 1979, Réné Blum, the district police chief at Mézière in northern France, was taken ill during a celebratory lunch. He collapsed and died and the post-mortem indicated that he might have been poisoned. Blum's death was followed by that of two others, the town mayor and secondary school headmaster.

Three deaths of prominent people, all associated with meals, dinner or lunch, and all showing similar post-mortem indications, presented the police with a mystery. Laboratory tests on the victims' stomach contents showed the presence of the death cap mushroom, mixed with edible fungi. *Amanita phalloides* has a fierce reputation as a deadly poison and accounts for many accidental deaths. One or two death caps will certainly kill an adult.

The question uppermost in the minds of investigators was whether there was any link between the three deaths. While exploring this avenue of enquiry, it was discovered that a mixture of death cap and other fungi had been previously used in the 1930s by a religious sect in Belgium. This group used a mushroom concoction as a tonic and a means of attaining a higher state of divine awareness.

Enquiries received a fresh impetus after a fourth poisoning when a woman librarian collapsed during dinner. Fortunately, prompt action saved her life and she was able to provide police with the linking evidence for which they had been searching. It appeared that the three dead men and the librarian who survived had all been members of the community's picnic committee, which arranged an annual children's day out.

It seemed that recriminations had arisen from the committee's decision not to award the bus contract for the children's outing to the usual firm. The head of the bus firm, Anna Fort, remonstrated angrily with the mayor over the loss of the contract. Meanwhile, the laboratory testing samples from the poisoning victims came up with the observation that traces of bronze indicated the toxic mixture had been prepared in a bronze container.

When detectives called on Anna Fort, they found that she was a thirty-year-old woman who helped run her invalid father's bus firm but who also worked part-time for a catering company. It was also made known that she was subject to epileptic seizures and given to violent outbursts. While questioning Fort, an astute detective noticed a bronze pot in the kitchen and also a picture of a woman named Adèle Jouve. Investigators began to feel that their enquiries were getting somewhere, especially with the knowledge that Jouve was the founder of the Belgian sect that promoted the use of toxic concoctions.

Questioned further, Anna Fort broke down and described how she targeted her victims out of revenge. She enlisted the help of Max Fargue, one of her firm's drivers. With careful timing, the pair turned up at the murder venue where Fargue created a diversion at the front door. This allowed Fort to slip round to the back door, enter the kitchen and add her deadly poison to the plate of food waiting to be eaten by her intended victim.

Fort was judged to be mentally unfit to stand trial for her crimes and was committed to an institution for the criminally insane. Fargue was convicted of murder and sentenced to life imprisonment.

"... If I Did It ..."

Flora Haskell was a single mother who made a living doing other people's laundry. She lived in a small cottage in Salisbury in the UK with her twelve-year-old son, Teddy. Despite the loss of one leg below the knee, he got around on crutches and even played football. He was well known locally and was popular on account of his cheery personality.

On 31 October 1908, Teddy went to bed after supper at around 9.00 p.m. At about 10.30, Percy Noble, Flora Haskell's nephew, knocked on the door of her cottage intent on repaying a small loan. He was greeted by his aunt, clearly distraught, who cried out to him, "Go and stop that man! He has killed my poor Teddy! Go for a doctor quick!"

The boy was found lying on his bed as if asleep, except that his throat had been cut. His mother explained hysterically that she had encountered a man coming down the stairs towards the front door and he threw a knife at her, spattering her with blood. Stirred by Flora Haskell's story of a murdering intruder, the men of the locality formed themselves into search parties. Armed with sticks and lanterns, they scoured the surrounding lanes.

The searches came to nothing and the local police sought help from Scotland Yard. Detectives questioned Mrs Haskell and learned from her that a man had called at the house the day before Teddy died asking about lodgings. She told officers that money was missing from a locked drawer, which had been forced open. Flora Haskell was arrested and charged with murder. Teddy's funeral was well attended and a defence fund was set up for his mother.

Haskell appeared on trial at Devizes Assizes in February 1909. The prosecution maintained that she had murdered her child, "in one of those extraordinary abnormal conditions which overtake human beings sometimes." This was perhaps a veiled hint that she had killed the boy because of his disability. She was judged to be perfectly sane.

The prosecution's expert witness testified that the blood on Haskell's clothing could only have got there if she had been the murderer. Rayner Goddard, later Lord Chief Justice of England, conducted her defence. He asked the jury if they were prepared to "condemn a fellow creature to death on the evidence of the theories of doctors." As events turned out, the jury could not agree a verdict and a second trial was called for.

This took place in April 1909 and much of the evidence was repeated from the first trial. Goddard argued powerfully that the evidence of bloodstains could not, beyond any question of doubt, permit a guilty verdict. As he addressed the jury in his closing speech, Flora Haskell wept uncontrollably. The jury found her not guilty on the grounds of insufficient evidence and she left the court to cheering from the public gallery. While in custody, she told her wardress, ". . . if I did it, I don't remember it."

"Her Soul Wouldn't Leave The Body . . ."

Twenty-year-old Banaz Mahmod, a Kurdish woman, was last seen by her sister some time in 2005 when she thought she looked rundown. She disappeared in January 2006 having told the police that her family had threatened to kill her because the man she was in love with was seen as unsuitable and naming five men, including Mohamod Hama, who might be implicated.

On the morning she was murdered, her father, Mahmod Mahmod, left his house in Mitcham, west London, so that her killers would have freedom to carry out their mission. Over a period of two and a half hours, the young woman was subjected to degrading sexual abuse, torture and rape. Finally, she was strangled and her body buried in a pit.

This horrific killing was ordered by her father and his brother and led by Mohamod Hama, assisted by at least three other men. The details became known after Hama was arrested in February 2006. While he was being held in Belmarsh Prison, he boasted about what had happened to Banaz to a visitor there. His conversation was secretly taped and eventually used at his trial.

Hama described how he stood with one foot on Banaz's back while one of his gang of thugs prepared the ligature that was used to strangle her. He also spoke of stamping on the victim's neck, "Her soul wouldn't leave the body . . . I was kicking and stamping on her neck to get her soul out," he said.

In another taped conversation, Hama described how they took her body from her father's house in a suitcase and placed it in a car. He said there were police cars in the area and there were people in the street. He laughingly described dragging the suitcase until the handle broke off.

The dead woman's sister, talking from behind a screen in court, spoke about Banaz as a caring person and also voiced fears for her own safety. The Mahmod brothers were found guilty of murder and sentenced to life imprisonment for a minimum of twenty-three years. Hama was also sentenced to life imprisonment with a minimum of seventeen years. Two other men thought to have been involved fled to Iraq. One of the suspects was arrested in northern Iraq in 2007 and awaits possible extradition to Britain.

The killing of a person to restore a family's honour, as in the case of Banaz Mahmod, is often a brutal affair carried out by hitmen. It is estimated that there are twelve honour killings a year in Britain and an estimated 300 such killings every year in Pakistan. In 2008, it was reported that three teenage girls had been buried alive in "honour killings" in the province of Baluchistan.

"Systematically Selected And Murdered"

A reign of terror lasting six weeks descended on Suffolk in East Anglia in the UK at the end of 2006. During that time, five prostitutes were murdered and, with a serial killer at large, there was talk of a new Jack the Ripper.

Young women began disappearing from the red light district in Ipswich at the beginning of November. The first body turned up on 2 December. Twenty-five-year-old Gemma Adams was found in a brook at Hintlesham, Suffolk. In the following weeks leading up to Christmas, four other bodies were found.

The victims and the circumstances in which they were found had common characteristics. The women were all young prostitutes from the same area of Ipswich and they were regular drug users. When discovered, they were naked, showed no mutilating injuries nor were there any signs of a struggle. All had been strangled or suffocated and there were no indications of sexual assault.

The public were alarmed at having a serial killer in their midst and frightened by the speed of his actions. Police warned prostitutes to keep off the streets and large rewards were offered for information leading to the capture of the murderer.

The hunt for the serial killer involved over ten police forces and a trawl was made through the database of known sex offenders. DNA was found on three of the victims and a match was quickly found with a forty-eight-year-old truck driver whose DNA had been recorded after he was convicted of theft five years previously.

Steven Wright lived in Ipswich where he had a home in the red-light area, which he shared with his partner. He was arrested on 19 December. CCTV footage showed a red Ford Mondeo cruising in the district on significant dates when murder victims disappeared.

Wright worked in and around Ipswich as a fork-lift driver. He openly admitted to using prostitutes although he denied killing them. His partner worked a night shift and during the time that she was away, Wright took prostitutes back to the house for sex. This partly explained why local streetwalkers were unafraid of him, even when the murder scare was at its height – because they knew him.

He appeared on trial for murder at Ipswich Crown Court in January 2008. He denied the charges, but the forensic evidence against him was compelling, particularly the DNA. The prosecution drew attention to the vulnerability of the prostitute victims, all of whom needed money to fund their drug habit. Wright, it was contended, "systematically selected and murdered" five of them.

While Wright admitted picking up four of the five women, he denied killing them. He asked the court to believe it was a matter of coincidence. He drove around at night because he couldn't sleep and began taking prostitutes home because he was prone to cramp in his leg when having sex in the car. His defence was that he was a victim of misfortune.

The man who had terrorized a city for several weeks with echoes of Jack the Ripper was found guilty on 21 February 2008 and sentenced to life imprisonment. While there were similarities with the infamous nineteenth-century murderer, especially with the killing of five victims, there was also a major difference. Whereas the Ripper, as his name suggested, mutilated his victims, Wright hardly left a mark on their bodies.

He incapacitated them with drugs and then suffocated them. One unresolved mystery concerns his motive for killing.

Derby Day Execution

Alfred Webb was found dying from a gunshot wound outside his flat in Bayswater, London, on 9 February 1928. He did not regain consciousness and died in hospital. The flat had been expertedly broken into and ransacked by the intruder.

The circumstances leading up to the shooting were that Webb and his son returned to the flat during the evening. The break-in was evident and the intruder was still inside. Webb sent his son to fetch the police and, as the boy ran off, he heard a shot and saw a dark figure leave the building.

It appeared that the thief had been disturbed by the arrival of the occupier and, finding his escape blocked, shot his way free. Detectives made house-to-house enquiries and learned from one householder that a man had knocked on her door saying he was from "Warwick Garage" and asking to speak to the chauffeur. The woman did not employ a chauffeur and had no knowledge of a garage by that name. She sent the man away.

Convinced that they were looking for a professional thief, detectives believed they recognized the tactics of someone looking for an opportunity. One of the officers in a moment of inspiration mentioned that a housebreaker known to them lived at Warwick Mews. Was there any connection, he wondered?

The thief in question was Frederick Stewart whose affinity for the racetrack gave an indication of where he might be found. As the horseracing season had not started, the dog-track was the most likely. Stewart was located in a pub near the dog-track at Southend and was invited to answer some questions relating to the shooting of Alfred Webb.

Stewart admitted entering the flat at Bayswater and claimed that when he found his escape route blocked by Webb, there was a struggle and his gun discharged accidentally. Diligent police work undermined his story. While searching gardens in the neighbourhood of the shooting, officers found the murder weapon, a small calibre pistol. Crucially, firearms examiners found that a second shot had been fired but the bullet had jammed in the gun. Clearly, the gunman was prepared to do more than frighten the house-owner.

Stewart was tried for murder at the Old Bailey when his account of accidental shooting failed to convince the jury. He was found guilty and sentenced to death by Mr Justice Avory. His execution was due to take place at Pentonville on 6 June 1928, which happened to be Derby Day. Stewart asked if his hanging could be delayed so that he would know who won the race. His request was declined and it was reported that he had correctly tipped the winner before mounting the scaffold.

The Threepenny Piece Murders

At the end of a long sea voyage, the SS *Dorset* berthed at London Docks on 15 March 1909. The ship's crew went ashore, heading for pubs and prostitutes. The seamen had money in their pockets and it was common practice to carry a supply of threepenny bits, which they would give to any beggars they encountered.

Among those making their way to Whitechapel and Stepney were second engineer William Sproull and an engine-room hand called McEachern. The two men encountered a couple of prostitutes in Rupert Street and went with them to a lodging house. A drunken dispute arose over money. The seamen were unaware that their movements were being observed from across the street at No. 3 by two men who controlled the prostitutes.

Marks Reubens and his brother, Morris, both in their early twenties, were well-known to the police for their thieving and protection rackets. The brothers rushed across the street and attacked the two seamen. Morris was armed with a *sjambok* (whip) made of hippopotamus hide with which he set about McEachern. Meanwhile, Marks Reubens used a knife to stab Sproull repeatedly.

McEachern managed to escape from this onslaught, which left Morris free to join his brother's attack on Sproull. Mortally wounded, the second engineer, staggered into the street where he collapsed. The police were called to the scene led by the redoubtable Inspector Frederick Wensley. Sproull was found to be dead and there was a trail of threepenny bits leading from his body across the street to No. 3. Wensley and his men raided the house where they found the Reubens brothers and two women.

Questioning had hardly begun before Morris accused his brother of stabbing Sproull. A broken *sjambok* provided ample evidence of his part in the affair and the dead man's watch was found in his pocket. He admitted robbing Sproull as he lay dying in the street. Marks Reuben, did not say very much but his bloodstained clasp knife was found hidden behind a stove. In a desperate appeal to Wensley, Morris Reubens declared, "We never meant to kill the man, and you wouldn't want to see a couple of young fellows like us lopped."

The two women who made up the foursome gave a graphic account of the night's events. "Morrie had the stick," said Emily Allen, "and Markie the knife." The Reubens brothers were sent for trial at the Old Bailey in April 1909. The case against the two women was dropped on the grounds that they had been used by the brothers. Emily Allen proved to be a good witness for the prosecution.

Morris Reubens put on a display of histrionics in the dock and a doctor was called to attend to him. This did not elicit any recommendation to mercy from the jury which took ten minutes to return a guilty verdict and Mr Justice Jelf sentenced the pair to death. The Reubens Brothers were hanged at Pentonville Prison on 20 May 1909.

"I'm Sorry To See You Here Again"

Wherever she went, Louise Peete seemed to be followed by the Grim Reaper. Seven men died as a result of knowing her.

Lofie Louise Preslar was the daughter of a publisher and was brought up in Louisiana in the US. She received a private education and married Henry Bosley in 1903 when she was twenty years old. They moved to New Orleans where she began to pursue extra-marital activities. After finding her in bed with an oilman from Dallas, Bosley was so heartbroken that he took his own life.

She moved to Shreveport and then to Boston under a different name and led the life of a call girl, supplementing her earnings by stealing from her clients. Her next adventure occurred in Waco, Texas, where she met another oilman, Joe Appel, who was found dead soon afterwards. When questioned, Louise admitted killing him on the grounds that he had tried to rape her. She was tried and acquitted of murder.

In 1913 it was back to Dallas where she married Harry Faurote. When his new wife proved unfaithful, he hanged himself. Not letting the grass grow under her feet, she moved to Denver where, in 1915, she married Richard C. Peete, a sales representative. They had a daughter but argued constantly and decided to separate in 1920.

Louise Peete decided to seek her fortune in Los Angeles and, looking for somewhere to rent, came across Jacob Charles Denton, a millionaire industrialist. She moved in with him as housekeeper-companion but was irked when he declined to marry her.

In May 1920 Denton vanished and Louise's colourful explanation was that he had gone into hiding after being injured in an argument with another woman. At about this time, Louise arranged for a delivery of soil to be placed in the basement of the house where she intended growing mushrooms. Meanwhile, she set about forging Denton's name on cheques and selling off his art collection.

The police began to take an interest in Denton's disappearance and decided to search the house. Lying under a heap of soil in the basement, they found his mouldering corpse with a bullet wound in the back of the head. Louise was tried for murder in January 1921 and, this time, was convicted and sentenced to life imprisonment. Mr Peete remained faithful, however, visiting her in jail but when she became fed up with him he committed suicide.

After serving thirteen years, Louise was released from prison on parole. She moved to Pacific Palisades, California, where she met Arthur and Margaret Logan, her parole sponsors, who took her into their home. In 1944, she married Lee Borden Judson, an elderly widower but they did not live together. Louise continued to reside with the Logans and trouble loomed when money started disappearing. Diverting possible accusations, Louise set about persuading Margaret Logan that her husband was deranged and should be admitted to a psychiatric hospital.

On 30 May 1944, Margaret Logan went missing. Louise explained her absence by saying that she was critically ill in hospital. Meanwhile Arthur Logan died and Louise set up home in the Logan's house with Judson. She began wearing Margaret Logan's clothes and produced an insurance policy on Mrs Logan's life that made Louise the chief beneficiary.

By December 1944, the parole authorities became suspicious about Margaret Logan's reports and discovered that the signatures on them had been forged. A search of the Logans' home followed and the body of the missing lady of the house was found buried in the garden. Never short of an explanation, Louise said that Arthur Logan had killed his wife, and she tidied up by burying the corpse and having old man Logan committed for psychiatric treatment.

Louise was charged with murder and put on trial in Los Angeles. It was all too much for Judson who committed suicide by jumping off a building. Louise revelled in the attention she was receiving and commented that her personal charms were so powerful that her lovers were driven to distraction and suicide.

At the age of sixty-four, Louise Peete was found guilty of first-degree murder and sentenced to death. All appeals failed and she was sent to San Quentin to await her fate. Thirteen years after her first appearance at the prison, the warden greeted her by asking, "Mrs Peete, I'm sorry to see you here again. Is there anything I can do for you?" She died in the gas chamber on 11 April 1947.

Axe Woman

A young married couple faked an accident to collect on the insurance. Later, Martha Marek resorted to poisoning as a way of making a living.

She had been an orphan in Vienna at the beginning of the 1900s but her poor circumstances improved considerably when she met an elderly man who looked after her. When he died, Martha inherited his estate, which amounted to a small fortune. She married a young engineer, Emil Marek, in 1924 and they lived in style until Martha's money ran out.

In order to boost their flagging funds, they devised an insurance fraud. Emil took out a large accident insurance policy and soon afterwards tragedy struck when he lost a leg while chopping wood. Their pre-planned scheme was that Emil should sever his leg with the axe and claim that it was an accident. He had difficulty executing this part of the plan and had to call on his wife to finish the job.

The couple claimed on the insurance but encountered difficulties because the doctor who examined the injured Emil said his leg showed three separate cuts in what he believed was a contrived accident. The Mareks were charged first with fraud and then bribery when it was shown that Martha had offered money to a hospital nurse to say that the doctor was responsible for the cuts on Emil's leg.

The couple appeared in court to answer the charges and, while the fraud case was dropped, they were convicted of bribery and sentenced to four months' imprisonment. In due course, they accepted a greatly reduced settlement from the insurance company.

After trying their hands unsuccessfully at running a business venture, the Mareks were again in reduced circumstances. Things got even worse when Emil died of tuberculosis in 1932, followed by the death of one of their children. For Martha, it was now a matter of survival and she went to look after an elderly aunt, Susanne Lowenstein, whose demise quickly followed. Martha inherited money from her relative but, as before, her spending soon outstripped her assets. Her next move was to take in lodgers, one of whom died mysteriously. Meanwhile, Martha was busy scheming a new fraud involving paintings belonging to the late Frau Lowenstein which she claimed had been stolen.

Her latest scheme was soon uncovered and after she was arrested, stories began to emerge that she had poisoned her lodger. Exhumation of the body proved that death had been caused by thallium poisoning. Further exhumations followed and it was shown that Susanne Lowenstein, Martha's husband and her two children had all been poisoned.

Martha Marek had bought thallium, an unusual poison only discovered in 1861, from a pharmacy in Vienna. She was tried for murder in 1938 at a time when Germany ruled Austria and the death penalty had been reintroduced. Despite her special pleadings of innocence, she was found guilty and sentenced to death. She was executed on 6 December 1938 when, ironically, she was beheaded with an axe.

Case Of The Torn Glove

Frederick and Alice Wiltshaw lived in a fourteen-room mansion at Barlaston, Staffordshire in the UK. Mr Wiltshire was a wealthy businessman and headed a pottery firm. When he returned home from work in the early evening of 16 July 1952, he found his wife lying dead in a pool of blood in the kitchen. She had been severely beaten with an ornamental poker, which lay next to the body, and also stabbed.

Several items of value had been stolen, including a gold cigarette case and the rings from Alice Wiltshaw's fingers. There was no sign of a forced entry and the murder could be timed fairly accurately between 5.20 p.m. when the staff left for the day and 6.30 p.m. when Mr Wiltshaw found his wife's body. Detectives surmised that the intruder was someone who knew the household routines.

A search of the garden produced a pair of gloves with blood on them and also a small tear on the thumb. The garden gave access to a footpath leading to the railway station at Barlaston.

Curiously, Mr Wiltshaw noticed that an old raincoat he used when gardening was missing.

Working on the theory that the murderer was someone known to the Wiltshaws, detectives learnt that their chauffeur-handyman had been dismissed earlier in the year for using one of the cars for his own purposes without permission. Twenty-nine-year-old Leslie Green had left after six months' employment.

Crime scene investigators believed that the murderer, whose clothes were heavily bloodstained, had taken the old raincoat to cover them up, left the house by way of the garden, dropping his gloves as he went, and headed for the railway station. It was known that Green had a girlfriend who lived in Leeds, a city that was served by trains running through Stafford. Enquiries revealed that he had stayed at the Metropole Hotel in Leeds using Mr Wiltshaw's name and describing himself as a traveller for a pottery firm.

With the help of the transport police, detectives found Mr Wiltshaw's raincoat, which had turned up in the lost property office at Holyhead. The bloodstains on it were confirmed as the murder victim's. As the net closed around Green, it was discovered that he had proposed marriage to his girlfriend, giving her rings stolen from Mrs Wiltshaw. The rings were later recovered from the place where he had hidden them when he realized the police were looking for him. In another flamboyant gesture, he had shown the stolen gold cigarette case to a colleague of his girlfriend.

With reports in the press naming Green as the man police wished to interview, he decided to respond and presented himself for questioning by detectives. It was noted that a scar on his thumb marked exactly the tear in one of the gloves discarded by the murderer. His line was that he did not commit the murder and he claimed that the rings were given to him by two men he met in Leeds.

Green was charged with murder and the magistrates committed him for trial. He professed his innocence throughout, but the trail of evidence he had left behind, although circumstantial, was enough to convict him. He was sentenced to death and hanged at Winson Green Prison, Birmingham, on 23 December 1935.

"The Neighbour From Hell . . ."

On Good Friday, 6 April 2007, twenty-two-year-old Krystal Hart, a mother-to-be, was shot dead on her doorstep in Battersea, south London.

This was to be the final act in a long-running dispute with her neighbour, who lived in the flat above. Angela Brewer had made complaints about her neighbour and relations were such that both women had installed CCTV cameras to spy on each other. Court proceedings had been initiated to resolve their differences.

The men friends of the two women had stayed above the dispute but a crisis developed over an incident involving Brewer's companion, David Hughes, whose car was parked outside the terrace house. He took exception to Hart's friend making a note of the registration number. There was an argument and Hughes went off to his home nearby where he armed himself before returning. What happened next was captured on CCTV. First, Hughes tried to confront Hart's boyfriend and then he shouted "come out, you bitch". When Krystal Hart appeared at the door, Hughes shot her twice in the head. She died instantly. The whole incident from the first act of provocation to the fatal shooting had taken less than an hour.

Hughes, aged forty, was tried for murder at the Old Bailey in February 2008. He was a petty criminal who made a living selling drugs and stolen goods. He was besotted with fifty-three-year-old Angela Brewer and had been heard telling her that he would do anything for her. The prosecution said that Brewer was an emotional bully and her behaviour had earned her the local title of "the neighbour from hell". Hughes assimilated Brewer's animosity and the judge said she had made life unbearable for her neighbour by making false accusations.

He told Hughes that he had tried to curry favour with Brewer and it was a mark of her warped personality that he took her rantings seriously. Brewer was cleared of any criminal involvement but moral issues remained. The judge sentenced David Hughes to life imprisonment for what to all intents and purposes was "a ruthless execution and a truly evil act".

"I Only Want Some Matches"

At the age of twenty-six, Huibrecht Jacob de Leeuw was a popular appointee to the job of town clerk in Dewetsdorp, South Africa. He was married, ambitious and soon began to live beyond his means. When he lapsed into debt, he decided to dip into the town's exchequer of which, as town clerk, he was the custodian.

He kept the account book in arrears so that the true state of the town's finances was hidden. When rumours began to circulate that de Leeuw had personal financial problems, the mayor decided it would be prudent to cast a critical eye over the accounts. He found them in disarray with many receipts missing and confronted the town clerk, accusing him of incompetence. De Leeuw's defence was that the books were only in arrears because he was overworked. He promised to set everything straight.

His position was perilous and he attempted to borrow money to make up the losses. This ploy failed and he was unable to fulfil his promise to rectify the accounting faults. He was given a week to put things in order or face dismissal.

The thought of losing his job and endangering his marriage led de Leeuw to think that murdering his accusers might be the answer. He made enquiries about explosive devices using petrol and dynamite and carried out a few secret experiments.

The day fixed for the final reckoning was 8 April 1927 when he would face Mayor von Maltitz and two members of the finance committee at a meeting in the town hall. After scrutinizing the ledgers, von Maltitz accused de Leeuw of misusing the town's funds. The meeting then broke up to be reconvened after lunch when the town clerk would almost certainly be dismissed from his post.

Shortly after the finance committee reconvened, there was a terrific explosion which blew the roof off the town hall and shattered every window. The mayor died instantly and his two colleagues, both badly burned, died later in hospital. Unfortunately for de Leeuw, the two fatally injured men made dying declarations implicating him in theft.

De Leeuw had succeeded in destroying his accusers, along with the damning evidence of the account books but was now a prime murder suspect. He was sent for trial at Bloemfontein in August 1927. A town hall employee testified that he saw two cans of petrol in the town clerk's office on the day of the explosion. And a local shopkeeper described how de Leeuw had appeared in her shop that afternoon in an agitated state saying, "I only want some matches."

The trial judge sitting with two assessors found the former town clerk guilty of murder and sentenced him to death. De Leeuw, who it was later shown could easily have paid off his debts, told the court, "I am prepared to go to meet my Creator." He was hanged on 30 September 1927.

On The Run

Thirty-one-year-old William Hughes, a man with a violent record, was being escorted to Chesterfield magistrates' court to answer a charge of rape. He was put in a taxi accompanied by two prison warders at Leicester Prison on 12 January 1977. When the taxi was on the motorway, despite being handcuffed, Hughes produced a knife and violently attacked one of his escorts. He managed to grab the key to his handcuffs and release himself. He told the driver to keep driving. When they reached Stone Edge, near Chatsworth Park, he ordered the driver to stop and forced him and the two injured men out of the car. He then drove away but came off the road near Beeley and collided with a wall. At this point, he took to his feet and walked out on to the moors.

A manhunt ensued involving the police and army, aided by helicopters. They failed to capture their quarry who was now holed up in a remote cottage where he held its owners hostage.

The Moran family were intimidated by Hughes's threats of violence and an extraordinary interlude developed during which he allowed individual members to leave the cottage to shop for newspapers and cigarettes. They did not use these periods of freedom to raise the alarm because they were too fearful of what he might do.

On 14 January 1977, he let Gill Moran out of the cottage to fetch a car intended for his getaway. She chose this moment to raise the alarm via a neighbour and returned with the car. Hughes realized what she had done and forced her into the car at knifepoint. He then drove away, having left behind a trail of death. Gill Moran was unaware that the man beside her in the car had stabbed to death her mother and father, her husband and her ten-year-old daughter.

The police set up roadblocks and Hughes was spotted heading towards Peak Forest. After a chase he lost control of the car. Surrounded by police, he stepped out of the vehicle holding Gill Moran as hostage. He demanded they give him a car and he set off again in a police vehicle. A further chase ensued in the direction of Macclesfield. A bus was commandeered and used as a roadblock.

When Hughes came into view, he swerved past the bus and crashed the car. He was heard shouting, "I'm going to stab her. I'm going to kill her." Over the next forty-five minutes, officers sought to calm Hughes and tried to persuade him to leave Gill Moran in the car and they would provide him with another vehicle. He demanded a Land Rover for his getaway and such a vehicle was duly brought to the scene.

As Hughes stepped out of the crashed car, police marksmen killed him with four shots. He was dragged away bleeding from the head and Gill Moran, who had suffered knife wounds, was released from her ordeal. Later, she would learn about the tragic deaths of her family.

An inquiry into the murders raised many questions. The first was why the police had given up their search on the moors when Hughes was less than a mile away in the Morans' cottage. The second was the practice of transferring a dangerous prisoner using a taxi. The Home Secretary promised that security would be tightened up. Other questions hinged on how Hughes had managed to obtain a knife and apparently had not been searched.

The Fate Of "Daddy Samples"

Walter Lewis Samples, a retired engineer who lived alone in Memphis, Tennessee, had been ill for a couple of days and, when his condition worsened on 21 February 1941, he asked his doctor to call round urgently. He was clearly in great pain and before he was rushed off to hospital, he mentioned that the last meal he had eaten was breakfast when he had cooked bacon and eggs and drank two glasses of milk. The milk was delivered to his doorstep as usual but he noticed that the supplier was not his regular dairy.

Soon after admission to hospital, Samples died, and an autopsy determined that he had been poisoned with phosphorus. Analysis of the milk in the opened bottle taken from his refrigerator was also positive for the poison. The dairy that supplied the milk had impeccable bottling procedures, which ruled out accidental contamination. This left suicide or murder as the options open for investigation.

Suicide was thought unlikely leading to the conclusion that someone wanted him out of the way and had planted the poisoned milk with the intention of killing him. A search of Samples' bungalow provided a few surprises indicating that the military veteran had been leading a double life. A horde of photographs was found of images depicting partially clothed women and his address book was filled with telephone numbers of ladies, many of whom were married. Some of the photographs were signed by the ladies in question and dedicated to "Daddy Samples". It seemed that the veteran had a robust sex life.

Knowledge of this background provided the possibility that a disenchanted lover might have wanted to eliminate "Daddy Samples". Detectives interviewed some of the ladies and formed the impression that his personal magnetism was such that they would do anything for him.

Another line of enquiry bore fruit. Samples had been active in the property market and investigators checked court records to see if he had been involved in any litigious disputes. It seemed that he had some unresolved business with a man named Le Roy House. Enquiries showed that Mrs House had been involved romantically with Samples and a woman answering her description had been seen by neighbours at his property.

The plot thickened when a search of Le Roy House's property turned up several milk bottles belonging to the same Memphis dairy that supplied Samples. Mrs House, apparently unbeknown to her husband, was in possession of a will whereby Samples made her his sole beneficiary. The signature on the document was a forgery, however, and the Houses were charged with murder.

At this point, Le Roy House confessed that he had left the bottle of poisoned milk on Samples' doorstep and absolved his wife from any blame. Nevertheless, they were both tried and convicted of murder, each being sentenced to twenty years imprisonment. By this time, Le Roy had withdrawn his confession and, following an appeal, a new trial was granted in 1943. Mrs House caused a sensation by declaring, "My husband is innocent, I did it alone and he's trying to protect me." Her conviction and sentence were upheld while the charges against Le Roy were dismissed.

Poisoned Stout

When a poison concoction disguised in a bottle of stout was left unattended and sampled by three people, two of whom died as a result, the case illustrated the legal point that someone who attempts to murder person A, and by mischance kills B, is still guilty of murder.

Richard Brinkley was a jobbing gardener who hit on a get-rich-quick scheme involving murder and fraud. He befriended a seventy-seven-year-old widow, Johanna Maria Louisa Blume, who lived with her granddaughter, Caroline, in a house she owned in Fulham, London.

In December 1906, Brinkley put his cunning plan into action by making out a will whereby Mrs Blume left all her assets and property to him. On the pretext that he was collecting signatures for an outing to the seaside, he presented the widow with the paper on which was written the will and carefully folded to obscure the nature of the contents. He then persuaded her to put her signature at the bottom of the paper.

Using the same ploy, Brinkley next procured the signatures of two witnesses. Two days later Mrs Blume died and the examining doctor attributed her death to apoplexy. A verdict of death from natural causes was recorded by the coroner.

Brinkley now appeared at the house in Fulham with the intention of taking possession under the terms of the late Mrs Blume's will. He produced her will to prove his right of ownership and moved in at the expense of her granddaughter who was dispossessed.

Thinking he had achieved his aims, Brinkley began selling off some of the contents of the house but was in for a shock when Mrs Blume's relatives contested the will. He was told that the two witnesses to the document would be required to swear on oath that they were both present when the testator signed.

This development provided Brinkley with a dilemma. Realizing that the witnesses would be questioned, he decided to eliminate them. He began with Mr Parker, an accountant's clerk, who was already beginning to smell a rat. After a couple of visits involving the pouring of drinks and attempts on Brinkley's part to adulterate them when Parker was out of the room, he resorted to another ruse.

This involved the purchase of a dog that Parker had for sale. Brinkley called at Parker's lodgings on 20 April 1907 to discuss terms. When he arrived, he produced a bottle of stout and vigorously proclaimed the health-giving qualities of the drink. At this point, Parker's landlord, Mr Beck, called at the house but made himself scarce when he realized the two men were discussing business.

Parker and Brinkley went out into the yard to look at the dog, leaving the bottle of stout on the table. Meanwhile, Mr Beck returned, accompanied by his wife and daughter. Persuaded by Brinkley's advocacy of the drink they decided to sample it. Within minutes, Mr and Mrs Beck were struck down with convulsions and died soon afterwards. Their daughter was taken ill but recovered later in hospital.

Brinkley was quickly arrested after Parker told the police what had happened. The dregs of liquid remaining in the bottled stout were analysed and found to contain prussic acid. Mrs Blume's body was later exhumed but no traces of poison were found. Brinkley protested his innocence and attempted to put up an alibi but it quickly unravelled on questioning.

Asked about his possession of prussic acid, strychnine, arsenic and chloroform, Brinkley said they were used for electrical and photographic experiments. His trial at Lewes Assizes for the murder of Mr and Mrs Beck was notable for the fact that they were not his intended victims. The jury had little difficulty in returning a guilty verdict and Brinkley was sentenced to death by Mr Justice Bigham and was executed at Wandsworth Prison on 13 August 1907.

Poison Pie

Thirty-five-year-old Michael Barber worked in a factory warehouse at Westcliff-on-Sea in the UK. He was married to Susan and they had three children. While he liked the quiet life, his wife preferred to be socially active. The marriage got into difficulties when Susan proved unfaithful. Returning from a fishing trip, Michael surprised Susan in bed with a neighbour. There were harsh words and a few blows exchanged.

Early in June 1981, Michael became unwell with severe headaches and was off work. When he experienced cramps and nausea, his doctor treated him for an infection. His health continued to go downhill and after he had breathing problems, he was admitted to hospital at Southend. When his kidneys began to fail, he was transferred to Hammersmith Hospital where doctors began to suspect that he had been poisoned.

Michael Barber died on 27 June from cardiac arrest and kidney failure. On the same day, Susan's neighbour moved in with her. Michael's body was duly cremated but not before tissue samples had been taken. After a long delay, laboratory test results showed that he had been poisoned with paraquat, a powerful herbicide.

Police enquiries led to the arrest of Susan Barber and her twenty-five-year-old paramour, Richard Collins. They denied any involvement in Michael's death but, slowly, a picture began to emerge of a failing marriage and an unfaithful wife. Neighbours provided colourful testimony of Susan's lustful ambitions, which included making dates by radio using "Nympho" as her call sign. Probing questioning resulted in a confession.

Susan Barber said she had found a supply of paraquat in the garden shed. She mixed some of it with Michael's dinner of steak and kidney pie. When this had no immediate effect, she repeated the procedure, reducing Michael to a state where his organs started to fail.

Ironically, Michael had brought the paraquat into their home at a time when he worked in landscape gardening. Paraquat is a highly effective herbicide which, if ingested, produces severe headaches and gastro-intestinal problems. In the secondary phase of poisoning, the liver and kidneys are affected and the lungs begin to fail.

Susan hardly played the role of a grieving widow, first bringing Collins into her life and then discarding him in favour of other men. In all this, Collins was believed to be her tool; he knew what was going on but had no part in the poisoning.

The pair were put on trial in November 1982. They pleaded not guilty to the charges of murder and conspiracy to murder. Susan's account was that she had poisoned her husband only to incapacitate him so that she could escape with her children from an abusive marriage. The jury found her guilty of murder and she was given a sentence of life imprisonment. Collins was found guilty of conspiracy and sentenced to two years' imprisonment.

"Lie In Wait For The Victim"

The teenage daughter of a millionaire devised a murder plan aimed to make her wealthy. She committed some of her plans to paper, outlining how she would target an elderly, wealthy woman to kill and rob; it was meant to be a perfect murder.

Kemi Adeyoola's murderous ambitions were nurtured while she was in a juvenile detention centre following a conviction for shoplifting.

Eighty-five-year-old Anne Mendel was found by her husband lying in a pool of blood at the bottom of the stairs in their home at Golders Green in north-west London. She had been stabbed fourteen times. The murder was committed in March 2005 a few months after Adeyoola's thesis, "Prison and After: Making Life Count", was found in her detention centre cell.

She set out her objective, which was to gain a minimum of three million pounds by killing an elderly woman who must be wealthy and defenceless. That person was Anne Mendel and Adeyoola's DNA was found on her body.

Adeyoola went on trial for murder in June 2006 when the full extent of her plans was revealed in what amounted to a murder manual. She drew up lists of equipment needed, including semi-automatic guns, wigs and dark glasses. The modus operandi was also mapped out: "lie in wait for the victim, creep up on her, and cover her mouth with a gloved hand." Once inside the house, her chilling mission was to use a butcher's knife "to remove her head" and wrap it in cling film to contain the bleeding. The "job", as she described it, was to be carried out by February 2005.

In court, Adeyoola said her handwritten notes were intended as a work of fiction to fulfil her ambition to be a writer. The young woman was the daughter of a successful property management businessman. Her parents were divorced and she had had a disturbed upbringing. She had a record for shoplifting and had worked as an escort, making £500 a night. Detectives found pornographic material, sex toys and stolen clothes when they searched her flat.

She pleaded not guilty to the charge of murder but the prosecution made convincing use of her "murder blueprint" and argued that the killing of Mrs Mendel was a rehearsal for her real aim which was to kill a really wealthy victim and gain the three million pounds she planned to gain. Adeyoola had attempted to set up a false alibi for the murder by eliciting help from a young accomplice. She admitted shoplifting from the age of fifteen and described it as a skill. The jury brought in a guilty verdict and the judge in his summing up dismissed the defence notion that her fractured family background was an explanation for her crime.

Judge Richard Hone described Adeyoola as "remorseless and cold-blooded", adding, "I think you wanted to experience what it felt like to kill someone in cold-blood, possibly so that you could write about it . . ." The eighteen-year-old was sentenced to twenty years' imprisonment.

"Pray For Me . . ."

Consumed with jealousy, a student made a diary entry referring to his girlfriend, writing, "Next time I suspect her of liking another man, I shall kill her quickly and without warning." Three months later, he fulfilled that promise.

Mohammed Abdullah and Sonja Hoff were students at the University of California in Berkeley. Sonya, a vibrant young woman who had an active social life, was pursuing a course of Persian studies and Abdullah studied Islamic culture. They were drawn together and there was talk of marriage.

Mohammed Abdullah had changed his name from Joseph Howk, reflecting his conversion from Roman Catholicism to Islam. He had a high IQ but had been a difficult child, which led to psychiatric assessment and a diagnosis of a schizoid personality at the age of fifteen.

The two students met in 1959 at Berkeley but their attraction began to founder when Abdullah took exception to Sonja's love of dancing and some of the clothes that she wore. But the main bone of contention was his jealous nature and suspicion that she was seeing other men.

They quarrelled and Abdullah's demands became more insistent. He made a diary entry on 6 April 1960 in which he wrote, "Tonight I tried to kill myself but Sonja put herself between my knife and my throat." He threatened to kill her if she saw another man.

Two weeks later, he threatened her directly and Sonja reported the incident to the police. He was ordered to leave the University. Sonja took a vacation job working for a while as a waitress in Berkeley. Then she chanced to meet Abdullah but declined his invitation to go with him to his apartment.

Two days later, on 13 July 1960, Abdullah obtained a .38 revolver and prepared some typewritten notes. He wrote, "In the name of God, beneficient and merciful, I have stolen a pistol to kill my beloved and myself" and ended, "Pray for me . . . I have done wrong, but forgive me . . ." Then he met Sonja and asked to talk with her. He told her he loved her before firing two shots into her head at close range, fatally wounding her. The next shot he fired into his own head.

Abdullah survived his bullet wound, although he lost the sight of an eye. His intention to kill Sonja was clear and when he came to trial for murder, he pleaded innocence by reason of insanity. He was tried with the man who had sold him the murder weapon in the knowledge that it was to be used to kill Sonja.

Abdullah was found guilty of first-degree murder and sentenced to death. This was later commuted to life imprisonment. The man who provided the murder weapon was convicted of involuntary manslaughter.

Feral Thuggery

On an August evening in 2007 a group of teenagers gathered at the entrance to Stubbylee Park in Bacup, Lancashire, UK. They had been drinking cider and other alcoholic drinks.

At about midnight, twenty-year-old Sophie Lancaster and her boyfriend, Robert Maltby, aged twenty-one, both students, went into the park. Their appearance excited the teenagers because they were dressed as Goths and this seemed to be a stimulus for what happened next.

The young couple, who were simply enjoying each other's company, were set upon in a violent, completely unprovoked attack by five teenagers. Maltby was thrown to the ground and the gang took running kicks at him until he was senseless. Sophie Lancaster attempted to protect her boyfriend, cradling him as he lay unconscious on the ground. She then became the target of a vicious sustained assault that left her bloodied and beaten. Witnesses later said that they kicked her head like a football.

Sophie Lancaster died two weeks later in hospital; Robert Maltby survived but with permanent injuries. Paramedics called to the scene were appalled at the injuries caused by this orgy of violence. The gang members responsible boasted to their friends, that they had ". . . done sommat good . . . you wanna see them – they're a right mess!"

Five teenagers involved in the attack were arrested within two weeks. Questioned about the incident, each blamed the others. A fifteen-year-old, not named, denied murder while his four companions pleaded guilty to causing grievous bodily harm.

Two of those involved in the attack who had not been identified because of their age were named by order of the judge at Preston Crown Court in April 2008. Brendan Harris, aged fifteen, denied murder, and Ryan Herbert, aged sixteen, who admitted it, were convicted and sentenced to life imprisonment. Three other teenagers who pleaded guilty to causing grievous bodily harm with intent on Robert Maltby were also identified by the judge. Each received a prison sentence.

It was brought out in their trial that the youths had both been drinking heavily; Harris admitted to drinking two litres of cider. He also said he initiated the attack because he was drunk and showing off. Four teenage witnesses to the assault came forward to testify. It transpired that Harris and Herbert had attacked a sixteen-year-old boy four months earlier and had been given community service orders.

The court heard evidence of the animal-like ferocity of the attack, which the judge described as "feral thuggery". Sophie

Lancaster's mother took a courageous view of the outcome of the trial and made a plea for tolerance in society.

Man In A Green Suit

A hospital worker walking his dogs in New York's Central Park on 2 November 1942 let them off their leashes in an area that was being prepared for landscaping. The dogs led him to a patch of grass where, as he discovered, they were sniffing around the corpse of a young woman.

She was neatly dressed but there was no identification on her body and her bag was missing. While there were no immediate signs of injury, an autopsy showed that she had been strangled. Files at the Missing Persons Bureau were checked in the hope of establishing her identity but to no avail. Then, a report came in from a man whose daughter was missing after going out on a weekend date.

The body in the mortuary was identified as twenty-three-year-old Louisa Almodovar. The young woman, who was married but separated from her husband, had been living with her parents. She had taken a telephone call arranging a date but did not say whom she was planning to meet.

Louisa's husband was Terry Almodovar whom she had met at a dance and they married in 1942 after a whirlwind romance. They separated within a few months. One of the sources of friction between the couple was Terry's love of dancing in an environment in which there were plenty of attractive partners.

Detectives learned that Terry had previously called at the home of his wife's parents complaining that Louisa had attacked one of his dancing partners. He had been ordered out of the house. When Terry was questioned about the evening of the murder, he said that he had spent it at the Rhumba Palace Dance Hall, an alibi that would be corroborated by several of the girls he had danced with.

When he was searched, a pawn ticket was found in Terry's pocket. This, he explained, was for a green suit, which happened to be the one he was wearing on the night in question. The suit was retrieved and tested for bloodstains, with negative results.

Scratch marks on his arms looked suspicious but he gave an innocent explanation for them.

Despite the lack of firm evidence, Terry Almodovar was indicted with first-degree murder and appeared on trial in February 1943. He strongly protested his innocence and things seemed to be going in his favour until the green suit made an appearance. The prosecution had consulted scientific experts and their evidence turned the case on its head.

The green suit had been re-examined for forensic traces and the trouser turn-ups revealed the presence of grass seeds. Not just any old grass seeds but a rare variety that was known to grow only in Central Park. Botanists established that the seeds and other traces of vegetation on the trousers could only have come from one place – the spot where Louisa Almodovar was murdered.

The trial jury returned a guilty verdict and, on 9 March 1943, Terry Almodovar was sentenced to death. He reacted angrily and had to be restrained. It appeared that he had secretly met Louisa in Central Park intending to kill her to make way for a new woman in his life. His mistake, and the flaw in his plan for the perfect murder, was to pick a location with distinctive vegetation that ultimately unmasked his crime.

". . . I Have No Regrets"

Pakistan's worst serial killings arose as one man's act of revenge against the police.

When Javed Iqbal complained to the police in Lahore that he had been mugged and robbed by two boys, he was furious because he believed his claim was not taken seriously. He resolved to take his revenge by killing 100 boys.

Iqbal recruited three accomplices to help him in his mission, two of whom were juveniles. Between June 1998 and December 1999, young boys were lured to his home with promises of food and money. Once under his control, the boys were systematically drugged, raped and strangled with a chain. The bodies were dismembered and put into a vat of acid. After they had been turned into sludge, their remains were poured into a sewer. Clothes and shoes were kept as trophies.

When he had reached his target of 100 victims, Iqbal wrote an anonymous letter to the police claiming that he had murdered runaway children at his home in Lahore. When police arrived to search his home they found evidence of his claim. His house was a virtual murder factory. Human body parts were recovered, together with piles of clothing belonging to his victims. He had also kept photographs of the boys he killed and the presence of an acid vat was a sinister reminder of their fate.

Iqbal was not at home and managed to avoid capture for a month, despite an intensive manhunt. Finally, he presented himself at the editorial office of a magazine and offered them a diary containing details of the abuse inflicted on his victims, which he said was revenge for the treatment he had received from the police in 1998. "I am Javed Iqbal," he told astonished magazine staff, "killer of 100 children."

Together with his accomplices, Iqbal appeared on trial in March 2000. Having admitted his crimes, he now withdrew his confession, which he said was intended to discredit the police. He pleaded not guilty, saying he had made up the story to put a spotlight on the problem of runaway children.

In his original confession, Iqbal said, "I am not ashamed of my actions and I am ready to die. I have no regrets." He got his wish when Judge Allah Baksh sentenced him to death and described the method by which it should be carried out. He said that Iqbal and his co-accused, twenty-year-old Sajid, should be publicly executed in the presence of the victims' relatives. They should be strangled with the same chain they had used to kill their child victims, after which their bodies should be dismembered and destroyed with acid.

Applying Islamic Sharia Law, the judge ordered that the punishment be carried out in one of Lahore's public parks. While the controversial judgment was being debated at higher levels, Iqbal and Sajid took matters into their own hands by committing suicide in their prison cells on 8 October 2001.

No Apparent Motive

In the course of four days in 2000, three women were killed for no discernible motive.

The body of twenty-one-year-old Jodie Hyde, a recovering drug addict, was found near a recreation ground in Sparkbrook near Birmingham in the UK. She had been strangled and set on fire. Three days later, the badly beaten body of Rosemary Corcoran was discovered in a wooded area near Droitwich Spa. She had sustained severe injuries to her head. Within hours, a third woman was killed while walking to work. She was run over by a car, dragged away and battered about the head.

Philip Smith, whose modest claim to fame was that he had once lived in the same street as Fred West, the Gloucester mass murderer, lived in Birmingham where he worked as a cab driver and odd-job man. He was nicknamed "Bigfoot" on account of his considerable size, weighing in at twenty-three stone.

Jodie Hyde and Rosemary Corcoran were regulars at the Rainbow public house, which was also frequented by Smith who provided lifts home for customers. It was possible that the women knew him. Smith was arrested after police viewed CCTV footage from a local club which showed him with Rosemary Corcoran a few hours before she was found dead. She appeared to be resisting him. Smith was also identified by CCTV as the attacker of the first victim. Images showed him in his car.

Smith was arrested on the strength of the visual evidence provided by surveillance cameras. A search of his bed-sit accommodation turned up articles which he had taken from two of his victims. A pair of blood-soaked jeans were found in the bath. DNA testing later showed matches to two of the dead women.

West Midlands Police believed Smith may have been responsible for serious unsolved crimes committed over a period of twenty years. That the three murders in Birmingham appeared to be without motive was a problem for detectives in linking Smith with other offences, especially as he had no previous convictions.

While initially denying involvement in the murders, Smith changed his plea during the trial at Leicester Crown Court. The forensic evidence and CCTV images placing him at two of the crime scenes conclusively proved his guilt. Sentencing him, Mr Justice Rafferty referred to the brutality with which he killed the three women. Underlining the lack of apparent motive, he said, "I suspect their families will suffer the more, as they simply don't understand why you did it." Smith received a life sentence.

CHAPTER 14

Simply Bizarre

All murders may be called bizarre for one reason or another. They may be particularly strange, grotesque or weird in some aspects of their execution, detection or punishment. Most can be fitted into some broad category defined by motive or method, for example, while others remain simply bizarre.

Even a cursory look at a collection of murder cases provides an insight into the lethal excesses of which the human species is capable. Within every human being there lurk primitive instincts related to survival. When threatened, the biological temptation is for protection and self-preservation.

In the modern world, a social veneer hides the dark forces of nature and the restraining influence of nurture acts as a counter-balance. Yet the bounds are easily crossed when a combination of forces erupt into violence or murder.

The circumstances of every murder represent a unique occurrence. A coming together of time and place in combination with elements of chance and opportunity. When this is overlaid with an eruption of emotion and the nuances of the unexpected, a murder matrix is created.

Some murders are so bizarre in their incidents that they might fairly be described as unbelievable. But if murder teaches us anything, it is that the unbelievable can happen. Who would conceive that a successful lawyer would kill his wife by wiring up her car with explosives? Yet Arthur D. Payne did precisely that. Or that Graham Coutts kept his victim's body in a storage unit so that he could visit it at his leisure.

Some murderers revel in their devilish work, such as George Stephenson, who after an orgy of violence in which five people were killed asked if his exploits put him in "the top ten". Others trawl the depths of their imagination to find excuses that might absolve them of guilt. Karl Taylor asked the trial jury to believe that his victim committed suicide by deliberately falling on his knife. And Mark Dixie tried to explain the traces of his DNA on his victim by describing how he came across her lifeless body by chance and performed sex on it.

Also in the realms of the unbelievable was indestructible Mike Malloy who defied a murder gang's best efforts to poison him with car antifreeze, horse liniment and rat poison. He finally succumbed to their murderous intent when they gassed him.

And the ultimate mystery is murder in a locked room. Isidor Fink was found dead from gunshot wounds in his locked tenement room. There was no murder weapon and no fingerprints, just an abiding mystery and another bizarre murder.

Home Sweet Home

Arthur D. Payne was a successful lawyer with a practice in Amarillo, Texas, living a comfortable life with a wife and three children. On 27 June 1930, he decided to leave the car at home for his wife to use and walked to work. Later that morning, Mrs Payne took her nine-year-old son to go shopping. They travelled only a short distance when the car began to trail smoke before disintegrating in an explosion. Mrs Payne was killed and her son badly injured.

It appeared that explosives in the car had been detonated by a time fuse. While the police were baffled by the incident, the campaigning editor of the *Amarillo News* reported it as a murder and hired a well-known private investigator to hunt down the killer. Arthur Payne offered a $5,000 reward for information.

A.B. MacDonald was an experienced reporter on the *Kansas City Star*. He was a dogged investigator who learned that ninety per cent of Amarillo's citizens believed Payne had killed his wife. Without supporting evidence, the claim seemed unfounded. Payne had built up a successful law practice defending criminals whose company he particularly sought out. MacDonald soon discovered that the lawyer had taken out life insurance on his wife and children, with himself named as the beneficiary. When the reporter interviewed Payne, he found him shifty and, instinctively, felt there was a case to answer.

Public opinion was strongly prejudiced against Payne. Enquiries revealed that he had been unfaithful to his wife and he had confided to his lover that he would marry her if he could be rid of his spouse. He had a reputation as a philanderer and was defensive when questioned about his love life.

Under pressure on account of the revelations about his extra-marital activities, Payne broke down and made a full confession which ran to 60,000 words, probably a record of its kind. He admitted trying to poison his wife and then setting up a shotgun to kill her in a simulated accident. When these attempts to eliminate her failed, he resorted to dynamite, with devastating consequences.

Sent for trial and aided by his confession, a Texan jury lost no time in finding him guilty and he was sentenced to death by electrocution. Two days before he was due to be strapped to the electric chair, however, he blew himself up. The blast was strong enough to leave a gaping hole in the wall of his cell. His last wish was that "Home Sweet Home" should be played at his funeral.

While Arthur D. Payne blew himself to extinction, A.B. MacDonald later capped his career as an investigative journalist by being awarded a Pulitzer Prize.

Trophy Cabinet

Jane Longhurst, a thirty-one-year-old music teacher went missing from her home in Brighton in the UK on 14 March 2003. Some weeks later, a walker in woods at Pulborough, Sussex, noticed something burning in the undergrowth and discovered her body. The young woman, who had been strangled, was identified by her dental records.

Following this grim discovery, staff at a storage facility in Brighton reported their suspicions of a man calling himself

Paul Kelly who made frequent out-of-hours visits to the unit he had rented. This man had rented a storage space on 25 March, explaining that he needed it urgently to store personal belongings.

Footage from security cameras showed that Paul Kelly had made repeated visits over a three-week period. When police realized this was a false name and he was identified as Graham Coutts, a part-time musician, the next step was to open and examine the storage unit. Officers found a box containing Jane Longhurst's mobile phone and purse, a bloodstained rope and a shirt stained with blood and semen.

Coutts had kept his victim's body in the storage unit so that he could view it as a trophy at his leisure. It was only when the remains began to putrefy that he was forced to remove them. He had a history of fascination with violent sex and harboured a fetish for strangulation. He was addicted to violent pornography and acted out some of his fantasies with co-operative partners. He confided to one of them that the time would come when he would rape and strangle a woman.

At his trial for murder in Lewes Crown Court in February 2004, he denied murder, claiming that Jane Longhurst's death was an accident that occurred during a sex game. Evidence of his taste for sexual violence had been found on his computer and he frequently viewed pornographic programmes. The prosecution argued that Coutts was fixated on images of helpless women who ended up being strangled.

The trial jury found thirty-six-year-old Coutts guilty of murder and the judge passed a sentence of thirty years' imprisonment.

". . . Am I In The Top Ten?"

On 1 September 1986, Joseph Cleaver and his wife Hilda were enjoying a family dinner party at their country home when five intruders burst in. Cleaver and his wife, their son Thomas and daughter-in-law Wendy, were dragged away from the dining room by armed men. Also taken was Margaret Murphy, a live-in nurse who looked after Mrs Cleaver, a stroke victim. They were taken upstairs into the bedrooms where they were tied up and strangled. The daughter-in-law was raped, strangled and mutilated. Having ransacked the house, the gang then started fires with petrol poured over their victims before fleeing into the night.

The carnage that had occurred at the Cleavers' home, Burgate House near Fordingbridge in Hampshire in the UK, was discovered the next morning when the gardener and cleaner arrived to begin work. They found half-eaten food still on the plates on the dining room table, mute testimony to the violence that had occurred.

Police had an early lead when a red car believed to have been used by the gang was traced to Coventry. It had been rented by a George Stephenson who returned it to the hire firm on the day after the murders. Within forty-eight hours, Stephenson and two associates, George and John Daly, were being questioned. Stephenson had worked for the Cleavers as their handyman but had been dismissed for drunkenness. George Daly had convictions for burglary and theft.

Since his teenage years, Stephenson had a history of casual employment mixed with periods of detention for theft and handling stolen goods. He also had a violent temperament and his wife of six weeks deserted him after he abused her. Once arrested, Stephenson said he had been shocked to see his face on television as a wanted man. He thought he might be questioned about a robbery but he did not realize anyone had died. He put the blame on the Daly brothers who wanted the shotguns that Joseph Cleaver kept in his house. He said John Daly was drunk on the night of the robbery. Stephenson drove them down to Bournemouth where they celebrated by drinking a bottle of wine.

Stephenson and the Daly brothers were sent for trial at Winchester Crown Court in October 1987, when the full extent of what happened at the Cleavers' home the previous year was exposed. Wearing stocking masks the trio had burst into the house armed with pickaxe handles and two cans of petrol. They started their night of horror by beating the family's dog. After tying up their victims, they each raped Wendy Cleaver and then strangled her. Finally, dousing their helpless victims with petrol, they threw firelighters into the bedrooms burning them alive.

When questioned by detectives, Stephenson had asked, "Is this the worst murder of all time? . . . Am I a star? . . . Am I in the top ten?" The three defendants were found guilty of murder and manslaughter and given a total of thirteen life sentences. Mr Justice Hobhouse told Stephenson, "In all that occurred that night you showed no mercy. You deserve none." Facing a minimum of twenty-five years' imprisonment, Stephenson smirked and shrugged his shoulders.

Unlikely Excuse

On 18 May 2007, Kate Beagley, a thirty-two-year-old manager at a utility company, went to the CC Club in central London for drinks with friends. During the evening she became acquainted with Karl Taylor, a fitness instructor, and they exchanged telephone numbers. Later they agreed to go on a date.

The couple met at the Roebuck public house, Richmond Hill on 30 May. They were noticed by fellow customers and Beagley was observed to be busy using her mobile phone. When she did not turn up for work, her friends and family began telephoning around in efforts to locate her.

Karl Taylor was arrested on suspicion of kidnap, and when questioned, admitted that he had killed Beagley and told police officers where to find her body. She was found in Oxhey Woods, near Watford, lying in a drainage ditch. She had been stabbed in the face and neck.

Tayor said he only wanted to steal her car and had put the knife to her neck in order to take the ignition key. He put her body in the boot of her VW Golf and drove to the spot where he dumped her. He was careful to strip the body and wash it with mineral water to remove any forensic traces. He then drove back to London where he had a flat in Covent Garden. On the way, he threw the murder weapon and some of Beagley's clothes out on to the motorway. He also telephoned his girlfriend and, later, showed off the new car he had acquired. Taylor's route was confirmed by CCTV images recorded at a filling station in Shepherd's Bush where he stopped to re-fuel the VW.

Enquiries into Taylor's background showed that he had a conviction for obtaining property by deception and that he had talked of taking his own life. He was sent for trial at the Old Bailey in March 2008. The prosecution accused him of concealing a knife in his coat sleeve when he met Beagley on their first date. They sat on a park bench overlooking the river when he threatened her with the knife.

Taylor's version of events was that he produced the knife and told her he only wanted her car. When she resisted and grappled with him, he cut her "because she was going for my face." He claimed that Beagley had committed suicide by pushing her head on to the knife after discussing some of her personal problems with him.

The jury convicted twenty-seven-year-old Taylor of murder and Judge Giles Forrester sentenced him to a minimum of thirty years' imprisonment. The judge described him as arrogant and highly dangerous and said, "This was murder done for gain. You went to meet this girl equipped with a knife. You took advantage of her vulnerability for your own ends." Taylor's suggestion that the dead woman had committed suicide by throwing herself on to his knife did not merit a great deal of discussion.

Sexual Predator

Eighteen-year-old Sally Anne Bowman, an aspiring model, became a murder victim on 25 September 2005. Her body was found with stab wounds lying on the driveway at her home in Croydon, south London.

The post-mortem showed that she had been repeatedly stabbed. There were bite marks on her body and she had been sexually assaulted. The hunt for her attacker led to one of the UK's largest mass screenings for DNA. Appeals for information were broadcast on the BBC's "Crimewatch" programme and an e-fit was issued of a possible suspect. The police had a strong idea that the attacker lived locally.

Mark Dixie, aged thirty-seven, was arrested on 15 June 2006. He had been involved in a bar brawl after a football match. The police exercised powers they were given in 2000 to take DNA samples from anyone arrested and held at a police station. Dixie's DNA matched that left on the body of Sally Bowman.

He lived in south London, was estranged from his family, and worked as an itinerant pub chef. He had a long history of sexual offences with convictions going back over twenty years. He had worked in Holland and Spain and also in Australia where he was linked with an unsolved rape and attempted murder in 1998.

In his circle of acquaintances, Dixie was known to use aliases and to be a recreational drug user. On the night before Sally Bowman was killed, he had celebrated his birthday, drinking beer and using cocaine. When detectives searched his accommodation they found a copy of the *Sun* newspaper dated 23 February 2006 with semen traces on the front page. That issue of the newspaper carried a report of the murder that had occurred five months previously.

During his trial at the Old Bailey, a nineteen-year-old woman from Perth, Australia, described being raped in 1997 by a man who broke into the house where she was living. He knocked her unconscious and left traces of semen on her clothing. DNA recovered from those traces belonged to Dixie. He denied the attack.

His explanation for his DNA being found on Sally Bowman was that coming home from his party, he found her lying on the driveway of her home and decided to have sex with her lifeless body. He also left bite marks on her. Dixie's counsel contended that while the evidence showed he had sex, it did not prove that he was a murderer. The jury thought differently and took only three and a half hours to bring in a guilty verdict. Mr Justice Gordon, saying there were no mitigating circumstances in Dixie's case and he had shown no remorse, sentenced him to life imprisonment.

Dixie's conviction and that of Steven Wright (*see page 382*), the Suffolk murderer, in the same week, prompted the British police to call for a national DNA register. DNA had played a crucial role in bringing both murderers to justice.

Mister Indestructible

A five-man murder ring operating in New York during the Great Depression targeted individuals who were down on their luck whom they insured and then murdered to claim the money. When they selected Mike Malloy, his resistance to numerous attempts on his life earned him the nickname "Indestructible Mike".

The gang had claimed their first victim a year earlier and collected on the insurance. They got Betty Carlsen drunk, took her back to her room, stripped her, poured cold water over her body and left the window open. When she expired, the cause of death was indicated as pneumonia and no questions were asked.

Next in line was Mike Malloy who hung around the bars looking for a handout. He was easily persuaded to sign up for life insurance. The plotters' first tactic was to buy him enough drinks to kill him by alcoholism. When he seemed to thrive on this treatment, they tried car antifreeze, which Malloy consumed without hesitation and after being unwell, soon returned to his old routine.

The gang persisted with the antifreeze and laced it first with turpentine, then horse liniment and finally rat poison. Malloy thrived on these cocktails so the plotters switched to offering him adulterated food. He was still on his feet after consuming poisoned oysters and rotten fish. The next move was to get him drunk and expose him to the elements, a strategy that had worked with the first victim.

Amazingly, he survived, having been found wandering naked around a public park. The plotters were becoming desperate and opted for even more brutal tactics. A taxi-driver was bribed to run him down in the street, and after examining Malloy's senseless body, they decided they had succeeded this time. To their disappointment, he turned up three weeks later, saying he had been concussed and asking for a drink.

Running out of ideas, the gang resolved at this stage to go for direct murder. On 22 February 1933, the five-member gang visited Malloy in his rented room and gassed him. A doctor was persuaded to issue a certificate giving pneumonia as the cause of death and Mike Malloy was buried with indecent haste.

By now, rumours of a murder-for-profit gang operating in the city had reached the New York Police Department. Following enquiries, Malloy's body was exhumed and the true nature of his death established. The gang members, when questioned, each blamed the others and one turned States Evidence. Tony Marino, Harry Green, Joe Murphy, Dan Kreisberg and Frank Pasqua were found guilty and all except Green sentenced to death. They were executed in the electric chair at Sing Sing in 1934.

A footnote to this affair was that the gang spent more on their efforts to kill "Indestructible Mike" than they re-couped by claiming on his insurance.

Murder In A Locked Room

A murder committed in a locked room is one of the crime world's classic mysteries. The death of a laundry operator in New York in 1929 teased the imagination of film director, Alfred Hitchcock, and writer Ben Hecht. Neither came up with an explanation.

Isidor Fink, orphaned in his native Poland, emigrated to America where he worked hard and saved enough money to start his own laundry on East 123rd Street. He occupied one large ground-floor room in a tenement block which served both his business and domestic needs. He also had two rooms at the rear of the building, which he sub-let to an elderly woman who lived on her own. There was a connecting door to these rooms, which was permanently bolted shut on both sides.

Fink was very conscious of the need for security in an area where crime was commonplace. Accordingly, every door and window was secured with locks, bolts and bars. On 9 March, after making a few local laundry deliveries, he returned home about 10.15 p.m. A neighbouring shopkeeper noticed that Fink's premises were closed up with no lights showing.

At about 10.30, the tenant in the rooms adjoining the laundry heard three shots, followed by a heavy thud. She raised the alarm by running into the street and calling for help. A police patrolman on duty nearby responded within a minute. After listening to the woman's explanation of what she heard, the officer tried the door and found it locked. Next, he tried the connecting door from the rented rooms. It too was locked on the laundry side.

The patrolman's next brainwave was to ask a boy among the crowd that had gathered if he would crawl through a small window, enabling him to gain access to the front door and release the bolt. This proved difficult because the window had been nailed to the frame and did not, therefore, open. Finally, by breaking the glass, the officer made an opening for the boy to get through.

Once inside the laundry, the patrolman saw the body of Isidor Fink lying on the floor. He was dead with two bullet wounds in the chest and another in his arm. The immediate reading of the scene suggested suicide, but where was the gun?

A thorough search of the premises failed to find the weapon, which the medical examiner thought was probably .38 calibre. The doctor thought the death was a murder because of the distance from the body that the firearm had been discharged. Robbery did not appear to be the motive as no money had been taken. The only fingerprints found at the scene were those of Isidor Fink.

After months of investigation, detectives came no nearer to solving the laundryman's death. They were satisfied that the room and every conceivable entry or exit point had been locked and bolted when the shots were fired. Searches were made for possible secret panels that might conceal a weapon. None was found. The violent death of the thirty-year-old laundryman remained a mystery as far as crime scene investigators were concerned. The only hope of solving it lay with the ingenuity of fiction writers.

Hats Off!

Ernest Key, a sixty-four-year-old jeweller who had been in business in Surbiton, Surrey, for twenty years, was found unconscious in his shop on Christmas Eve 1938. His son and daughter discovered their father lying in a pool of blood after a savage knife attack. He had sustained thirty-one wounds and died on the way to hospital.

It was evident that the murder had occurred in the course of a robbery as jewellery was missing from the shop. Intriguingly, the murderer had appeared to leave his bowler hat behind when he fled from the crime scene. One of the first officials to arrive at the premises in Victoria Road, Surbiton, was the County Pathologist, Dr Eric Gardner. He made a preliminary assessment of the scene pending the arrival of the Home Office expert, Sir Bernard Spilsbury.

Dr Gardner looked at the abandoned headgear and gave the police some ideas about the likely wearer. As events unfolded, these clues proved unnecessary because the murderer, who had injured his hand in the attack on Ernest Key, presented himself at Kingston County Hospital seeking treatment. As it happened, he saw the same doctor who, an hour earlier, had been called out to attend Mr Key. Twenty-nine-year-old William Butler, an unemployed driver with convictions for house-breaking, had taken a taxi to the hospital where he gave a false name and said he had injured his hand in an accident using a wood-cutting machine.

When questioned by the police, he changed his story, claiming that he had been knocked down by a motorcycle in the street. He had given false information at the hospital he said, because he could not afford to pay for treatment.

Butler was charged with murder and appeared on trial at the Old Bailey in February 1938. His contention that he had acted in self-defence did not find favour with the jury who brought in a guilty verdict. He was sentenced to death and hanged at Wandsworth Prison on 29 March 1939.

The bowler hat left at the crime scene was something of a red herring but Dr Gardner's observations made international news and prompted the Berlin police to enquire about the British clairvoyant crime expert.

A Man Who Knew Too Much

Recognized as a knowledgeable local man, Paul Belvin was flattered to be asked by detectives if he would help them reconstruct a murder. He accepted whole-heartedly, and in the process, revealed knowledge possessed only by the crime investigators and the murderer himself.

Twenty-four-year-old Jean Burrows was a British journalist working in Bermuda. On 3 July 1971, she and her husband, together with two friends, dined at a harbourside restaurant in Hamilton. After their meal, they decided to return to the Burrows' home for coffee and set off on their mopeds around 1.00 a.m. Jean Burrows never arrived.

A search was mounted at daylight and her body was found floating in the harbour. She had sustained severe head injuries and been partially strangled; she had also been raped. The pathologist believed that after being rendered unconscious, she was held under water until she expired.

A search of the area discovered several of her possessions scattered about on swampy ground and her moped was recovered from a patch of long grass. Local enquiries produced useful information including the name of a man who had been noticed on the beach because of the attention he paid to young women swimming and sunbathing. He was twenty-eight-year-old Paul Belvin, who was something of a drifter with no fixed address.

Belvin had become a minor local celebrity when he won a prize in a competition and attracted a good deal of publicity. Detectives decided to question him and were impressed by the extent of his knowledge of the locals and of peoples' comings and goings.

One of the detectives suggested that Belvin might be able to help in the reconstruction they were planning to stage of Jean Burrows' murder. No doubt flattered, he agreed, and accompanied officers to the harbour area. He proceeded to give a graphic portrayal of how and where the killer might have hidden in order to ambush his victim. Indeed, he indicated the exact spot where she was found.

Asked about the injuries Burrows had sustained, Belvin's view was that the murderer had probably used an iron pipe to batter her into submission. No mention had previously been made about such a murder weapon. Belvin made the helpful suggestion that the pipe had probably been thrown into the sea. His prediction proved to be entirely accurate when naval divers retrieved a metal pipe from the sea within throwing distance from the shore.

Belvin had already revealed knowledge of the crime known only to the police and he quickly found himself under arrest. Forensic examination of some of his clothing showed trace evidence connecting him to the victim. He was charged with murder on 1 September 1971 and made a full statement.

The man who knew too much for his own good was put on trial for murder and found guilty. The death sentence imposed on Belvin was subsequently commuted to life imprisonment.

Not A Good Place

David Chenery-Wickens was a spiritualist minister known as "The Reverend". He killed his wife and dumped her body. Then, using her mobile phone, he sent text messages for her friends to make it appear she was still alive. He also left a message for his dead wife: "I'm trying to tune into you. You seem to be in not a good place . . ."

The "not in a good place" was a bramble patch about ten miles from their home in East Sussex where Diane Chenery-Wickens' decomposed body was found five months later. She had confronted her husband on 22 January 2008 with the discovery of a telephone bill itemizing calls to one of his mistresses and to a gay chatline.

Fearing exposure of his secret life, he killed Diane and, two days later, reported her missing. He told the police that they had gone together to London where she had an appointment at the BBC and they agreed to meet up afterwards. According to him, she failed to turn up. CCTV evidence proved that Diane had travelled alone to London and there was no scheduled appointment at the BBC where she worked as an accomplished television make-up artist.

He subsequently changed his story, directing blame on to Diane for the breakdown of their marriage, and claiming she was going to start a new life in Spain. Meanwhile, within days of her disappearance, he was busy pawning her jewellery.

Fifty-two-year-old Chenery-Wickens came to believe, when he was still in his early twenties, that he had the gift of communicating with the dead. In due course, he gained accreditation as a spiritual healer and began to call himself "The Reverend". To his workmates at the time, when he was driving trucks, he was known as "Cosmic Dave".

By 2003, he had given up truck driving and began to work as a healer offering counselling. When a spiritual church was established at Crowborough in Sussex, he led a teaching group of mainly female participants. He learned a great deal about their private lives, which enabled him to control his relationships with them. He was a sexual predator and had a string of affairs. He was also constantly short of money and, by spinning tales about needing funds to pay for medical treatment, persuaded some of his conquests to lend him money.

Diane, a respected professional in her field, was the breadwinner with a high salary who paid for everything in their home. When she learned of her husband's deception, he killed her without hesitation and manufactured a web of lies in his attempt to cover up his crime.

Chenery-Wickens was tried for murder at Lewes Crown Court in March 2009. He was found guilty by a unanimous decision of the jury and Mr Justice Cooke sentenced him to imprisonment for at least eighteen years.

"Murder In Their Hearts"

Gerry Tobin, a thirty-five-year-old mechanic and member of the Hell's Angels, was driving home to London riding his Harley-Davidson motorcycle on 12 August 2007. He was returning from the Bulldog Bash biker festival in Warwickshire, travelling down the M40 motorway when he was followed by a fast-moving car. As the car drew level, two shots were fired at Tobin. He died instantly and the car sped away.

CCTV images at a motorway filling station picked up a green Rover car believed to have been used by the gunman. Such a car was later found abandoned as a burnt-out wreck, denying investigators any hope of retrieving forensic material. By tracing previous owners of the car, however, police were led to forty-four-year-old Sean Creighton from Coventry. He was described as Sergeant-at-arms of the South Warwickshire chapter of the Outlaws, a rival biker gang to the Hell's Angels.

Public enquiries identified six other members of the chapter and, along with Creighton, they were charged with the murder of Tobin. Creighton appeared to have been the instigator of a plan to kill a Hell's Angel biker after the festival held at Long Marston, which the Outlaws regarded as their territory.

When the festival closed on 12 August, Tobin set off home, riding his Harley-Davidson, in convoy with two other bikers. Creighton, together with Dave Garside and Simon Turner, waited in the Rover at a lay-by on the A46. They were looking for a passing biker wearing the Hell's Angels' insignia. Karl Garside and two others waited as back-up in another vehicle and a third vehicle driven by Malcolm Bull. Tobin was targeted as he drove past for no better reason than that he was a Hell's Angel biker and a member of a rival group.

Charges were brought against seven of the Outlaws and they were sent for trial at Birmingham Crown Court in October 2008. Creighton pleaded guilty to murder at the outset and did not give evidence. Dave Garside said he drove the car on the day of the shooting but was unaware that violence was planned. Simon Turner from Nuneaton, Malcolm Bull, Karl Garside, Dean Taylor and Ian Cameron, all from Coventry, were in the other cars. They pleaded not guilty to murder.

The prosecutor described the killing of Tobin as "a thoroughly cold-blooded business" which had been planned in considerable detail. The victim had been targeted, selected and, he suggested, some might say, executed. Tobin was hit in the neck by a shot which penetrated his skull. Bearing in mind that the car containing the gunman, and Tobin on his Harley-Davidson, were all travelling at around 80 mph, indicated that the shooting was carried out with skill and precision.

The jury at Birmingham Crown Court deliberated for eight days and gave their judgment in stages. When all the verdicts were in, the outcome was that six members of the Outlaws were found guilty of murder and Creighton, who admitted guilt at the outset, made it seven convictions. Mr Justice Treacy, who described the Outlaws as having "murder in their hearts", sentenced all seven accused to life imprisonment with varying terms to be served.

Private Eye Gets His Man

When the German freighter, *Gertrude Schultz*, encountered a storm in the Atlantic, high winds damaged one of the oil tanks that were part of the deck cargo. A seaman sent to inspect the damage found more than an oil spill. The leaking oil tank contained the naked bodies of two young women who had evidently been shot.

The vessel had been at sea for six days, sailing from Galveston, Texas, and heading for the German port of Hamburg. The year was 1914 and the USA was still exporting oil to the country that was about to precipitate a world war. The captain of the *Gertrude Schultz* decided to continue his journey to Europe.

On reaching his destination, the captain reported the discovery of the two bodies on his ship. The owners of the vessel decided on the unorthodox step of not pursuing an enquiry through usual channels but to hire a private investigator in the United States. When the ship next traversed the Atlantic, heading for Houston, the services of Joe Hunter were obtained to enquire into the curious affair of the two corpses found on the previous voyage.

He contacted the authorities in Hamburg and established that there were no reports of missing twenty-year-old women at the time in question. Next, he turned his attention to

Chicago where the rail tanker cars had originated. There were no reports of missing women there either. Hunter was nothing if not doggedly determined in his enquiries. His next move was to check the stations on the route that the rail cars had taken from Chicago to Galveston. Here he found something positive; a report of a woman who had gone missing two weeks before the *Gertrude Schultz* left port. She was twenty-three-year-old Adele Drucker whose disappearance had been reported by her aunt, Ella Abington. The young woman was the daughter of Hans Drucker who with his brother, Oscar, were the sons of a wealthy German steel producer. Hans had died and Oscar emigrated to America where he married Ella.

After Hans died, his two daughters, Adele and Ida went to America to stay with Abington who, by this time, was divorced from Oscar. He had remarried and gone to live in Chicago. Adele and Ida went to see him but he claimed they never arrived.

With this new information, private detective Hunter traced Adele to an address in St Louis. There he located a house which had been rented by Oscar Drucker in a false name. By the time Hunter called, the bird had flown but crucial evidence was found among the rubbish he left behind. This consisted of half-burned letters indicating that Adele and Ida had been invited to visit him.

Hunter eventually caught up with Oscar Drucker and confronted him with his suspicions. Drucker explained that he had been the victim of a family grievance whereby his brother left everything to his daughters. He resolved to lure the two young women into his sphere of influence in order to gain access to their inheritance. Adele suspected her uncle's motives so he shot her and Ida suffered the same fate. He put their bodies into the rail tanker carrying oil en route to the docks at Galveston.

The private detective arrested Drucker but his suspect escaped while they were travelling to St Louis by train to report to the authorities. But, in the end, Hunter got his man. A year later, he tracked him down to Tijuana in Mexico. Accompanied by a US Marshal, he confronted his quarry in a bar. Drucker pulled a gun, shot at Hunter and missed. The private eye then carried out rough justice by shooting Oscar Drucker dead.

Trail Of Blood

A farmer and his wife preparing to bale hay in their fields near Dunstable in Bedfordshire in August 1960, made a grisly discovery. In a shed on their property, they found the body of a man who had been shot dead. He was readily identified as Keith Arthur from the Army pay book in his jacket pocket.

It was apparent that Arthur had been killed elsewhere and his murderer had dumped the body in the farm shed hidden under some sacks. Keith Arthur was a local man, an ex-soldier, who worked as a factory machinist and dealt in secondhand cars. He had a reputation as a drinker and an idle boaster.

A murder investigation was mounted and local officers were put on alert. A woman police officer in the centre of Dunstable drew her colleagues' attention to a trail of blood which she had spotted in the street leading to a public WC. While the significance of this was being discussed, a woman from a nearby house explained that she was a dentist and it was quite common for her patients to spit out blood after an extraction. She advised the officers not to waste their time.

Shortly afterwards, the same policewoman spotted another trail of what looked like blood leading in an entirely different direction. The trail of what proved to be red paint led to a house in Edward Street and to some startling developments. A householder came forward to ask if the officers were investigating the recent murder. She told them that her daughter had witnessed the killing and pointed out the house where it had taken place.

The house indicated was occupied by Jack Day and his family. The neighbour's daughter, Patricia, babysat for them and played with the children. She told the police that on her last visit Mrs Day sent her on an errand and when she returned there was a strange man in the house. He was talking about a gold bracelet when Jack Day appeared on the scene. He asked the man what he was doing. The atmosphere was tense and Patricia prepared to leave when Day produced a gun, there was a shot and the man collapsed.

Other witnesses talked of seeing two men in the street, one of whom was injured and bleeding. His companion was supporting him. All attention was now focussed on Jack Day who owned an unlicensed .38 revolver.

When Day was questioned, he said, "You've got the wrong man." But forensic traces on his shoes and clothes confirmed his contact with the dead man. A search of the garage where he worked turned up a .38 revolver and a spent bullet. It came out that he had told a neighbour that he believed his wife was seeing another man and had vowed to kill him.

He made a statement to the effect that he had encountered Keith Arthur in his home and that his gun, which he made a practice of carrying with him at all times, discharged accidentally. When he realized that Arthur was wounded, he tried to get him to a doctor but he died before he could get him into his car. He panicked and decided to dump the body in the farm shed.

Jack Day was tried at Bedford Assizes in January 1961 and found guilty of murder. Sentenced to death he declined to seek a reprieve on the grounds that he did not commit the murder. He was duly executed.

Cowboys And Indians

Twenty-one-year-old Drummer James Ellis served with the Leicestershire Regiment and was based in barracks at Aldershot. In May 1923, he went missing and was believed to have deserted. Several months later, on 23 September, his body was found lying in bushes at Long Valley near Aldershot.

The body had been reduced to a skeleton but the manner of the young man's death was apparent. His wrists and ankles were bound with a drum-rope. There was a handkerchief stuffed in his mouth and an army greatcoat covered his head and face. This was held tightly in place with a belt secured around the head. Doctors had little difficulty determining that he had suffocated.

One of the dead man's friends, Albert Dearnley, made it known that Ellis had talked about emigrating to Australia. When questioned by the police, he was more forthcoming and admitted that the two had quarrelled over a girl. When he came to make a written statement, he accepted responsibility for Ellis' death.

His story was that he and Ellis had walked together on the common close to their barracks and decided to play a game of "Cowboys and Indians". This involved tying up Ellis with a drum-rope at his own request. The idea was supposed to be that he would wriggle free of his bonds and they would meet up later at their barracks. When Ellis failed to re-appear, Dearnley kept quiet, believing his friend had gone back to his home in Yorkshire.

Sir Bernard Spilsbury examined the remains and took the view that the binding and gagging had been done at the request of the victim but had been done so effectively as to ensure suffocation resulted. Dearnley was arrested and charged with murder.

The trial took place at Winchester Assizes. A great deal emerged about the relationship between Ellis and Dearnley. It seemed that although they were friends, there was also a history of quarrels. On the day of the "Cowboys and Indians" episode, Dearnley admitted that once he had trussed up Ellis, he gagged him as punishment for having insulted his girlfriend. He did not intend to kill him though, and his defence was one of manslaughter and of a game that got out of hand.

The jury took only thirty minutes to find Dearnley guilty of murder and he was sentenced to death. A public petition containing over 20,000 signatures failed but the emergence of new information led to the execution being halted. What had apparently been common knowledge at the Aldershot barracks was drawn to the attention of the Home Office. This concerned homosexual activities involving Ellis, Dearnley and a non-commissioned officer. The view was that Ellis had made Dearnley's life a misery with his sexual demands and threats of blackmail regarding the third man.

A reprieve was granted and Dearnley served nine years in prison before being released on parole in 1932.

A Callous And Evil Act

Victor Farrant was a man with a past when he met forty-five-year-old Glenda Hoskins, an accountant, at Haddy's nightclub in Portsmouth in the UK in August 1993. They began an intense affair, which was interrupted when he explained that he was due to go abroad to work in Belgium. In fact, he returned to Albany Prison on the Isle of Wight to resume his prison sentence.

Glenda Hoskins did not know when she met her silver-haired charmer that he was a convicted rapist whose attack on a woman in 1987 had earned him twelve years in prison. They kept up their relationship and, in due course, he confided in her the real reason for his absences. This resulted in a parting of the ways when Glenda said she would have no more to do with him.

Farrant served his time and achieved his release on 7 November 1995. His first instinct was to re-visit some of his old haunts and, by coincidence, he saw Glenda Hoskins. They renewed their affair, which proved to be somewhat stormy and short-lived. On Christmas Day, they split up once more.

Farrant reacted angrily and took out his rage on a forty-three-year-old prostitute. Working as a casual builder and armed with a chisel he made an assignation with Ann Fidler at her home in Eastleigh. When she declined some of his sexual demands, he subjected her to a savage beating, causing severe injuries that left her brain-damaged.

He was drawn again to Glenda Hoskins and insisted that he wanted to pick up where they had left off. She took the easy option of acquiescing to avoid confrontation. Their relationship followed the previous pattern; he was abusive, plaguing her with telephone calls and harassing behaviour.

Glenda made it plain to him that enough was enough and at this point their affair had completely broken down. On the evening of 7 February 1996, Farrant visited her at her home in Portsmouth and gave her letters in which he threatened to use violence if she did not comply with his wishes. The encounter ended with Glenda being drowned in her bath. Her body was found the next day by her daughter.

Farrant escaped to Belgium and a year passed before he was brought back to Britain to face charges. He was sent for trial at Winchester Crown Court in January 1998. Questions were asked why a convicted rapist, known to be a danger to the public, had been given his freedom with no supervision. The law in the UK has now been changed to ensure that this loophole could not be exploited in future.

The judge, sentencing Farrant after the jury returned its guilty verdict, referred to his "mercilous assault" on Ann Fidler which left her permanently damaged. Of the murder of Glenda Hoskins, he said, "It was a ruthless, callous and evil act, committed by a highly dangerous man," who showed "not a shred of remorse, compassion or pity." He sentenced Farrant to life imprisonment with the recommendation that he should never be released.

Sentenced To Life And Death

Twenty-nine-year-old Harrison Graham lived in a two-room apartment on the third floor of a house in Philadelphia in the US. His home was known as the "shooting gallery" on account of the drug addicts who regularly used the premises. It was well known to the police who made frequent visits.

On 9 August 1987, Graham was evicted from his apartment following complaints from neighbours about the smell. The occupant of the premises on the floor below was disturbed when blood began dripping through the ceiling.

A week later, Graham surrendered to the police and what they discovered almost defied description. In a filthy, stench-ridden room they found six bodies in varying states of decomposition. Some had been reduced to skeletons. A seventh body had been dismembered. The door of the room in which the corpses were stored had been nailed shut.

The bodies were those of female drug users who had been strangled. That some of the bodies had been reduced to skeletons indicated they had been in the house a considerable time. When he was questioned by the police, Graham confessed to killing the seven women.

Graham stood trial on seven counts of first-degree murder in February 1988. He appeared in the Common Pleas Court at Philadelphia, presided over by Judge Robert A. Latrone, sitting without a jury. The prosecution case was that Graham lured women to his apartment with the promise of drugs and strangled them during sex. He disposed of the corpses on an out-of-sight, out-of-mind basis by throwing them into his back room and nailing the door shut.

Graham's defence team argued that he did not go out targeting women to kill – they came to him. He was described as a "dumb, passive conduit", used by women who wanted access to drugs in his "shooting gallery". The fact that he lived in an apartment surrounded by decomposing corpses indicated a mentally and emotionally disturbed individual. The defence ran a "not guilty by reason of insanity" strategy. Reference was made to his traumatic childhood and mental impairment.

Graham sat through the trial showing little animation apart from playing with his finger puppets, small brown monkeys. The judge rejected the insanity defence and ruled that the defendant was guilty of first-degree murder. When it came to determining the penalty for his crimes, the judge explained at length that he had the right to request a jury to decide. Graham's only response was to ask the judge if he could have his "Monster Cookie" puppet back?

The defence argued against the death penalty, saying that Graham's life should be spared to allow scientists to study his behaviour and personality. Judge Latrone's sentence was unusual. He ruled that Graham should serve seven life sentences and six death penalties. This was a legal strategem which would ensure the convicted serial killer would remain in prison with no prospect of release. Thus, Graham was sentenced both to life and death in one judgment.

Searching For The Perfect Sex Slave

Gerald Armand Gallego was so reviled on account of his crimes that he was moved from prison in California, which was soft on the death penalty at the time, and taken across the border to neighbouring Nevada where it was believed he would get his "just deserts".

Gerald Gallego had a pedigree of violence. His father was executed in 1955 in Mississippi at the age of twenty-eight for murdering a prison guard. Gerald showed criminal tendencies at an early age and developed an insatiable sexual appetite. He committed his first offence at the age of thirteen, he was married at eighteen and had an incestuous relationship with his daughter. By the time he reached thirty-two, he had been married seven times.

In 1978, he bigamously married twenty-one-year-old Charlene Williams. She admired his macho personality and went along with his stated desire to find "the perfect sex slave". She helped him in his quest, luring young women into his clutches, which involved keeping them captive in the back of their van so that Gallego could rape them while Charlene kept watch in the cab.

Between 24 June 1979 and 17 July 1980, the Gallegos abducted six women in the Sacramento area. After being beaten and raped, the victims were driven to remote spots where they were shot dead and their bodies dumped. Some of the bodies were later discovered near Lovelock, a small town in Nevada.

On 2 November 1980, a young couple leaving a restaurant in Sacramento were accosted by the marauding Gallegos. Charlene ordered them at gunpoint into the van where Gallego was waiting. Craig Miller and Beth Sowers, both in their twenties, had been at a dance and a friend saw them with Charlene and thought the situation looked suspicious. He informed the police about the incident and officers interviewed Charlene at her parents' home, receiving evasive answers.

In the meantime, the body of Craig Miller was found in nearby Eldorado County with three gunshot wounds to the head. By now, Charlene had fled but detectives realized they were looking for both her and Gerald Gallego. They caught up with the pair in Omaha, Nebraska, and a few days later the body of Beth Sowers was discovered. She was found in a field with three gunshot wounds in the back of her head.

While Gallego proved to be an unco-operative prisoner, Charlene endulged in plea-bargaining and made a complete confession to their crimes. Her story was that she was Gallego's sex slave and felt compelled to find new slaves for him. The couple were returned to California to face trial where, in return for her testimony, Charlene was sentenced to sixteen years in prison. Gerald Gallego was sentenced to death for the murders of Miller and Sowers.

The fact that there had been no execution in California for seventeen years upset the citizens of Lovelock, Nevada, where some of Gallego's victims had been killed. In a deal between state officials, Gallego was removed from San Quentin and transferred across the border to Nevada.

When it became known that Lovelock could not afford to stage the trial, the public responded by contributing money. Thousands of citizens throughout the USA sent donations to the town clerk to ensure that Gallego would be tried in a state that supported the death penalty. A note attached to one offering said simply, "Hang the bastard by his toes".

Charlene and Gerald Gallego were tried at Lovelock for two murders. She received two prison sentences of sixteen years to run concurrently and he received a second death sentence. He was scheduled to die by lethal injection but, in 1977, a higher court decided Gallego was entitled to a new sentencing hearing due to an irregularity in earlier proceedings. Charlene was released in 1977 while he remained on Death Row awaiting the outcome of various appeals.

Red Light Killer

Poughkeepsie, a normally quiet college town in New York State, was terrorized by a serial killer in the late 1990s. The victims were mostly drawn from the red light district where they worked as prostitutes or frequented drug-dealing premises.

In October 1996 a thirty-year-old woman was reported missing and, in the ensuing months, seven other women disappeared. No bodies were discovered and there was no evidence of any crimes having been committed. There were though, common factors linking the missing women. First, there was the sex trade connection and the women were mostly in their twenties; second, all were of short, slim build, white with brown hair. Another consideration was that they lived independently and had few links with their families.

The police suspected a serial killer was at work and as the number of disappearances mounted, so tensions rose in Poughkeepsie and citizens became fearful. Investigators scrutinized offender files and they started to focus on a local man who had been charged with assault on a prostitute.

Francois Kendall, aged twenty-seven, worked as a hall monitor at a community school. His personal habits left something to be desired and the children called him "stinky". Kendall was co-operative with investigators and was willing to admit them to his home. He lived in a two-storey house with his parents and a sister. Officers found nothing incriminating, possibly being deterred by the state of the property, which was strewn with litter and distinguished by an offensive smell.

No action was taken until Kendall's name came up again in an assault complaint from a woman who said she had gone to his house and been abused. She talked her way out of a threatening situation and reported it to the police.

Kendall's home was searched and, braving the appalling smell, officers solved the mystery of what had happened to the missing women of Poughkeepsie. The remains of eight bodies were found in the house in various stages of decomposition. Some had been dismembered and put into plastic boxes or trash bags. Others had been stored in the attic and in the crawl space under the house.

Kendall had begun picking up women in downtown Poughkeepsie since 1996 and taking them home. Over a period of nearly two years, he took prostitutes back to his house and had sex with them in the garage. Some escaped his worst predations but others were strangled and dismembered with saws. The house was filthy, littered with discarded clothing, personal effects, old newspapers and used condoms. Neighbours thought the stench arising from Kendall's home was simply due to the filthy living conditions. No one suspected the real horrors to be found there.

Medical teams pieced together the human remains recovered from the house and made identification of the victims by means of tattoos and dental records. In due course, Kendall was charged with the murders of eight women and sent for trial. He was convicted of first-degree murder and sentenced to life imprisonment.

Six-Six-Six

Ambulance personnel called to a crime scene in Scotland found sixteen-year-old Luke Mitchell calmly sitting beside the mutilated body of his girlfriend.

Fourteen-year-old Jodi Jones lay dead in woods near Roan's Dyke at Dalkeith, Midlothian. She had been bludgeoned, strangled and mutilated with cuts to her breast and abdomen. Mitchell, who said he had found the body while out walking with his dog, busied himself with his mobile phone while the ambulance crew went about their routines.

Mitchell's indifference raised eyebrows among investigators and this hardened into suspicion as they learned more about the teenager. He came from a broken home and lived in a state bordering on squalor, not washing himself or his clothes regularly. He was interested in the occult and fascinated by knives and drugs. When questioned, he was defiant and showed no guilt over his girlfriend's death.

There was no evidence of sexual assault and no DNA evidence to provide a link between the victim and Mitchell, who by now was the main suspect. Information filtered through from his school about his fractious behaviour, defying teachers and exerting an unhealthy influence over other pupils. It also emerged that he had threatened a fellow pupil with a knife. His fascination with violence and satanism was well known.

Detectives questioning Mitchell found themselves up against a cunning and unemotional individual. A knife pouch found in Mitchell's possession bore the initials of the dead girl, JJ and the legend 666, the supposed mark of the "Great Beast". The teenager was a fan of American goth rocker Marilyn Manson who had an obsession with the notorious Black Dahlia murder case in California in 1947 (*see page 329*). The Black Dahlia, whose real name was Elizabeth Short, had been killed and mutilated in a way that had echoes in the death of Jodi Jones.

When it became known that Mitchell was planning on taking another girlfriend on holiday, the scenario in which he had a confrontation with Jodi became apparent. On 21 November 2003, police investigators reported to the prosecutor fiscal that Luke Mitchell was their prime suspect. The teenager was arrested in April 2004 and charged with murder.

He was tried at Edinburgh High Court in January 2005. The case against Mitchell was that he had a violent confrontation with Jodi Jones over his admission that he had another girlfriend. With no DNA evidence or murder weapon, the prosecution relied on circumstantial evidence. Reference was made to Mitchell's interest in the occult and satanism. In his summing-up, the judge, Lord Nimmo-Smith, said the resemblance between the injuries inflicted on Jodi Jones and those shown in Marilyn Manson's painting of the Black Dahlia could not be ignored. "I think," he said, "that you carried an image of the paintings in your memory when you killed Jodi."

Mitchell showed no emotion when the judge sentenced him to imprisonment for at least twenty years. In August 2009 doubts were expressed about the circumstantial nature of the evidence used to convict Mitchell and, in particular, questions regarding new DNA evidence.

Opportune Killer

A long-distance truck driver raped and strangled a nineteen-year-old French girl who asked him for a lift. He kept her body hidden in his cab while he travelled around the UK making deliveries and celebrating Christmas.

Celine Figard, an accountancy student, was making her way to Fordingbridge in the New Forest where she planned to spend the Christmas holiday. On 19 December 1995, she had travelled from Kent and reached the Chieveley service area on the M4 near Newbury. She was seen talking to the driver of a white Mercedes truck and enquiring about a possible lift to Salisbury.

When the young woman failed to turn up at Fordingbridge as expected, she was reported missing. The police mounted an intensive search for the driver of the white truck. They contacted road haulage contractors and began interviewing the owners of over 7,000 white Mercedes vehicles.

Celine's body was found on 29 December by a motorist who stopped at a lay-by on the A449 near Worcester. Her naked body had been dumped in the undergrowth. The search for the missing woman became a murder hunt and the breakthrough came when officers interviewed thirty-seven-year-old Stuart Morgan.

Morgan drove a white Mercedes truck and lived with his wife and son in Poole, Dorset. He denied being at the Chieveley service area and refused to give a DNA sample. Examination of his mobile phone records indicated that he had been at Chieveley on the day Celine Figard disappeared. Morgan was arrested in February 1996 and a driver picked him out on an identity parade. Once his truck was examined and his home searched, his denials collapsed. His DNA matched that found in his truck cab and the contents of his victim's rucksack were found hidden in his garden. The garage contained the blood-soaked mattress that he had removed from his vehicle.

To all intents and purposes, Morgan was a respectable individual, although some who knew him described him as a womanizer and petty criminal. His occupation as a truck driver gave him the opportunity to travel to different places on legitimate business. His usual routine was to leave his home on Sunday and return at the end of the week. He was leading a double-life as a family man in Poole and an itinerant philanderer.

Morgan was tried for murder at Worcester Crown Court in October 1996. He denied harming Celine Figard although he admitted that they had sexual intercourse which he claimed was consensual. The prosecution had a case in which the victim was seen leaving Chieveley in Morgan's white Mercedes truck on the last day she was known to be alive. He had raped and strangled her and then concealed her body in his vehicle, driving about his normal business before parking outside his home where he spent Christmas. When the festive holiday ended, he drove up to Worcester where he dumped the body.

Mr Justice Latham told Morgan he considered him a dangerous man. The jury brought in a unanimous guilty verdict and the defendant was sentenced to life imprisonment. The police said they were also looking at two unsolved murders of women whose bodies had been found close to motorways in the Midlands.

Small Change

A Canadian former soldier adopted an unusual criminal scheme that could hardly be described as a money-maker. Herbert McAuliffe set out with the single-minded aim of counterfeiting his national currency, choosing the Canadian half-dollar coin as the object of his forger's skill.

Having served in the Canadian armed services during the Second World War and achieving non-commissioned rank, McAuliffe also acquired workshop skills that might have been useful to him in a legitimate civilian occupation. He chose instead to use his talents in another direction and, following his dishonourable discharge from the army on charges of theft, he prepared for a career in crime. Perhaps in anticipation of trouble ahead, he equipped himself with a Thompson sub-machine gun and several automatic pistols.

Settling in Windsor, Ontario, he rented garage premises as a workshop, telling the owner that he was working on weapons research for the government. In order to fulfil his counterfeiting plans, McAuliffe needed some precision machinery such as lathes and die presses. His answer to the problem of raising funds was to rob a few filling stations and grocery outlets. By these means, he funded his research into the process of making fifty-cent pieces that would pass as genuine currency. Learning the art of the counterfeiter more or less from scratch, he perfected a method of using base metal die-stamped and finished with silver electro-plating. Thus, he became the first person successfully to forge Canadian half-dollar coins.

In order to test his coins, he took a supply across the US border to a gambling joint in Detroit, which accepted Canadian currency. The McAuliffe half-dollars were accepted with no problems. Emboldened by this success, he determined to make more coins but began to realize that his operating costs were too high – in fact, it cost him forty cents to make each fifty-cent coin.

His answer to this dilemma was to acquire funds to buy new counterfeiting machinery by robbing a bank. He selected a branch of the Imperial Bank of Canada in the small town of Langton, Ontario. Having stolen a car and armed himself with his Thompson sub-machine gun, he walked into the bank and in classic gangster style told the counter clerk, "This is a stick-up."

While customers recoiled in horror he ordered the clerk to open the vault and scooped over $20,000 into a holdall. He then ordered the customers to move into the vault so that he could make his getaway. His mistake, as it turned out, was not securing the vault door.

No sooner had McAuliffe made his getaway than two bank customers were in hot pursuit. He stopped his car brandishing his Tommy gun and directed bursts of fire at his pursuers, killing both of them outright. If he had a plan, he now abandoned it, leaving the stolen car and proceeds of his robbery behind. The bank robber and now murderer fled into the countryside where he became the target of a large manhunt.

After three days on the run, McAuliffe was discovered holed up in a farm building. He was put on trial for murder at Simcoe and, in due course, was convicted of double murder, for which he received a death sentence. This was carried out on 19 December 1950. What drove him to counterfeiting remained a mystery, especially as the rewards were so small but, in the end, it was his bungled bank robbery that sealed his fate.

Budapest To Vienna Express

Sylvestre Matushka was a Hungarian businessman in Budapest after the First World War. He had served in the army during the war and, on release, developed a number of business interests including a delicatessen. He also dabbled in the post-war black market and, in 1927, was charged with fraud and acquitted.

This seemed to be a turning point in his life. He moved to Vienna where he began to buy explosives and made several attempts to derail trains. On 1 January 1931, he tried unsuccessfully to derail the Vienna-Passau express and, later in the year, succeeded in overturning several carriages of the Vienna-Berlin express, injuring sixteen people.

He finally made his mark on 12 September 1932 when he set off an explosion that derailed the Budapest-Vienna express as it crossed a viaduct at Bia-Torbagy. In the chaos that followed, Matuschka smeared himself with blood and lay down among the victims. Twenty-two people lost their lives that day.

Following this tragic incident, Matushka sued Hungarian Railways for compensation because of alleged injuries. In the course of their enquiries, investigators found that he had not been a passenger on the train. Suspecting a fraudulent claim, investigators visited Matuschka at his home where they found detailed maps of rail networks in Holland, France and Italy.

When questioned, Matuschka said he had begun attacking trains when the railway authorities failed to implement a safety procedure he had invented. His real reasons were more deep-seated, as it transpired later in court. He was put on trial in June 1932 in Vienna.

Matuschka mounted an insanity defence based on a childhood incident at a fairground when a hypnotist put the idea of crashes in his mind. His antics in court seemed designed to support his insanity plea as he wept, ranted and trembled by turns. The prosecutor argued that Matuschka's motive lay in a sadistic impulse. The jury could not agree a verdict and a second trial was called for.

At the second hearing, incriminating evidence was brought out concerning the rail maps found in Matuschka's home which had been annotated in red ink, apparently planning future disasters. His response was to exploit his insanity defence by offering prayers and then claiming he had been instructed to kill by a spirit voice. This availed him nothing and the jury found him guilty. On 20 November 1934, he was sentenced to death. There seems some doubt over whether he was hanged or had his sentence commuted to life imprisonment.

Butcher's Boy

Penelope Mitchell married young to escape from an unhappy home. She and her husband, Alan, seemed a contented couple with two children and a home in Paarl, in South Africa's wine-growing region. But underneath the serene exterior lurked unfulfilled passions in so far as Alan Mitchell, approaching middle age, had lost interest in sex, to the frustration of his wife.

In 1981, tragedy struck the Mitchell household when Alan was murdered, practically on his own doorstep. Penelope heard the car door slam when Alan returned home and left the car on the driveway. When he did not enter the house she went out to investigate and found him lying on the path with a grievous head wound. He died in hospital from what doctors concluded was an injury inflicted with an axe.

He appeared to have been struck down by someone lying in wait who disappeared immediately after the blow was struck, taking the murder weapon with him. The strength and height needed to inflict the wound suggested that the assailant was a man. Robbery did not appear to be the motive and Alan Mitchell had no known enemies.

When detectives began to delve more closely into the Mitchells' domestic life, they found that Penelope had a reputation as a hypnotist. She held regular sessions in her home which, to all intents and purposes, were light-hearted affairs.

When the police received an anonymous tip-off suggesting they made enquiries of the local butcher, the investigation took a different turn. The butcher proved to be both elderly and small in stature and not likely to be the axe murderer. His delivery boy, though, was a vigorous and strong young man. Noel Hatting was invited to answer a few questions.

The delivery boy admitted that he had been having sex with Penelope Mitchell at times when her husband and children were away. He claimed that she had seduced him. This explained why none of the neighbours had reported seeing any strangers in the vicinity. Noel Hatting was a familiar figure doing his delivery rounds.

He had baulked when Penelope suggested murdering her husband to clear the way for their otherwise furtive lovemaking. Hatting maintained that on the day Alan Mitchell was killed, he had been hypnotized by Penelope and found himself standing outside the house holding a hatchet with Alan lying wounded on the ground. He said Penelope told him he had killed her husband while he claimed to have no memory of the event.

Penelope had a different version of events. She claimed that Hatting made the running and that she had tried to end their affair. She alleged that he threatened to inform her husband about their relationship. On the day of the murder, she went out to welcome her returning husband and found Noel Hatting, bloody axe in hand, standing over his stricken body.

When thieves and lovers fall out, there are always two different stories. Their trial jury believed they had acted in concert and both knew what they were doing. It was made clear that someone acting under hypnosis would not commit an act that they instinctively found abhorrent. The implication was that Noel Hatting fully understood what he was doing and that Penelope had provided the murder weapon. The trial jury in January 1982 convicted them of murder and they were sentenced to fifteen years in prison.

"... I Can't Pull Away"

Adele Kohr, a young nurse driving home to East Islip on Long Island, New York State, on 20 July 1970, was bothered by a car which was tailgaiting her. Sensing danger, she drove faster to pull ahead of the following vehicle but she could not dislodge the driver. When he drew alongside, she realized she was in trouble.

With great presence of mind, Adele pulled a notebook from her bag and, while driving with one hand on the steering wheel, scribbled a note with her free hand. "A man in a car pulled alongside me . . . he wants me to stop . . . he is following me in the same lane and I can't pull away . . . doing sixty-five . . ." She described the driver as a hippy type wearing a beard, glasses and a blue shirt. She even noted the model, colour and part registration number of his car.

When she was less than a mile from home, the driver succeeded in forcing her off the road. He blocked her possible escape route by backing up in front of her car. As he approached, she made one last scribbled entry in the pad beside her noting that he was wearing dark-coloured trousers.

Adele's car was found abandoned by the roadside with the engine still running and the headlights on. Her notebook lay on the passenger's seat. Her body was found next day some twenty miles away. She had been beaten, raped and strangled; in a final brutal act, her killer had driven over her body.

Crime scene investigators realized that the notes made by the murdered woman provided the likely key to the identity of her killer. Using her brief description of the car that pursued her, they made a short list of car owners and began the process of elimination.

Enquiries led to the female owner of a green Pontiac Tempest who lived in Islip and, through her, to Robert Meyer, her husband. He broadly corresponded to the description Adele had written down of a bearded individual wearing glasses. Meyer did not demur at being taken to police headquarters for questioning, and before he reached the interview room, admitted that he was sick and needed help.

Detectives discovered that Meyer had previous convictions for attacks on women, including the kidnapping, robbing and raping of a young woman a few weeks previously. Meyer was sent for trial and pleaded a defence of temporary insanity. He was judged guilty of second-degree murder and sentenced to twenty-five years to life imprisonment.

Adele Kohr's quick thinking under pressure failed to save her life but it did help to bring her killer to justice.

". . . I Think You Will Find My Wife Dead"

The difference between suicidal and homicidal strangulation stood between a death sentence and life imprisonment.

In the early hours of 21 November 1931, Peter Queen, a Glasgow bookmaker, appeared at a police station in the city and said to the duty officer, "Go to 539 Dumbarton Road, I think you will find my wife dead." Twenty-one-year-old Chrissie Gall, his common-law wife, was found lying in bed with a ligature made from a clothesline around her neck. She was dead from strangulation.

An immediate source of controversy was what exactly Queen told the police. He claimed to have said, "Don't think I killed her." The police version of what he was alleged to have said was, "I think I have killed her." Within hours of the discovery of the body, Queen was charged with murder.

Peter Queen was the son of a bookmaker in a family of six children. His father hired Chrissie Gall as a nursemaid. She and Queen fell for each other, but the young woman's addiction to alcohol was a burden. He tried to break her of the habit and they moved in together, living as man and wife.

Chrissie was disturbed by her unmarried status, which she referred to as "living in sin" and was upset about deceiving her family. She increasingly found solace in drink and threatened several times to commit suicide. At the beginning of November, visitors to their house noticed that the coat peg behind the kitchen door was broken. Curious, they asked Queen about it and he said that Chrissie had tried to hang herself.

On 19 November, Chrissie met her brother and they drank considerable quantities of beer and whisky. The following day Chrissie stayed at home and when Queen returned from work, she was quite drunk. Her in-laws came round and advised Queen to fetch a doctor. They left at about 11 p.m., no doctor was available and a few hours later Queen reported that Chrissie was dead.

The dead woman lay in her bed with the sheets pulled up around her. The ligature around her neck was plainly visible and secured with a half-knot. The room was remarkably well ordered. There were no signs of a struggle; nothing seemed to have been disturbed and Chrissie was still wearing her night bonnet. Post-mortem examination confirmed death by strangulation with sufficient force to break the cricoid cartilage. Two pathologists concluded that she had been murdered.

Peter Queen was put on trial at Glasgow in January 1932. He denied saying the words attributed to him by the police. The prosecutor made much of the fact that he had not attempted to loosen the cord around Chrissie's neck, did not take her pulse and did not call for a doctor. Queen had two leading forensic experts on his defence team; Sir Sydney Smith and Sir Bernard Spilsbury. They believed the death was suicidal, because in their opinion, there was little evidence to support homicidal strangulation.

Suicidal strangulation is relatively uncommon but cases have been recorded even with a ligature tied in a half-knot. The key issue is whether the knot is strong enough to hold the ligature after consciousness is lost. In homicidal strangulation, injuries to the neck are usually extensive as assailants apply more force than is necessary to cause death. Sydney Smith, writing in his memoirs, wryly remarked, ". . . in the only case where Spilsbury and I were in pretty complete agreement, the jury believed neither of us."

The jury returned a majority guilty verdict but added a recommendation to mercy. A death sentence was passed on Peter Queen but this was later commuted to one of life imprisonment. Sydney Smith said that when a person is found strangled, there is a strong presumption that it is murder. He thought there were very few indications of homicide in the circumstances of Chrissie Gall's death and believed that, although it was unusual, she had strangled herself.

When he was released from his life sentence, Peter Queen returned to his job as a bookmaker in Glasgow. He died in 1958 but he had been spared a death sentence, and in a strange way, justice was served.

War Of The Clinics

For two decades, the French city of Marseilles has been consumed with what the press have called "The War of the Clinics". A sequence of events has brought together doctors and the criminal underworld in a combination of avarice and murder.

Crisis point was reached on 16 January 1990 when the Mayor of the city's seventh district, Dr Jean-Jacques Peschard, was shot dead in his car after dining at a restaurant. Peschard, a prominent surgeon, was part of a syndicate in the lucrative private health sector.

The doctor was known to the police for his part in the disappearance of his girlfriend in 1984. Christine Barras worked as his clinical assistant and they lived together in his house. The couple had disagreements over their future and Peschard tried to dump Christine. Her family were aware of the arguments and she told her mother that if Peschard threw her over she would tell the world about his money-laundering activities. She claimed to have smuggled money for him into France from Switzerland.

Christine's family became concerned when their attempts to talk to her on the telephone were blocked by Peschard. His excuse was that she was unwell. Eventually, her mother was admitted to his house and she immediately realized something was wrong. The doctor appeared unnerved and he told her that Christine had moved out. This was strange because she had not taken her make-up and jewellery and, most important, bearing in mind that she was diabetic, she had left her insulin behind.

Christine's car was found by the police on 11 March 1984 in one of the poorer parts of the city. Peschard gave some elaborate explanations, saying that Christine had talked about joining a religious sect. Then he said she had been kidnapped.

In an extraordinary twist to the story, Christine's sister, Beatrice, took a job working for Peschard in his clinic. She used her position to question the doctor in unguarded moments. What she heard only increased her suspicions that he was involved in Christine's disappearance. In October

1985, investigators dug up Peschard's garden but nothing was found. Indeed, Christine was never found and enquiries were dropped in 1989. Nine months later, Dr Peschard was gunned down by an unknown assassin.

Police had made a connection between the death of Peschard with that of another doctor earlier. In May 1988, Dr Léonce Mout, director of the Polyclinique du Nord, was murdered late at night when he went to his car parked near the clinic. His way was blocked by another car and a gunman shot him through the windscreen, killing him with two bullets. The murder of Dr Peschard nearly two years later was almost identical in its execution.

The police arrested an Algerian businessman, Jean Chouraqui, who had been negotiating with Dr Mout to buy his clinic and add it to the four he already owned. After Peschard's murder, a man called Marcel Long came forward and said he had been the gunman's driver. He named Roger Memmoli as the hitman and said they had been instructed by Chouraqui. When questioned, Memmoli confessed to killing both doctors.

Fears of an influx of drug money have not been substantiated, although it was rumoured that General Manuel Noriego, former dictator of Panama, had connections at a high level in the civil administration of Marseilles. Meanwhile, Memmoli, self-confessed assassin remains in police custody as murky rumours continue to circulate.

". . . Order To Execute"

A drifter who travelled on the French rail network without buying a ticket confessed to killing three women, two of them on trains.

When Isabel Peake, a twenty-year-old university student, boarded a train at Limoges on 13 October 1999, she was beginning her return to England after an exchange visit in France. The overnight express passed through Chateauroux on its way north. It was near that town that Isabel Peake's semi-clothed body was found beside the rail tracks; she had evidently been thrown from the moving train.

The investigation into the young woman's death was sloppy. The train compartment used by Isabel Peake was cleaned before the police mounted a forensic investigation and it was over a week later before they decided a murder had taken place. Several witnesses described a man of North African origin wearing a baseball cap back-to-front seen boarding the train at Limoges. He was one of two passengers on that journey travelling without a ticket.

Police issued a photofit image of this individual and began a manhunt for him. The search was given fresh impetus in December when the body of Corinne Caillaux was discovered in a toilet on the sleeper service from Calais to Ventimiglia. She had been stabbed fifteen times. A blood-soaked baseball cap was found on the train and ticket inspectors identified a male passenger travelling without a ticket.

A few days later, the body of Emilie Bazin, who had been missing since October, was found hidden in a cellar under a heap of coal at a house in Amiens. She was the former girlfriend of a man identified as Sid Ahmed Rezala who had stayed at the house. Rezala was picked up in Lisbon on 11 January 2000 as a result of a phone-tapping exercise. He was held in custody by the Portuguese authorities pending a request for his extradition to France.

Twenty-one-year-old Rezala, described by the French police as a lawless drifter, had been released from prison in May 1999 following a conviction for assault. He lost his appeal against extradition to France, and in May 2000, made a confession in an interview published in a French magazine. He admitted killing the three women and claimed he saw flashes that he interpreted as "an order to execute".

When he murdered Corinne Caillaux he said he had been drinking whisky and taking drugs. He described his actions as "pure madness" and said he killed his ex-girlfriend, Emilie Bazin, to revenge her boyfriend. Again, he said he saw a "flash", like an order that has to be carried out. Rezala said he had tried to commit suicide several times because he felt unwanted as a person.

On 29 June 2000, Rezala achieved his wish when he set

fire to the mattress in his cell and suffocated. He had been admitted to the psychiatric wing of the prison where he was being held in Lisbon. In letters to his parents and friends he said he wanted to end his life and he did not want to cause suffering. He was quoted in a magazine article as saying he had lost everything in life and his only escape was to return to his creator.

"Why Should I Want To Kill My Wife?"

A woman dying of a terminal illness in a sanatorium drew attention to the actions of her husband who she suspected was poisoning her in order to speed up her demise.

Marjery Radford had been ill for seven years with tuberculosis and was nursed at a sanatorium in Godalming, Surrey in the UK. She was visited regularly by her father and her husband, Frederick, who worked as a laboratory technician at nearby St Thomas' Hospital.

Frederick was in the habit of taking his wife various food and drinks to stimulate her appetite and provide an alternative to the sanatorium's catering. He sometimes gave things to his father-in-law to take in, including soft drinks and fruit.

A few days before she died, Marjery Radford had a visit from a woman friend in whom she confided some of her concerns. She said she thought she was being poisoned because she had experienced vomiting after eating some of the things brought to her by her husband. Referring to a fruit pie she had eaten, she said, "I am sure it has been poisoned." She had been vomiting several times a day.

Mrs Radford asked her friend to send the fruit pie to Scotland Yard for analysis. Her wishes were carried out but not to the letter. What her friend did was to send the fruit pie to the superintendent of the sanatorium with an explanation in a following letter. This course of action was to have a dramatic outcome.

Unaware of the provenance of the fruit pie that had landed on his desk, the superintendent took it home, thinking some well-intentioned person had sent it to him for his enjoyment.

After eating a few mouthfuls, he was ill with vomiting and became extremely unwell. He lost no time in calling the police.

Marjery Radford died on 12 April 1949, the same day that analysts found arsenic in the pie eaten by the sanatorium's superintendent. Post-mortem examination of the dead woman showed that her body, already weakened by illness, was riddled with arsenic.

When he was interviewed by the police, Frederick Radford asked, "Why should I want to kill my wife? I knew she was going to die anyway." He pointed out that he was a laboratory technician and would not have been so foolish as to use arsenic as it was easy to detect. He challenged the police to charge him and let a jury decide the outcome.

Radford had asked a very good question, but his motive probably lay in his desire to speed up his wife's demise because he was having an affair with another woman. But for Marjery's suspicions that she was being poisoned, her eventual death would have been put down to tuberculosis and her murder would have gone undetected.

The day after he was questioned by the police, Frederick Radford was found dead in bed. He had taken his own life, opting for fast-acting prussic acid (cyanide) rather than a lingering death with arsenic.

Bearing A Grudge

The irony of a military marksman who trained US soldiers to kill, turning his weapon on fellow workers and killing fourteen of them, was not lost on the US anti-gun lobby.

On 20 August 1986, just before seven on a hot summer's day as rush-hour traffic began to build up, Patrick Sherrill reported for work. He entered the post-office building at Edmond, Oklahoma, where he was a part-time employee. He was dressed in his postal worker's uniform and he joined eighty colleagues in the building. Then he locked the exit doors before producing two .45 calibre automatic pistols and starting to shoot.

He first shot dead his supervisor at close range and began pursuing people who, as one eyewitness described it later, "scattered like flies". He chased them through the various work-stations and booths, firing as he went.

FBI and police SWAT teams surrounded the building but it was two hours before they entered the premises. They found fourteen dead postal workers and also Sherrill's body with three handguns and a mailbag full of ammunition lying close by. His final act had been to kill himself.

As reports of the shooting reached the news networks, the tragedy was described as the third worst one-day massacre in US history. Comparison was made with the McDonald's restaurant shootings in 1984 and the killings at the University of Texas in 1966. As always on these occasions, the bitter controversy over gun ownership was debated.

The Oklahoma shootings seemed to have a clear motive. It appeared that on the previous day, Sherrill had been warned by his supervisor that his work was unsatisfactory and he was threatened with dismissal. He had been suspended before and there was a history of disciplinary problems.

Sherrill, aged forty-four, was a marksman in the Oklahoma National Guard and had visited Britain a few weeks before the massacre to instruct soldiers in the use of the M16 rifle. As a member of the National Guard's shooting team, Sherrill was permitted to carry weapons for competition purposes. He checked out two .45 handguns at different times and 300 rounds of ammunition.

Following the massacre, the National Coalition to Ban Handguns commented that, but for the accessibility of handguns, Sherrill's disagreement with his supervisor might have been settled with a fist fight instead of the loss of fifteen lives.

Ronald Reagan, US President at the time, was not in favour of stricter gun controls. In 1985 the House of Representatives had voted to ease restrictions on gun control. This was against a background of an annual death toll using handguns of 21,000 shootings, including 8,000 homicides and 12,000 suicides. Patrick Sherrill, while described as a loner, had no history of mental instability and there was no evidence that he had been drinking or taking drugs. As events unfolded it seemed he was a man with a grudge.

Sinister And Deadly

Phil Spector, the 1960s music producer, was found guilty of murder by a Los Angeles court six years after the crime was committed at his rock-star mansion, the "Pyrenees Castle".

On 3 February 2003 Spector's chauffeur drove him to a local nightspot. There, he talked to the actor, Lana Clarkson, and invited her back to his mansion for a nightcap. They watched the James Cagney movie, *Kiss Tomorrow Goodbye*, which proved to be prophetic.

While sitting in his employer's car, the chauffeur thought he heard a gunshot from within the house. When he went to investigate, he encountered Spector who was holding a gun and declaring, "I think I killed somebody." The chauffeur called the police who found forty-year-old Lana Clarkson slumped in a chair, dead from a gunshot fired through her mouth. A .36 revolver lay on the floor.

Spector appeared to be disorientated and when he resisted police attempts to question him, he was felled by a charge from a tasergun. He was arrested and charged with murder. In an e-mail to a friend, he described Lana Clarkson's death as "accidental suicide".

Investigators discovered that Spector was obsessed with guns and owned many weapons. His behaviour at times was described as outlandish, possibly due to the effects of medication, lack of sleep and general depression.

Phil Spector was born in New York and moved to Los Angeles when still a teenager. He formed a band called the "Teddy Bears" and began a successful musical career. In the early 1960s he made his mark with his innovatory pop music productions and his Wall of Sound. His career began to decline in the next decade and his behaviour grew more eccentric. He had been married three times and survived a serious car crash in 1974.

When in 2007 Spector was tried for Lana Clarkson's murder, the prosecutor described him as "Sinister and Deadly". He was alleged to have put a loaded revolver into his victim's mouth and killed her with a single shot. He pleaded not guilty and his defence emphasized the lack of motive. When the jury failed to reach a unanimous verdict, the judge declared a mistrial and Spector was released on bail of one million dollars.

A retrial was ordered in 2009 when he again denied murder and his defence claimed that Clarkson was depressed and shot herself. Several women with whom he had been acquainted testified about his erratic behaviour and incidents when he confronted them with guns to reinforce his wishes. Spector spent millions on lawyers but refused to give testimony himself. He did though find time to tell a magazine that Lana "kissed the gun" before using it on herself.

The trial judge rejected demands to call another mistrial and on 13 April 2009, Spector was found guilty of second-degree murder. He was sentenced to life imprisonment with a minimum term of nineteen years.

A Leg Of Pork

On 23 November 1776, Cheshire farmer Newman Gartside was out on his land checking the boundaries. At a local beauty spot with a stream running close by he noticed something floating in the water. He fished it out and determined that it was a woman's garment stained with blood.

Helped by the young lad with him, he delved further into the water and to their horror retrieved a woman's head. A constable was sent for and further searches were made, resulting in the discovery of more body parts including an arm and a leg. These appeared to have been disarticulated with some skill.

The question everyone was asking as the news of the discovery spread concerned the identity of the woman. A shopkeeper from the nearby village of Astbury volunteered the information that a young woman dressed in blue had been in her shop. She knew her as Annie Smith, a singer of ballads who was supposed to perform at Congleton Fayre on 20 November but failed to turn up. The fact that copies of ballads had been found among the clothing dredged up from the stream, along with the body parts, confirmed the identification.

Gossip and various theories tended to focus on Sam Thorley, a man in his fifties who was thought by some to be simple-minded and observed to have a quick temper. He was also a butcher. More information came in from public sources including the discovery of blood on a stile leading to a cottage where Thorley had once lodged. One of the locals took on the role of sleuth and visited widow Hannah Oakes who lived in the cottage.

The widow related that Thorley had visited her on the night of the murder, furiously knocking on her door. He was wearing his trademark butcher's apron and his clothes were wet. He explained that he had fallen in the stream. From the folds of his apron, he produced a joint of meat, which he put on the kitchen table, declaring that it was a piece of pork. He urged Hannah Oakes to cook it straight away. She demurred, believing that it looked "off".

Thorley reappeared at the cottage the next day when he cooked the meat himself and sat down to eat it. The result was that he fetched it up, confirming the widow's opinion that it was indeed "off". She did not throw it away but kept it in store to render it down for the fat.

The amateur sleuth, now hot on the trail, examined the remains of the meat and thought it had the shape of a human leg muscle. A surgeon who scrutinized the flesh determined that it was of human origin.

Thorley appeared at an inquest held in Congleton Town Hall when Hannah Oakes, the star witness, retold her story. The jury returned a verdict of wilful murder against Sam Thorley and he was arrested and taken into the cells at Chester Castle. After spending four months in custody he was brought before the Chester Assizes in April 1777 and made a confession that sealed his fate. He said that he had been told human flesh was similar in taste to pork and decided to put theory into practice.

Thorley was sentenced to death and was hanged before a large crowd on 10 April 1777. Part of his punishment was that his dead body would be hung from a gibbet. The butcher, in death, provided carrion for the crows.

Not A Friend

John Tawell survived transportation to Australia as a young man where he established a successful business and returned to England as a man deserving respect. He aspired to be a Quaker and adopted The Friends' form of dress. He had a house in Berkhamsted, married and gave to charity.

But the would-be Quaker had a secret; he had made Sarah Habler his mistress. He set her up with lodgings in Paddington in London and he paid her maintenance. For her part, Sarah did everything to protect Tawell's reputation. She changed her name, cut herself off from her friends and family and moved from place to place. In due course, however, she became pregnant and thus an embarrassment to her lover.

Tawell decided to eliminate his mistress by getting her to drink stout laced with poison. In September 1843, Sarah, now living in Slough, was taken ill but survived. He made another attempt to kill her in January 1845 and prepared an elaborate alibi for himself. He was seen in a businessman's club in London and made a show of leaving his overcoat there. His next move was to make a dash to Paddington railway station where he took a train to Slough. He took some stout for Sarah, having laced it with prussic acid (cyanide), made a brief visit and hurried back to London by train. He arrived in time to retrieve his overcoat from the club at about 9 p.m., no doubt congratulating himself on having an alibi that placed him in London at the time Sarah Habler was succumbing to poisoning.

Unfortunately for him, a person wearing Quaker dress was seen leaving Sarah's house shortly before she was found dead. This description was telegraphed to the stationmaster at Paddington who related it to the police. Detectives observed his arrival by train from Slough and followed him to a coffee shop and thence to his lodgings.

When he was questioned the next day, Tawell denied having been in Slough and said he had not left London. His lies were easily disproved and he was arrested, the first murder suspect to be detained by means of a telegram. Enquiries showed that Tawell had bought a quantity of prussic acid on the morning of the murder from a chemist in Bishopsgate.

A post-mortem examination confirmed that Sarah Habler had been poisoned with prussic acid. Tawell's rather inadequate defence was that the poison had come from eating apples, the pips of which contained cyanide. He then claimed that she had taken her own life. A guilty verdict was returned at his trial for murder and he was sentenced to death.

He left a confession in which he stated his motive for poisoning Sarah was his constant dread that his association with her would become known and damage his exemplary character. He was executed in March 1845.

A Dying Declaration

Louisa Jane Taylor married a man considerably older than herself and became a widow at the age of thirty-six. In the spring of 1882, she moved into rented accommodation but was soon in trouble over rent arrears. As she sank deeper into debt, she visited friends who lived in Plumstead in south-east London.

Mary and William Tregillis were both in their eighties and Mary was not in the best of health. Louisa asked if she could stay with them while she sorted out her life following the loss of her husband. She intimated that she had come into money and planned to move into a new house.

The quid pro quo was that Louisa would act as nurse to Mary and indeed she slept in the same room as the old lady whom she called mother. About this time, Louisa began buying supplies of sugar of lead (lead acetate), a poisonous substance that also had a medicinal use in the treatment of skin rashes.

The purchases of sugar of lead coincided with a deterioration of Mary Tregillis' illness. Suspicion of Louisa also began to grow in William Tregillis' mind when he noticed that some of their possessions had disappeared. More significantly, the debt-ridden Louisa had designs on his pension money.

With his wife's health declining, Tregillis decided to call in the doctor who had been in regular attendance but now began to suspect poisoning. He involved the police and Louisa was asked some serious questions once it was known she had been buying sugar of lead from the local pharmacist.

On 10 October 1882, as Mary Tregillis was too ill to attend the magistrate's court, the proceedings were held in the sitting room of her home. Directing the focus of attention at Louisa she said, "I was always in good health till she came." Two weeks later, she was dead. In the meantime, Louisa had been charged with attempted murder and robbery.

Louisa Taylor, now charged with murdering Mary Tregillis, was tried at the Old Bailey in December 1882. The victim's deathbed statement was allowed in evidence and it was clear from this that she had been given white powder in her medicine every night. When she complained that the medicine made her throat burn, she was told it was good for her.

Having heard the evidence, the jury retired and came back within twenty minutes to deliver a guilty verdict. Mr Justice Stephen, describing Louisa Taylor's crime as a "treacherous murder", sentenced her to death. Still maintaining her innocence, she was executed at Maidstone on 2 January 1883.

Slept Like A Baby

Twenty-five-year-old Gerald Thompson worked as a toolmaker at a factory in Peoria, Illinois. Between November 1934 and June 1935, he committed sixteen rapes and possibly more. His technique was to pick up lone women and drive them out into the countryside. He kept his victim captive in his car by ensuring she received an electric shock if she touched the door handles. When he was ready he cut the victim's clothes off and tied her to the front of the car where he raped her. He took photographs of himself with the victim by means of a camera equipped with a self-timer.

In June 1935, rape turned to murder when Thompson picked up Mildred Hallmark as she waited at a bus stop near Peoria. It was a wet night and he offered her a lift. He drove to Springfield Cemetery where he parked his car intending to embark on his usual rape routine. But he had reckoned without his victim's fierce resistance. She fought him off and in the struggle he beat her and stabbed her. He left her, raped and dead, in the cemetery.

Peoria was shocked at this latest outrage and an anonymous tip off from an earlier rape victim led investigators to Thompson. He lived with his grandmother and a search of his room revealed the scope of his activities as a practised rapist. Detectives found a horde of obscene photographs featuring Thompson with his various victims. There was also a diary in which he had recorded the identities of the women he assaulted, together with descriptions of what had taken place. Blood-stained clothing was discovered which irrefutably linked him to the murder of Mildred Hallmark.

Following his arrest, there was an outburst of public anger and mobs demonstrated in Peoria threatening to string him up. Prior to his trial, Thompson had to be moved to a secret location to ensure his safety. There was extensive press coverage of his trial and his boast made to a friend that he averaged better than one rape a week for a year was revealed. He was also alleged to have said that after killing Mildred, he "slept like a baby".

Thompson's trial at Peoria was a formality. The evidence against him, most of which he had provided, including a confession, ensured his conviction. He was sentenced to death and the only question was whether he would reach the electric chair before the lynch mobs got their hands on him. The man who liked to confine his victims with electricity felt the full force of the massive charges sent through his body when he sat in the electric chair at Joliet State Penitentiary on 15 October 1935.

"We Shall Overcome"

Stanley "Tookie" Williams was a former Los Angeles gang leader and convicted murderer who spent twenty-four years in Death Row at San Quentin Prison. He won international recognition for his stand against violence and was judged by many to have earned redemption.

"Tookie" Williams was co-founder of the Crips gang in Los Angeles in 1971. Gang members were blamed for scores of killings in urban wars disputing control of the streets and drug business. He was convicted of killing a store clerk during a robbery in 1979 and, several days later, of killing three people in a motel robbery. He strongly protested his innocence but was convicted of murder and sentenced to death by lethal injection.

While on Death Row, he campaigned against gang culture and wrote children's books aimed at deflecting gang membership. He also appealed against his sentence, steadfastly maintaining his innocence, although he refused to apologise for crimes that he said he did not commit.

His execution, when it came in December 2005, had all the elements of a ritual. Williams's final appeal for clemency was refused by the Governor of California on 12 December on the grounds that without an apology there could be no redemption. The decision was received with fury in some quarters and concern was reflected around the world. A popularly expressed view was that if Williams did not merit clemency, what did clemency mean in California? The man on Death Row, in an interview with a news agency, retained his serenity, and said that fearing the end would not benefit him.

As the time of execution drew near, unprecedented numbers of people gathered outside the gates of San Quentin Prison, singing "We Shall Overcome". Even at this late hour, further appeals were made and rejected. Some protesters held up a banner featuring an image of California Governor, Arnold Schwarzenegger, and bearing the message, "Stop me before I kill again".

Nearly forty witnesses assembled in the death chamber as Williams received the lethal injection. At 12.35 an announcement was made to those mounting a silent vigil that "Tookie" Williams was dead. There were cries of "Long live Tookie Williams" and quieter suggestions that the rejection of clemency in this case was a moral failure.

Identity Thief

When a reclusive millionaire was found murdered in his north London home, the evidence pointed to identity theft as a motive. The investigation led to the first murder trial in Britain to be covered by a secrecy order on the grounds of national security.

Eighty-four-year-old Allan Chappelow lived in a dilapidated house with an overgrown garden in Hampstead. He was a scholarly man and writer, regarded locally as a harmless eccentric, not least because of his habit of riding a motorcycle in his dressing gown.

Concerns over his safety began to grow in May 2006 when there were reports that his bank accounts were being unlawfully accessed. When he did not respond to calls, the police became involved with what they thought might be a missing persons enquiry. It became known that when Chappelow returned home on 1 May after a visit to the USA, he found that the door of his house had been forced open and that mail had been stolen.

On 14 June, the police entered his home and discovered his body, which was lying under a four-foot-high pile of papers. He had been severely beaten about the head, with injuries inflicted by a heavy instrument. There was a great deal of blood spatter and his clothes were covered in wax burns, suggesting that he might have been tortured for information. The body was badly decomposed and it was believed Chappelow had been dead for three weeks.

Enquiries revealed that from mid-May until the middle of June, systematic attempts had been made to access the dead man's accounts using information gleaned by theft of mail delivered to his home. Twenty thousand pounds had been transferred out of one of his bank accounts.

The postman recorded a brief encounter he had with a Chinese person at Chappelow's house who had quizzed him about the mail he was delivering. The man was forty-six-year-old Wang Yam, a British subject born in China. Yam, made a bankrupt in 2006 with debts of over £1 million, lived with his girlfriend in a house two streets away from Chappelow's home. It seemed that the couple were behind with the rent and were facing eviction. Yam had set up an e-mail account in Chappelow's name at an internet café which he then accessed from his flat. Aware that a police investigation was gaining momentum, he fled to Switzerland.

Yam had graduated from a university in China and taken a lecturing post in Beijing. He became involved in the pro-democracy movement which alienated him from the Chinese government. He fled the backlash by escaping to Hong Kong where he was accepted as an asylum seeker in 1992 and later became a British citizen.

Following his extradition from Switzerland, Yam was charged with murder, theft and fraud, which he denied. His story was that a gang had murdered Chappelow and they had passed on to him the credit cards and bank details so that he could steal from the dead man's accounts. Forensic examination of the cigarette butts found at the crime scene established that the DNA on them was not Yam's.

He was tried at the Old Bailey in April 2008 when the Home Secretary ruled that most of the evidence would be heard in secret. This was because of Yam's background as a Chinese dissident when he worked as an informer for MI6. The jury failed to reach a verdict on the murder but he was found guilty of fraud. At his second trial in January 2009, he was found guilty of killing Allan Chappelow for the purpose of stealing his identity. Yam claimed that he had been framed. In a criminal case that made legal history, he was sentenced to a minimum of twenty years in prison.

Puppet Master

On New Year's Day 2008, fourteen-year-old Stefanie Rengel was stabbed to death outside her home in East York, Toronto.

She was in the family home with her brother when she was lured outside by a nineteen-year-old youth acting on instructions from his girlfriend. He stabbed Stefanie six times and left her dying on the snow-covered ground.

The instigator of the killing was a fifteen-year-old girl who could not be named because she was regarded as a youth offender. In March 2009, her boyfriend, referred to as DB, appeared in court to answer charges of murder. He pleaded guilty and was duly convicted.

The girl who had orchestrated the killing was tried as a youth offender and throughout the initial proceedings was referred to as MT. The prosecution case was that she was obsessively jealous of Stefanie whom she had never met, but regarded as a rival. Over several months, she used all her powers of persuasion to coerce her boyfriend to kill Stefanie. She pestered him with telephone calls and text messages until he finally gave in and agreed to do her bidding. In one message MT said simply, "I want her dead" and she turned the screw further by threatening to "block" DB "until you kill her".

The defence argued that MT suffered from a body-image disorder which made her anxious and insecure. She was obsessed about her appearance, believing she was fat, ugly and unattractive. Her insecurities, it was said, made her anxious about her self-image and she saw threats in others who she viewed as rivals. A forensic psychiatrist testified that she had a borderline personality disorder.

In March 2009 MT was convicted of first-degree murder. In further court proceedings in July, she read a tearful statement apologising to the family of the dead girl and admitting full responsibility for what had happened. Stefanie Rengel's mother made a moving victim-impact statement concerning the violent death of her young daughter. Her poignant words about her grief made a powerful impression on the public.

On 28 July, MT appeared in court to face her sentence. At issue was whether she would continue to be treated as a youth offender, in which case she would receive a lesser sentence than if she was sentenced as an adult. The prosecutor argued for an adult sentence. He said that MT had calculated the murder over several months and he dismissed the extenuating circumstances that the defence had proposed.

Defence arguments that MT did not wield the knife that killed Stefanie and was home at the time, carried little weight.

Mr Justice Ian Nordheimer ruled that MT should be given an adult sentence and, from that point, she became Melissa Todorovic. She was given an automatic life sentence. The judge commented that, "Put simply, the puppet master is not less blameworthy than the puppet."

In November 2009, the judge ruled that DB should be identified and treated by the court as an adult. Nineteen-year-old David Bigshaw, who had previously pleaded guilty, was sentenced to life imprisonment.

Select Bibliography

Books

BADAL, James Jessen: *In the Wake of the Butcher*, Kent State University Press, Ohio, 2001

BOWEN, David: *Body of Evidence*, Robinson, London, 2003

GAUTE, J.H.H. and ODELL, Robin: *Murder Whatdunit?*, Harrap, London, 1982
Murder Whereabouts, Harrap, London, 1986

GOODMAN, Jonathan (Ed.): *The Giant Book of Murder*, Magpie, London, 1995

HAINES, Max: *Doctors Who Kill*, Penguin, Toronto, 1993
Canadian Crimes, Penguin, Toronto, 1998
Murder Most Foul, Penguin, Toronto, 1999
Instruments of Murder, Penguin, Toronto, 2004

HAND, Derrick and FIFE-YEOMANS, Janet: *The Coroner*, ABC Books, Sydney, 2001

JESSE, F. Tennyson: *Murder and its Motives*, Harrap, London, 1924

LANE, Brian and GREGG, Wilfred: *The Encyclopaedia of Serial Killers*, Headline, London, 1992
The Encyclopaedia of Mass Murder, Headline, London, 2004

LEE, Sarah: *Classic Murders of The North West*, Pan Books, London, 1999

LINEDECKER, Clifford L. and BURT, William A.: *Nurses Who Kill*, Pinnacle, New York, 1990

MANN, Robert and WILLIAMSON, Miryam Ehrlich: *Forensic Detective*, Allen & Unwin, NSW, 2008

MARRINER, Brian: *Missing Bodies*, Arrow Books, London, 1994

MORTON, James: *Who's Who of Unsolved Murders*, Kyle Cathie, London, 1994

NASH, Jay Robert: *Compendium of World Crime*, Harrap, London, 1983

ODELL, Robin: *Landmarks in Twentieth-Century Murder*, Headline, London, 1995

The International Murderers' Who's Who, Headline, London, 1996

ODELL, Robin and GREGG, Wilfred: *Murderers' Row*, Sutton Publishing, Stroud, 2006

ROSE, Andrew: *Lethal Witness*, Sutton Publishing, Stroud, 2007

RULE, Ann: *If You Really Loved Me*, Simon and Schuster, New York, 1991

SCHREIBER, Flora Rheta: *The Shoemaker*, Simon and Schuster, New York, 1983

SIFAKIS, Carl: *The Encyclopaedia of American Crime*, Facts on File, New York, 1982

WHITTINGTON-EGAN, R. and M.: *Bedside Murder Book*, David & Charles, Frome, 1988

WILKES, Roger: *The Mammoth Book of Famous Trials*, Constable & Robinson, London, 2006

WILSON, Colin: *Order of Assassins*, Hart Davis, London, 1972

WILSON, Colin and PITMAN, Patricia: *Encyclopaedia of Murder*, Pan Books, London, 1961

WILLIAMS, Tony: *A Case of Murder*, Hodder Moa Beckett, New Zealand, 2000

WINCHESTER, Simon, *The Surgeon of Crowthorne*, Penguin, London, 1998

WOLF, J. Marvin and MADER, Katherine: *L.A. Crime*, Facts on File, New York, 1986

WYDEN, Peter: *The Hired Killers*, W. H. Allen, London, 1964

Newspapers

Baltimore Sun
New York Times
Straits Times
Daily Express
Scotland on Sunday
Sunday Times
Daily Mail
Guardian
Toronto Sun
Daily Mirror
Independent

Index of Names